Renegade

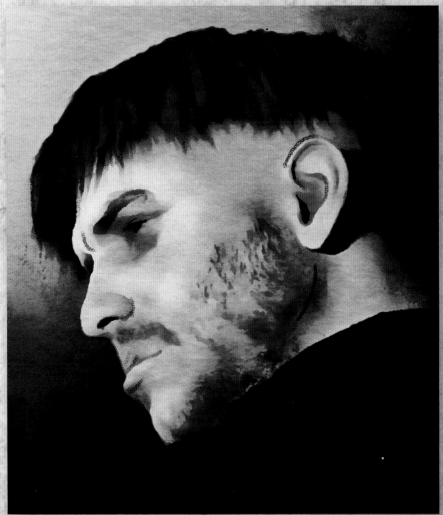

MARTIN LUTHER
THE GRAPHIC BIOGRAPHY

Andrea Grosso Ciponte

Text by Dacia Palmerino

Translation by Michael G. Parker

PLOUGH PUBLISHING HOUSE

Published by Plough Publishing House
Walden, New York
Robertsbridge, England
Elsmore, Australia
www.plough.com

Plough produces books, a quarterly magazine, and Plough.com to encourage people and help them put their faith into action. We believe Jesus can transform the world and that his teachings and example apply to all aspects of life. At the same time, we seek common ground with all people regardless of their creed.

Plough is the publishing house of the Bruderhof, an international community of families and singles seeking to follow Jesus together. Members of the Bruderhof are committed to a way of radical discipleship in the spirit of the Sermon on the Mount. Inspired by the first church in Jerusalem (Acts 2 and 4), they renounce private property and share everything in common in a life of nonviolence, justice, and service to neighbors near and far. To learn more about the Bruderhof's faith, history, and daily life, see Bruderhof.com. (Views expressed by Plough authors are their own and do not necessarily reflect the position of the Bruderhof.)

ISBN 978-0-87486-207-2
21 20 19 18 17   1 2 3 4 5 6

Based on the German edition, *Martin Luther,* published by Edition Faust in 2016, translated from the Italian by Nicoletta Giacon, edited by Harry Oberländer and Regine Strotbek in consultation with specialist advisors Eberhard Pausch and Jeffrey Myers.

Library of Congress Cataloging-in-Publication Data pending

Printed in the United States of America

Contents

In Dark Times

Martin Luther is born on
November 10, 1483 in the
German town of Eisleben.
It is a turbulent time;
the world is out of joint ...

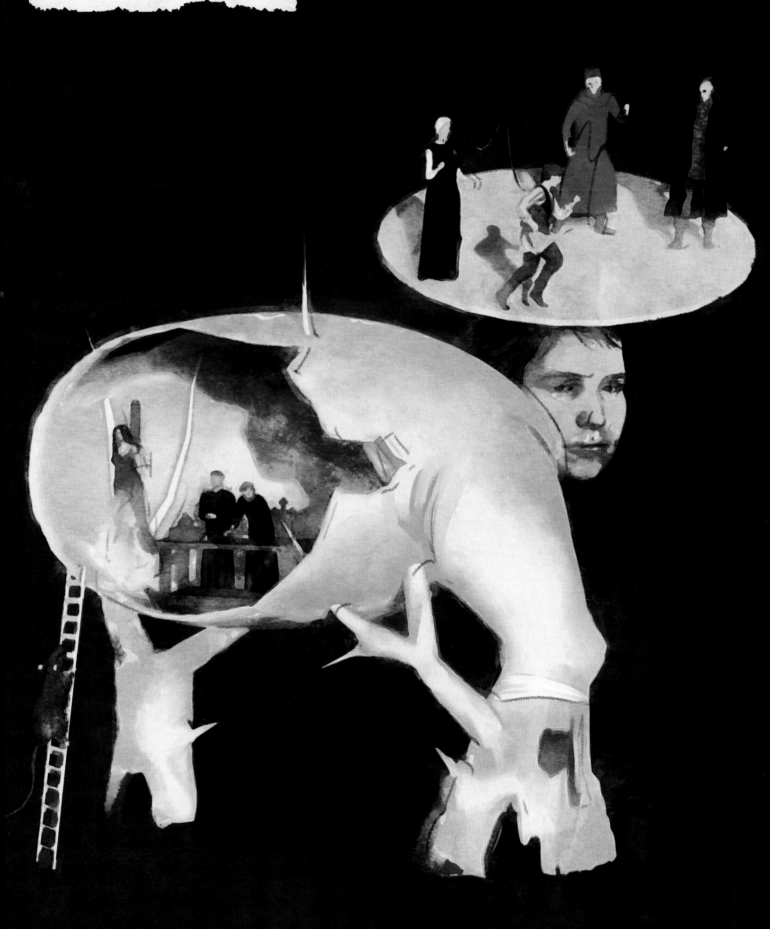

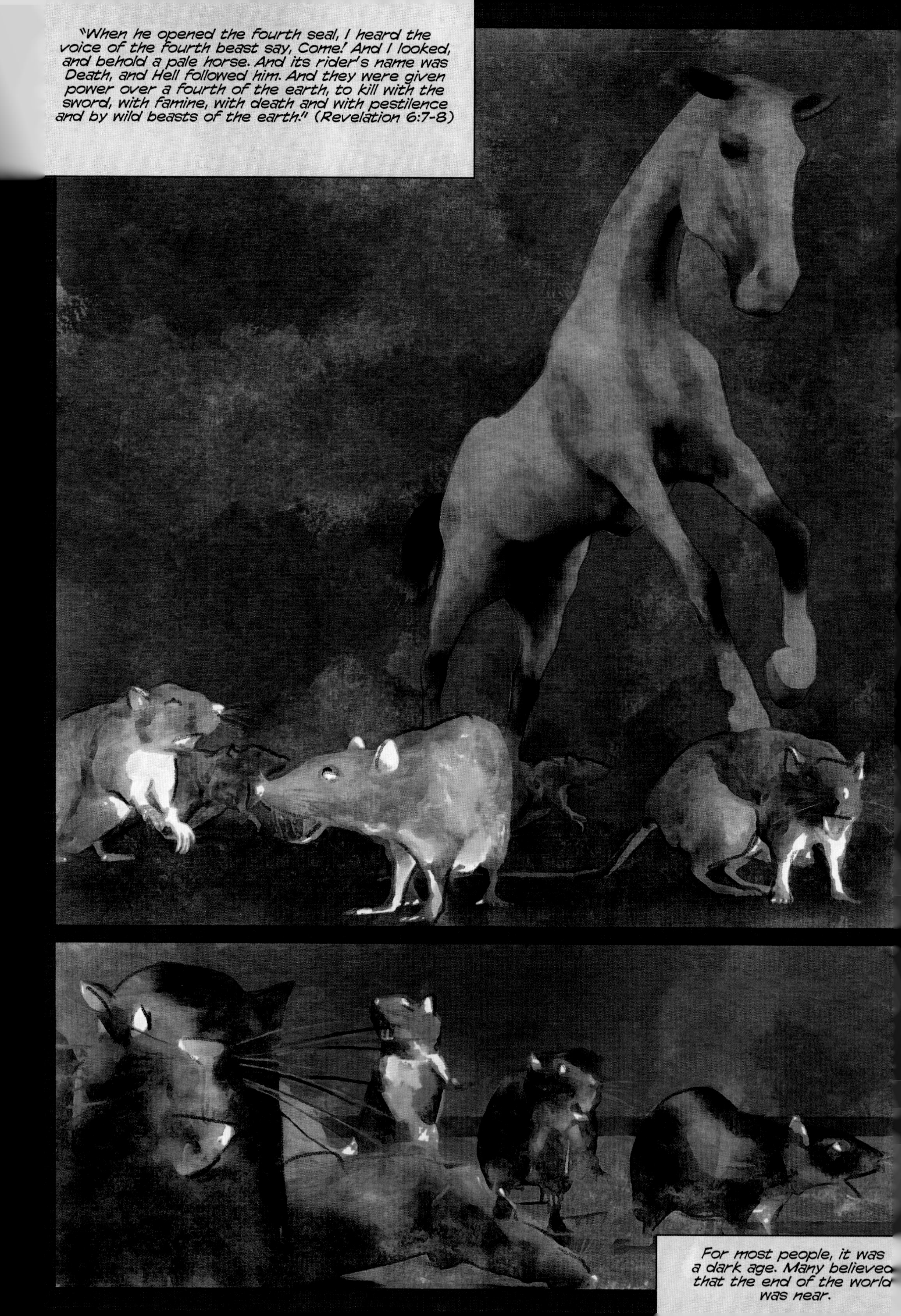
"When he opened the fourth seal, I heard the voice of the fourth beast say, Come! And I looked, and behold a pale horse. And its rider's name was Death, and Hell followed him. And they were given power over a fourth of the earth, to kill with the sword, with famine, with death and with pestilence and by wild beasts of the earth." (Revelation 6:7-8)
For most people, it was a dark age. Many believed that the end of the world was near.

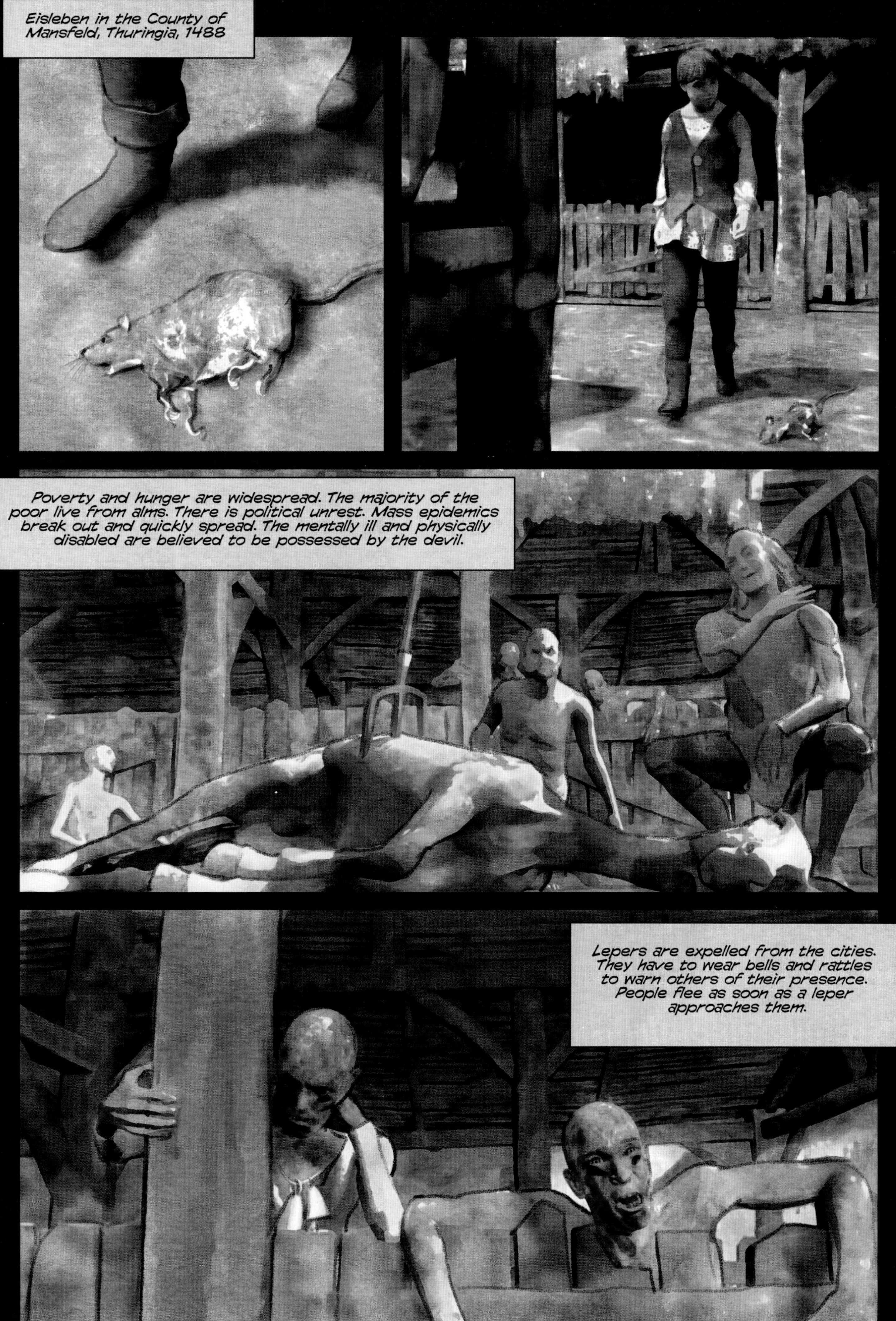
Eisleben in the County of Mansfeld, Thuringia, 1488
Poverty and hunger are widespread. The majority of the poor live from alms. There is political unrest. Mass epidemics break out and quickly spread. The mentally ill and physically disabled are believed to be possessed by the devil.
Lepers are expelled from the cities. They have to wear bells and rattles to warn others of their presence. People flee as soon as a leper approaches them.

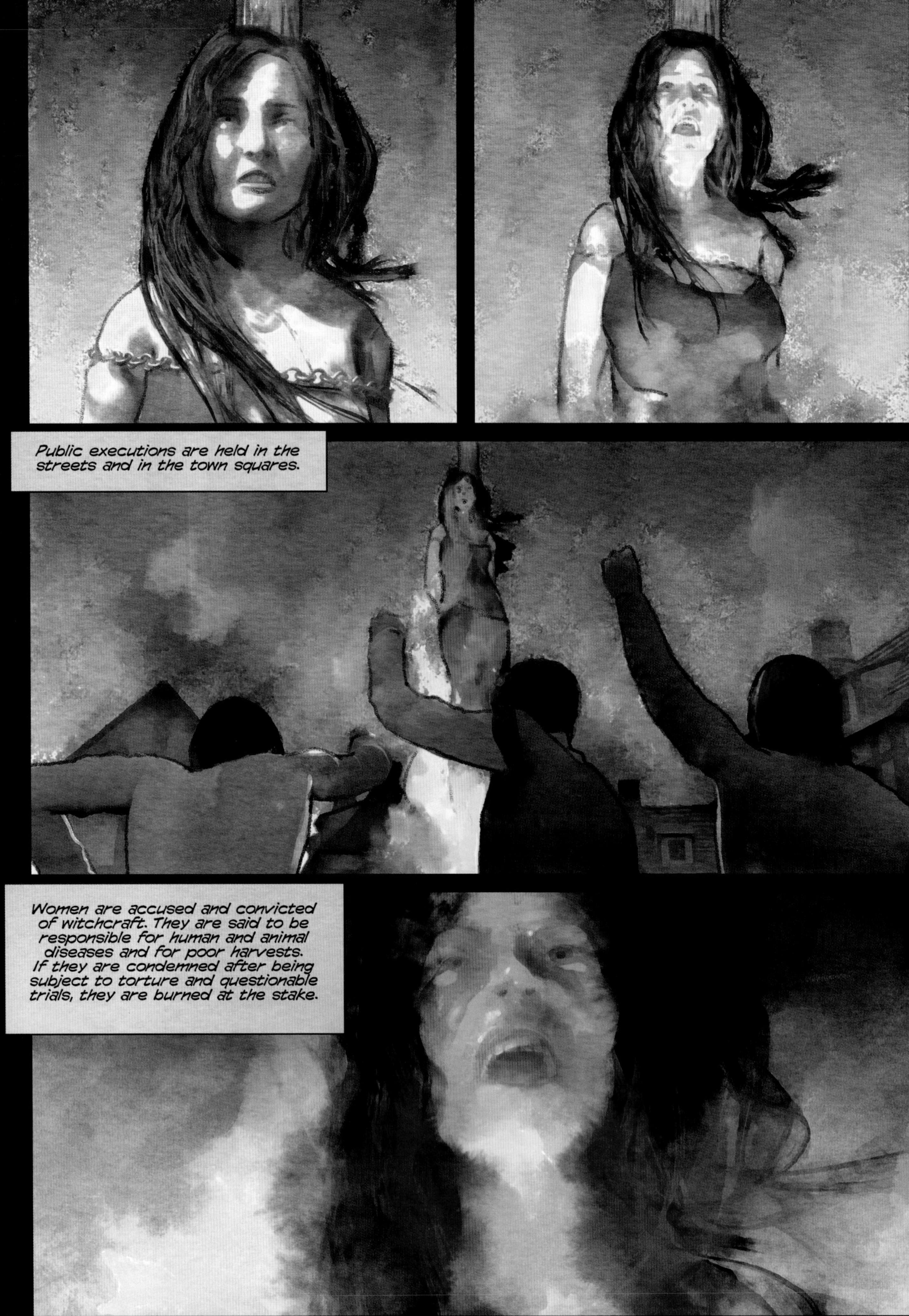

Public executions are held in the streets and in the town squares.
Women are accused and convicted of witchcraft. They are said to be responsible for human and animal diseases and for poor harvests. If they are condemned after being subject to torture and questionable trials, they are burned at the stake.

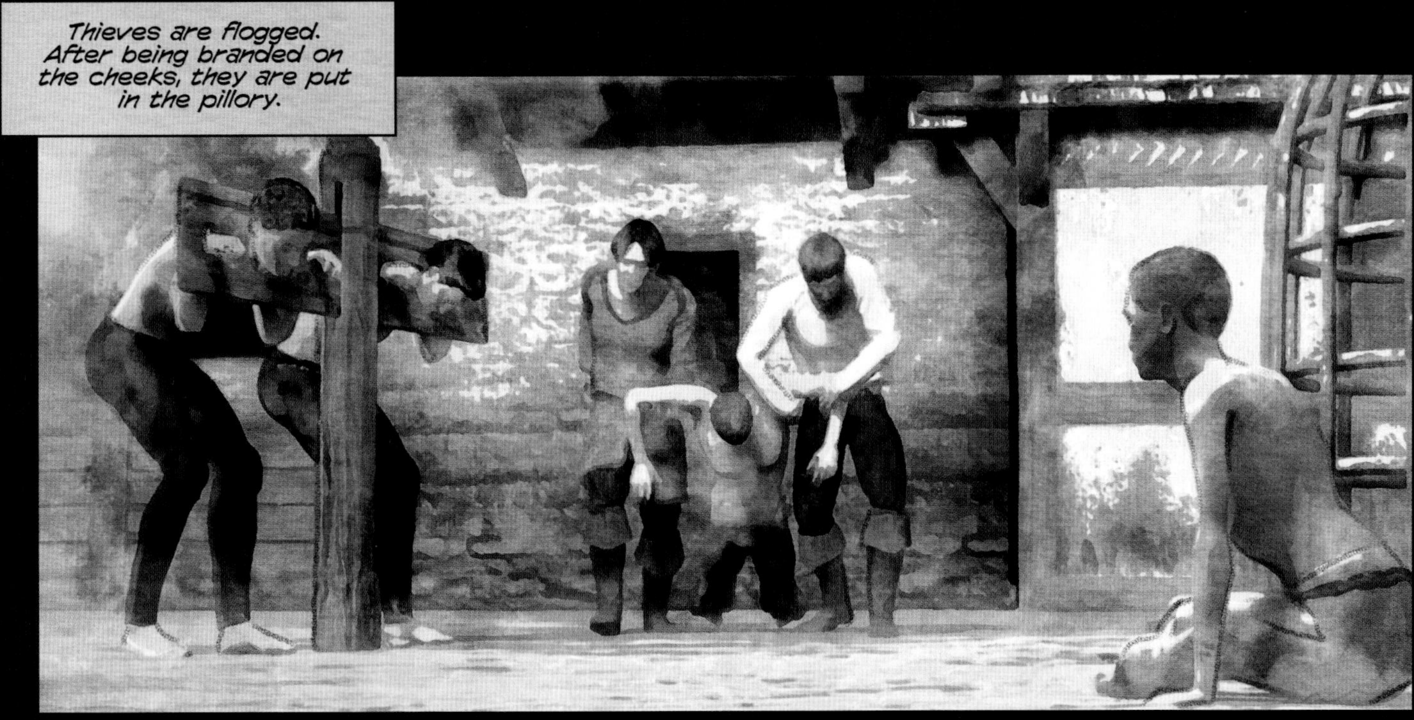
Thieves are flogged. After being branded on the cheeks, they are put in the pillory.

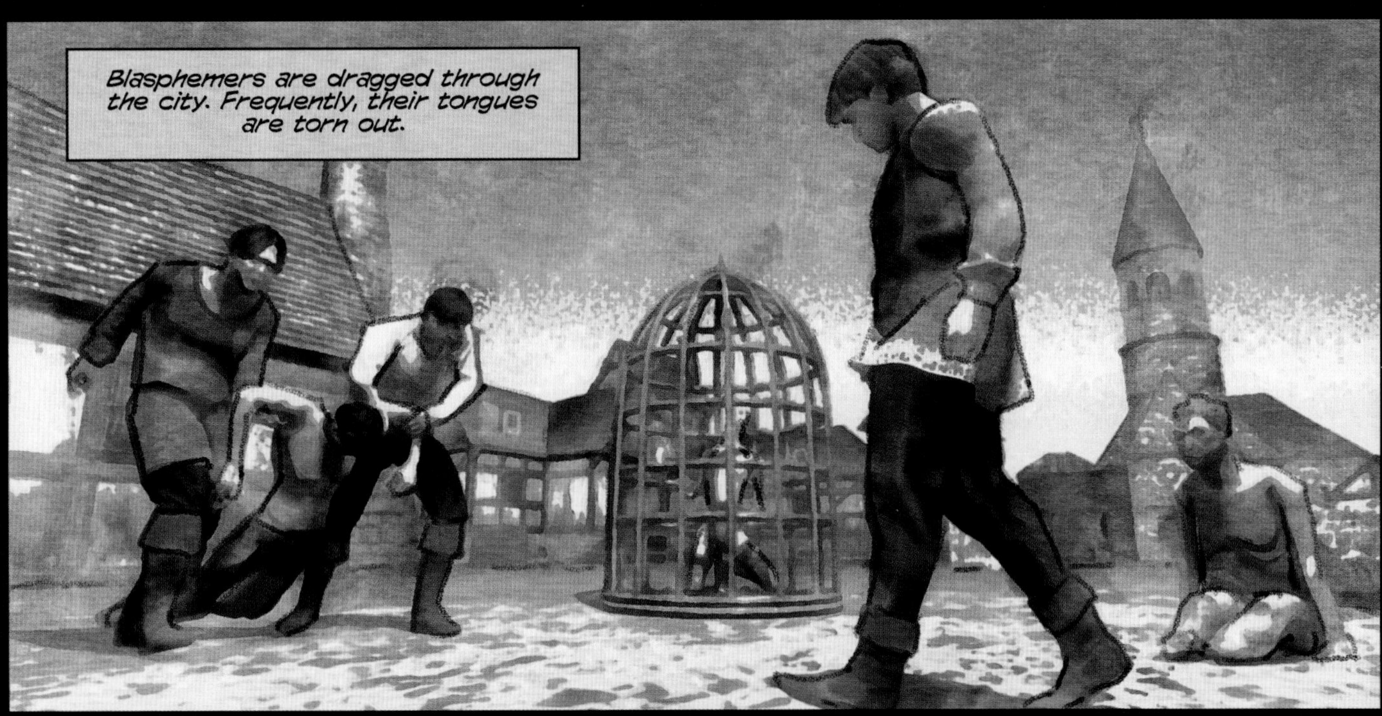
Blasphemers are dragged through the city. Frequently, their tongues are torn out.

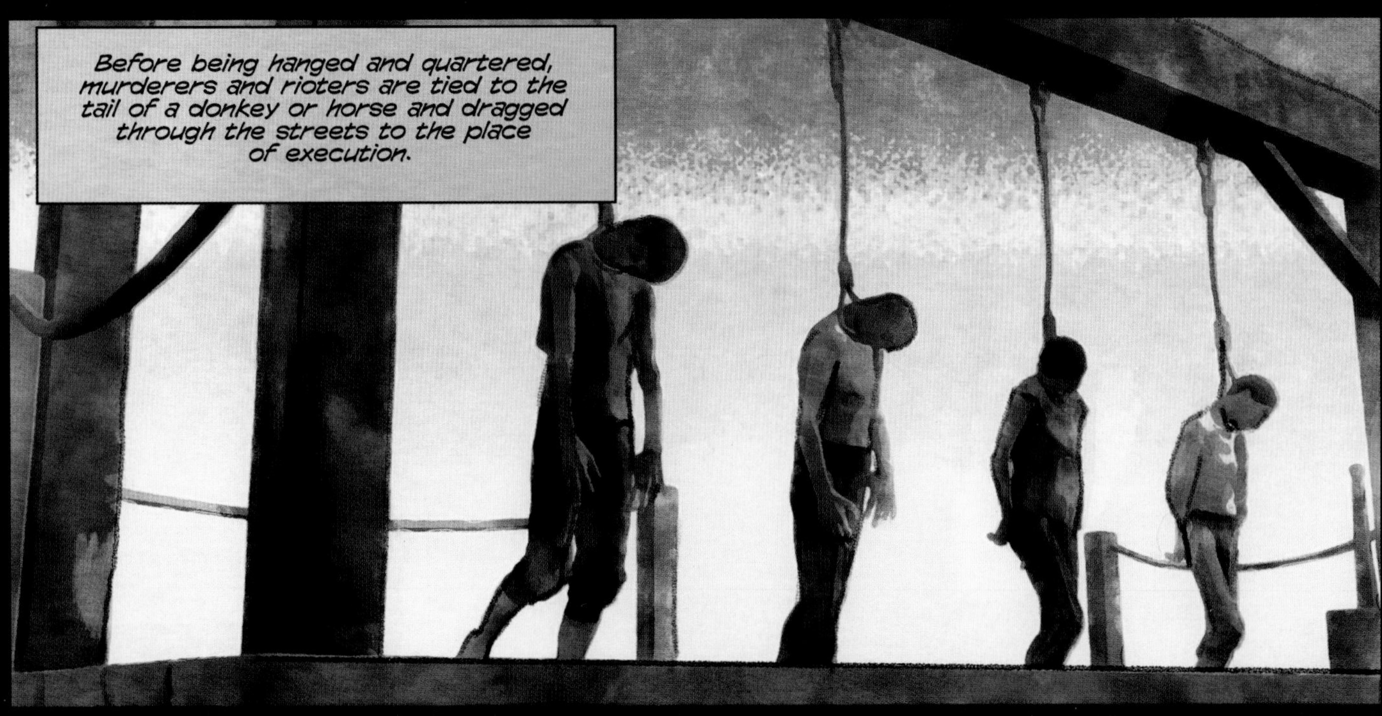
Before being hanged and quartered, murderers and rioters are tied to the tail of a donkey or horse and dragged through the streets to the place of execution.

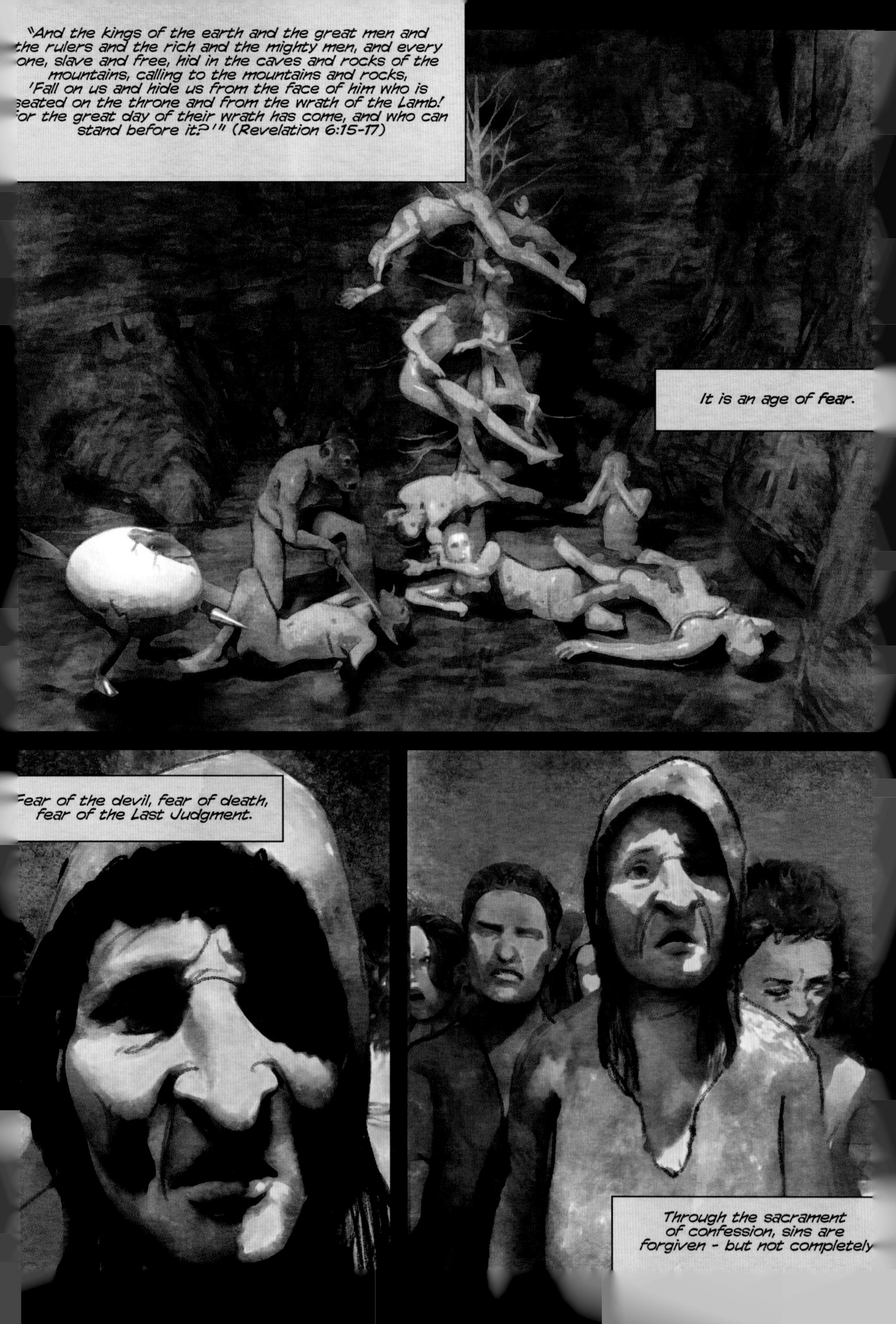
"And the kings of the earth and the great men and the rulers and the rich and the mighty men, and every one, slave and free, hid in the caves and rocks of the mountains, calling to the mountains and rocks, 'Fall on us and hide us from the face of him who is seated on the throne and from the wrath of the Lamb! For the great day of their wrath has come, and who can stand before it?'" (Revelation 6:15-17)
It is an age of fear.
Fear of the devil, fear of death, fear of the Last Judgment.
Through the sacrament of confession, sins are forgiven - but not completely

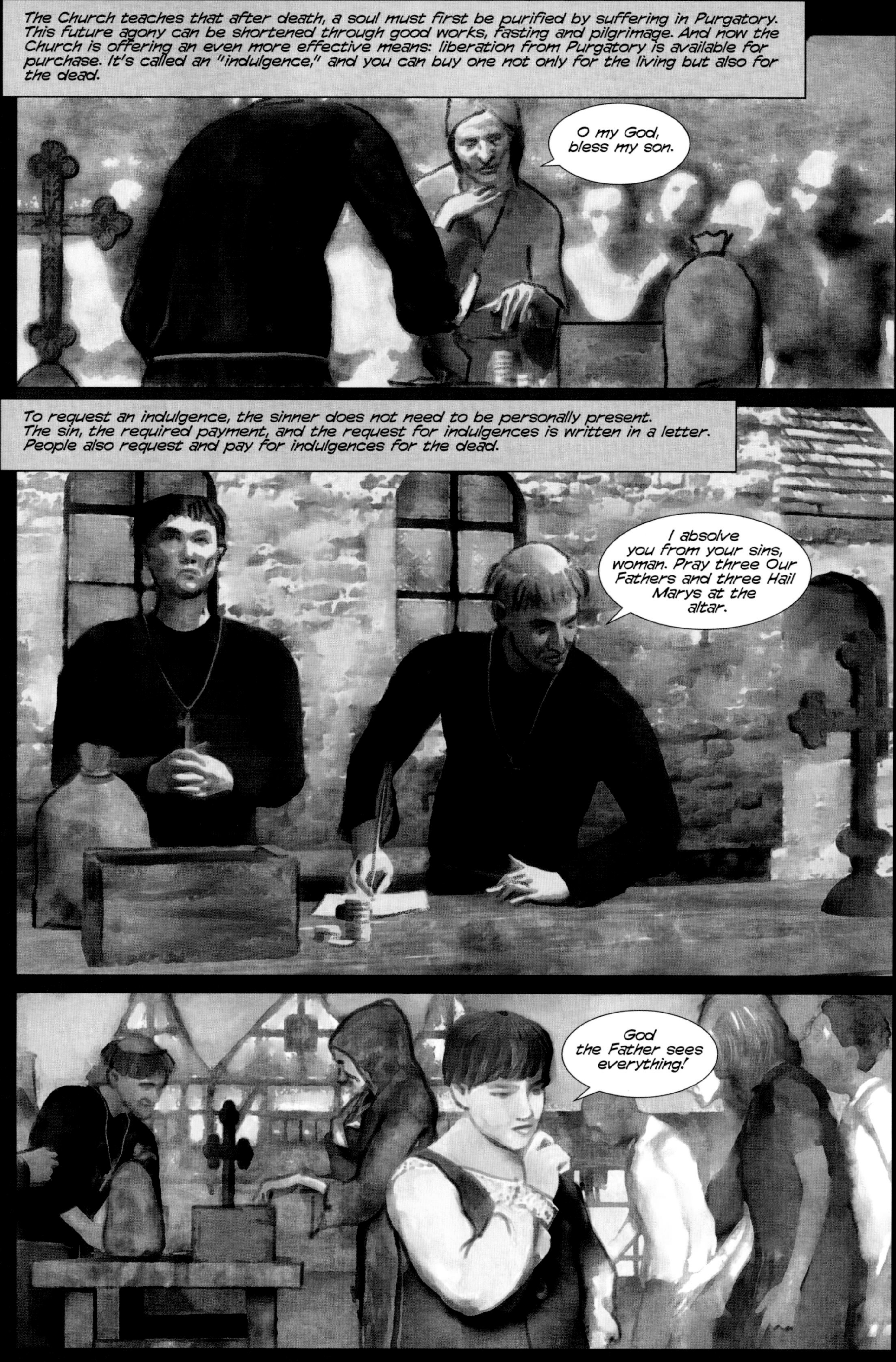
The Church teaches that after death, a soul must first be purified by suffering in Purgatory. This future agony can be shortened through good works, fasting and pilgrimage. And now the Church is offering an even more effective means: liberation from Purgatory is available for purchase. It's called an "indulgence," and you can buy one not only for the living but also for the dead.
O my God, bless my son.
To request an indulgence, the sinner does not need to be personally present. The sin, the required payment, and the request for indulgences is written in a letter. People also request and pay for indulgences for the dead.
I absolve you from your sins, woman. Pray three Our Fathers and three Hail Marys at the altar.
God the Father sees everything!

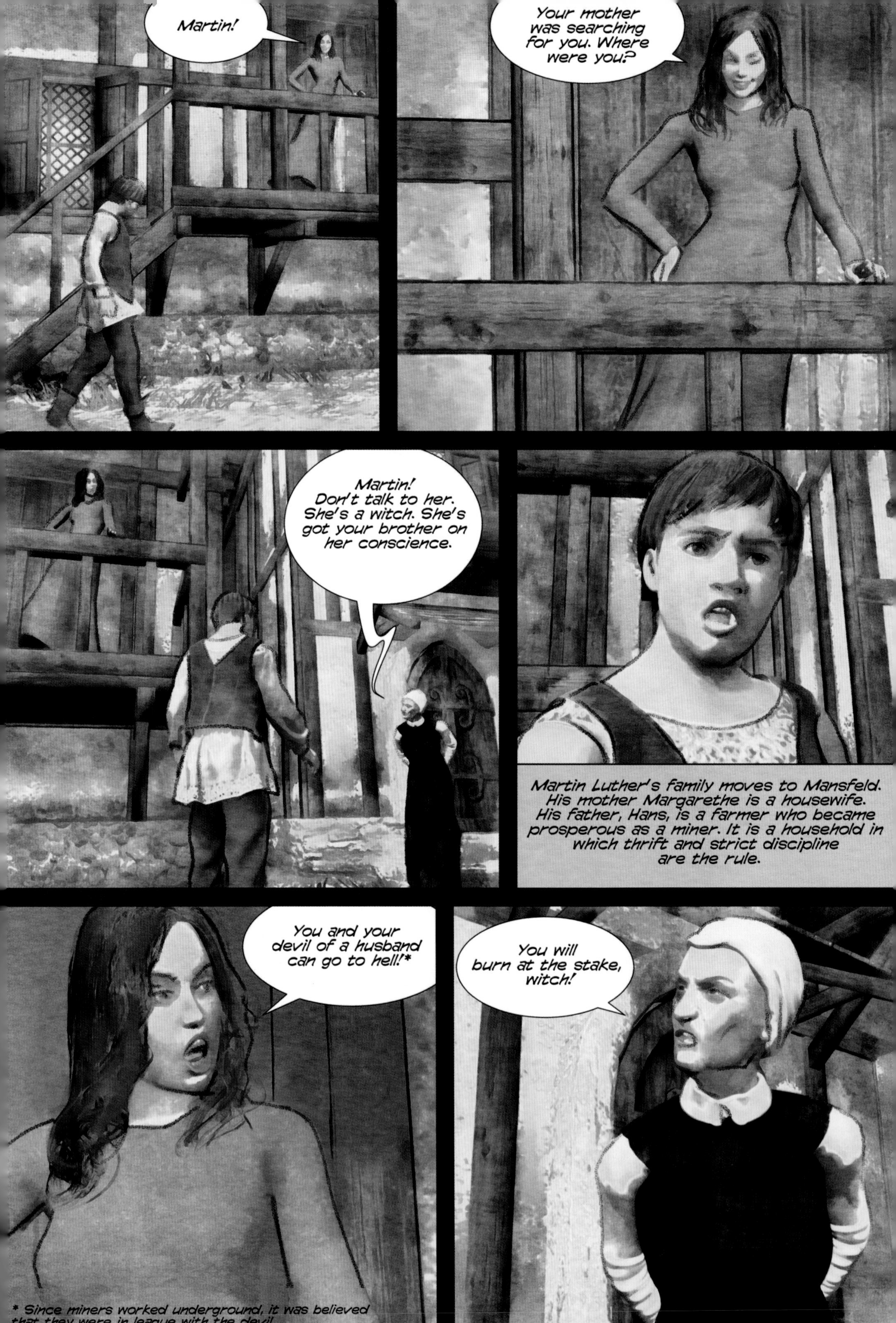
Martin!
Your mother was searching for you. Where were you?
Martin! Don't talk to her. She's a witch. She's got your brother on her conscience.
Martin Luther's family moves to Mansfeld. His mother Margarethe is a housewife. His father, Hans, is a farmer who became prosperous as a miner. It is a household in which thrift and strict discipline are the rule.
You and your devil of a husband can go to hell!*
You will burn at the stake, witch!

* Since miners worked underground, it was believed that they were in league with the devil.

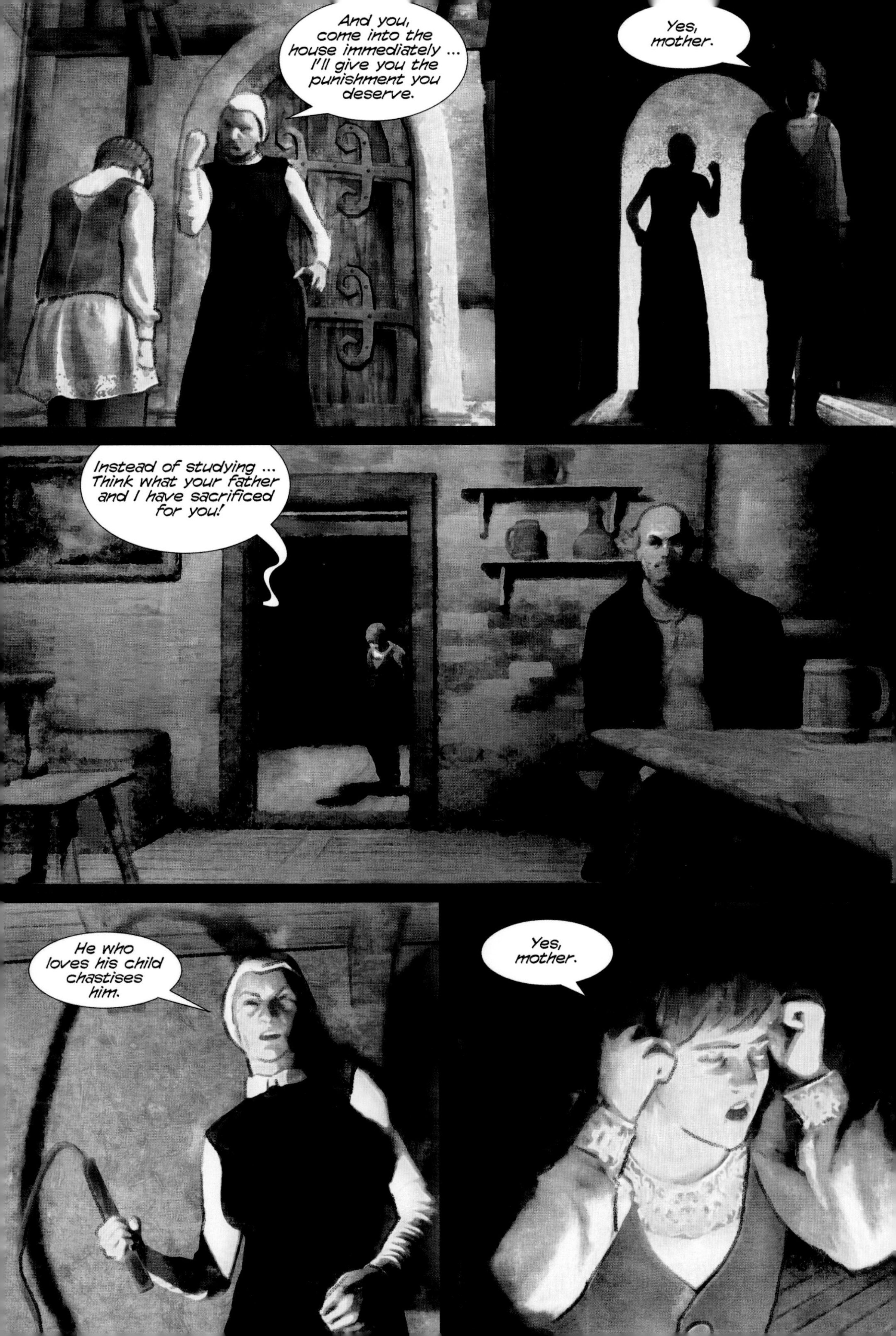
And you, come into the house immediately ... I'll give you the punishment you deserve.
Yes, mother.
Instead of studying ... Think what your father and I have sacrificed for you!
He who loves his child chastises him.
Yes, mother.

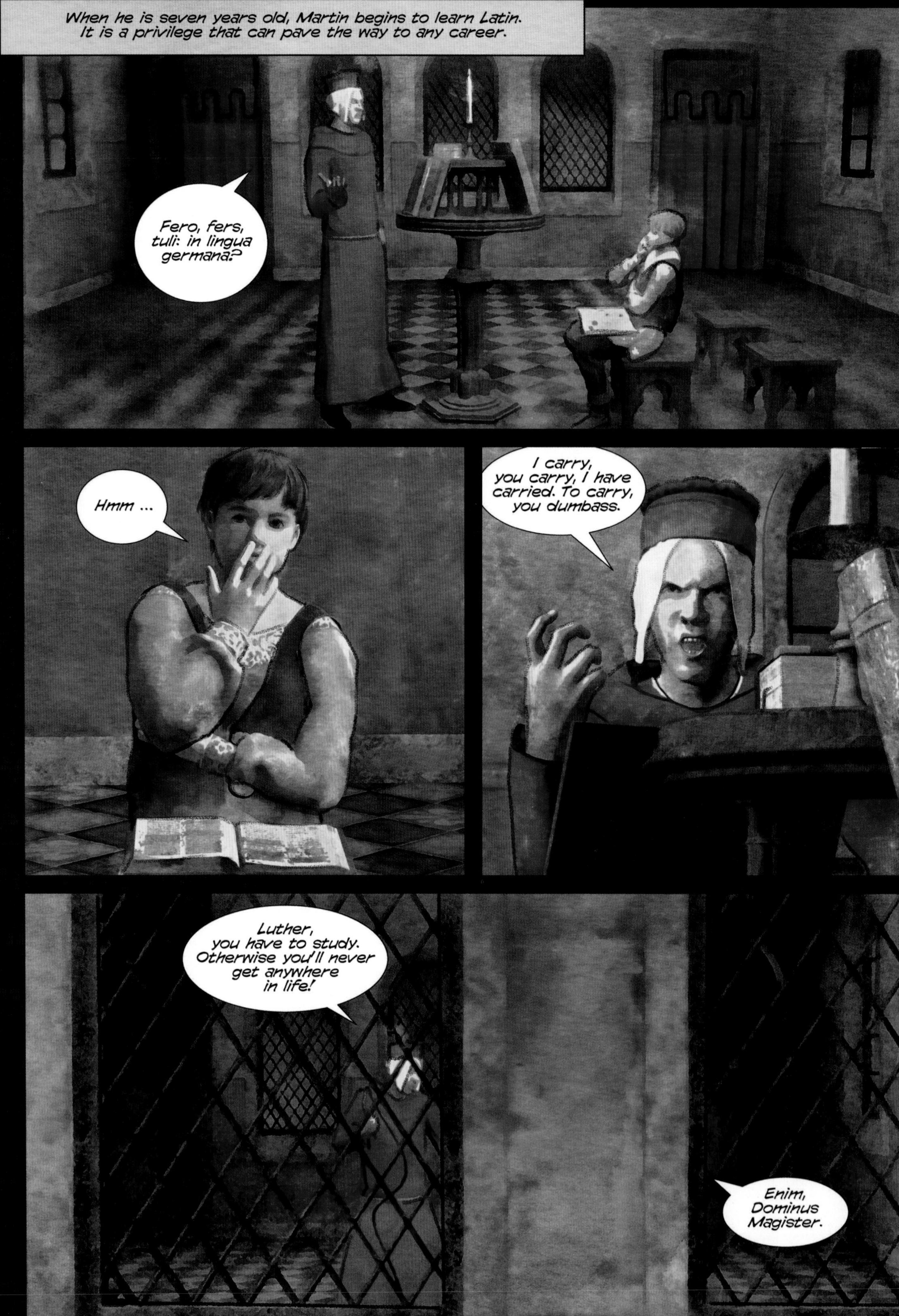
When he is seven years old, Martin begins to learn Latin. It is a privilege that can pave the way to any career.
Fero, fers, tuli: in lingua germana?
Hmm ...
I carry, you carry, I have carried. To carry, you dumbass.
Luther, you have to study. Otherwise you'll never get anywhere in life!
Enim, Dominus Magister.

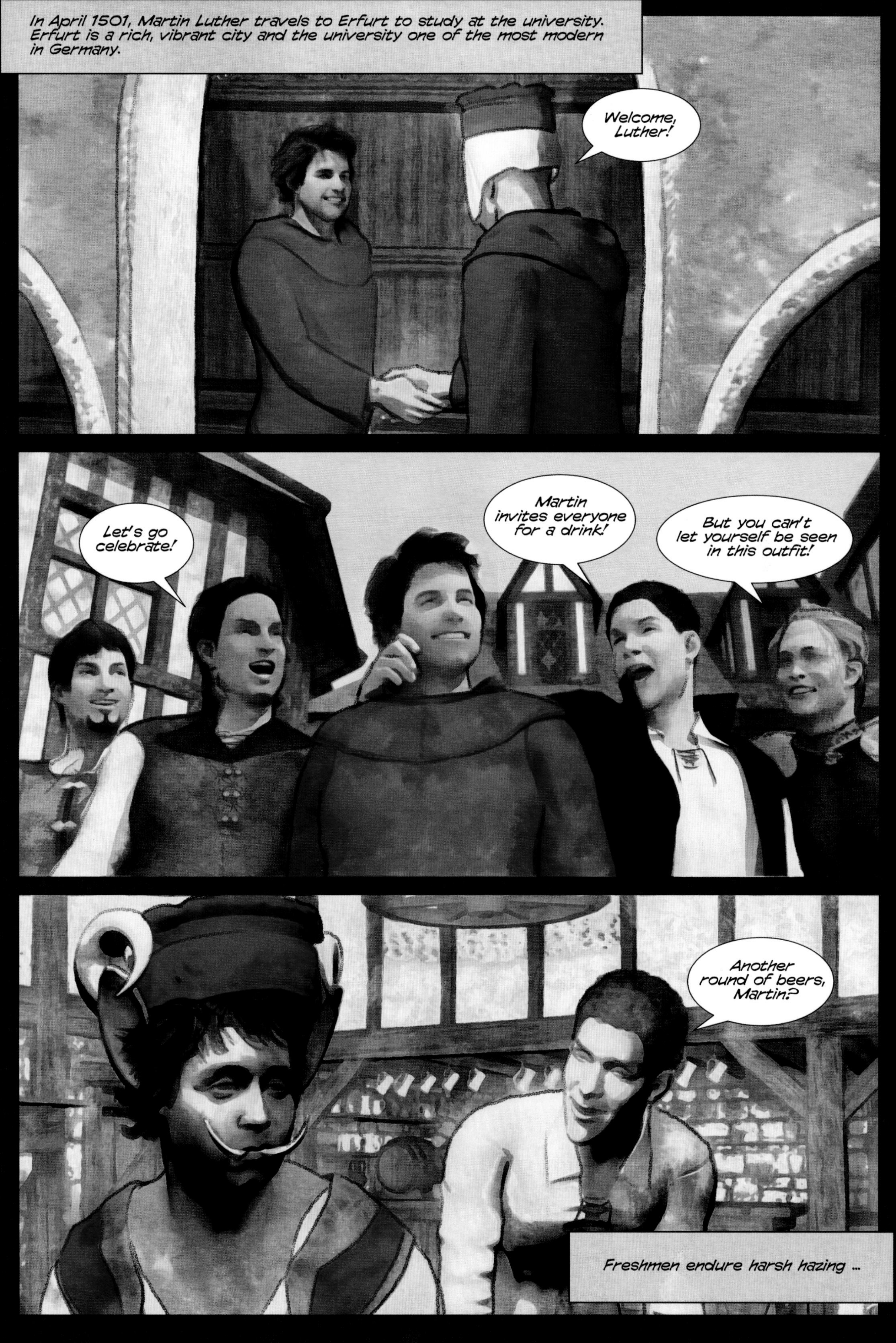
In April 1501, Martin Luther travels to Erfurt to study at the university. Erfurt is a rich, vibrant city and the university one of the most modern in Germany.
Welcome, Luther!
Let's go celebrate!
Martin invites everyone for a drink!
But you can't let yourself be seen in this outfit!
Another round of beers, Martin?
Freshmen endure harsh hazing ...

Luther never misses a lecture and spends much time in the library. Once, he is permitted to hold a Bible in his hands for a few minutes, a privilege usually reserved for masters. For him, it's a sign from God.

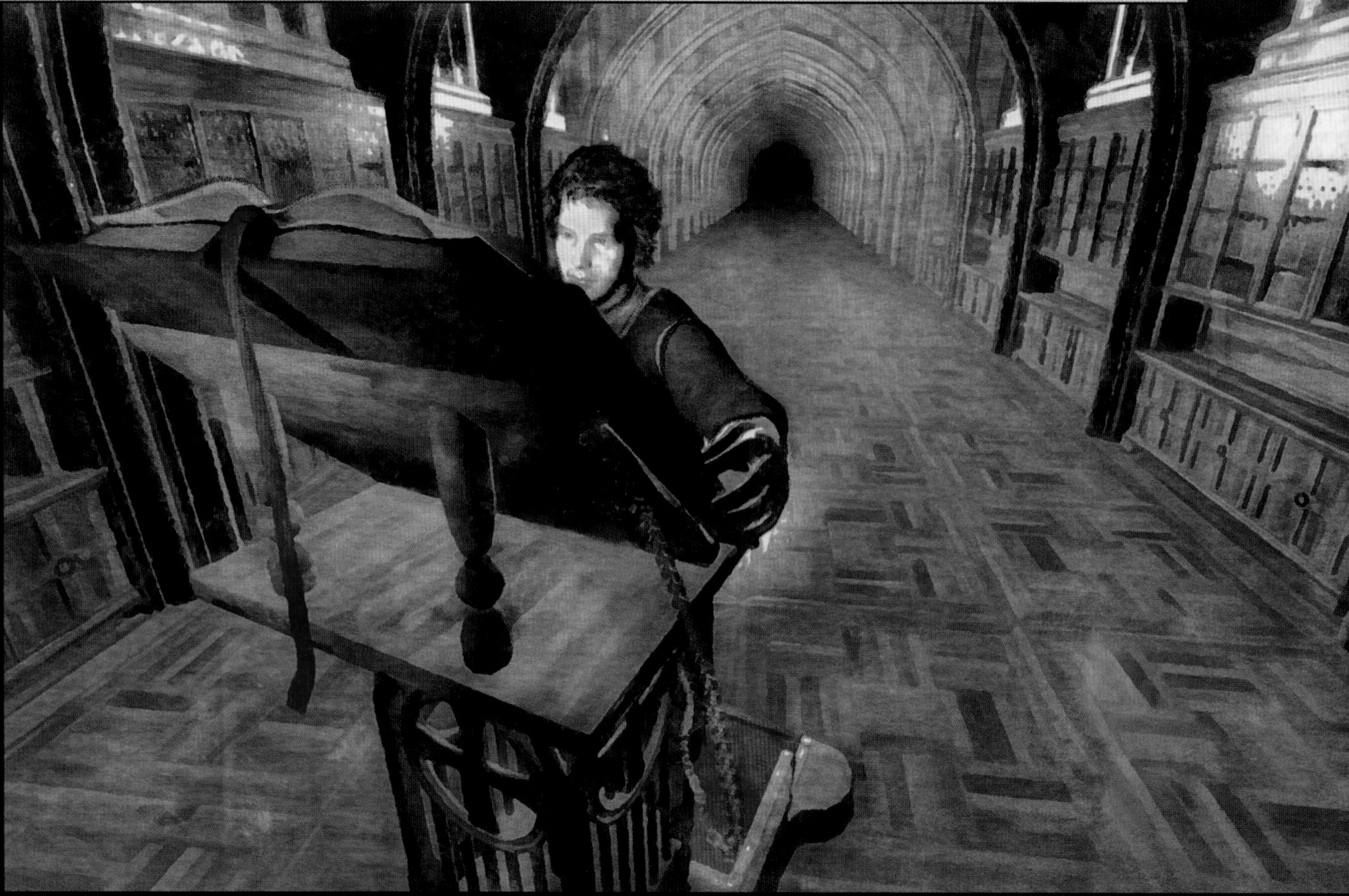

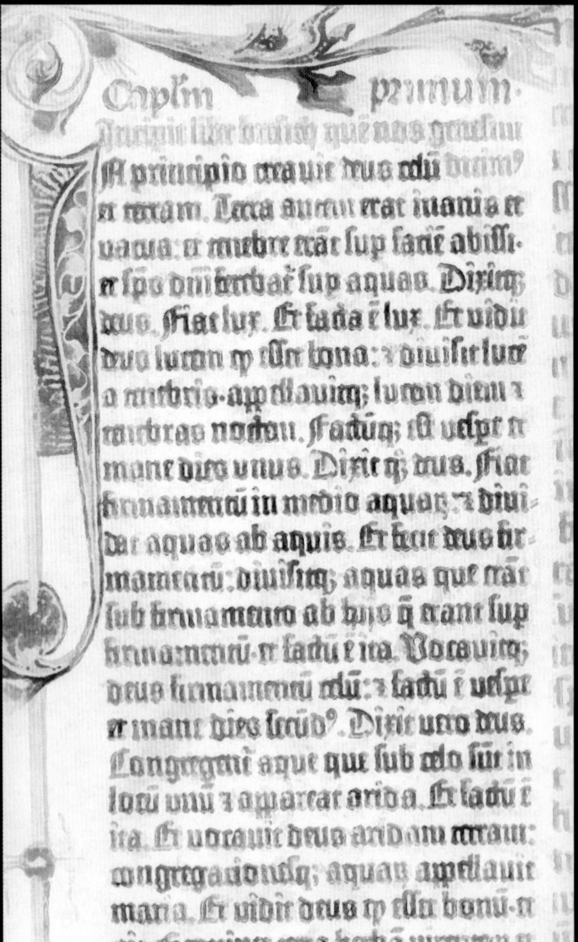
Caplm primum.
Incipit liber bresith quē nos genesim
In principio creauit deus celū dicim⁹
et terram. Terra autem erat inanis et
vacua: et tenebre erāt sup faciē abissi.
et sps dñi ferebat sup aquas. Dixitq;
deus. Fiat lux. Et facta ē lux. Et vidit
deus lucem q esset bona: et divisit lucē
a tenebris. appellauitq; lucem diem et
tenebras noctem. Factuq; est vespe et
mane dies unus. Dixit q; deus. Fiat
firmamentū in medio aquaꝝ: et divi-
dat aquas ab aquis. Et fecit deus firmamentū: divisitq; aquas que erāt
sub firmamento ab hiis q erant sup
firmamentū. et factū ē ita. Vocauitq;
deus firmamentū celū: et factū ē vespe
et mane dies secūd⁹. Dixit vero deus.
Congregent aque que sub celo sūt in
locū unū et appareat arida. Et factū ē
ita. Et vocauit deus aridam terram:
congregacionesq; aquaꝝ appellauit
maria. Et vidit deus q esset bonū. et
ait. Germinet terra herbā virentem et
facientē semen: et lignū pomiferū faciēs
fructū iuxta genus suū. cui⁹ semen in

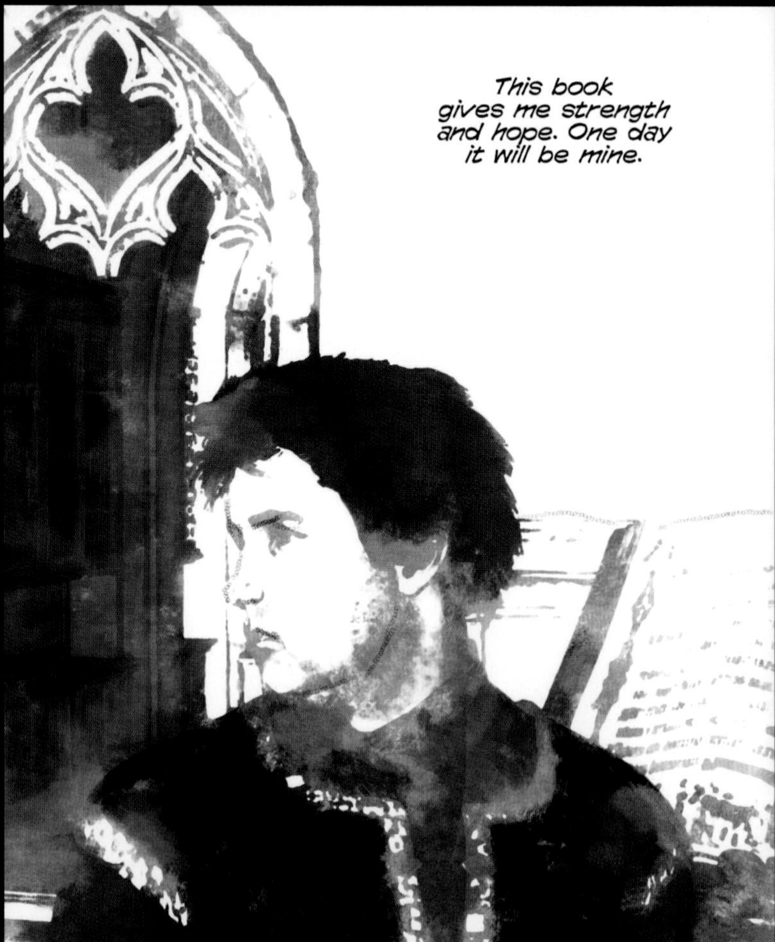
This book gives me strength and hope. One day it will be mine.

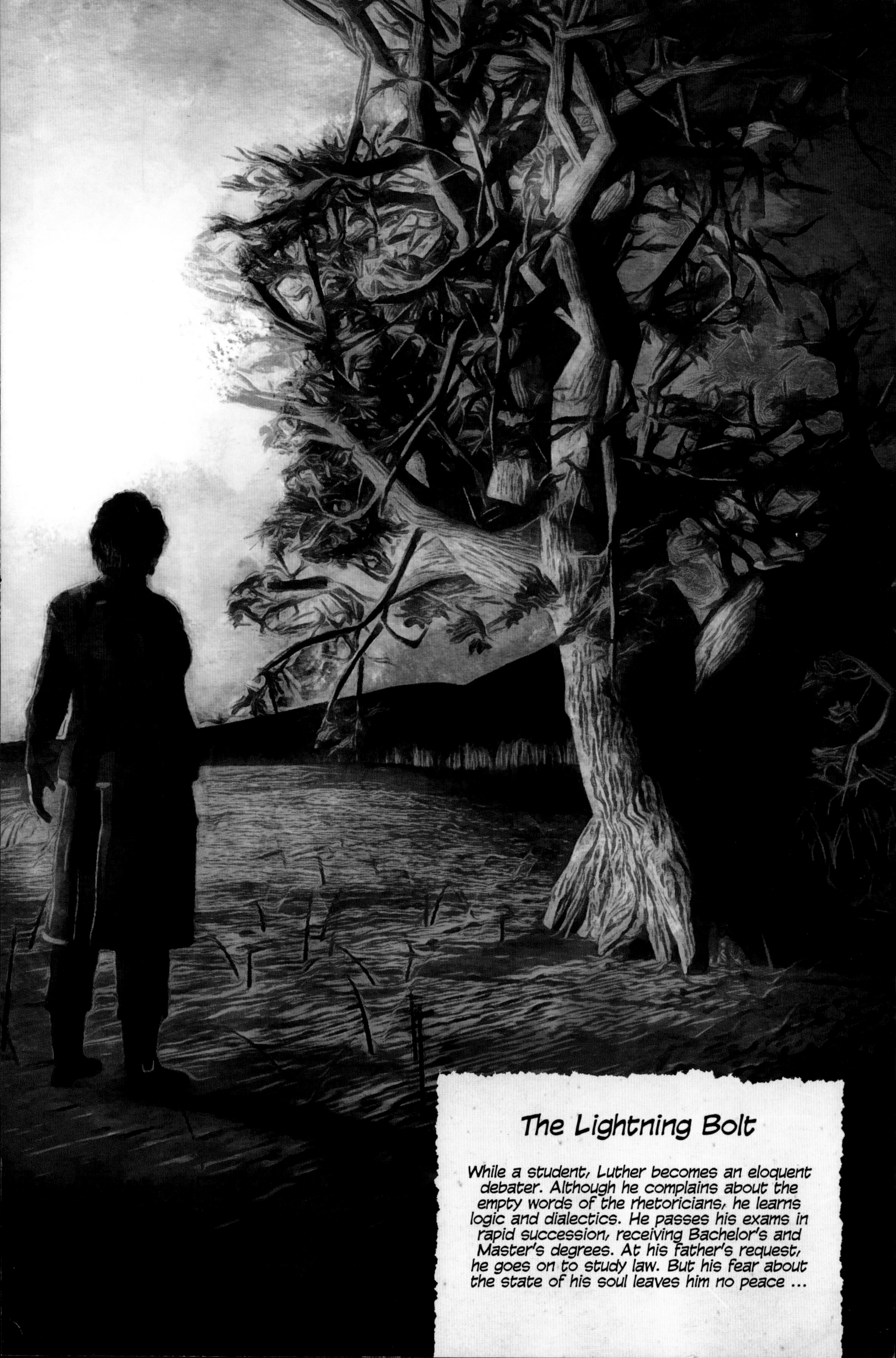
The Lightning Bolt
While a student, Luther becomes an eloquent debater. Although he complains about the empty words of the rhetoricians, he learns logic and dialectics. He passes his exams in rapid succession, receiving Bachelor's and Master's degrees. At his father's request, he goes on to study law. But his fear about the state of his soul leaves him no peace ...

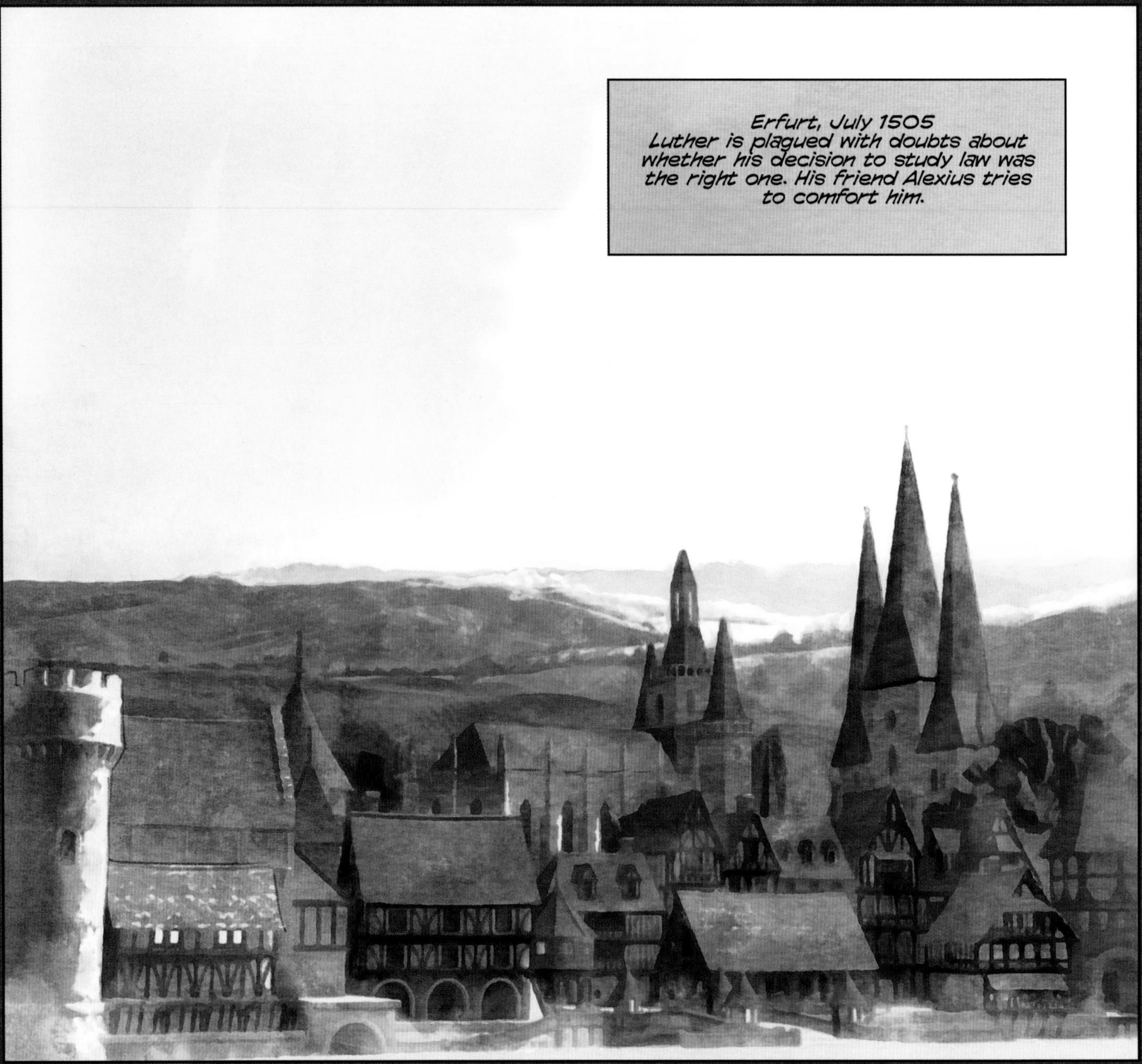
Erfurt, July 1505
Luther is plagued with doubts about whether his decision to study law was the right one. His friend Alexius tries to comfort him.

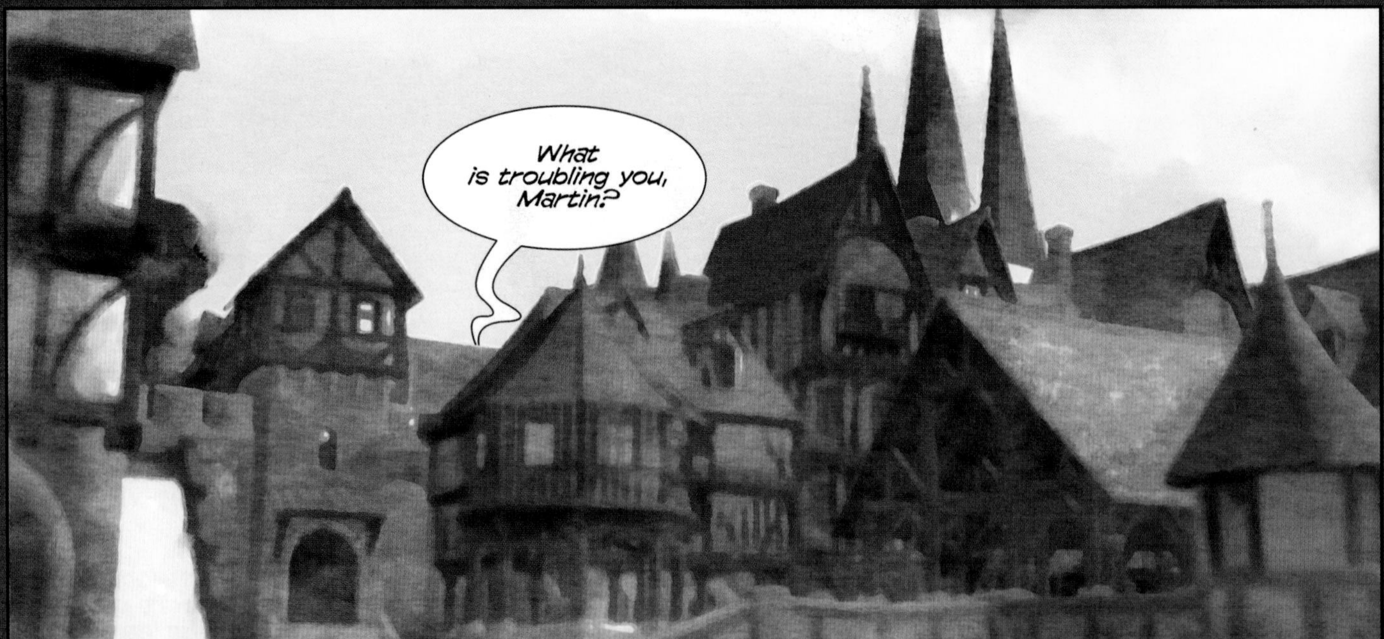
What is troubling you, Martin?

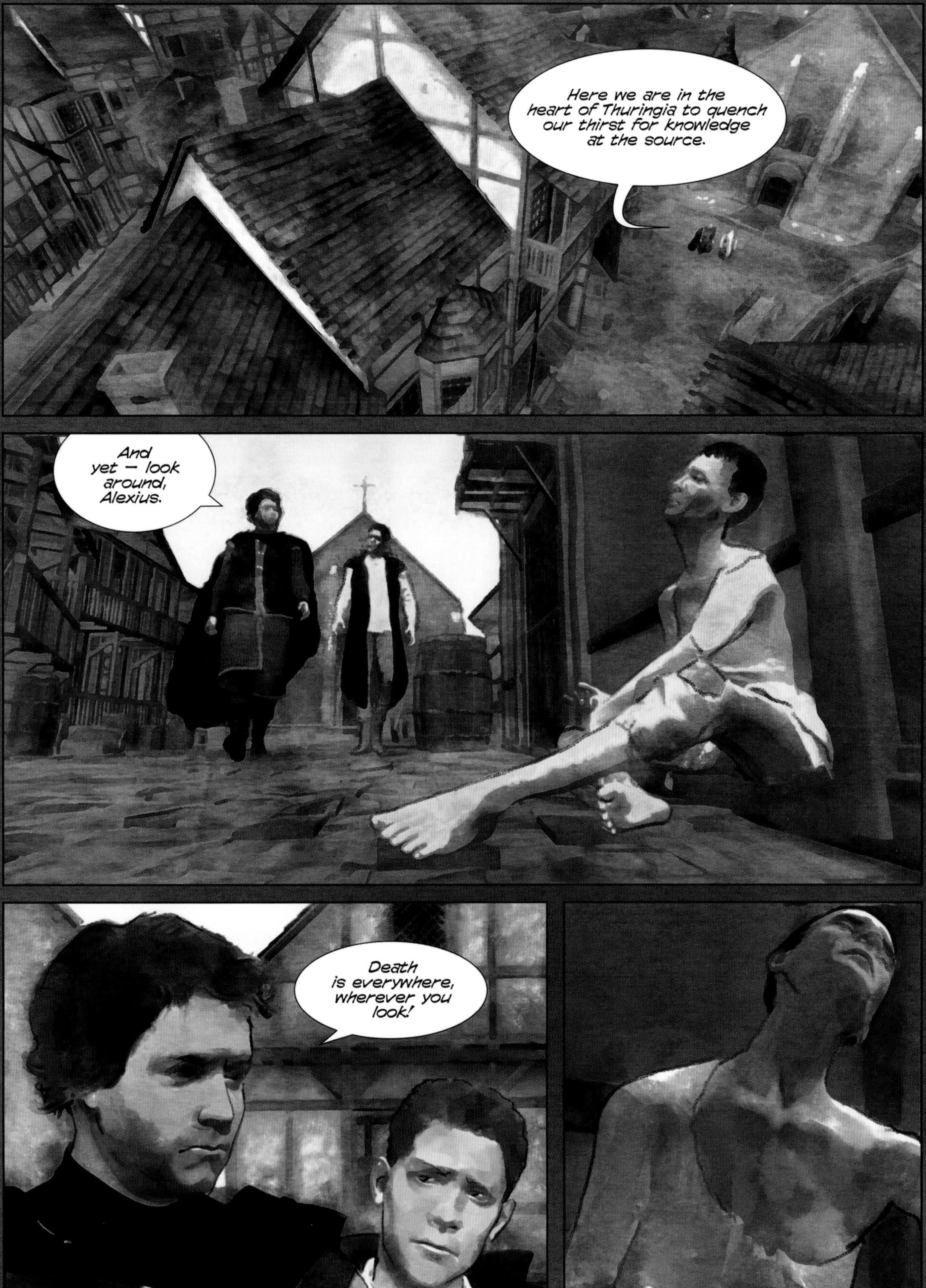
Here we are in the heart of Thuringia to quench our thirst for knowledge at the source.
And yet — look around, Alexius.
Death is everywhere, wherever you look!

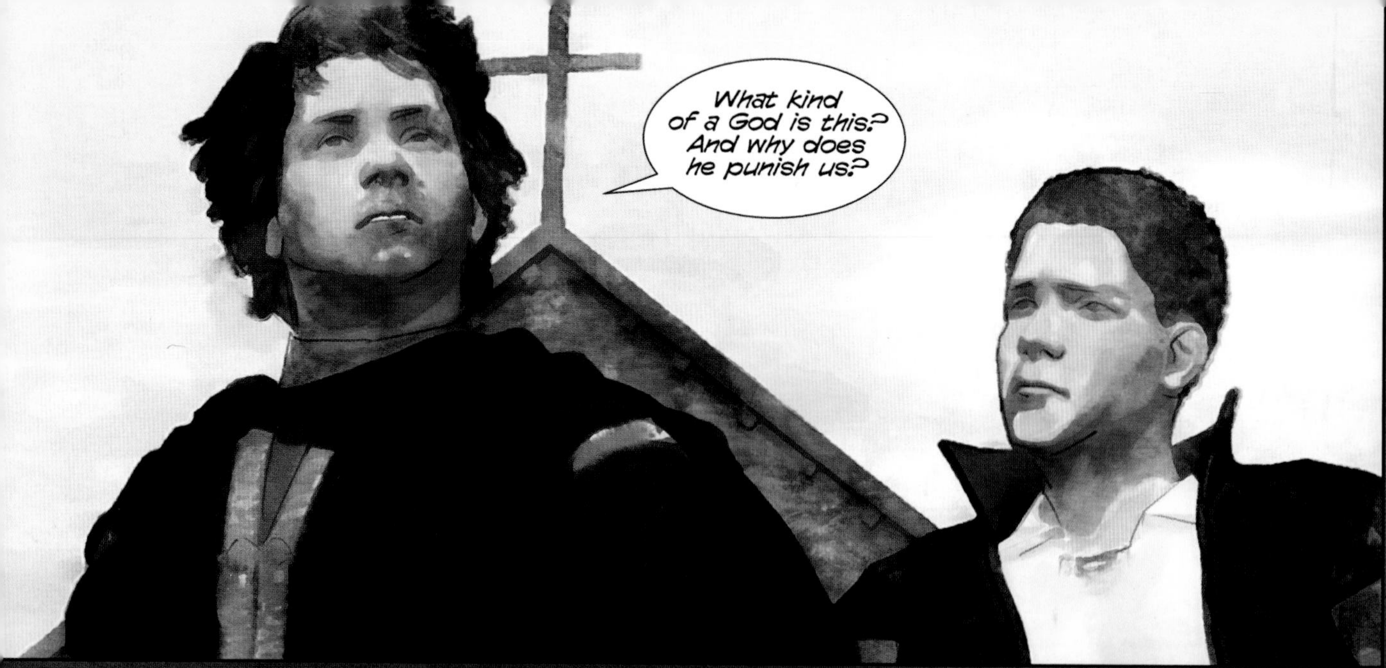
What kind of a God is this? And why does he punish us?

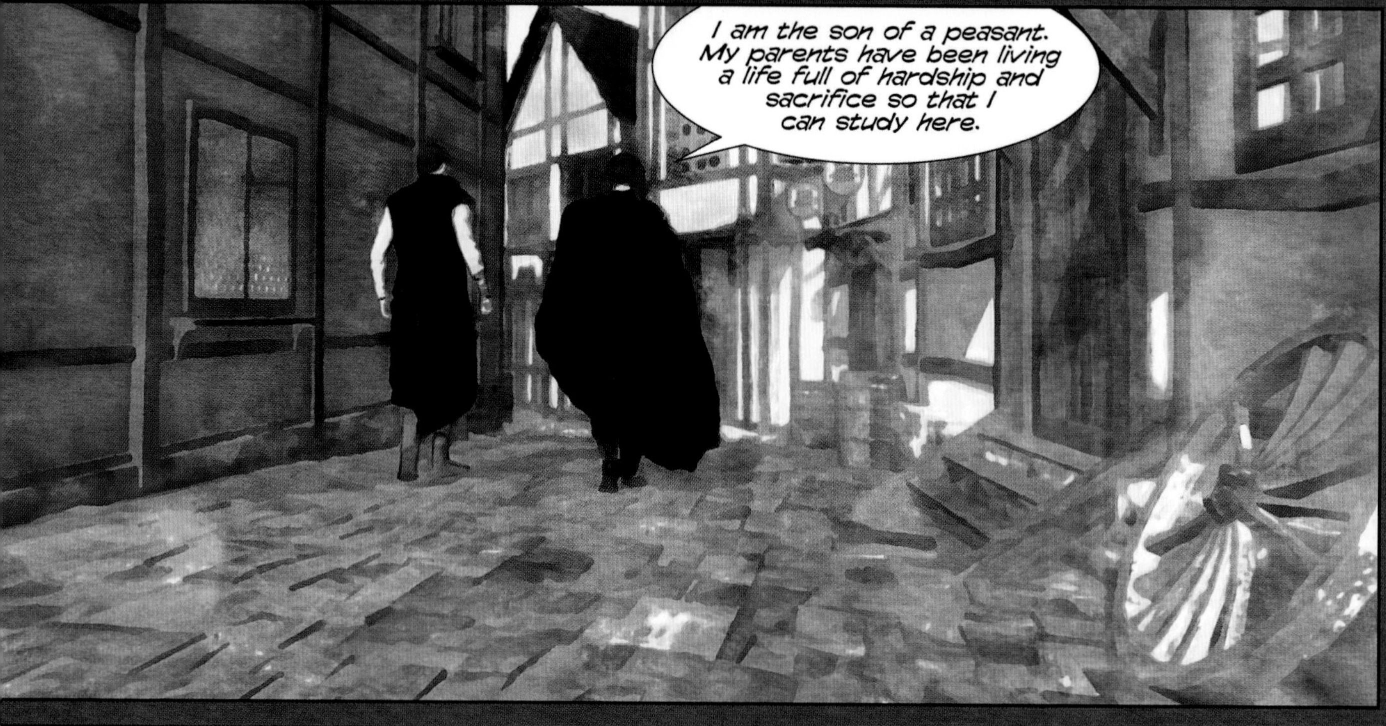
I am the son of a peasant. My parents have been living a life full of hardship and sacrifice so that I can study here.

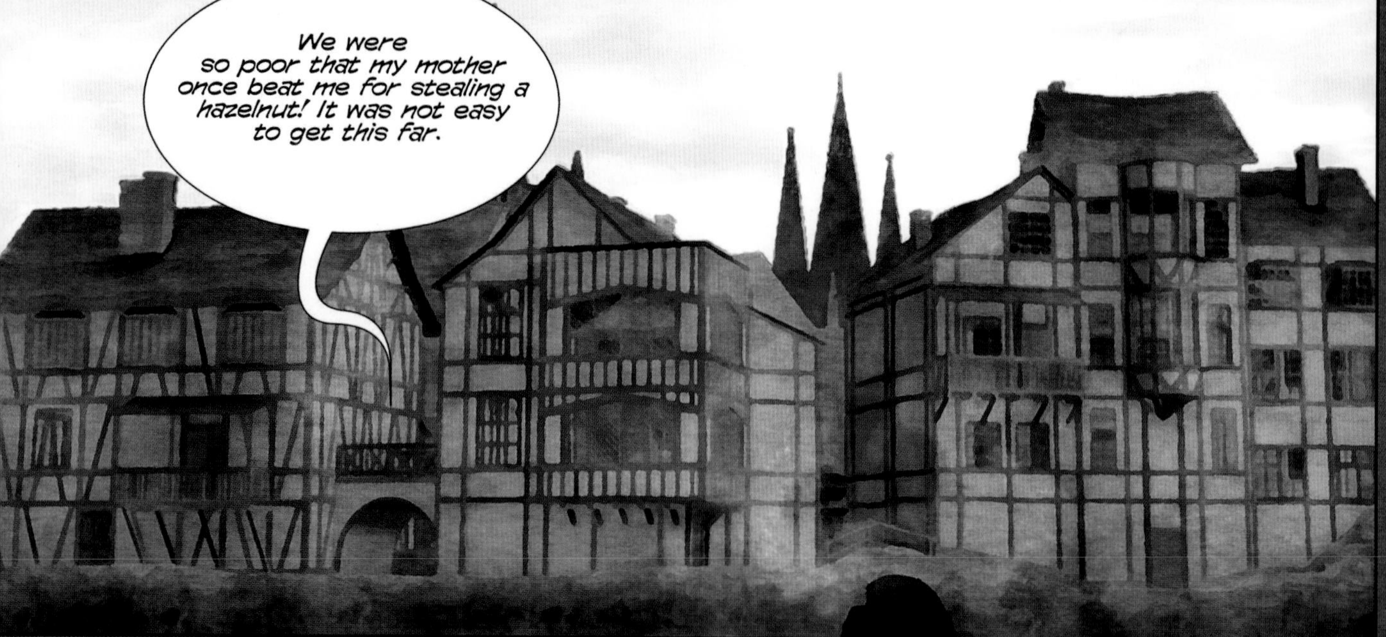
We were so poor that my mother once beat me for stealing a hazelnut! It was not easy to get this far.

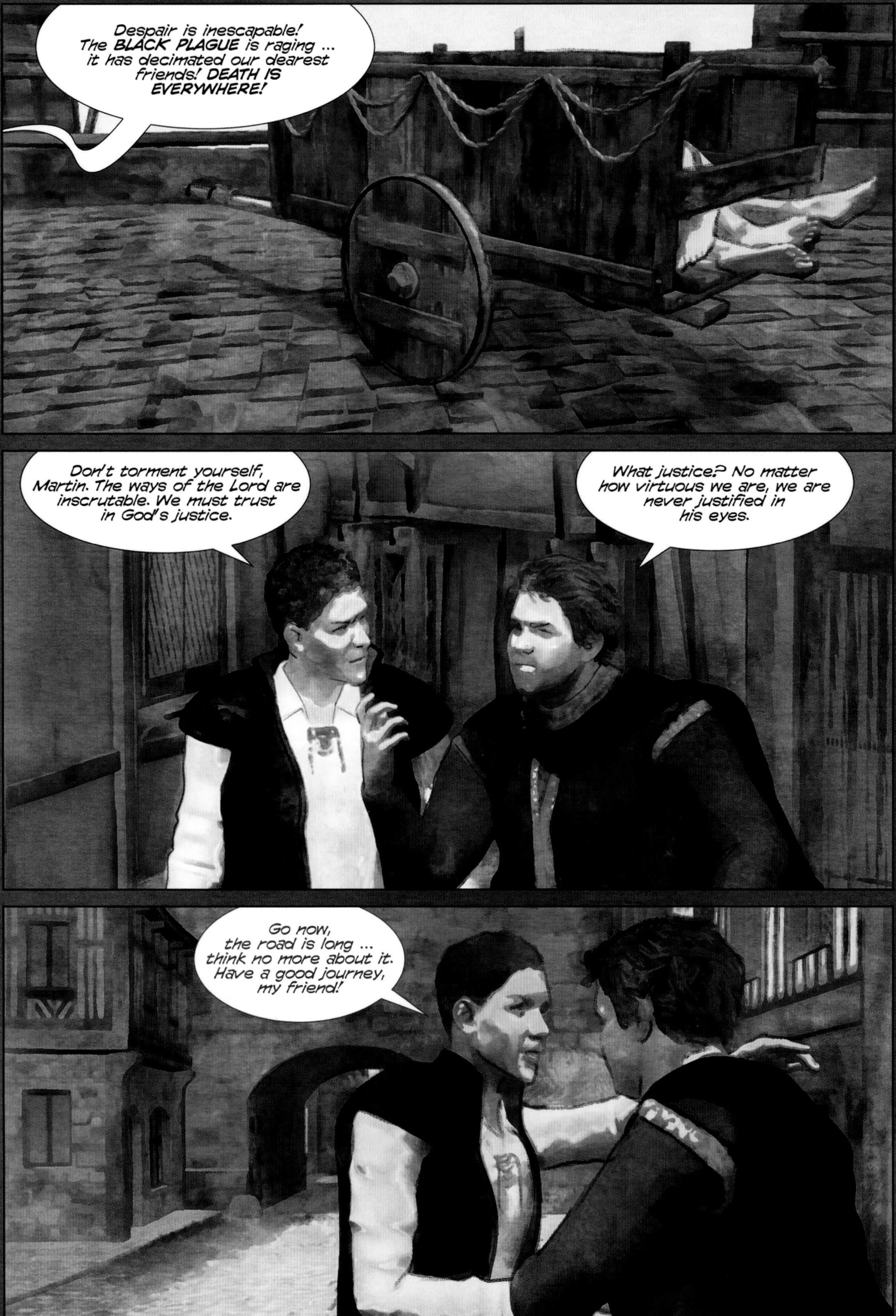
Despair is inescapable! The BLACK PLAGUE is raging ... it has decimated our dearest friends! DEATH IS EVERYWHERE!
Don't torment yourself, Martin. The ways of the Lord are inscrutable. We must trust in God's justice.
What justice? No matter how virtuous we are, we are never justified in his eyes.
Go now, the road is long ... think no more about it. Have a good journey, my friend!

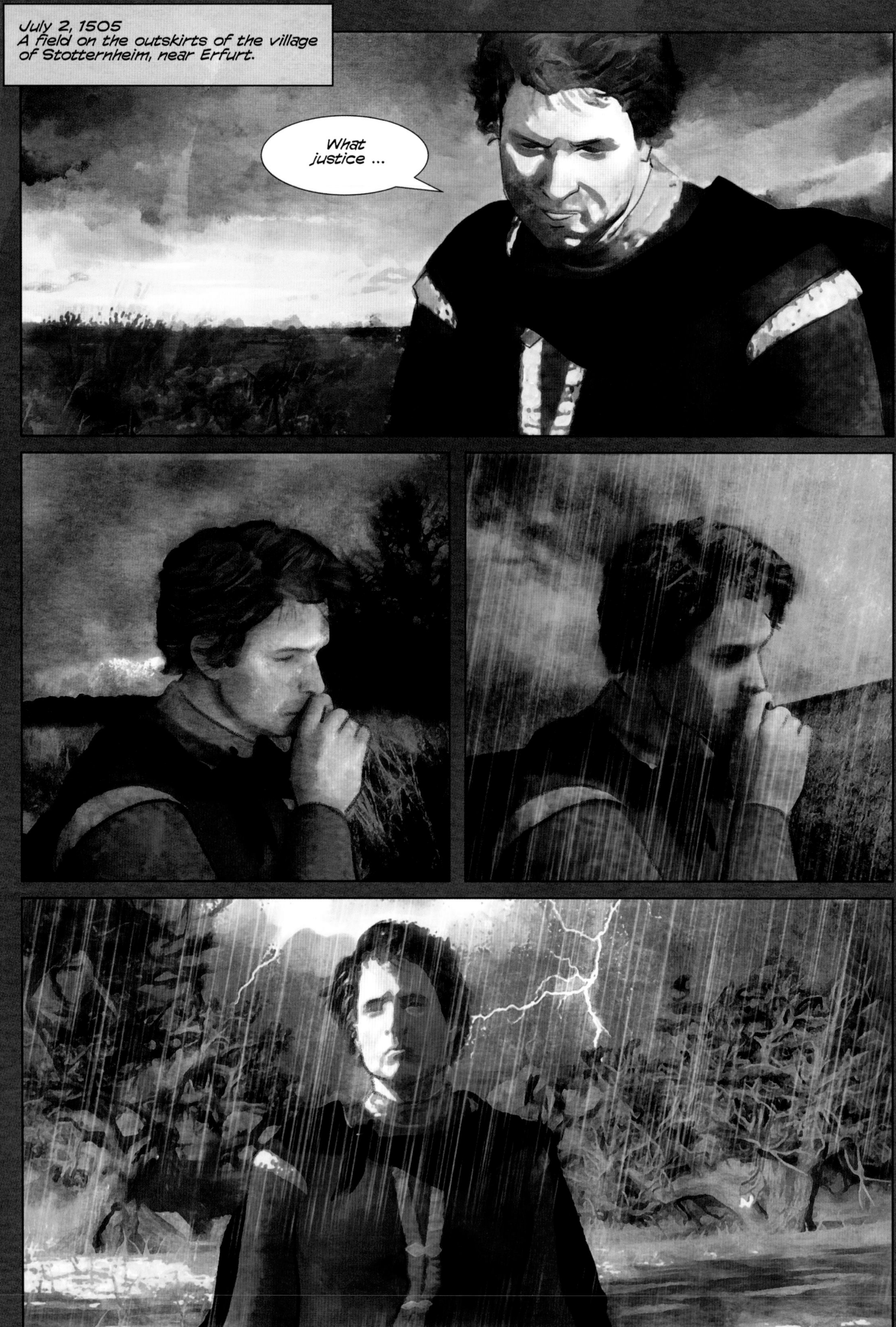
July 2, 1505
A field on the outskirts of the village of Stotternheim, near Erfurt.
What justice ...

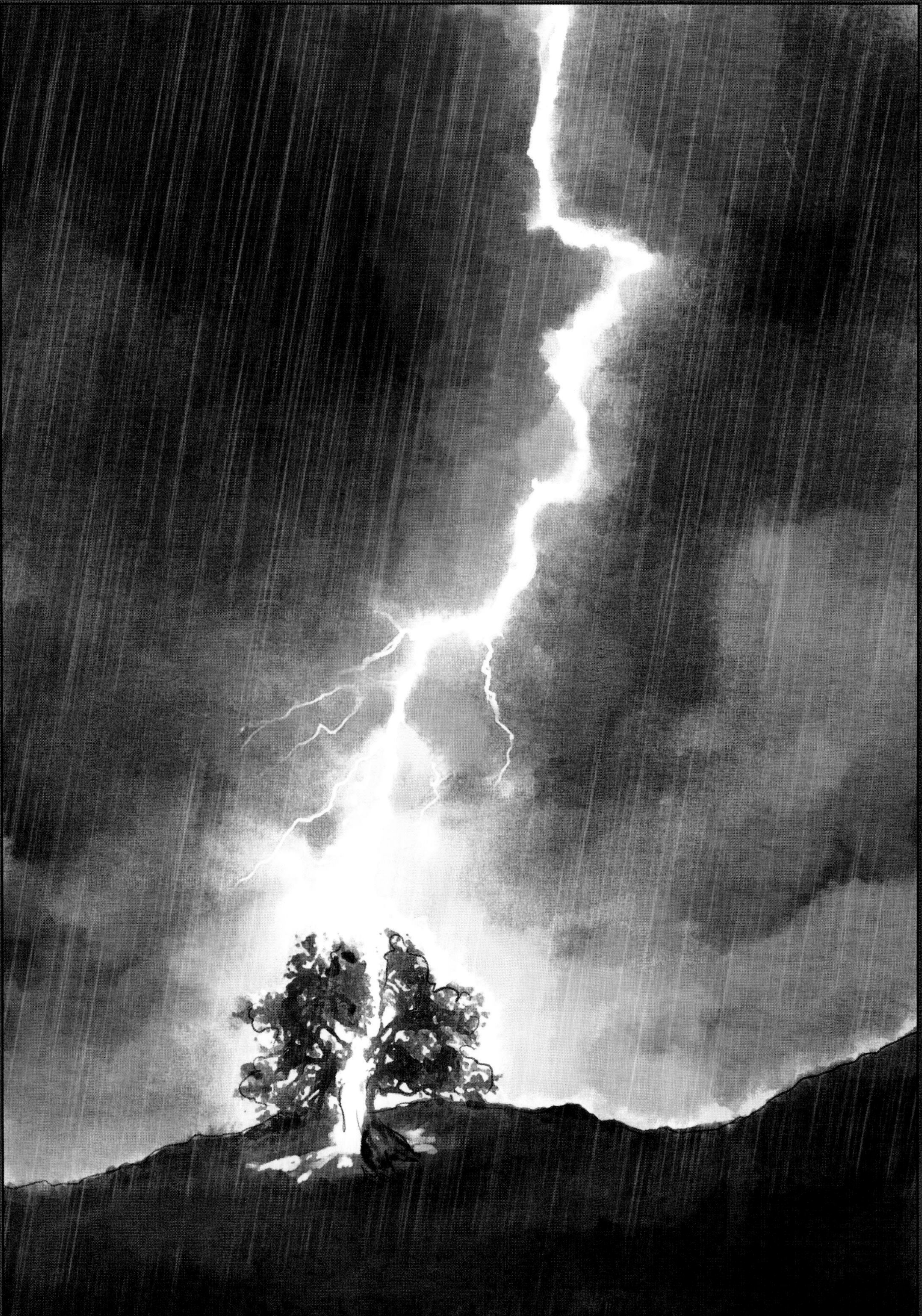

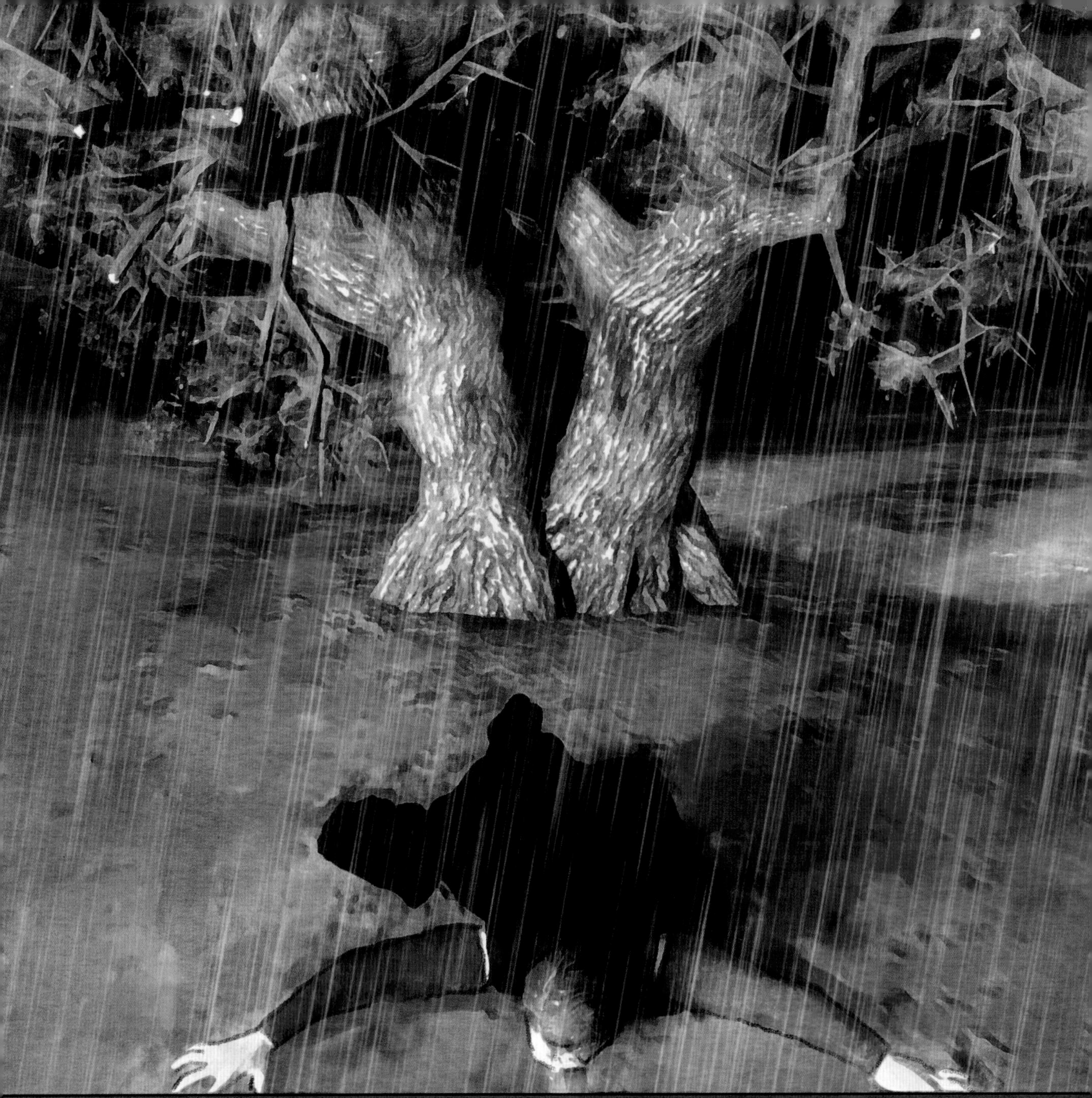

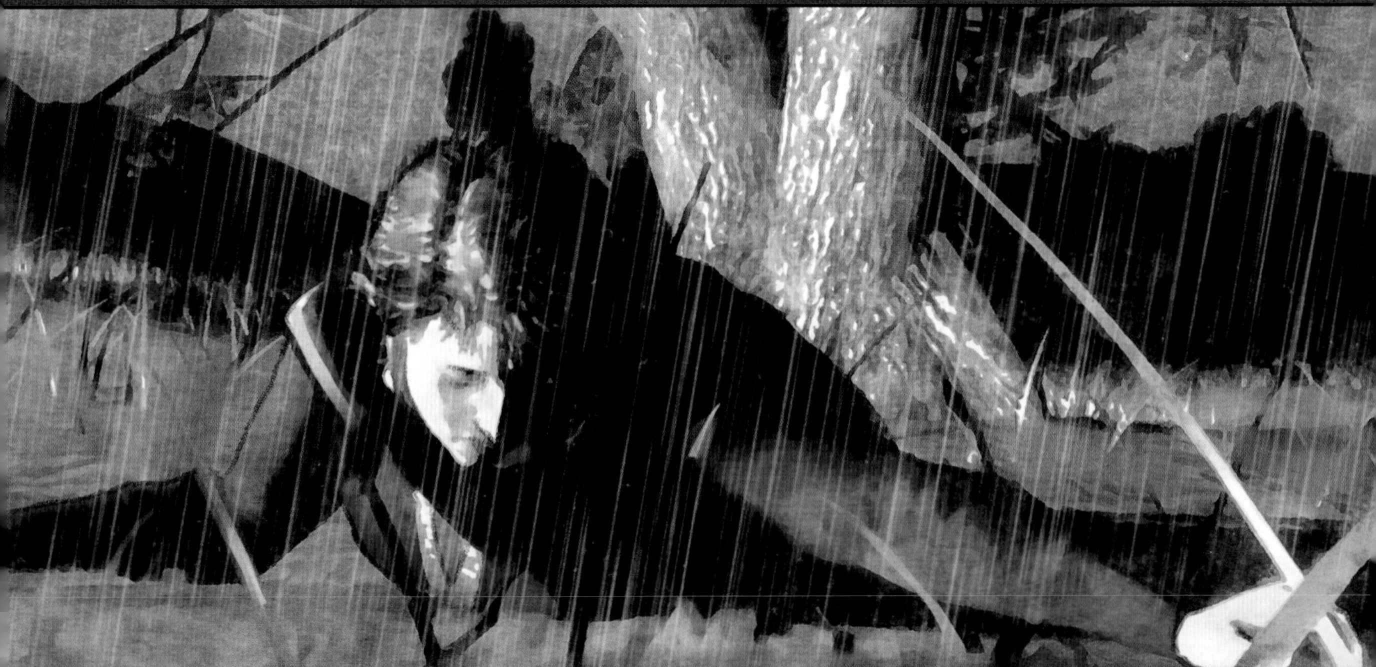

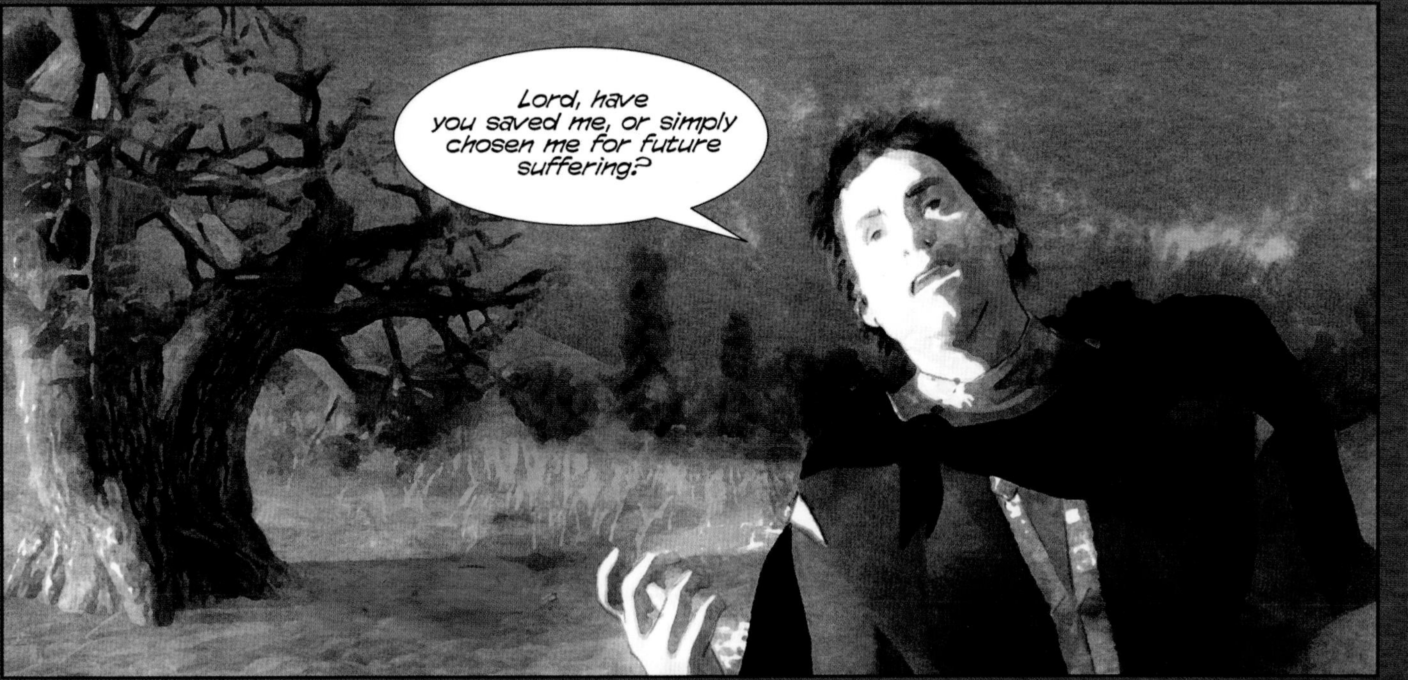
Lord, have you saved me, or simply chosen me for future suffering?

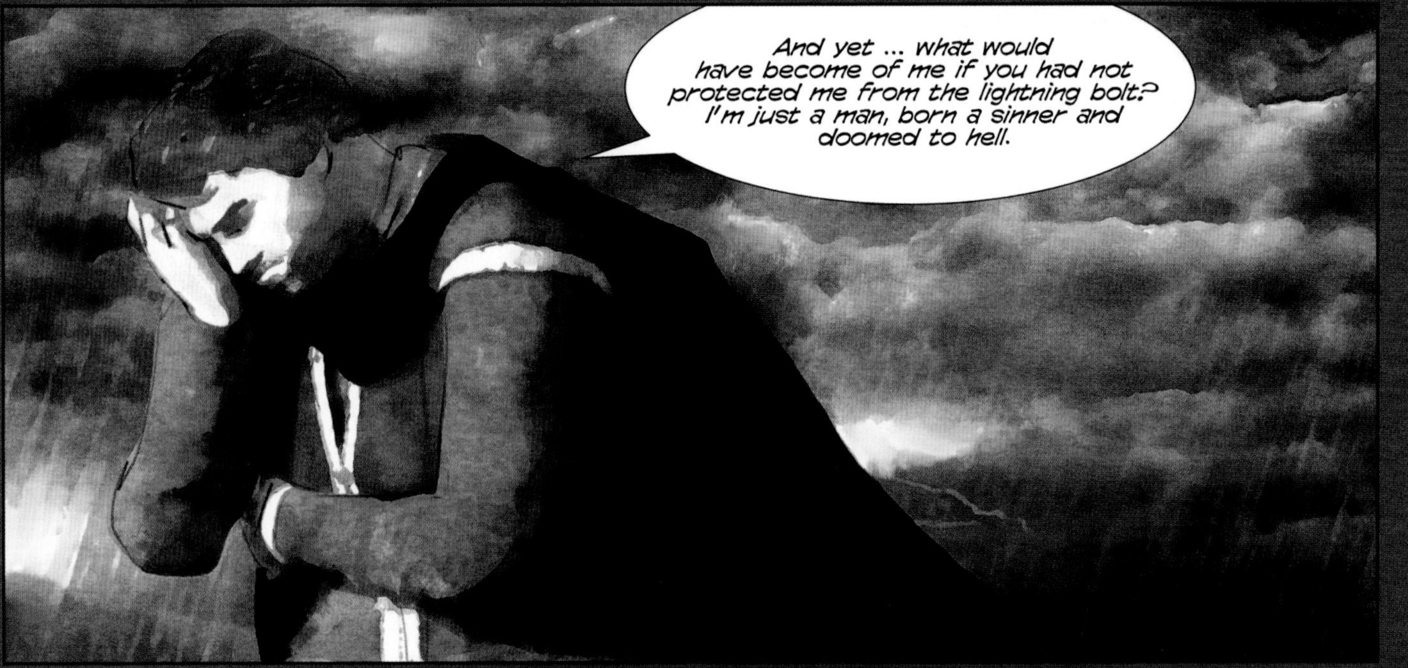
And yet ... what would have become of me if you had not protected me from the lightning bolt? I'm just a man, born a sinner and doomed to hell.

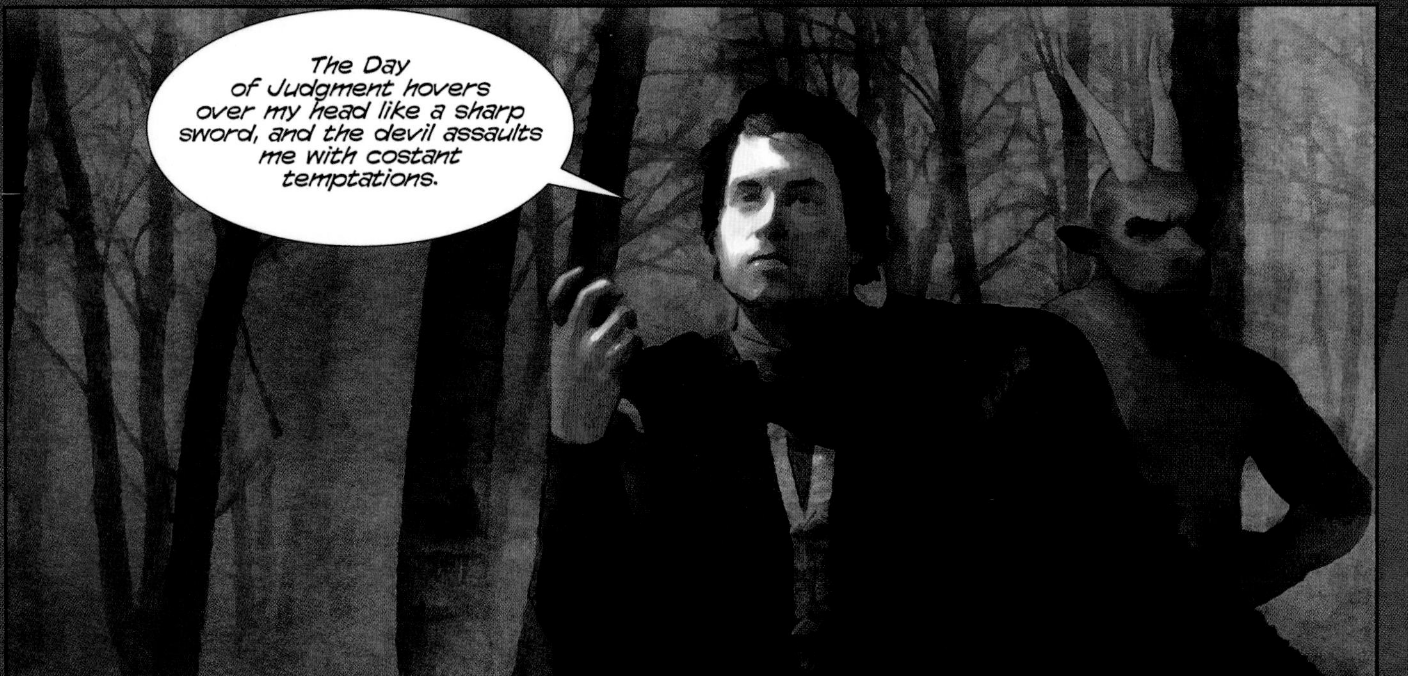
The Day of Judgment hovers over my head like a sharp sword, and the devil assaults me with costant temptations.

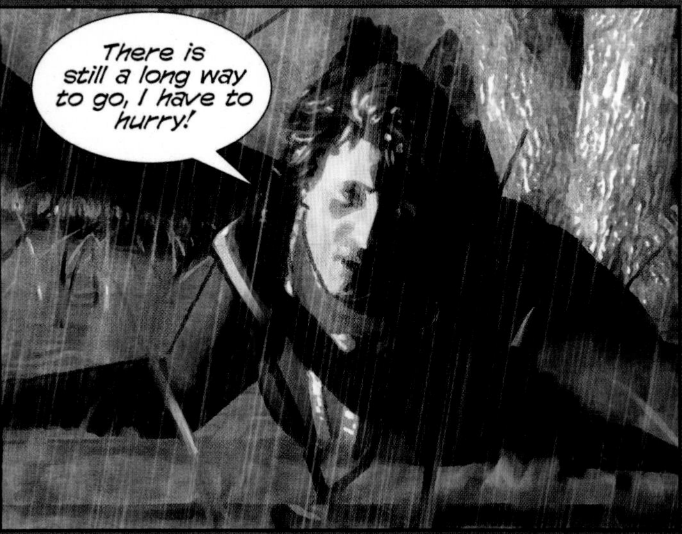
There is still a long way to go, I have to hurry!

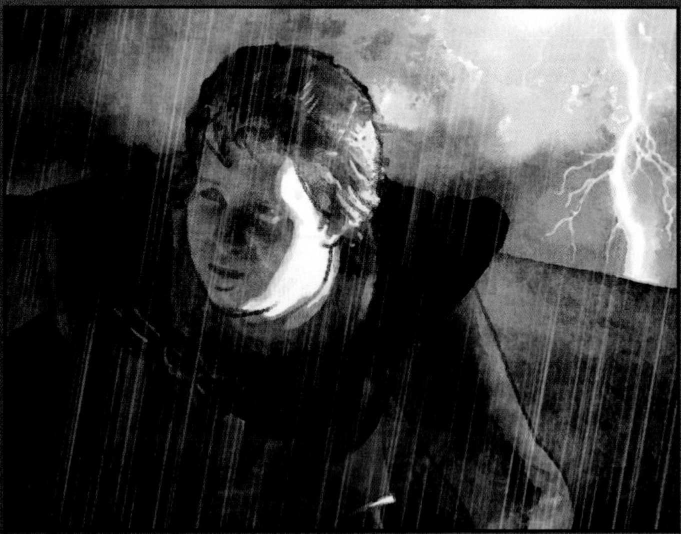

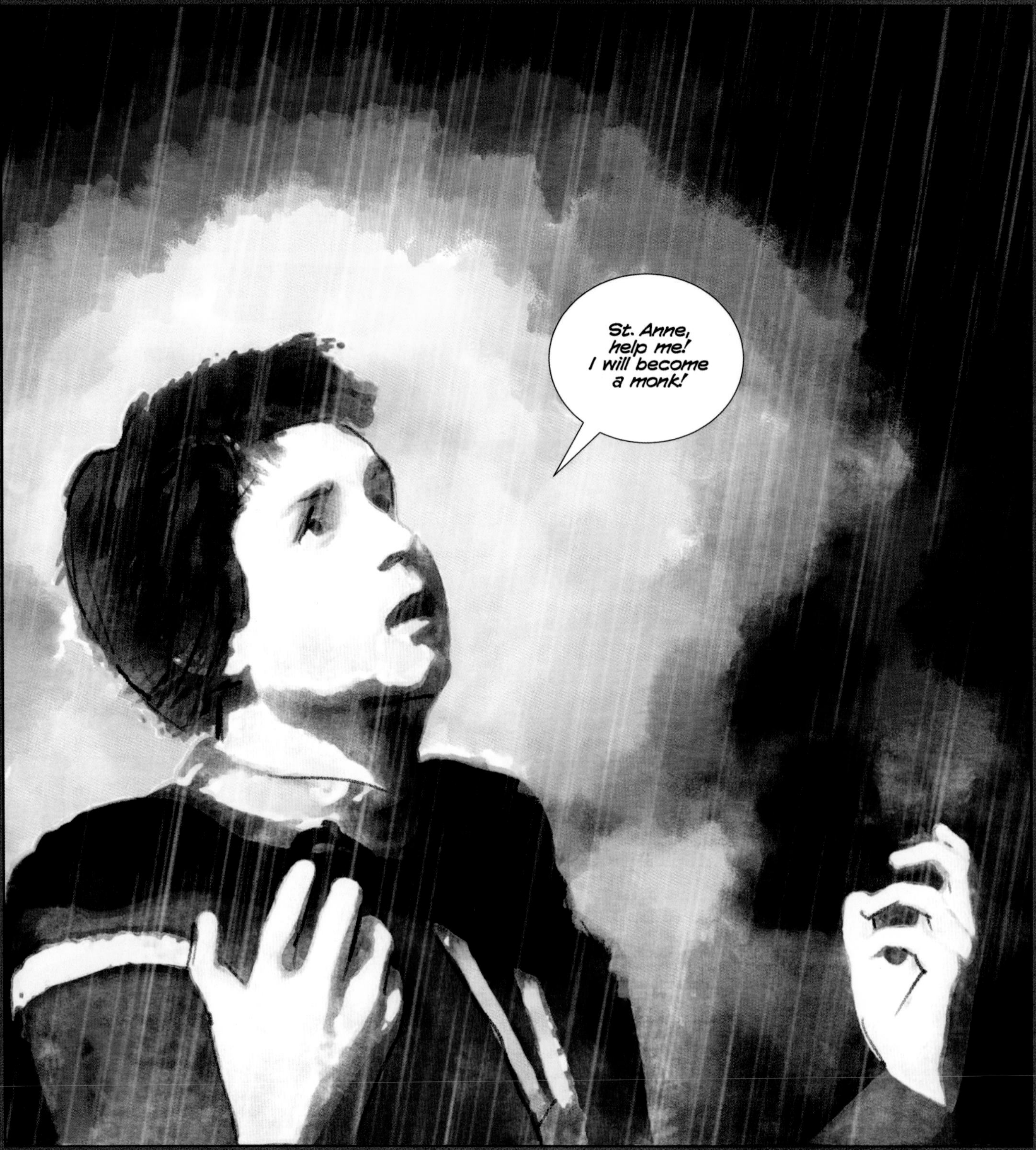
St. Anne, help me! I will become a monk!

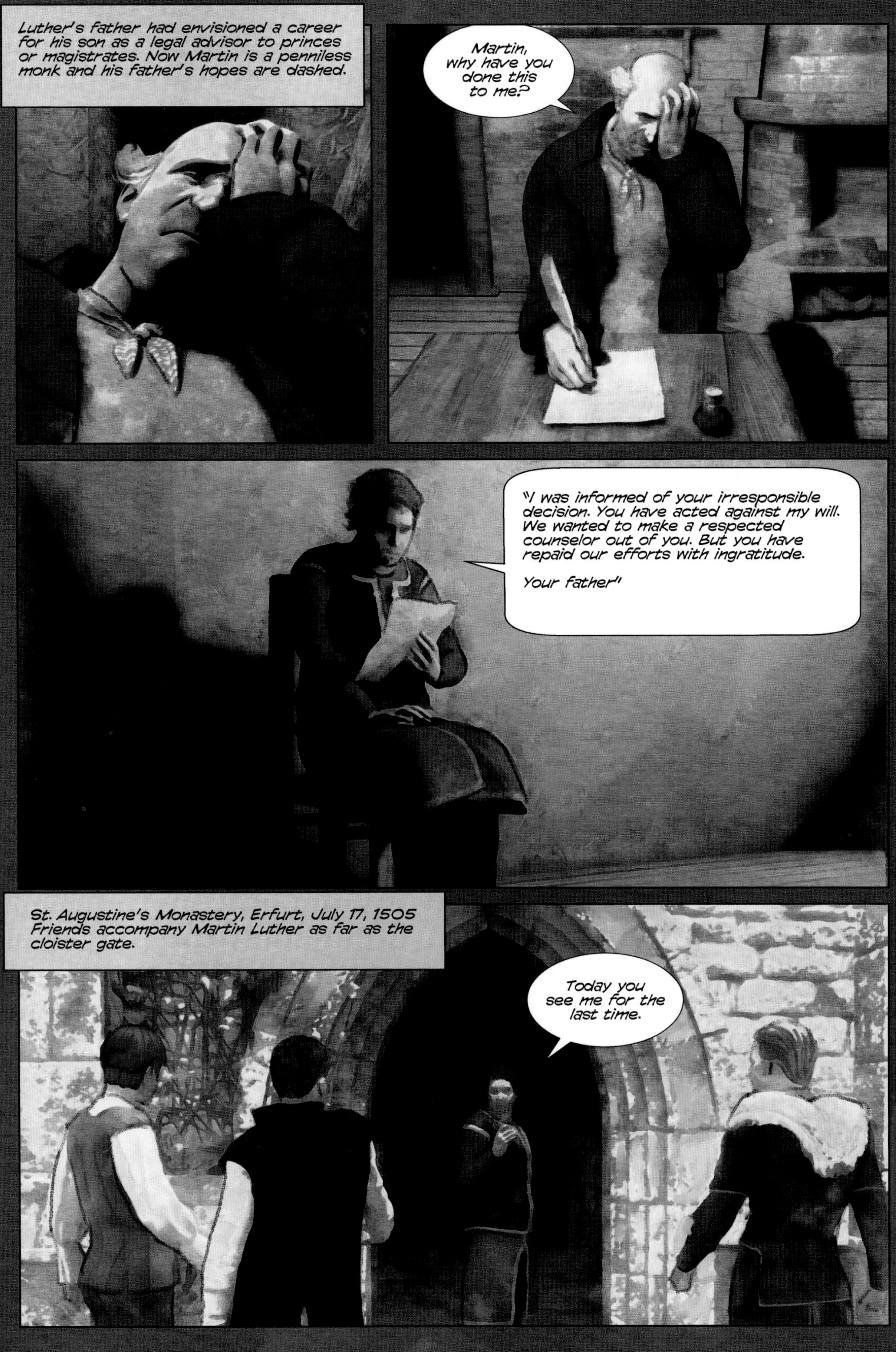
Luther's father had envisioned a career for his son as a legal advisor to princes or magistrates. Now Martin is a penniless monk and his father's hopes are dashed.
Martin, why have you done this to me?
"I was informed of your irresponsible decision. You have acted against my will. We wanted to make a respected counselor out of you. But you have repaid our efforts with ingratitude.
Your father"
St. Augustine's Monastery, Erfurt, July 17, 1505 Friends accompany Martin Luther as far as the cloister gate.
Today you see me for the last time.

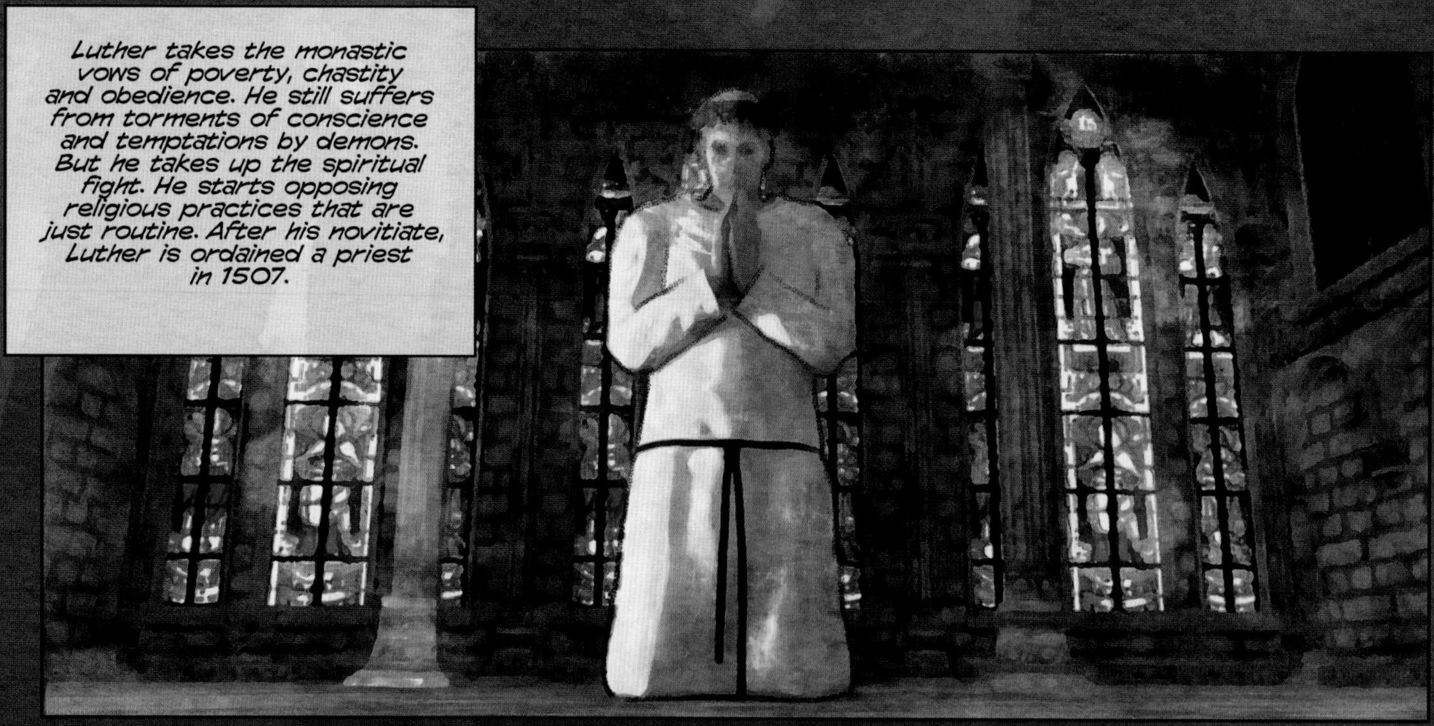
Luther takes the monastic vows of poverty, chastity and obedience. He still suffers from torments of conscience and temptations by demons. But he takes up the spiritual fight. He starts opposing religious practices that are just routine. After his novitiate, Luther is ordained a priest in 1507.

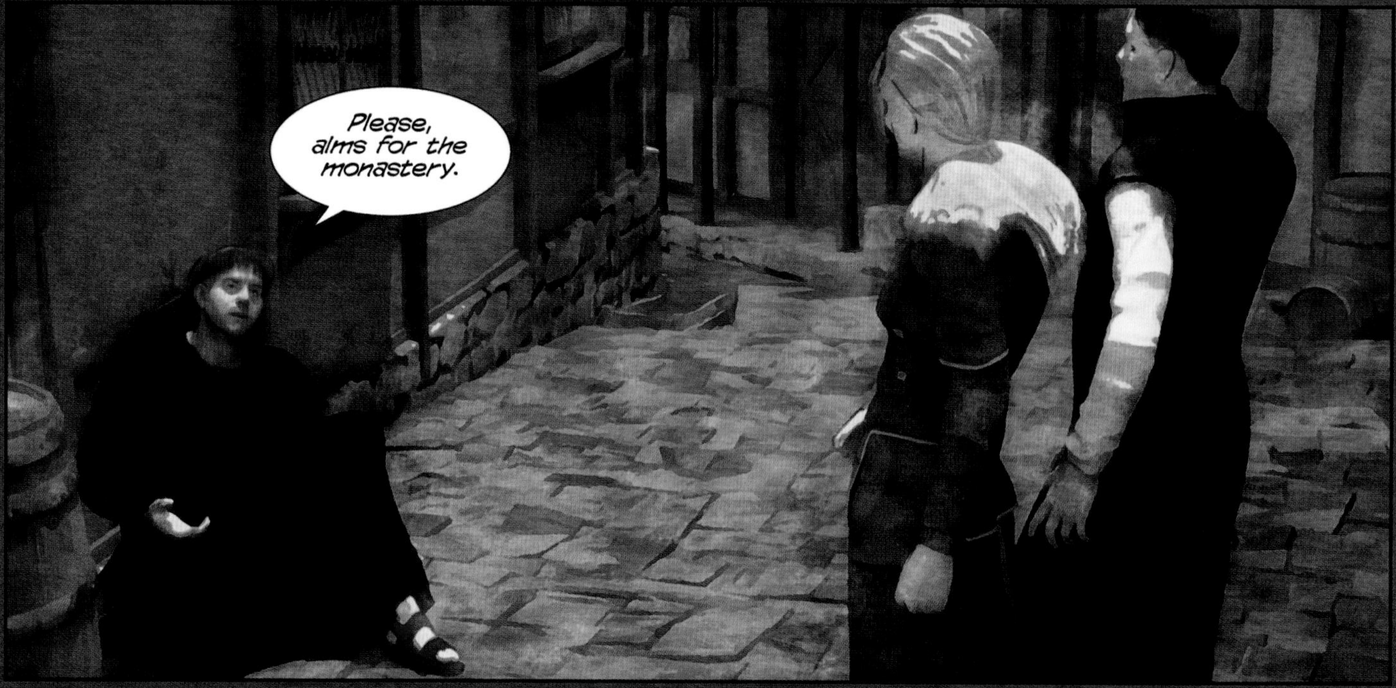
Please, alms for the monastery.

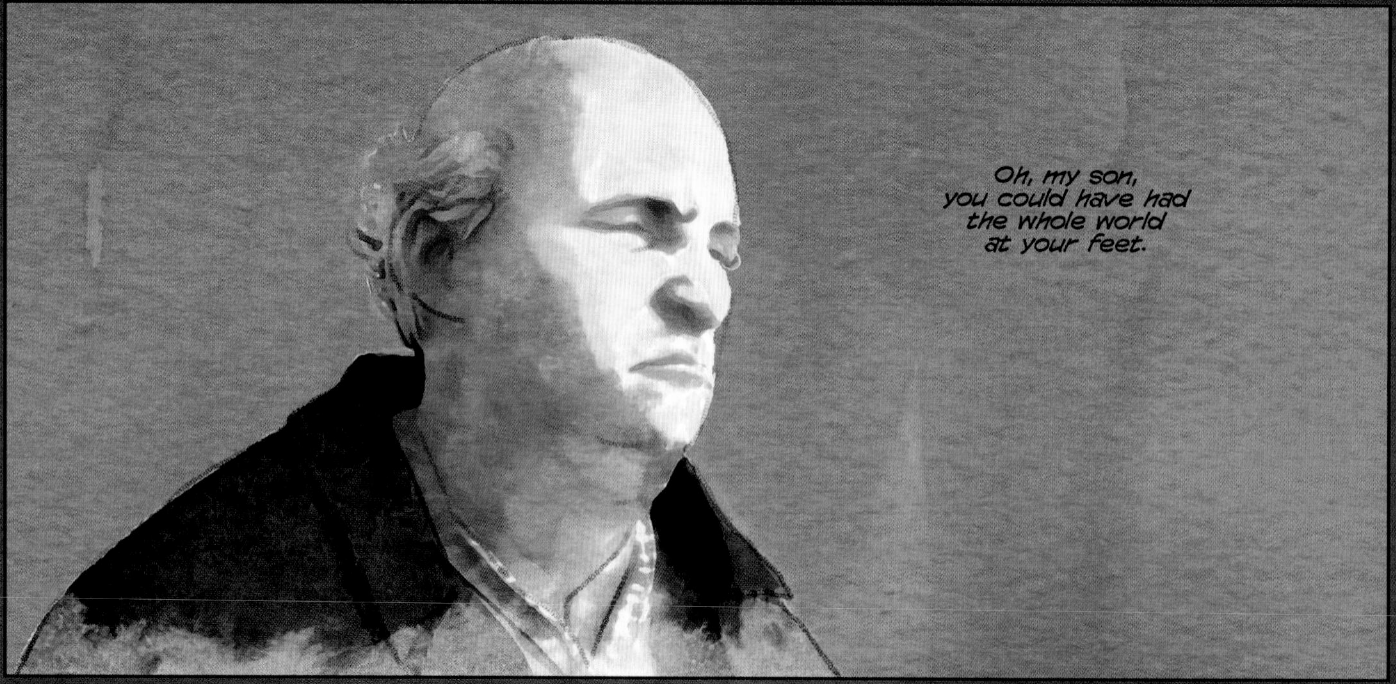
Oh, my son, you could have had the whole world at your feet.

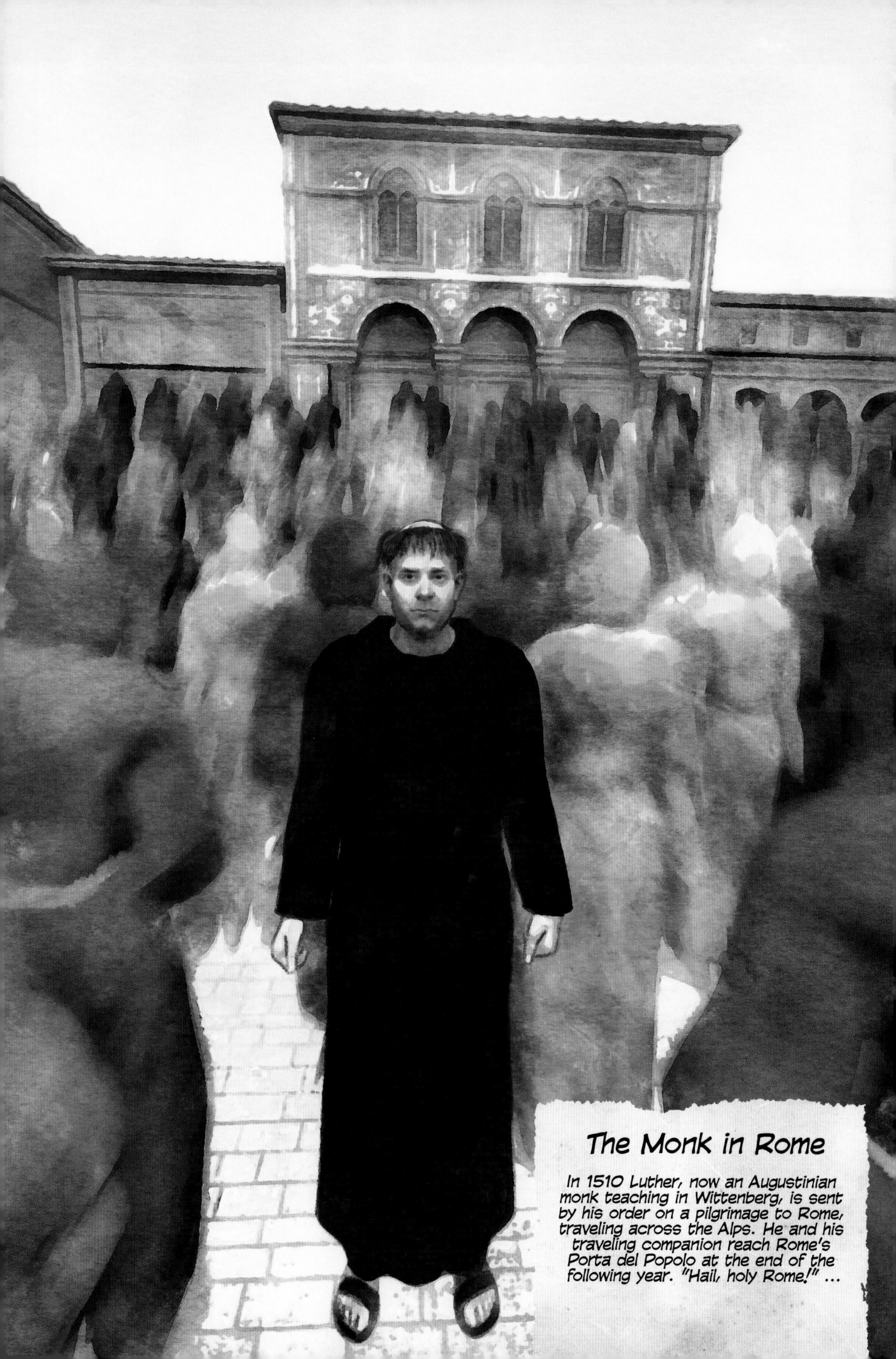
The Monk in Rome
In 1510 Luther, now an Augustinian monk teaching in Wittenberg, is sent by his order on a pilgrimage to Rome, traveling across the Alps. He and his traveling companion reach Rome's Porta del Popolo at the end of the following year. "Hail, holy Rome!" ...

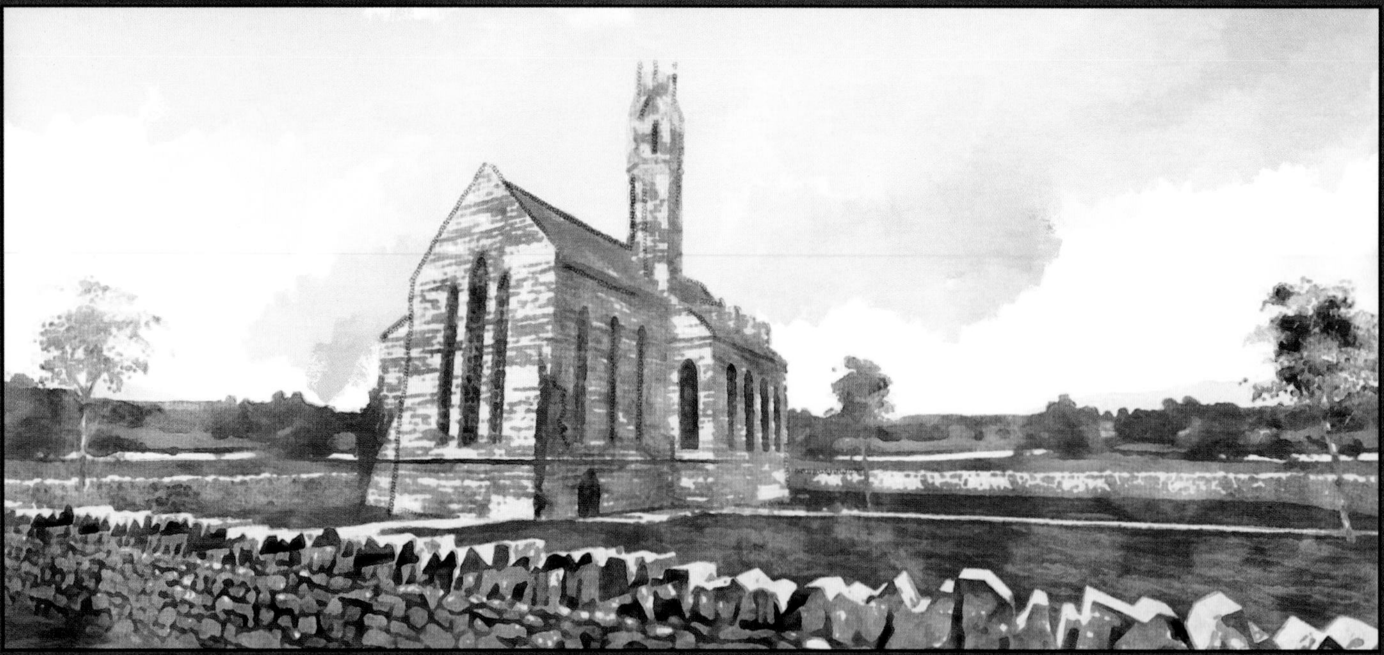

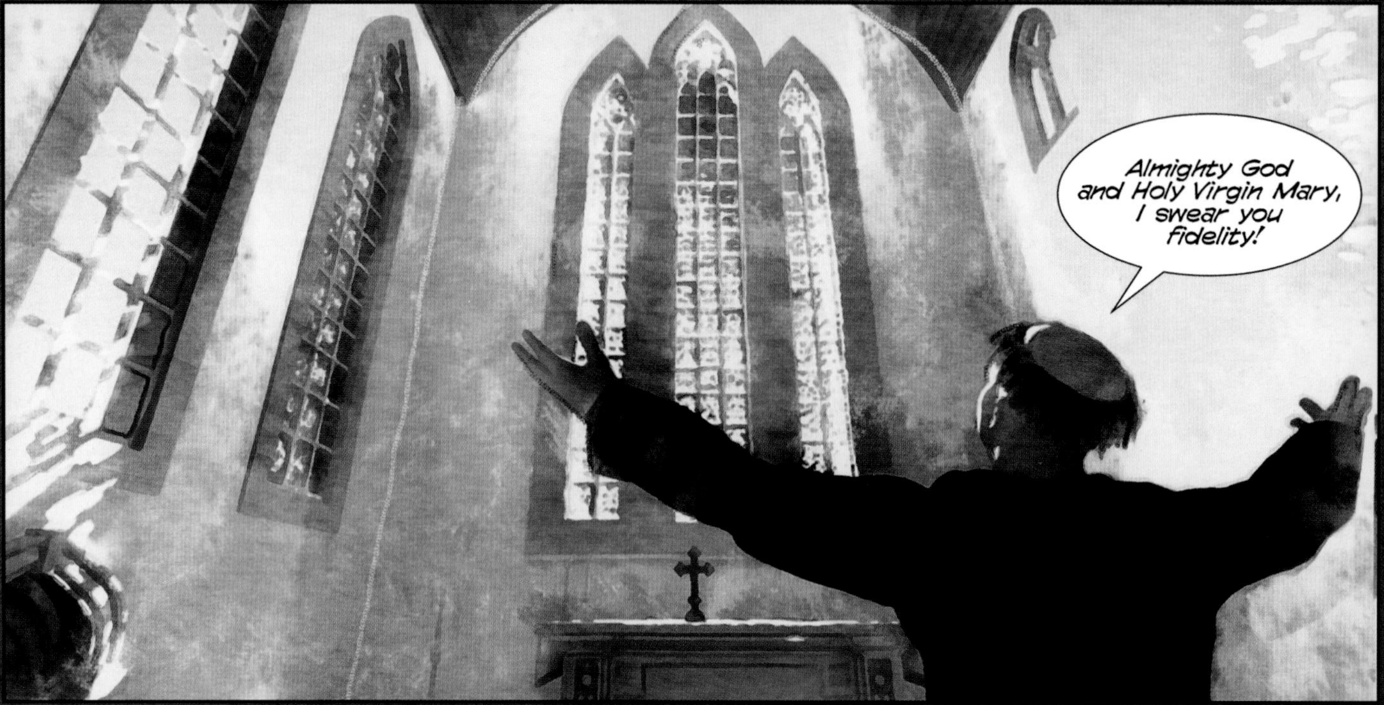
Almighty God and Holy Virgin Mary, I swear you fidelity!

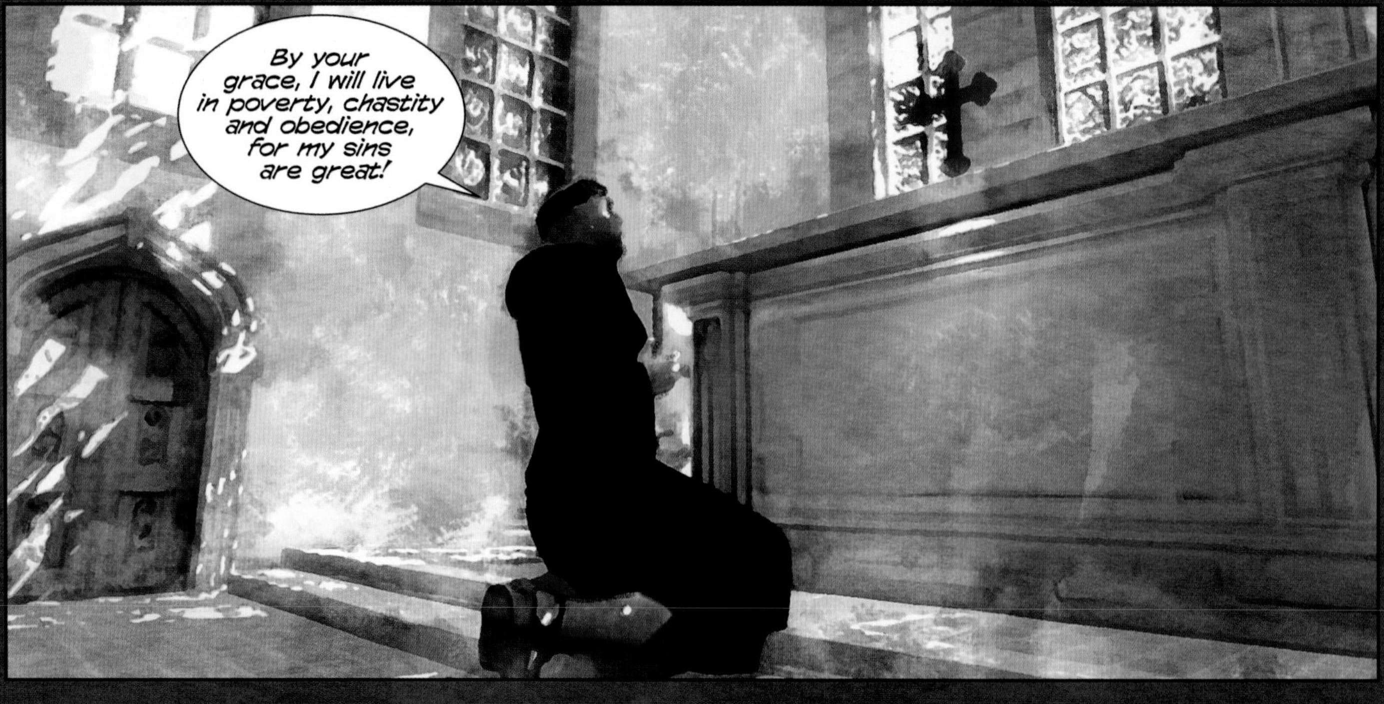
By your grace, I will live in poverty, chastity and obedience, for my sins are great!

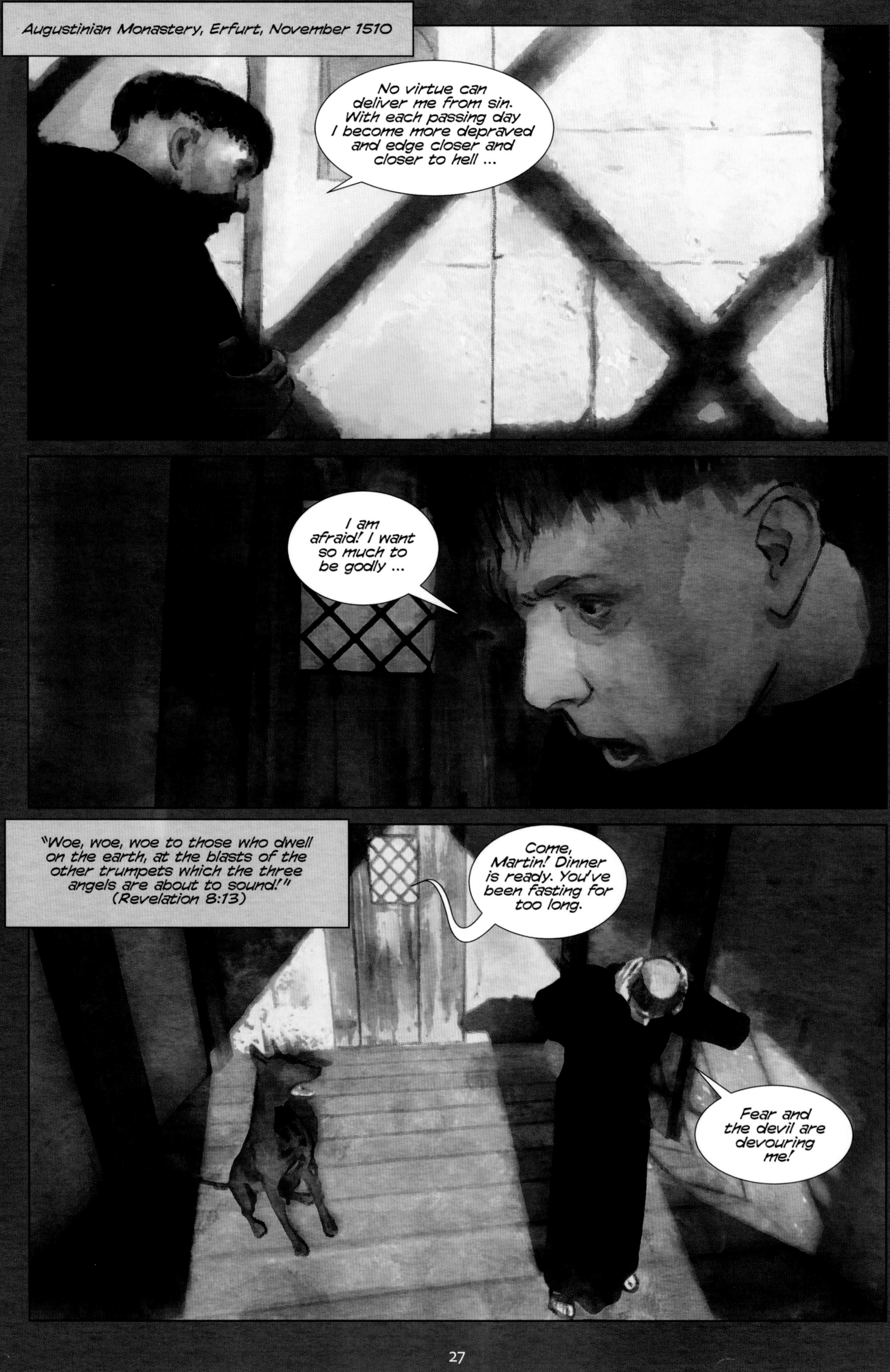
Augustinian Monastery, Erfurt, November 1510
No virtue can deliver me from sin. With each passing day I become more depraved and edge closer and closer to hell ...
I am afraid! I want so much to be godly ...
"Woe, woe, woe to those who dwell on the earth, at the blasts of the other trumpets which the three angels are about to sound!" (Revelation 8:13)
Come, Martin! Dinner is ready. You've been fasting for too long.
Fear and the devil are devouring me!

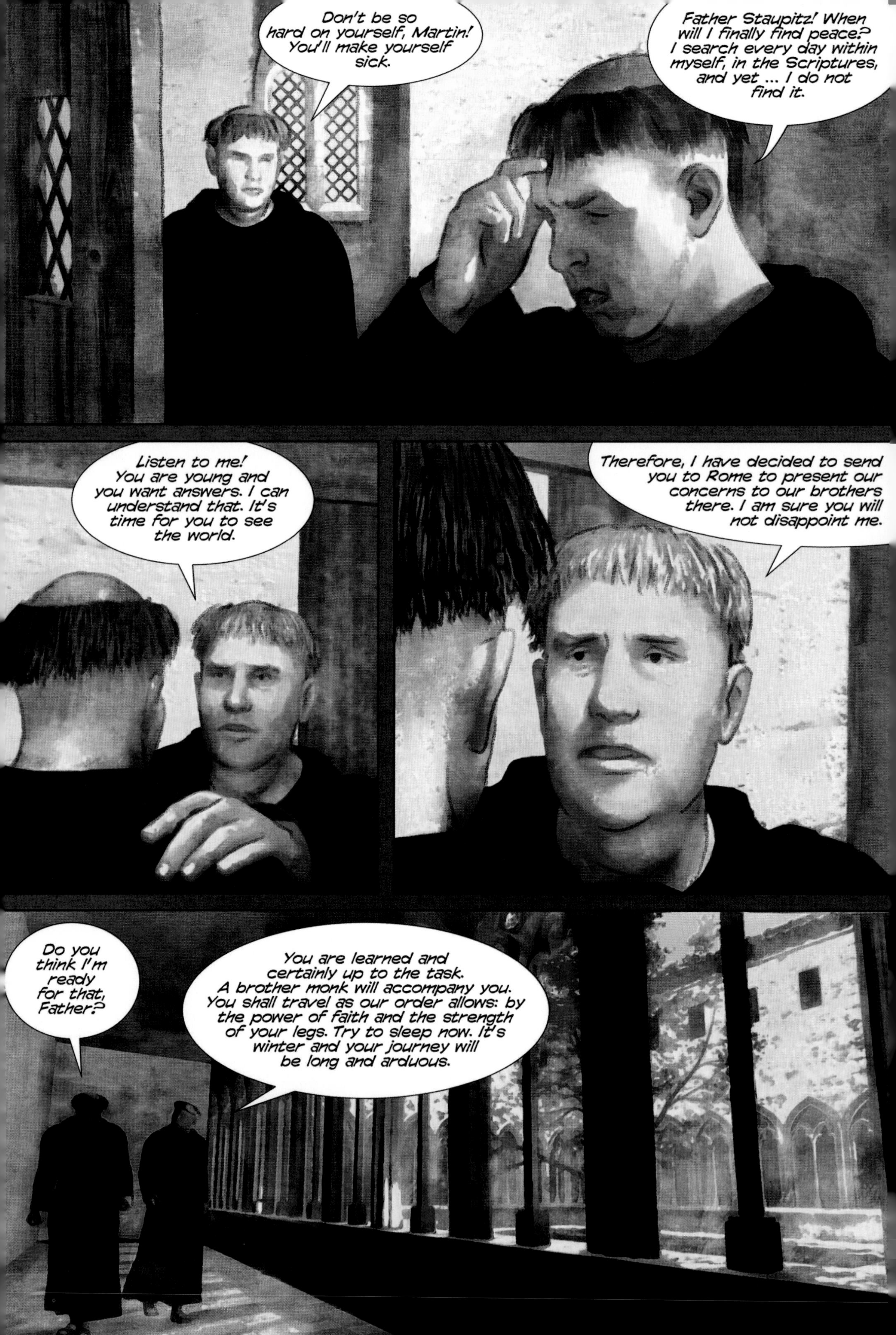
Don't be so hard on yourself, Martin! You'll make yourself sick.
Father Staupitz! When will I finally find peace? I search every day within myself, in the Scriptures, and yet ... I do not find it.
Listen to me! You are young and you want answers. I can understand that. It's time for you to see the world.
Therefore, I have decided to send you to Rome to present our concerns to our brothers there. I am sure you will not disappoint me.
Do you think I'm ready for that, Father?
You are learned and certainly up to the task. A brother monk will accompany you. You shall travel as our order allows: by the power of faith and the strength of your legs. Try to sleep now. It's winter and your journey will be long and arduous.

You will travel via Nuremberg over Ulm, Memmingen and Chur.

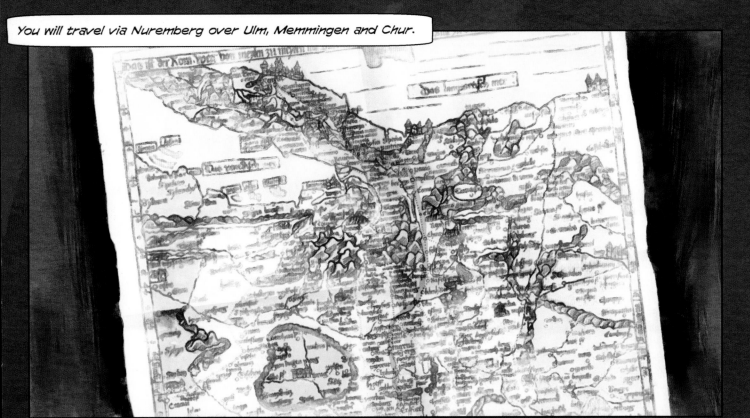

You will then cross the Alps and continue to Settimo.

Look around, Martin! Those are brothers who have died along the way! God bless them.

Come, brother, follow me. If we are caught in the storm, we too will die.

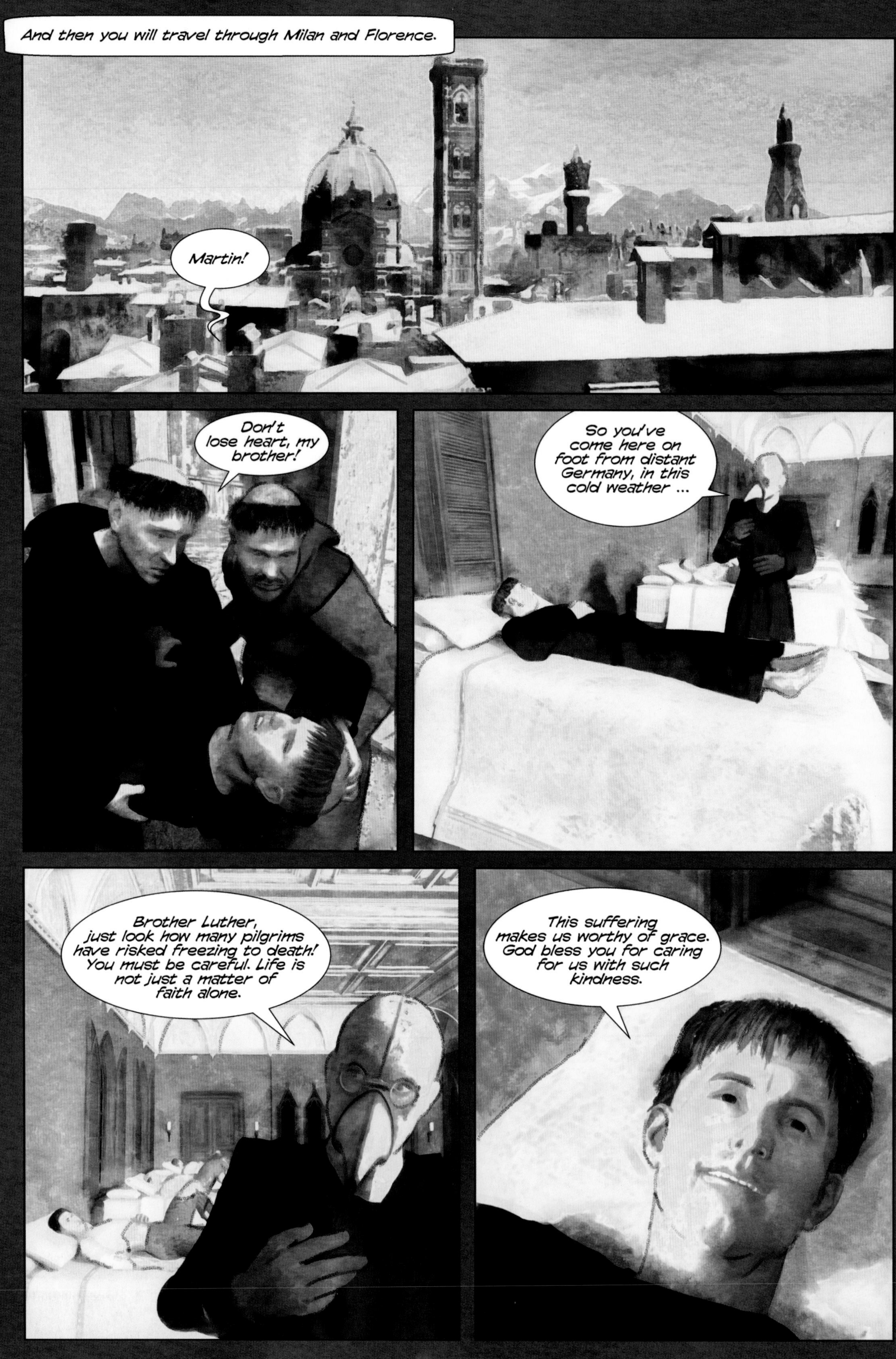
And then you will travel through Milan and Florence.
Martin!
Don't lose heart, my brother!
So you've come here on foot from distant Germany, in this cold weather ...
Brother Luther, just look how many pilgrims have risked freezing to death! You must be careful. Life is not just a matter of faith alone.
This suffering makes us worthy of grace. God bless you for caring for us with such kindness.

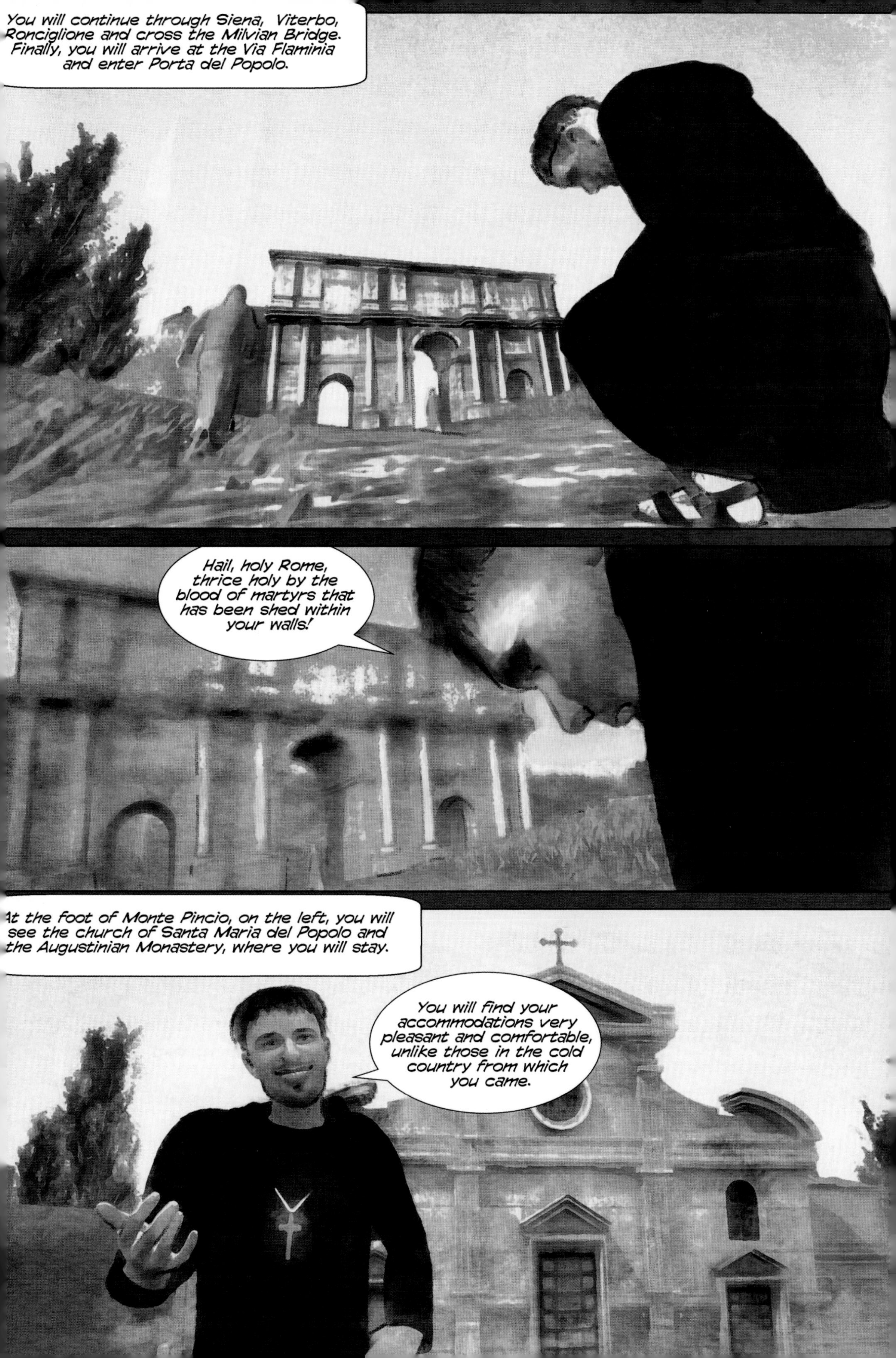
You will continue through Siena, Viterbo, Ronciglione and cross the Milvian Bridge. Finally, you will arrive at the Via Flaminia and enter Porta del Popolo.
Hail, holy Rome, thrice holy by the blood of martyrs that has been shed within your walls!
At the foot of Monte Pincio, on the left, you will see the church of Santa Maria del Popolo and the Augustinian Monastery, where you will stay.
You will find your accommodations very pleasant and comfortable, unlike those in the cold country from which you came.

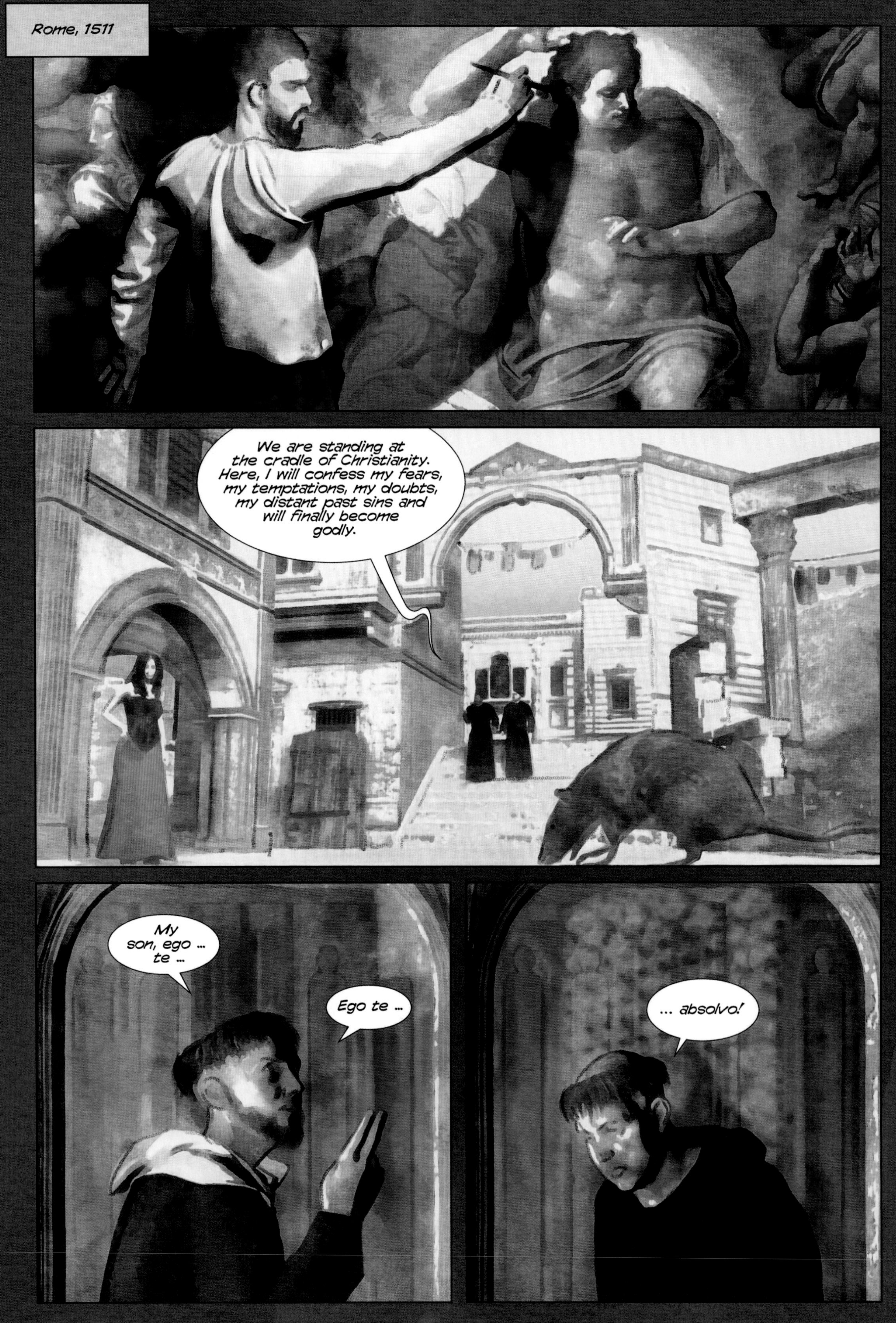
Rome, 1511
We are standing at the cradle of Christianity. Here, I will confess my fears, my temptations, my doubts, my distant past sins and will finally become godly.
My son, ego ... te ...
Ego te ...
... absolvo!

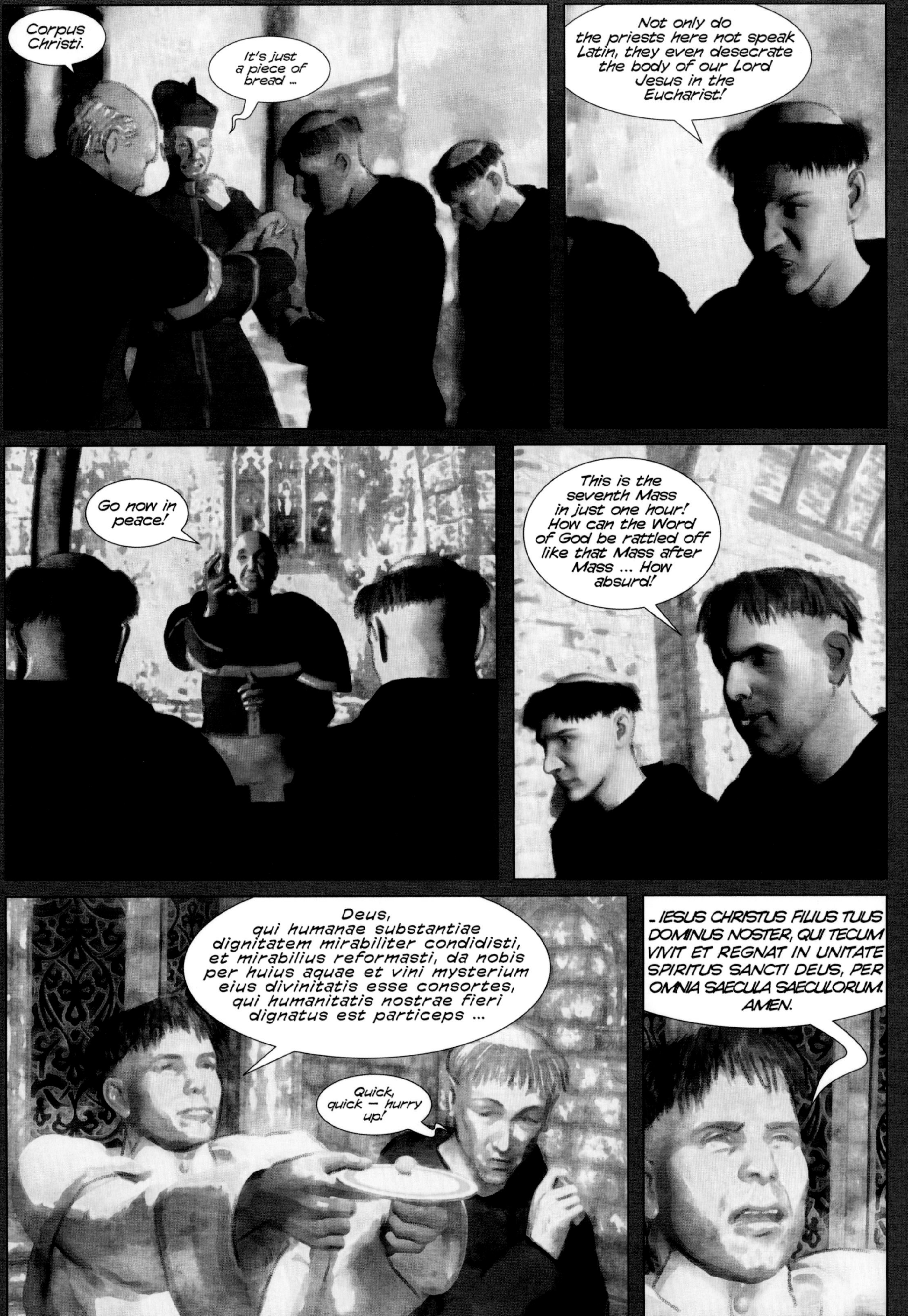

Corpus Christi.
It's just a piece of bread ...
Not only do the priests here not speak Latin, they even desecrate the body of our Lord Jesus in the Eucharist!
Go now in peace!
This is the seventh Mass in just one hour! How can the Word of God be rattled off like that Mass after Mass ... How absurd!
Deus, qui humanae substantiae dignitatem mirabiliter condidisti, et mirabilius reformasti, da nobis per huius aquae et vini mysterium eius divinitatis esse consortes, qui humanitatis nostrae fieri dignatus est particeps ...
Quick, quick — hurry up!
– IESUS CHRISTUS FILIUS TUUS DOMINUS NOSTER, QUI TECUM VIVIT ET REGNAT IN UNITATE SPIRITUS SANCTI DEUS, PER OMNIA SAECULA SAECULORUM. AMEN.

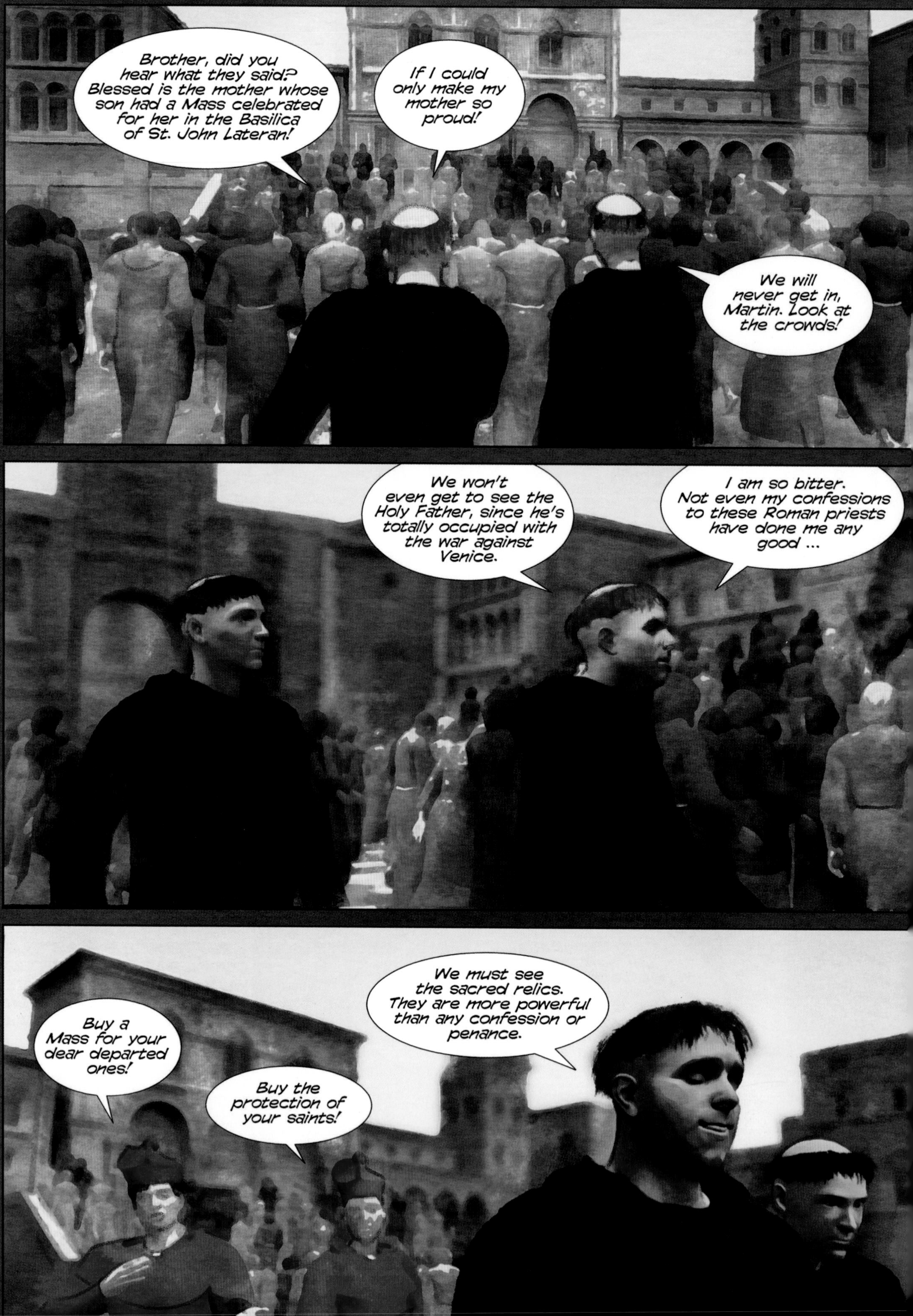
Brother, did you hear what they said? Blessed is the mother whose son had a Mass celebrated for her in the Basilica of St. John Lateran!
If I could only make my mother so proud!
We will never get in, Martin. Look at the crowds!
We won't even get to see the Holy Father, since he's totally occupied with the war against Venice.
I am so bitter. Not even my confessions to these Roman priests have done me any good ...
Buy a Mass for your dear departed ones!
Buy the protection of your saints!
We must see the sacred relics. They are more powerful than any confession or penance.

The seven pilgrim churches of Rome: St. Peter's, St. Paul Outside-the-Walls, St. Mary Major, St. Lawrence Outside-the-Walls, the Basilica of the Holy Cross in Jerusalem, St. Sebastian Outside-the-Walls, St. John Lateran.

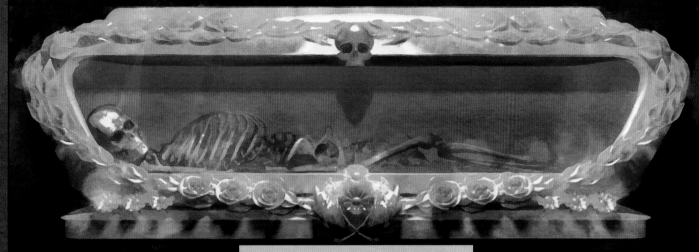

The bones of St. Peter.

The remains of St. Paul.

The scissors with which the Emperor Domitian cut off the hair of John of Patmos.

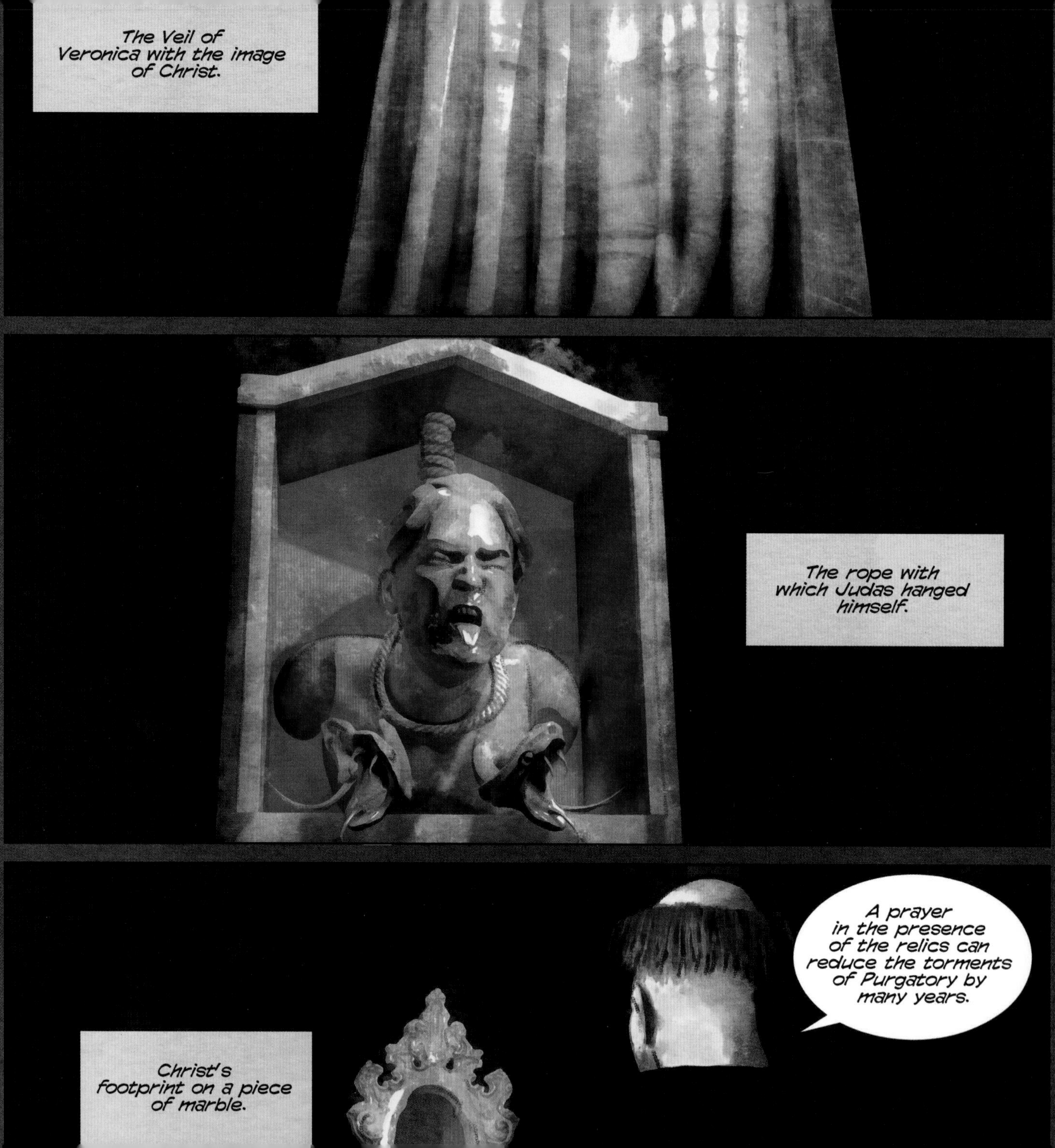
The Veil of Veronica with the image of Christ.
The rope with which Judas hanged himself.
A prayer in the presence of the relics can reduce the torments of Purgatory by many years.
Christ's footprint on a piece of marble.

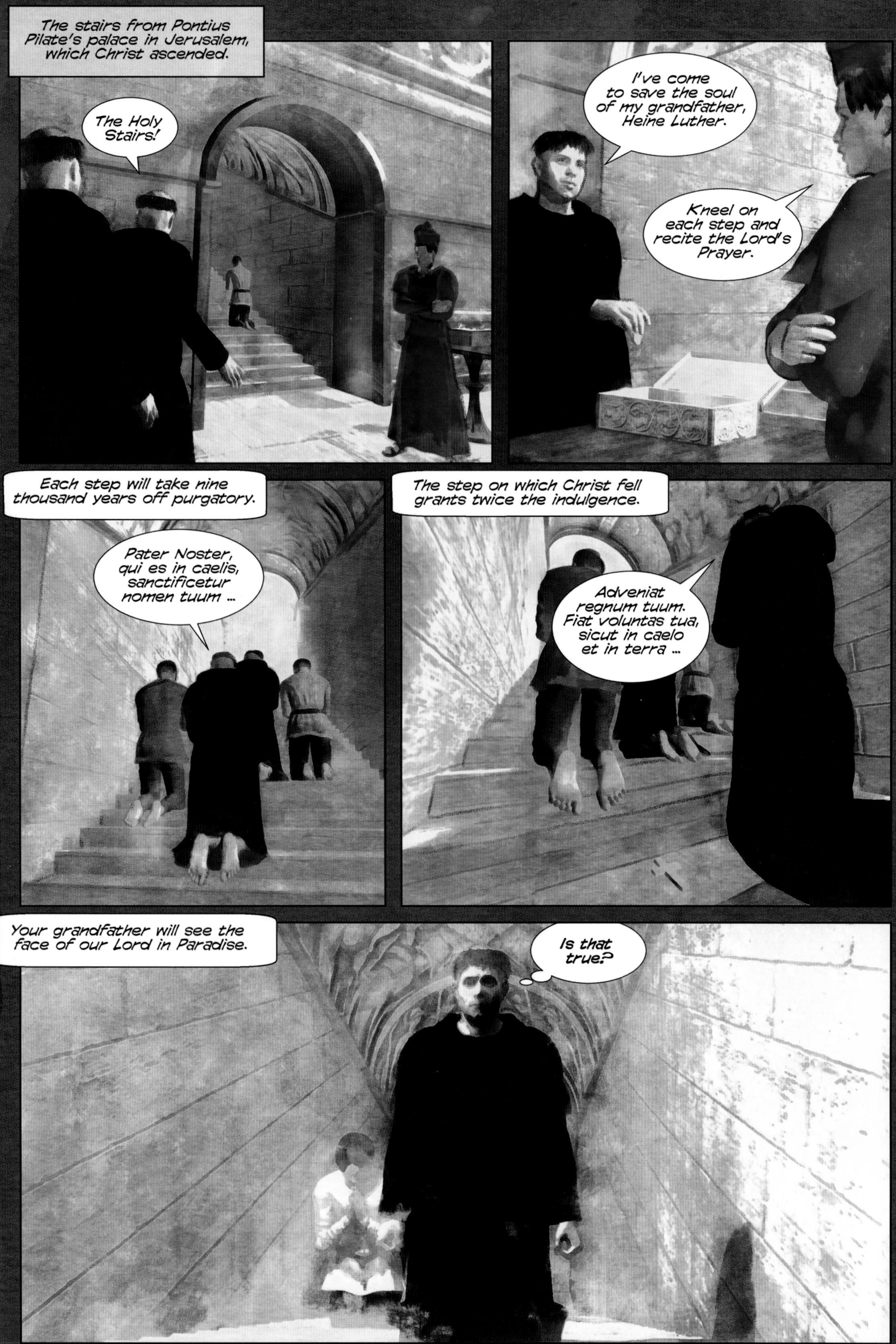
The stairs from Pontius Pilate's palace in Jerusalem, which Christ ascended.
The Holy Stairs!
I've come to save the soul of my grandfather, Heine Luther.
Kneel on each step and recite the Lord's Prayer.
Each step will take nine thousand years off purgatory.
Pater Noster, qui es in caelis, sanctificetur nomen tuum ...
The step on which Christ fell grants twice the indulgence.
Adveniat regnum tuum. Fiat voluntas tua, sicut in caelo et in terra ...
Your grandfather will see the face of our Lord in Paradise.
Is that true?

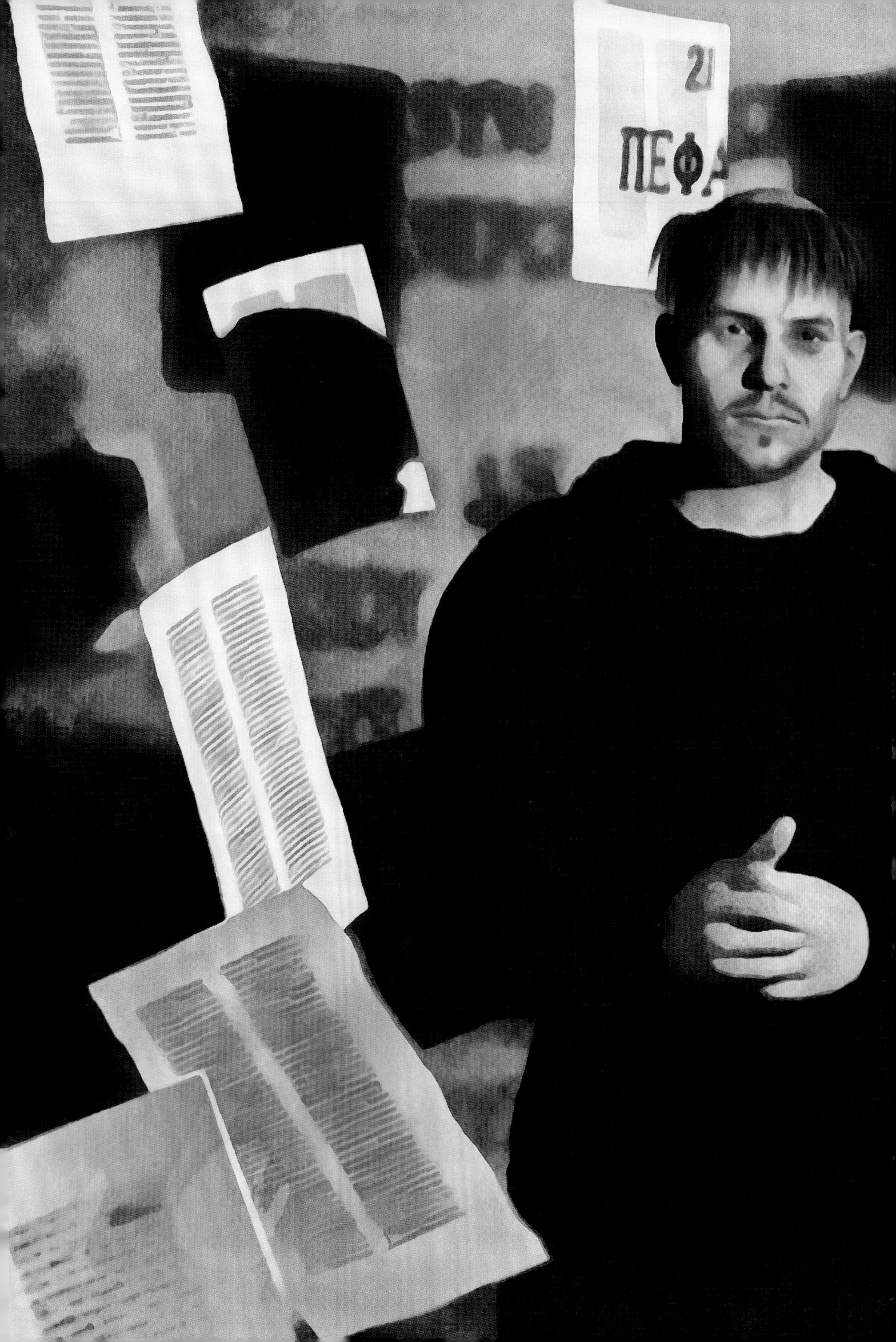
21

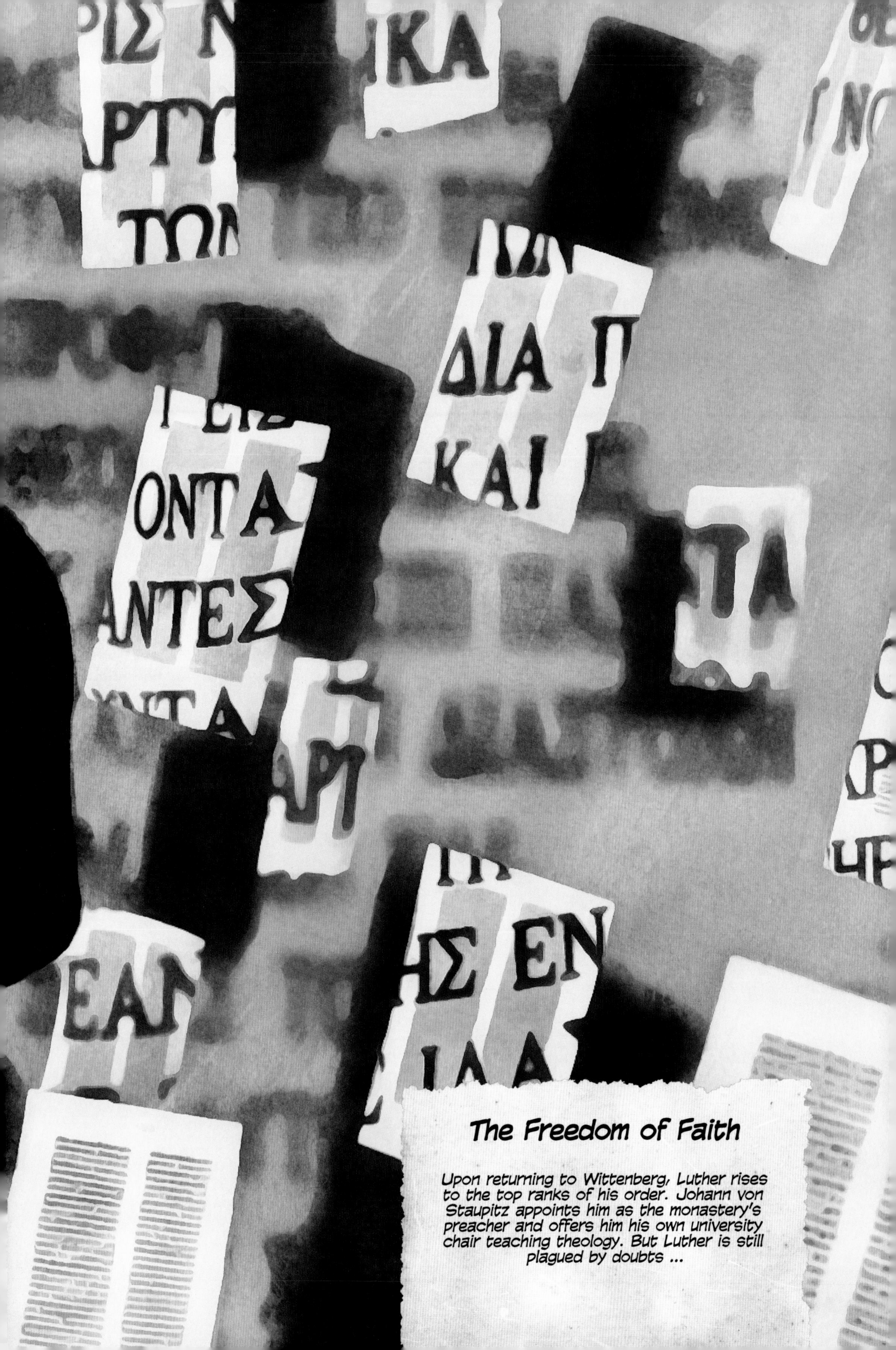
The Freedom of Faith
Upon returning to Wittenberg, Luther rises to the top ranks of his order. Johann von Staupitz appoints him as the monastery's preacher and offers him his own university chair teaching theology. But Luther is still plagued by doubts ...

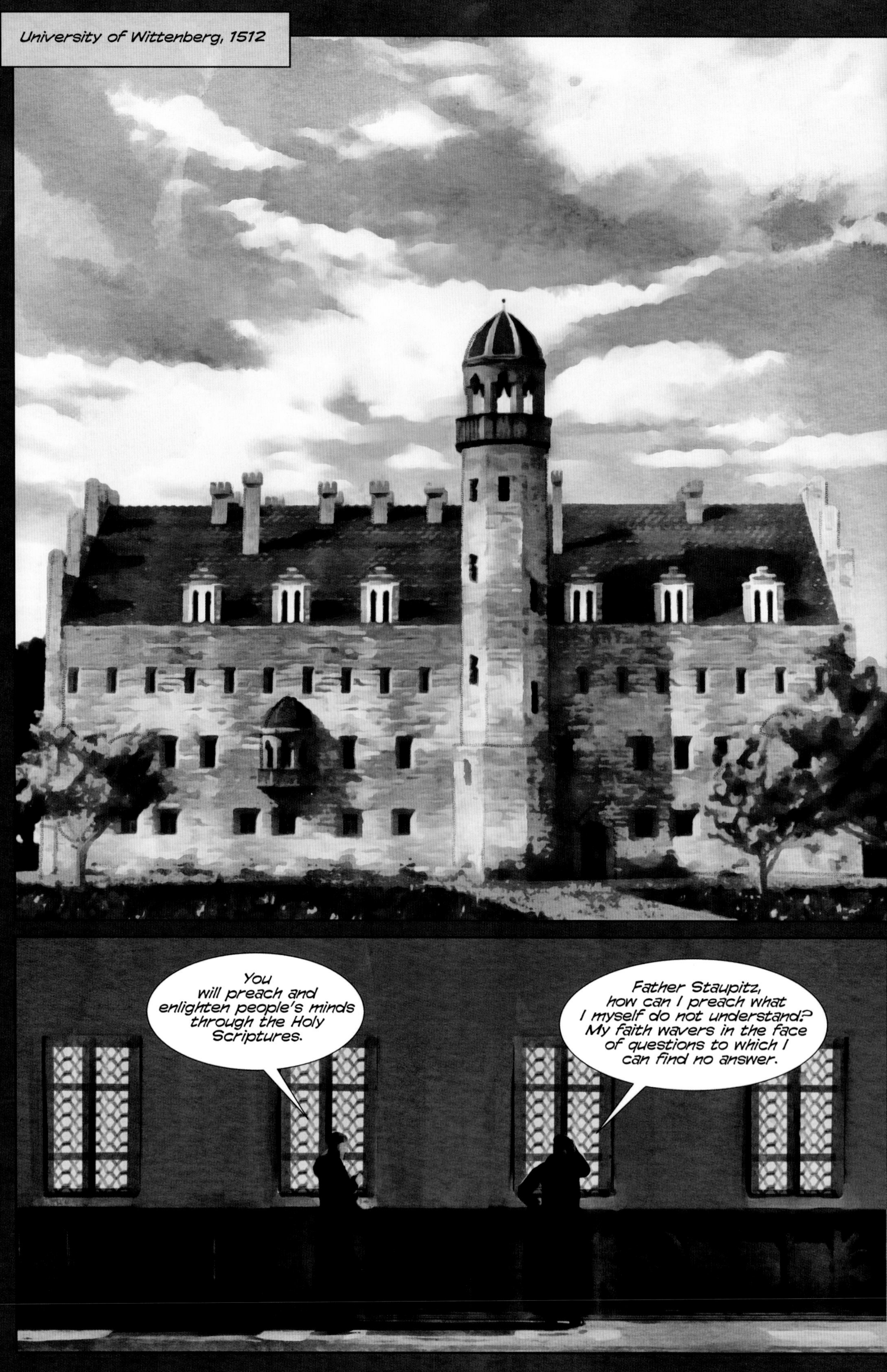
University of Wittenberg, 1512
You will preach and enlighten people's minds through the Holy Scriptures.
Father Staupitz, how can I preach what I myself do not understand? My faith wavers in the face of questions to which I can find no answer.

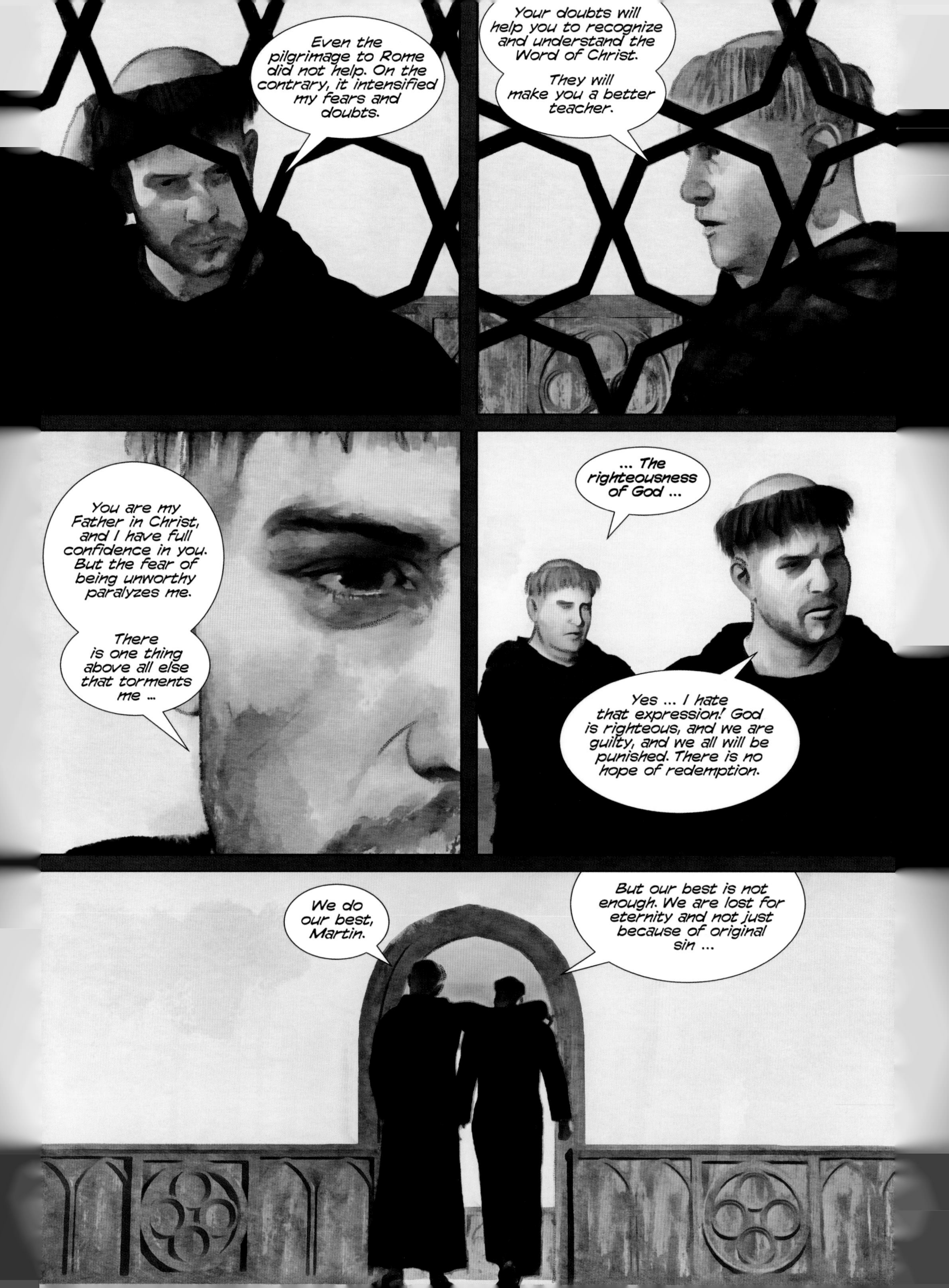
Even the pilgrimage to Rome did not help. On the contrary, it intensified my fears and doubts.
Your doubts will help you to recognize and understand the Word of Christ.
They will make you a better teacher.
You are my Father in Christ, and I have full confidence in you. But the fear of being unworthy paralyzes me.
There is one thing above all else that torments me ...
... The righteousness of God ...
Yes ... I hate that expression! God is righteous, and we are guilty, and we all will be punished. There is no hope of redemption.
We do our best, Martin.
But our best is not enough. We are lost for eternity and not just because of original sin ...

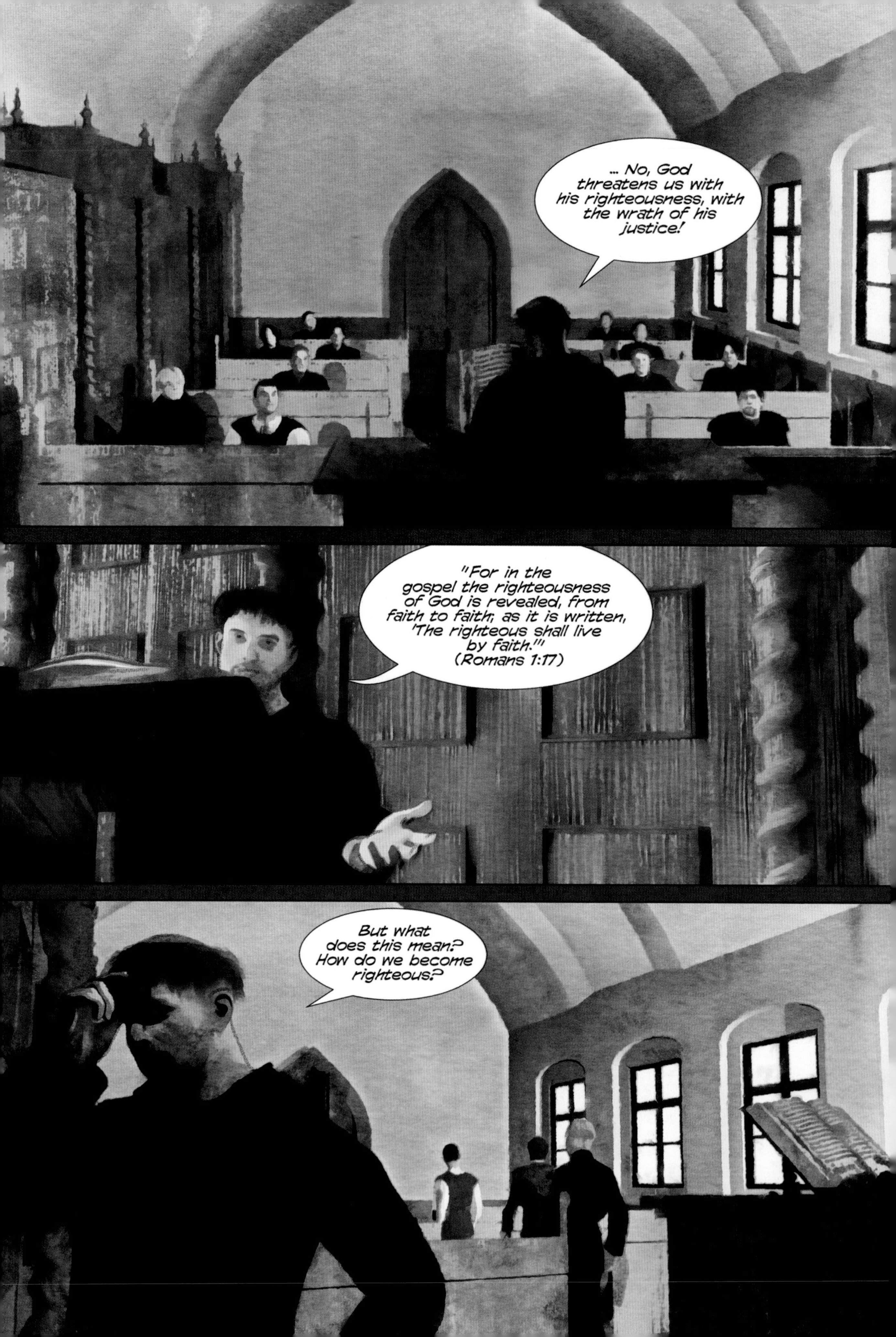
... No, God threatens us with his righteousness, with the wrath of his justice!
"For in the gospel the righteousness of God is revealed, from faith to faith; as it is written, 'The righteous shall live by faith.'" (Romans 1:17)
But what does this mean? How do we become righteous?

How can I please God and gain his favor?
How can I escape the fires of purgatory?
And what if fasting, prayer and pilgrimages are nothing but sweet forms of flattery in God's eyes?
Even after so many pious works, I feel no grace within me.

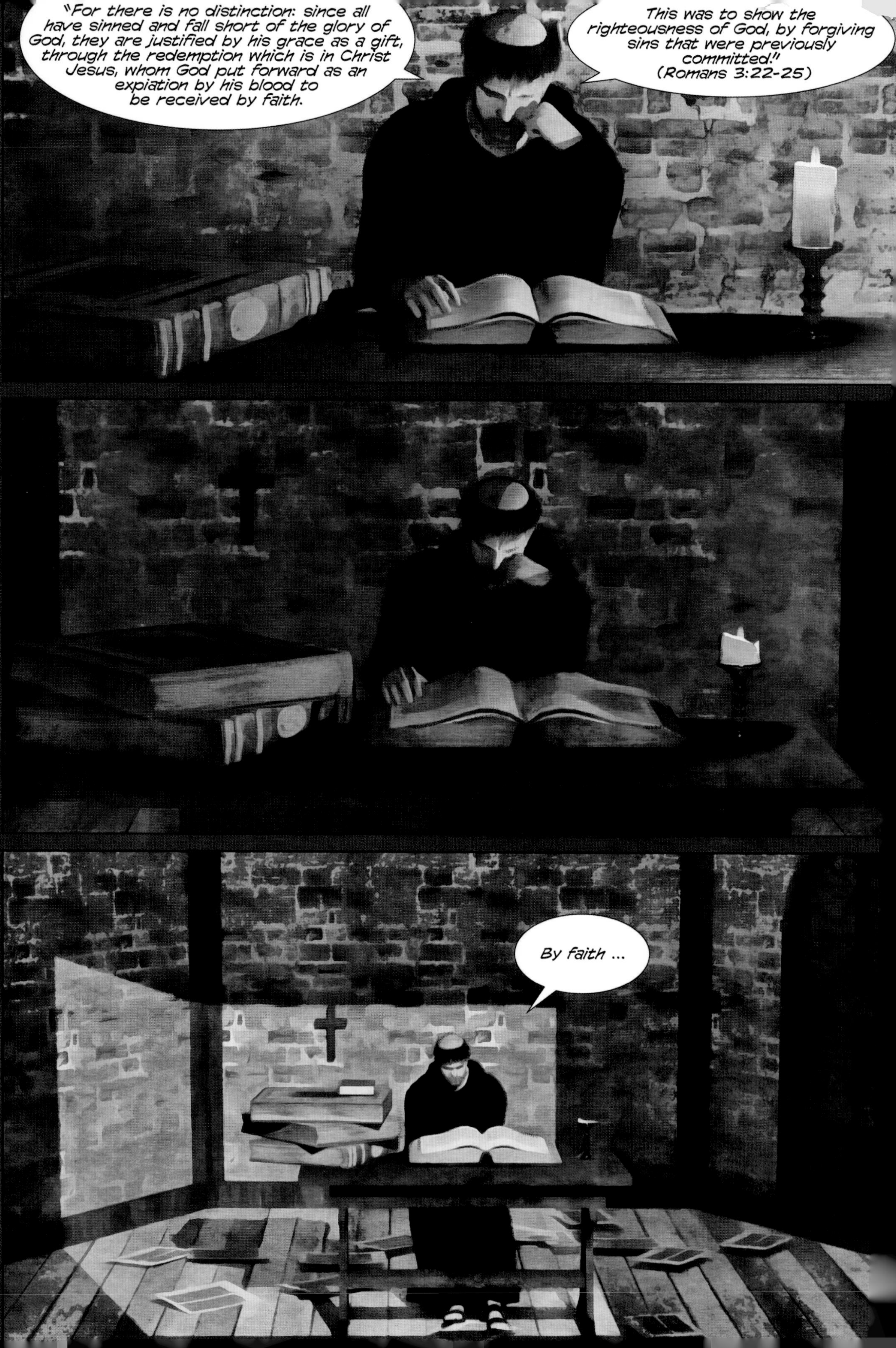
"For there is no distinction: since all have sinned and fall short of the glory of God, they are justified by his grace as a gift, through the redemption which is in Christ Jesus, whom God put forward as an expiation by his blood to be received by faith.
This was to show the righteousness of God, by forgiving sins that were previously committed."
(Romans 3:22-25)
By faith ...

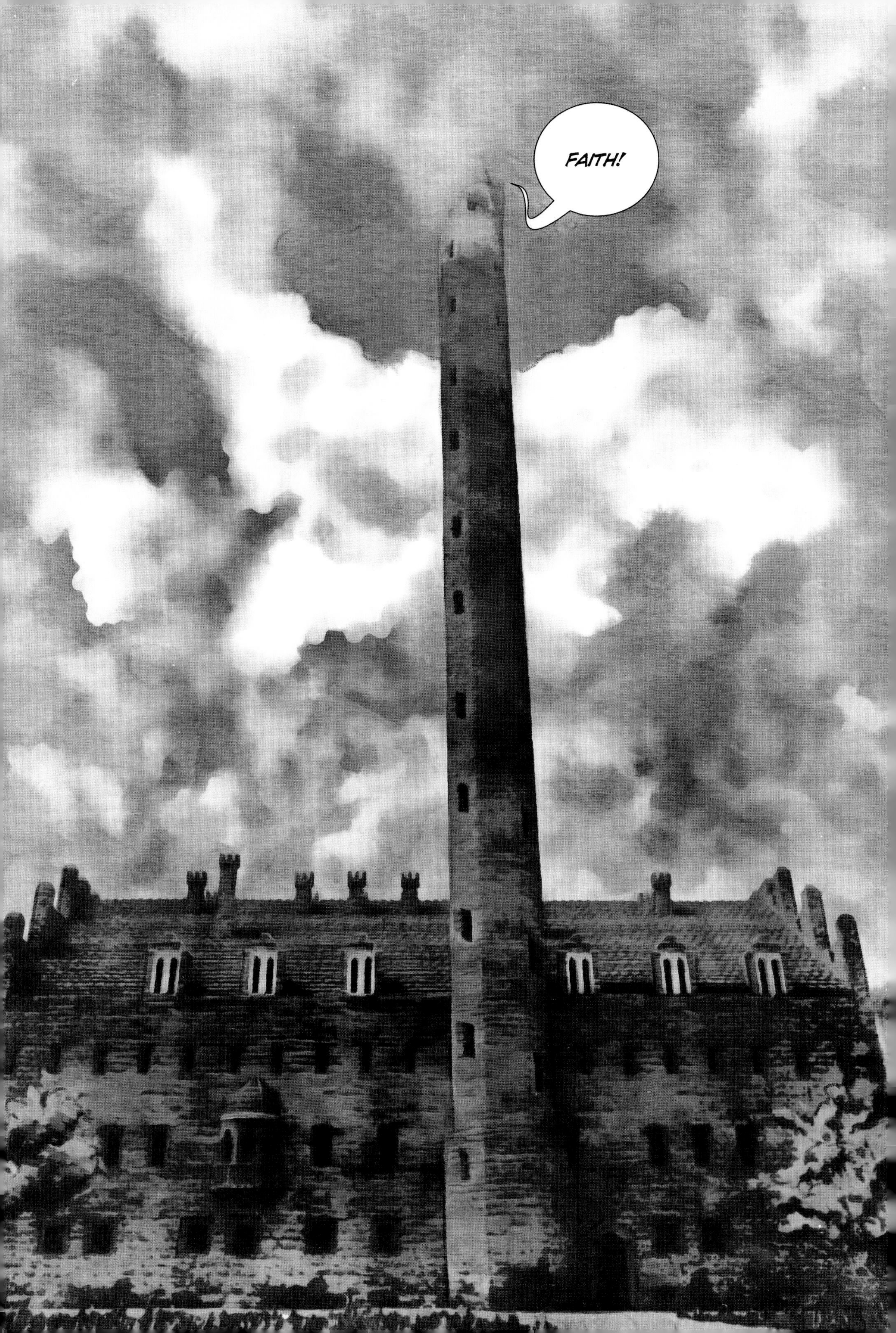
FAITH!

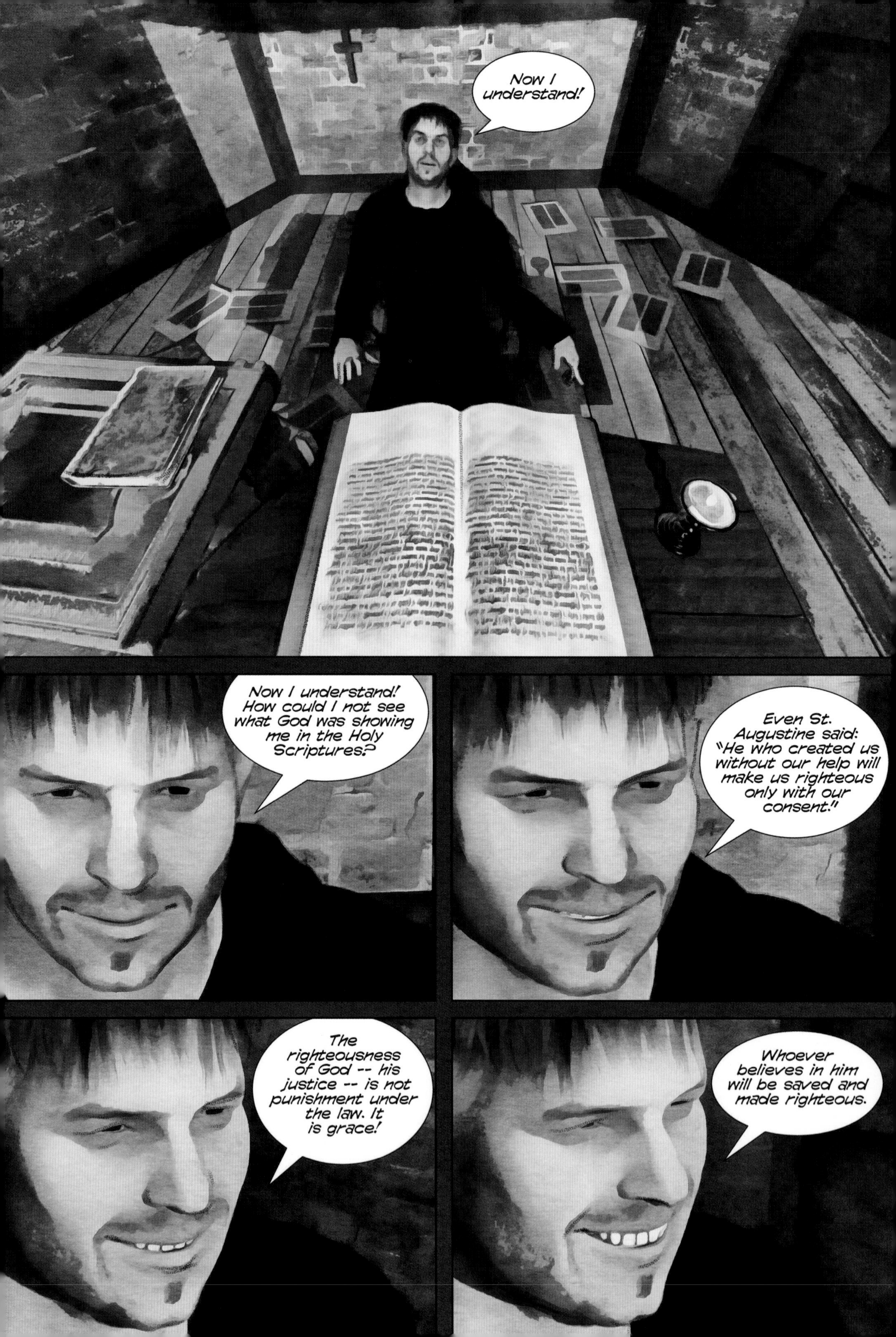
Now I understand!
Now I understand! How could I not see what God was showing me in the Holy Scriptures?
Even St. Augustine said: "He who created us without our help will make us righteous only with our consent."
The righteousness of God -- his justice -- is not punishment under the law. It is grace!
Whoever believes in him will be saved and made righteous.

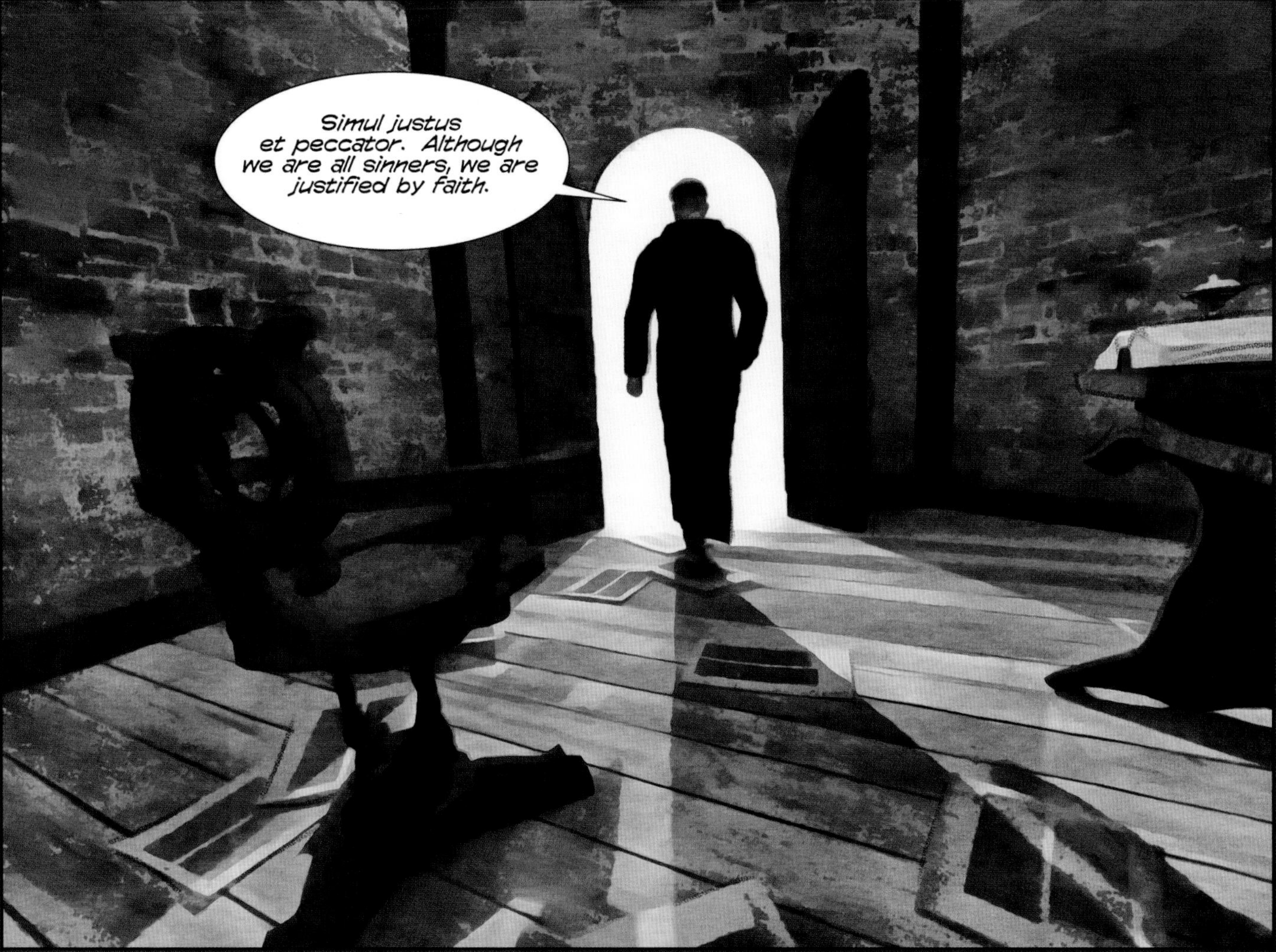
Simul justus et peccator. Although we are all sinners, we are justified by faith.

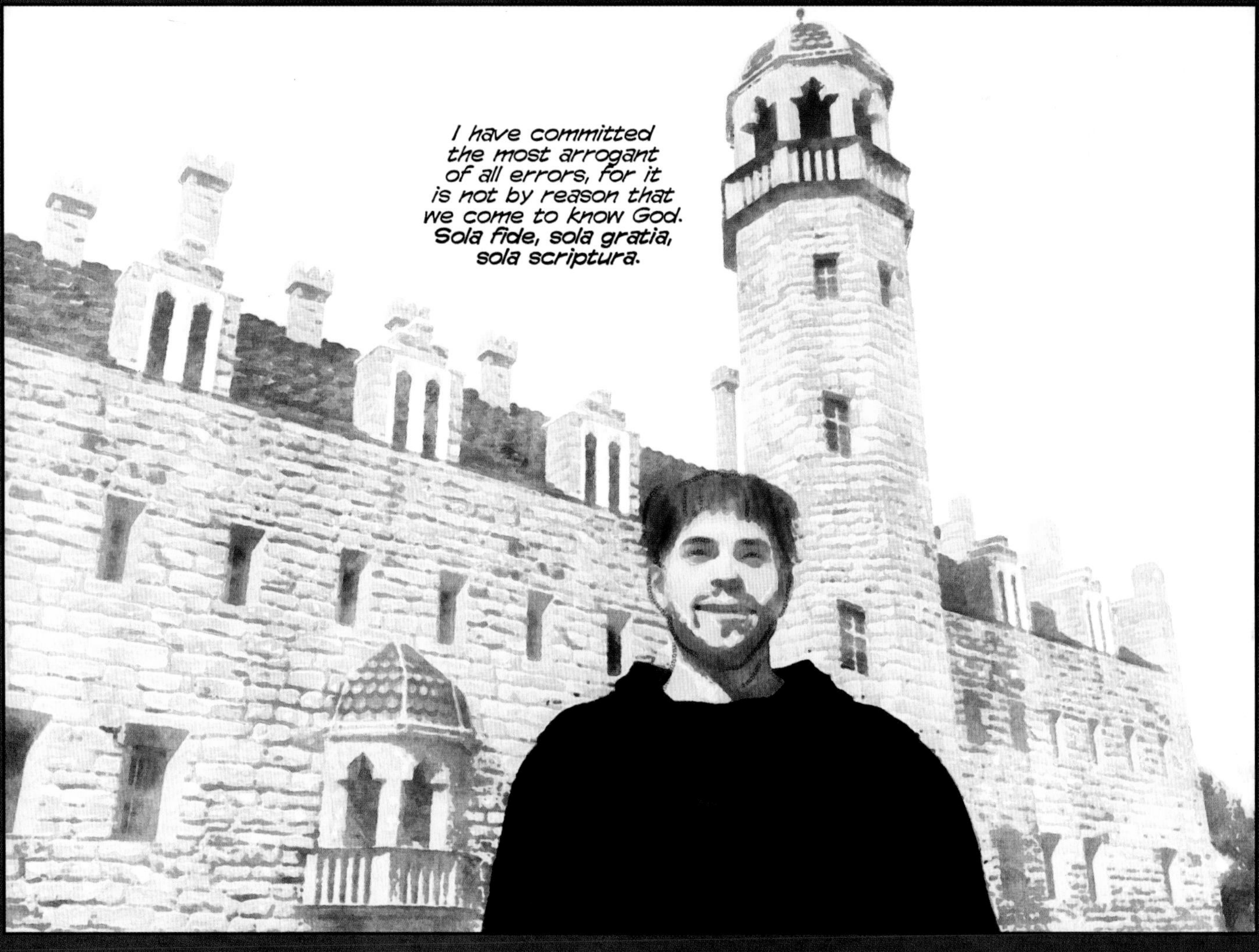
I have committed the most arrogant of all errors, for it is not by reason that we come to know God. Sola fide, sola gratia, sola scriptura.

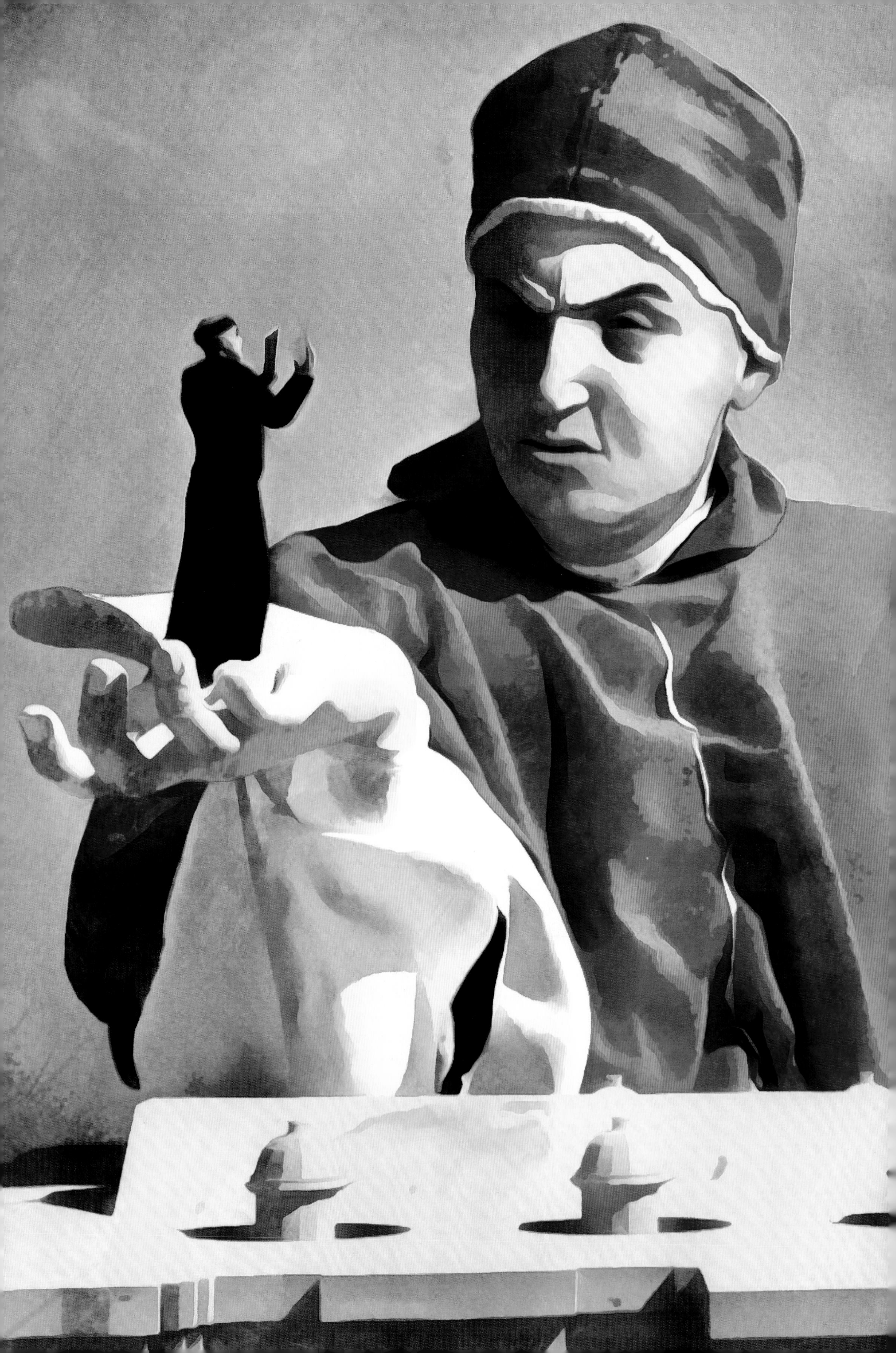

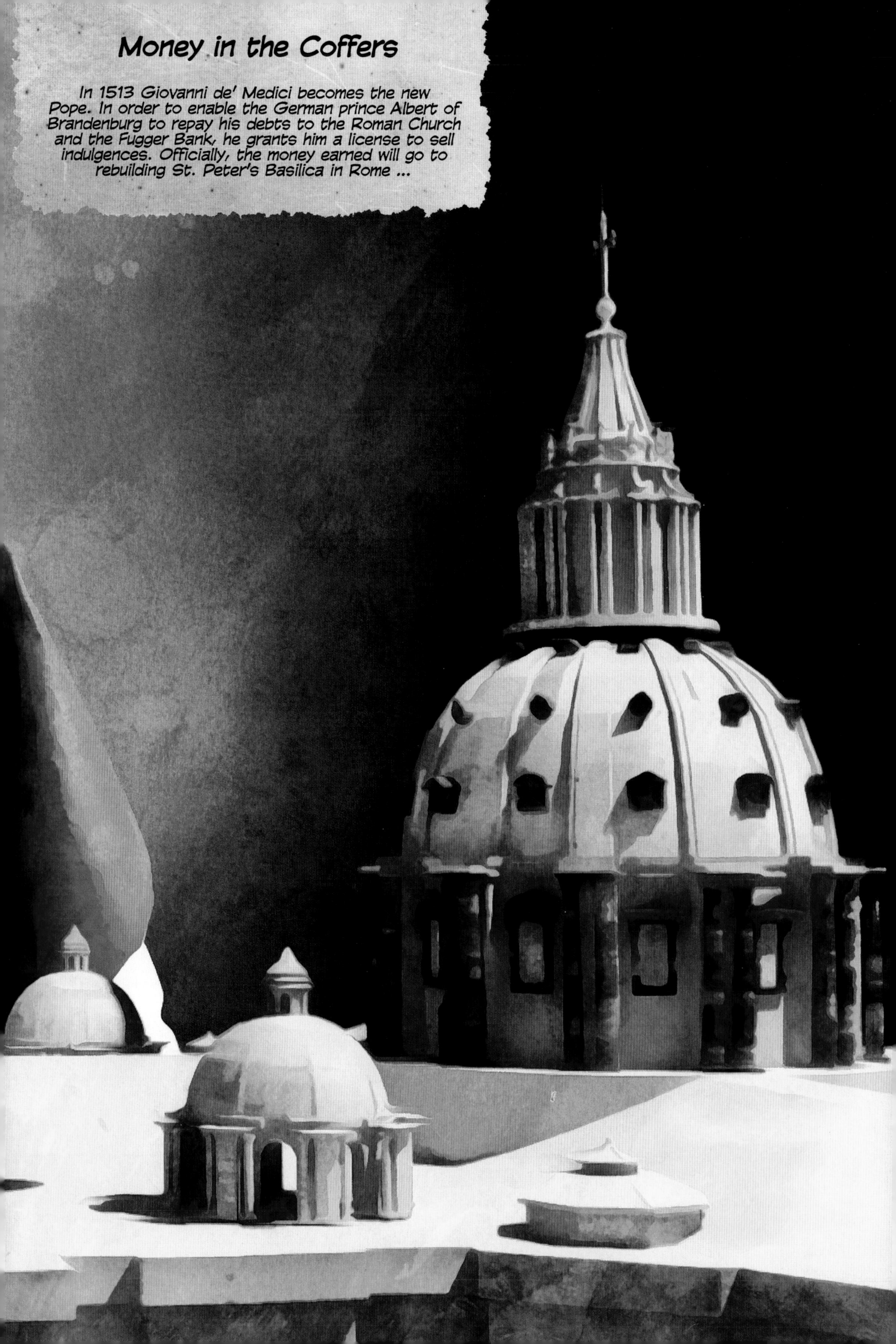
Money in the Coffers
In 1513 Giovanni de' Medici becomes the new Pope. In order to enable the German prince Albert of Brandenburg to repay his debts to the Roman Church and the Fugger Bank, he grants him a license to sell indulgences. Officially, the money earned will go to rebuilding St. Peter's Basilica in Rome ...

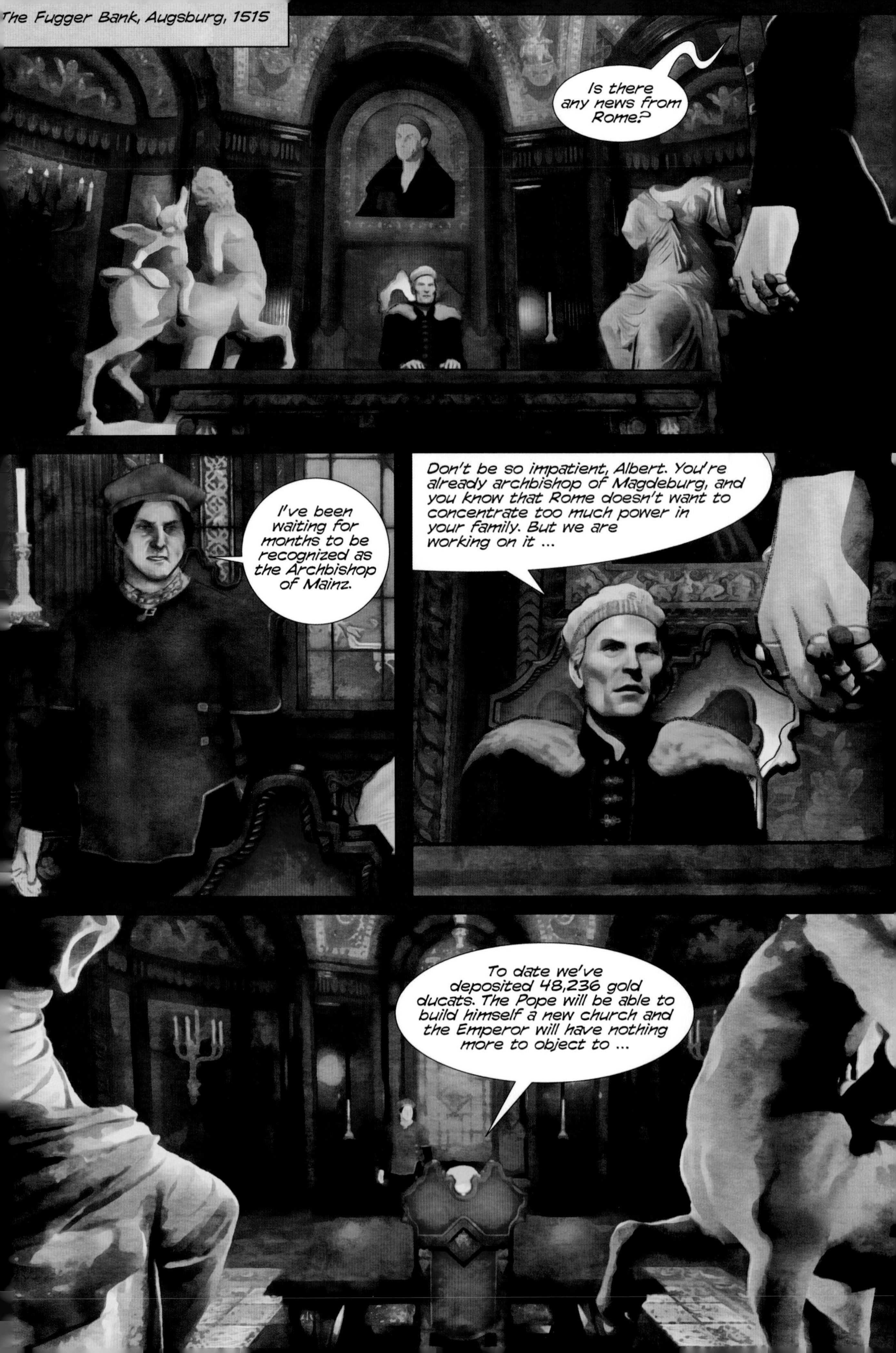
The Fugger Bank, Augsburg, 1515
Is there any news from Rome?
I've been waiting for months to be recognized as the Archbishop of Mainz.
Don't be so impatient, Albert. You're already archbishop of Magdeburg, and you know that Rome doesn't want to concentrate too much power in your family. But we are working on it ...
To date we've deposited 48,236 gold ducats. The Pope will be able to build himself a new church and the Emperor will have nothing more to object to ...

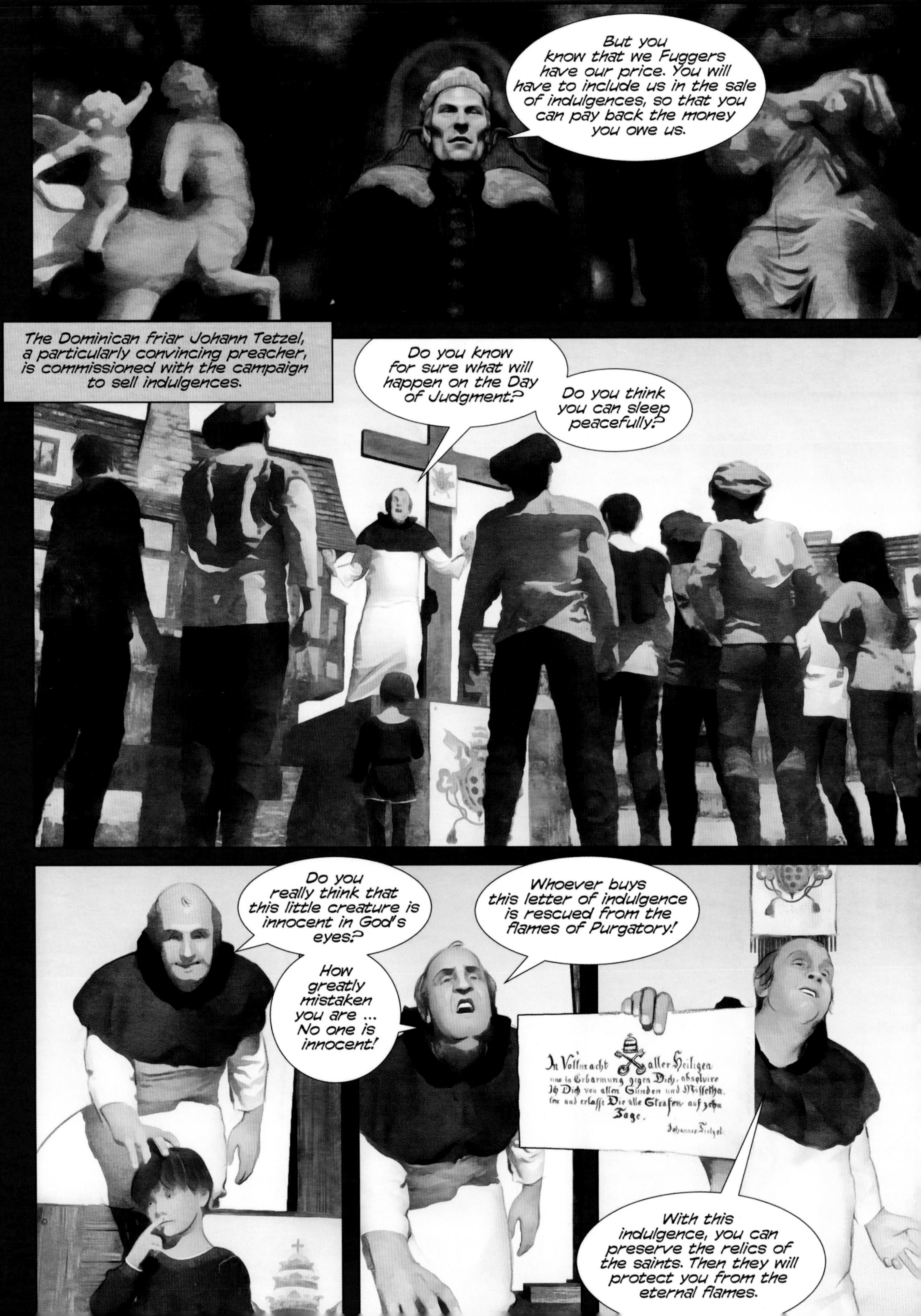
But you know that we Fuggers have our price. You will have to include us in the sale of indulgences, so that you can pay back the money you owe us.
The Dominican friar Johann Tetzel, a particularly convincing preacher, is commissioned with the campaign to sell indulgences.
Do you know for sure what will happen on the Day of Judgment?
Do you think you can sleep peacefully?
Do you really think that this little creature is innocent in God's eyes?
How greatly mistaken you are ... No one is innocent!
Whoever buys this letter of indulgence is rescued from the flames of Purgatory!
In Vollmacht aller Heiligen
und in Erbarmung gegen Dich, absolvire
Ich Dich von allen Sünden und Missetha,
ten und erlasse Dir alle Strafen auf zehn
Tage.
Johannes Tetzel
With this indulgence, you can preserve the relics of the saints. Then they will protect you from the eternal flames.

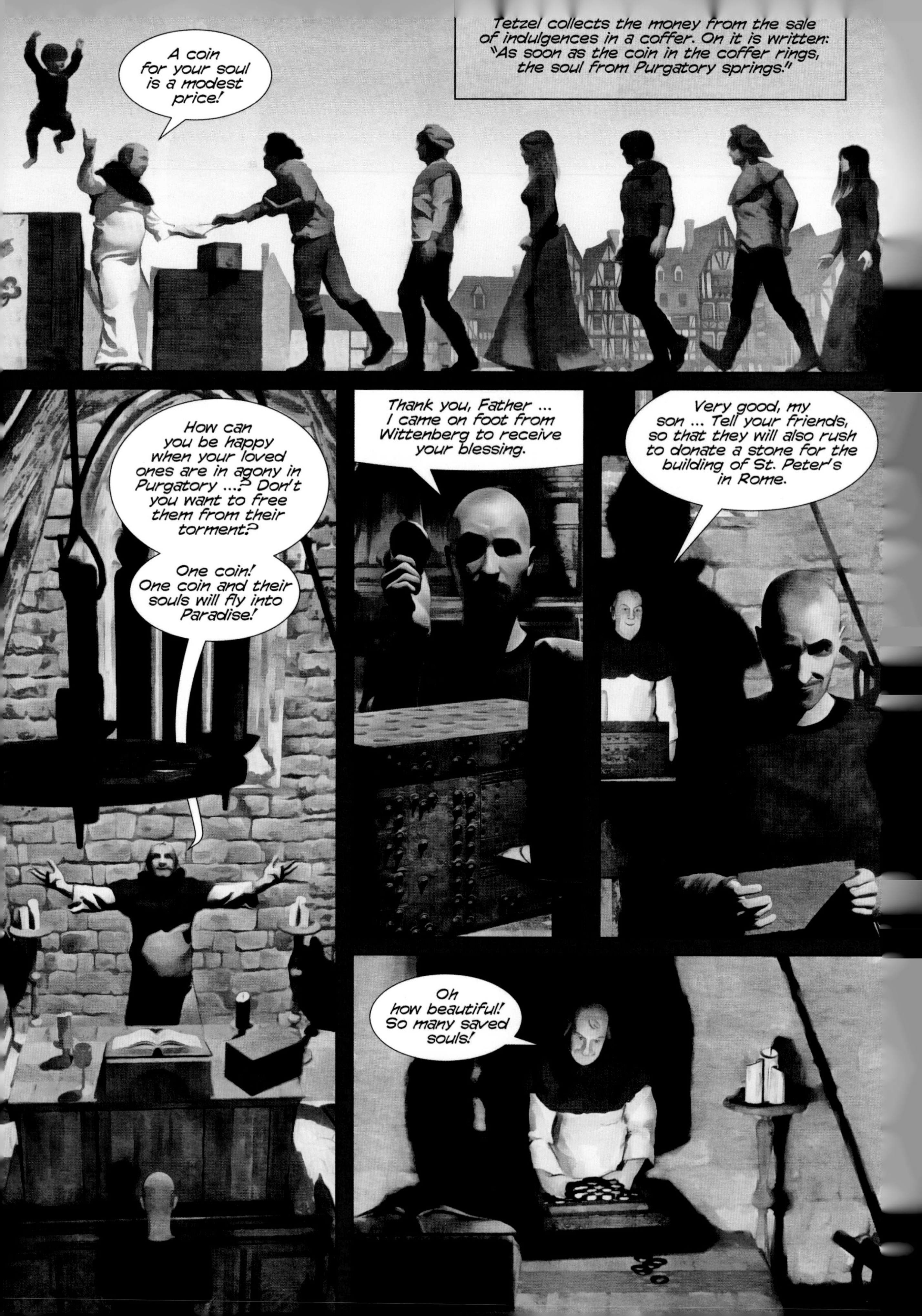
Tetzel collects the money from the sale of indulgences in a coffer. On it is written: "As soon as the coin in the coffer rings, the soul from Purgatory springs."
A coin for your soul is a modest price!
How can you be happy when your loved ones are in agony in Purgatory ...? Don't you want to free them from their torment?
One coin! One coin and their souls will fly into Paradise!
Thank you, Father ... I came on foot from Wittenberg to receive your blessing.
Very good, my son ... Tell your friends, so that they will also rush to donate a stone for the building of St. Peter's in Rome.
Oh how beautiful! So many saved souls!

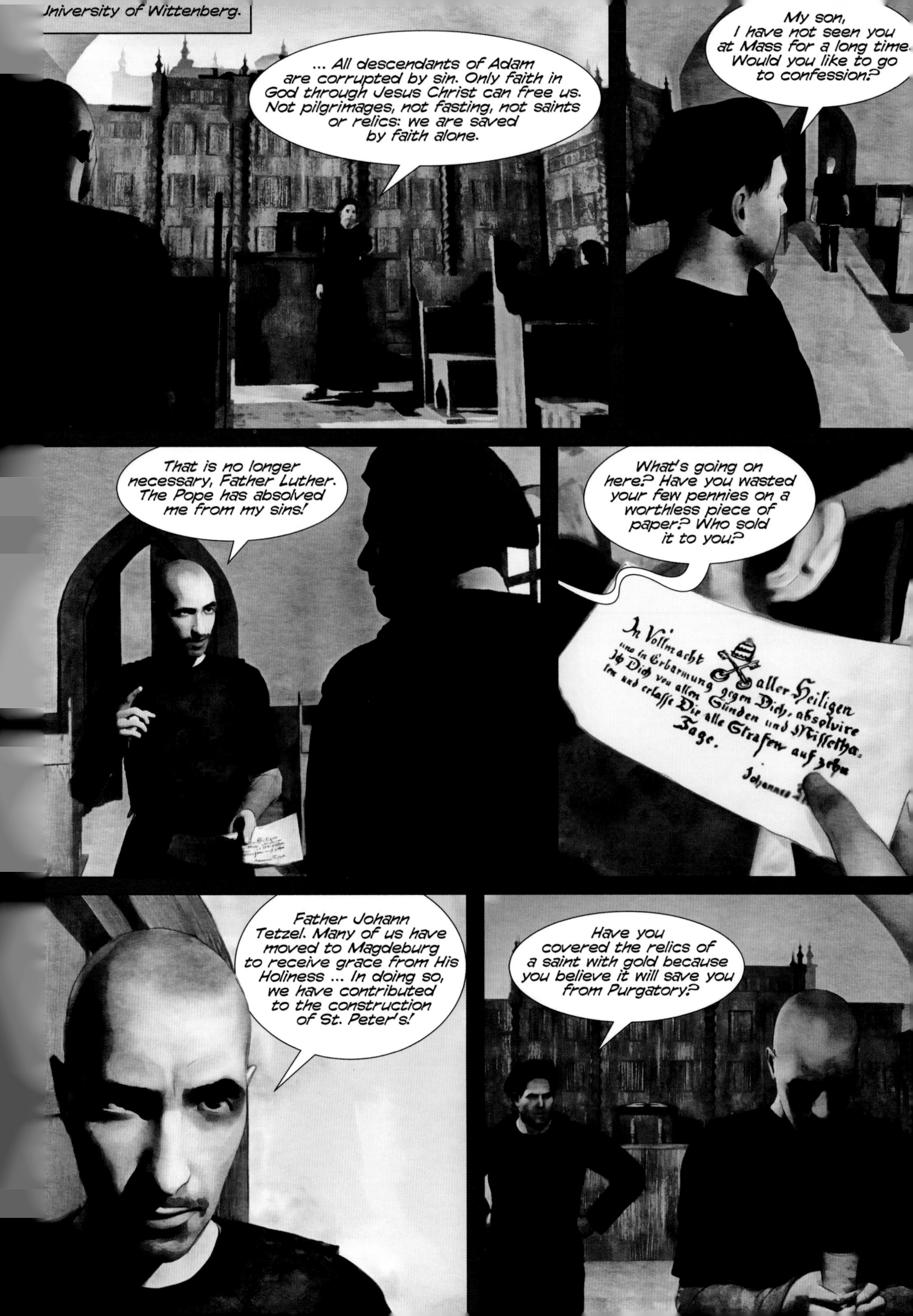

University of Wittenberg.
... All descendants of Adam are corrupted by sin. Only faith in God through Jesus Christ can free us. Not pilgrimages, not fasting, not saints or relics: we are saved by faith alone.
My son, I have not seen you at Mass for a long time. Would you like to go to confession?
That is no longer necessary, Father Luther. The Pope has absolved me from my sins!
What's going on here? Have you wasted your few pennies on a worthless piece of paper? Who sold it to you?
In Vollmacht aller Heiligen und in Erbarmung gegen Dich, absolvire Ich Dich von allen Sünden und Missethaten und erlasse Dir alle Strafen auf zehn Tage.
Johannes
Father Johann Tetzel. Many of us have moved to Magdeburg to receive grace from His Holiness ... In doing so, we have contributed to the construction of St. Peter's!
Have you covered the relics of a saint with gold because you believe it will save you from Purgatory?

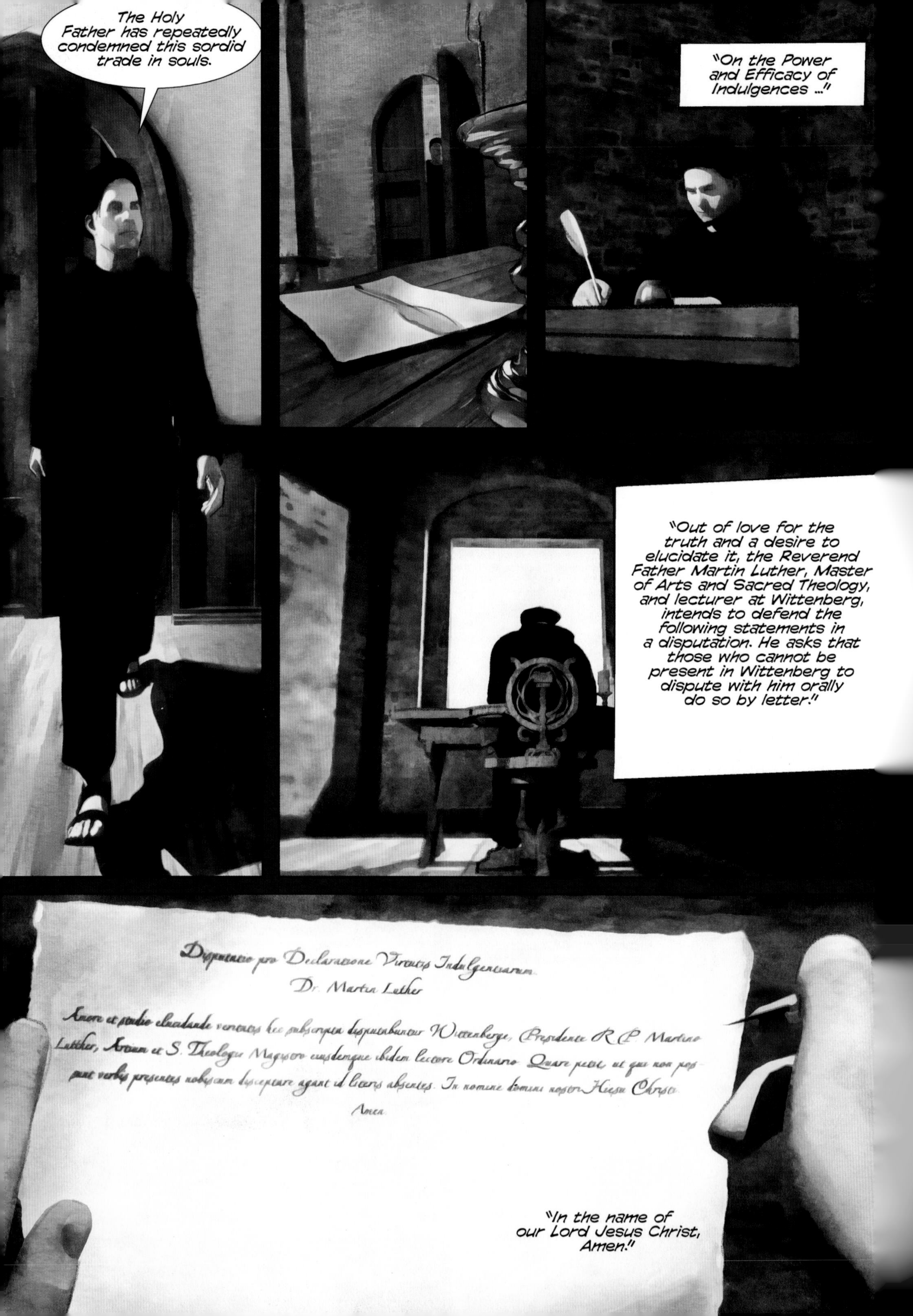
The Holy Father has repeatedly condemned this sordid trade in souls.
"On the Power and Efficacy of Indulgences ..."
"Out of love for the truth and a desire to elucidate it, the Reverend Father Martin Luther, Master of Arts and Sacred Theology, and lecturer at Wittenberg, intends to defend the following statements in a disputation. He asks that those who cannot be present in Wittenberg to dispute with him orally do so by letter."
Dr. Martin Luther
Amen
"In the name of our Lord Jesus Christ, Amen."

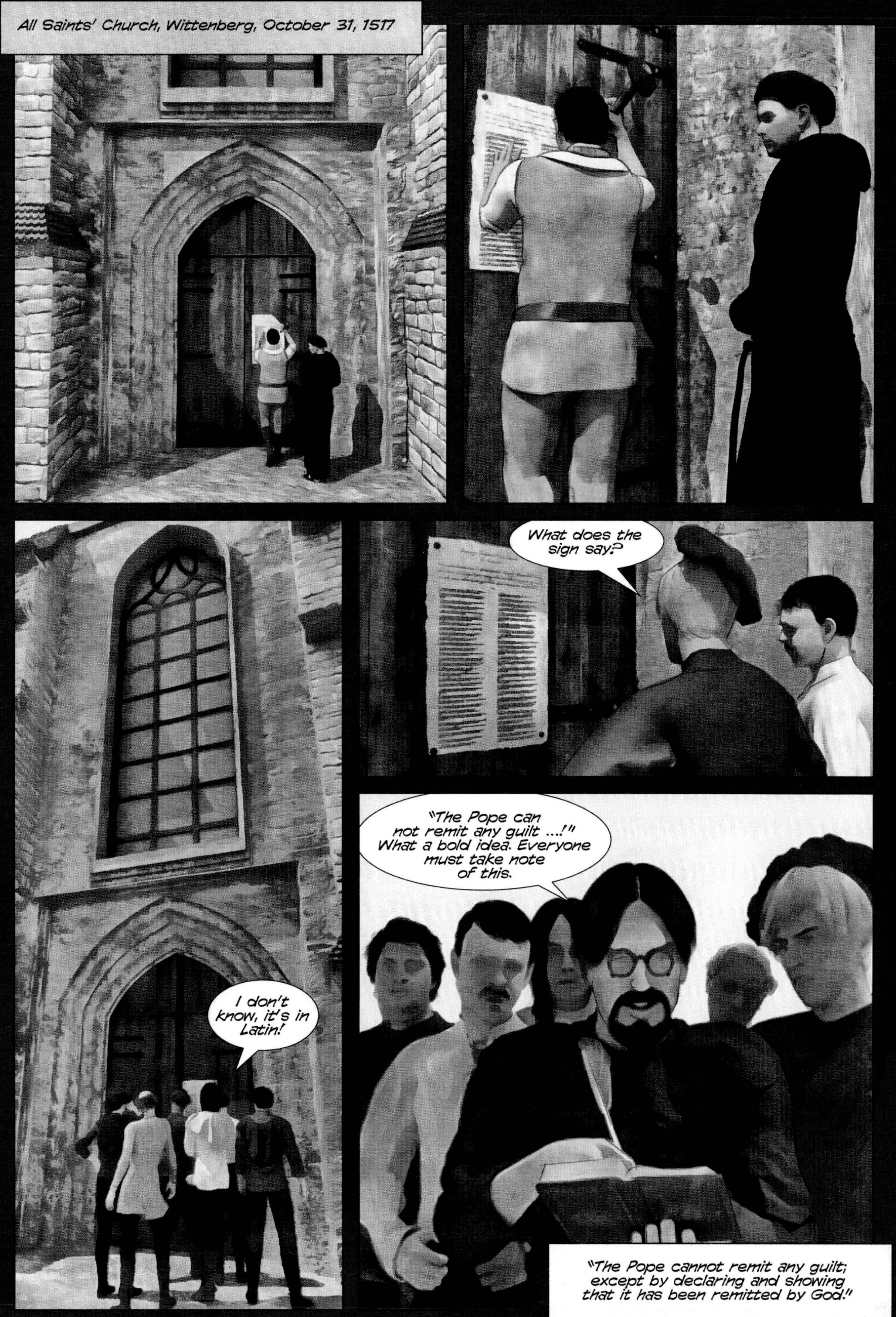
All Saints' Church, Wittenberg, October 31, 1517
What does the sign say?
I don't know, it's in Latin!
"The Pope can not remit any guilt ...!" What a bold idea. Everyone must take note of this.
"The Pope cannot remit any guilt; except by declaring and showing that it has been remitted by God!"

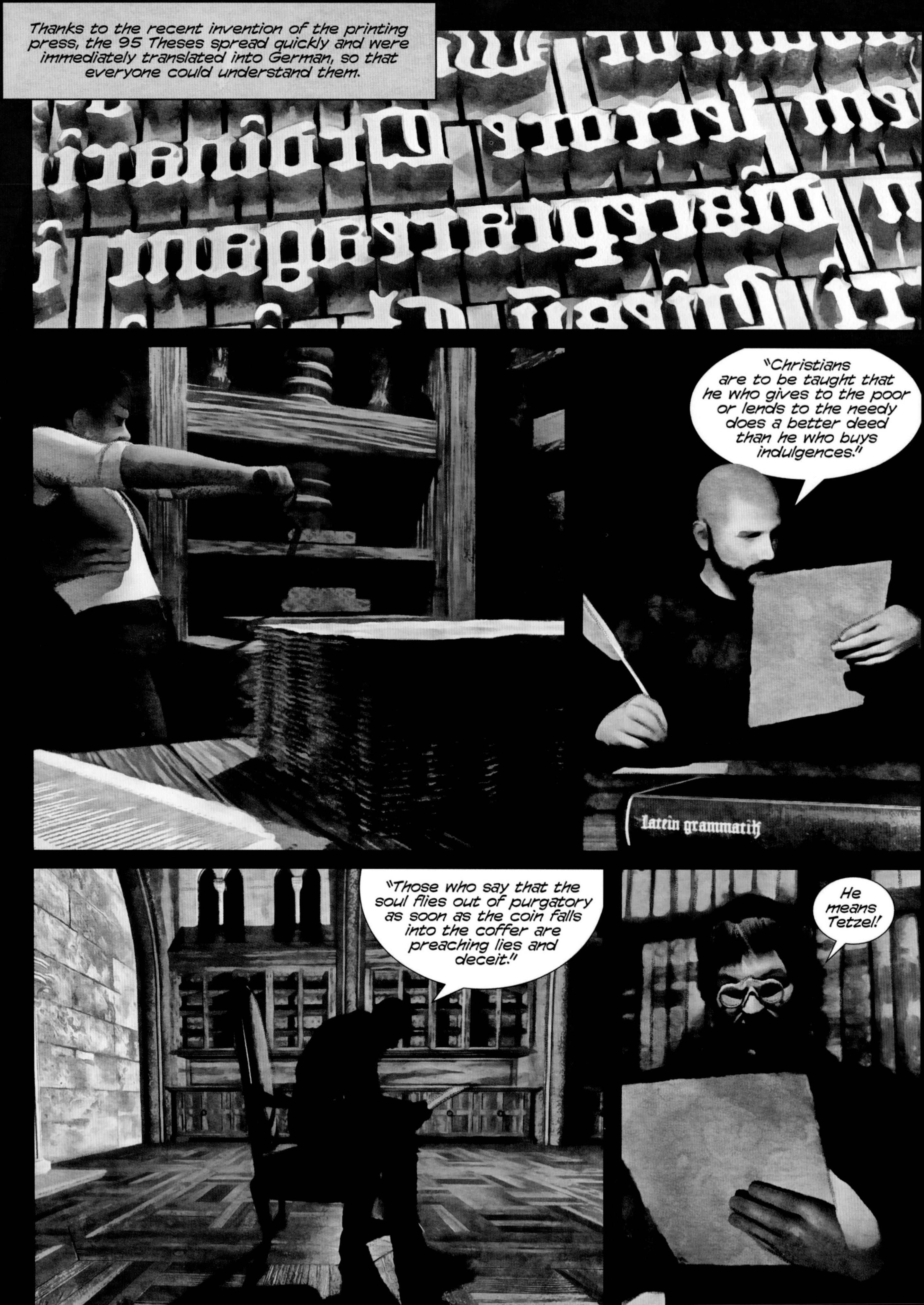
Thanks to the recent invention of the printing press, the 95 Theses spread quickly and were immediately translated into German, so that everyone could understand them.
"Christians are to be taught that he who gives to the poor or lends to the needy does a better deed than he who buys indulgences."
latein grammatik
"Those who say that the soul flies out of purgatory as soon as the coin falls into the coffer are preaching lies and deceit."
He means Tetzel!

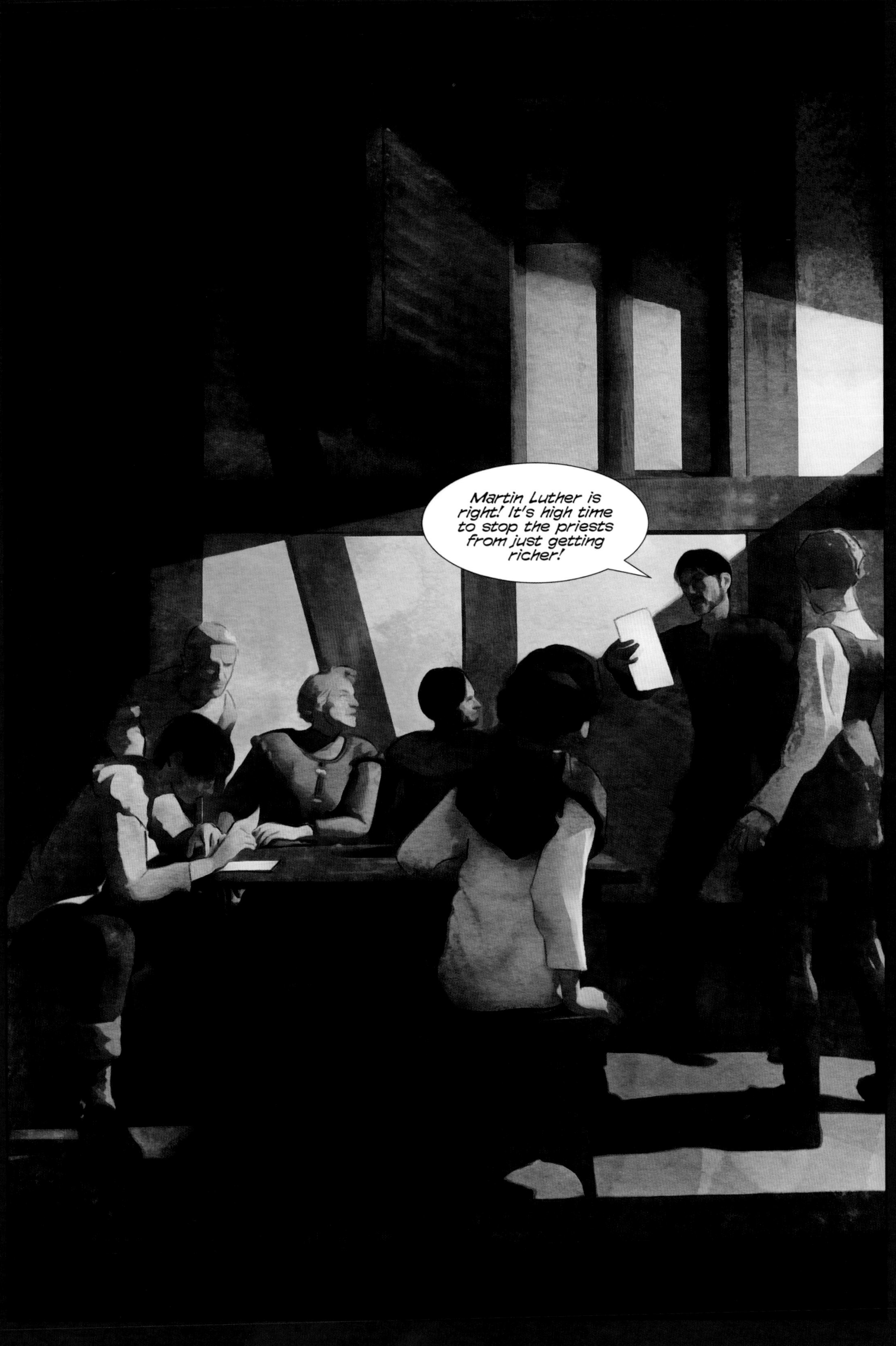
Martin Luther is right! It's high time to stop the priests from just getting richer!

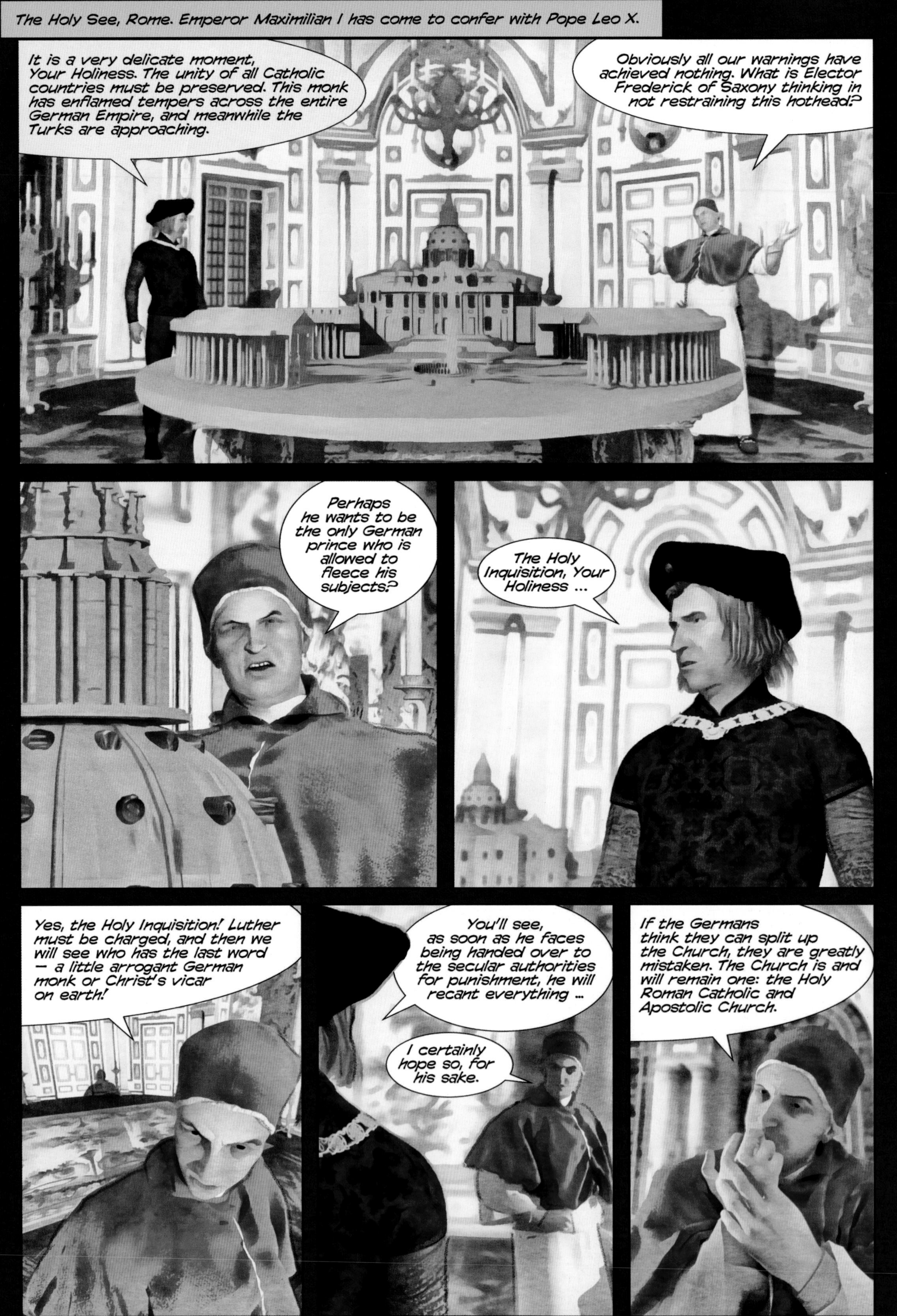
The Holy See, Rome. Emperor Maximilian I has come to confer with Pope Leo X.
It is a very delicate moment, Your Holiness. The unity of all Catholic countries must be preserved. This monk has enflamed tempers across the entire German Empire, and meanwhile the Turks are approaching.
Obviously all our warnings have achieved nothing. What is Elector Frederick of Saxony thinking in not restraining this hothead?
Perhaps he wants to be the only German prince who is allowed to fleece his subjects?
The Holy Inquisition, Your Holiness ...
Yes, the Holy Inquisition! Luther must be charged, and then we will see who has the last word – a little arrogant German monk or Christ's vicar on earth!
You'll see, as soon as he faces being handed over to the secular authorities for punishment, he will recant everything ...
I certainly hope so, for his sake.
If the Germans think they can split up the Church, they are greatly mistaken. The Church is and will remain one: the Holy Roman Catholic and Apostolic Church.

Augsburg, October 12, 1518. While the Diet of the Holy Roman Empire meets, consultations are taking place on the margins about who should succeed Emperor Maximilian I, who is critically ill. Cardinal Cajetan, the emissary of Pope Leo, urges Luther to recant his Wittenberg Ttheses.

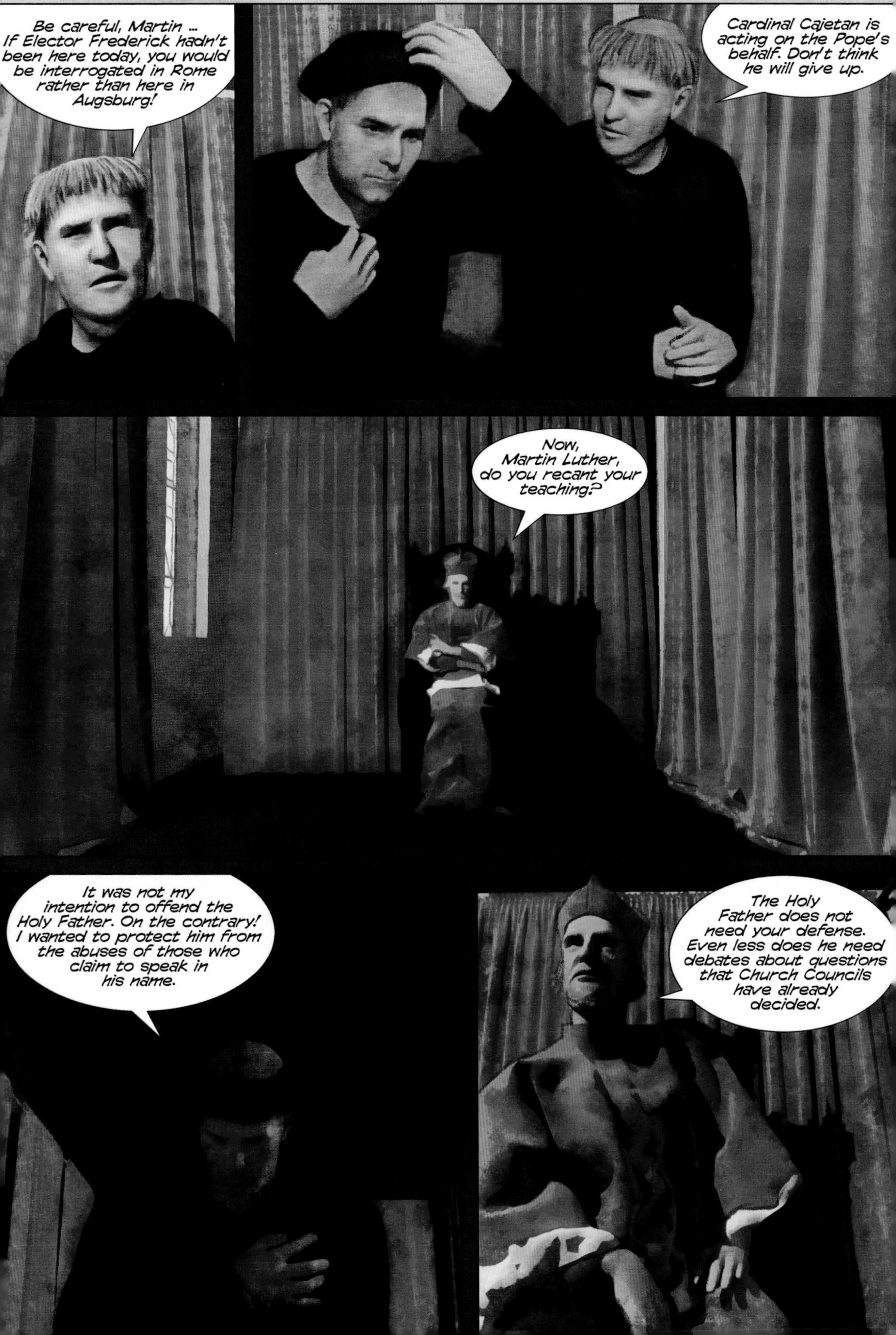

Be careful, Martin ... If Elector Frederick hadn't been here today, you would be interrogated in Rome rather than here in Augsburg!
Cardinal Cajetan is acting on the Pope's behalf. Don't think he will give up.
Now, Martin Luther, do you recant your teaching?
It was not my intention to offend the Holy Father. On the contrary! I wanted to protect him from the abuses of those who claim to speak in his name.
The Holy Father does not need your defense. Even less does he need debates about questions that Church Councils have already decided.

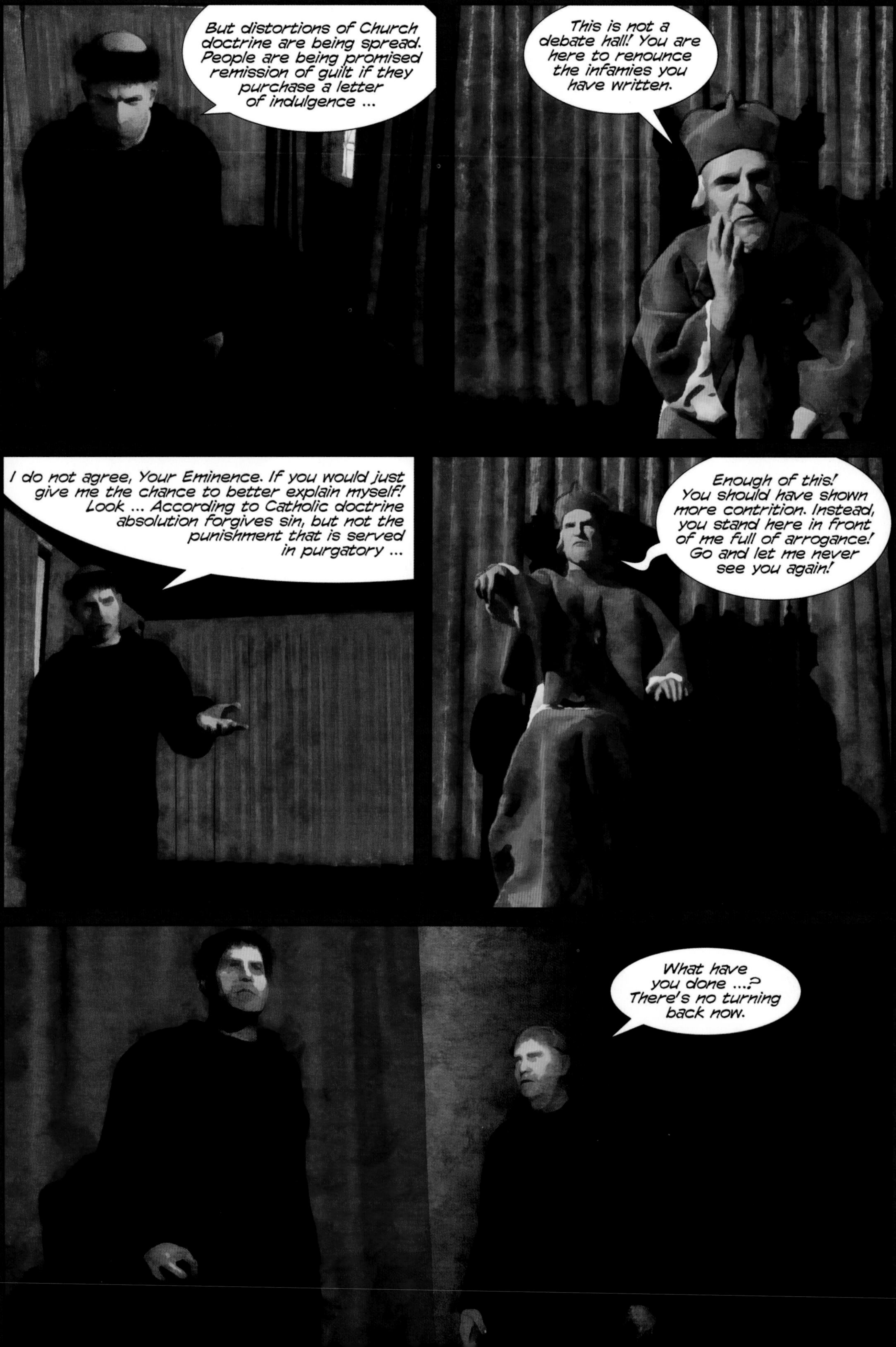
But distortions of Church doctrine are being spread. People are being promised remission of guilt if they purchase a letter of indulgence ...
This is not a debate hall! You are here to renounce the infamies you have written.
I do not agree, Your Eminence. If you would just give me the chance to better explain myself! Look ... According to Catholic doctrine absolution forgives sin, but not the punishment that is served in purgatory ...
Enough of this! You should have shown more contrition. Instead, you stand here in front of me full of arrogance! Go and let me never see you again!
What have you done ...? There's no turning back now.

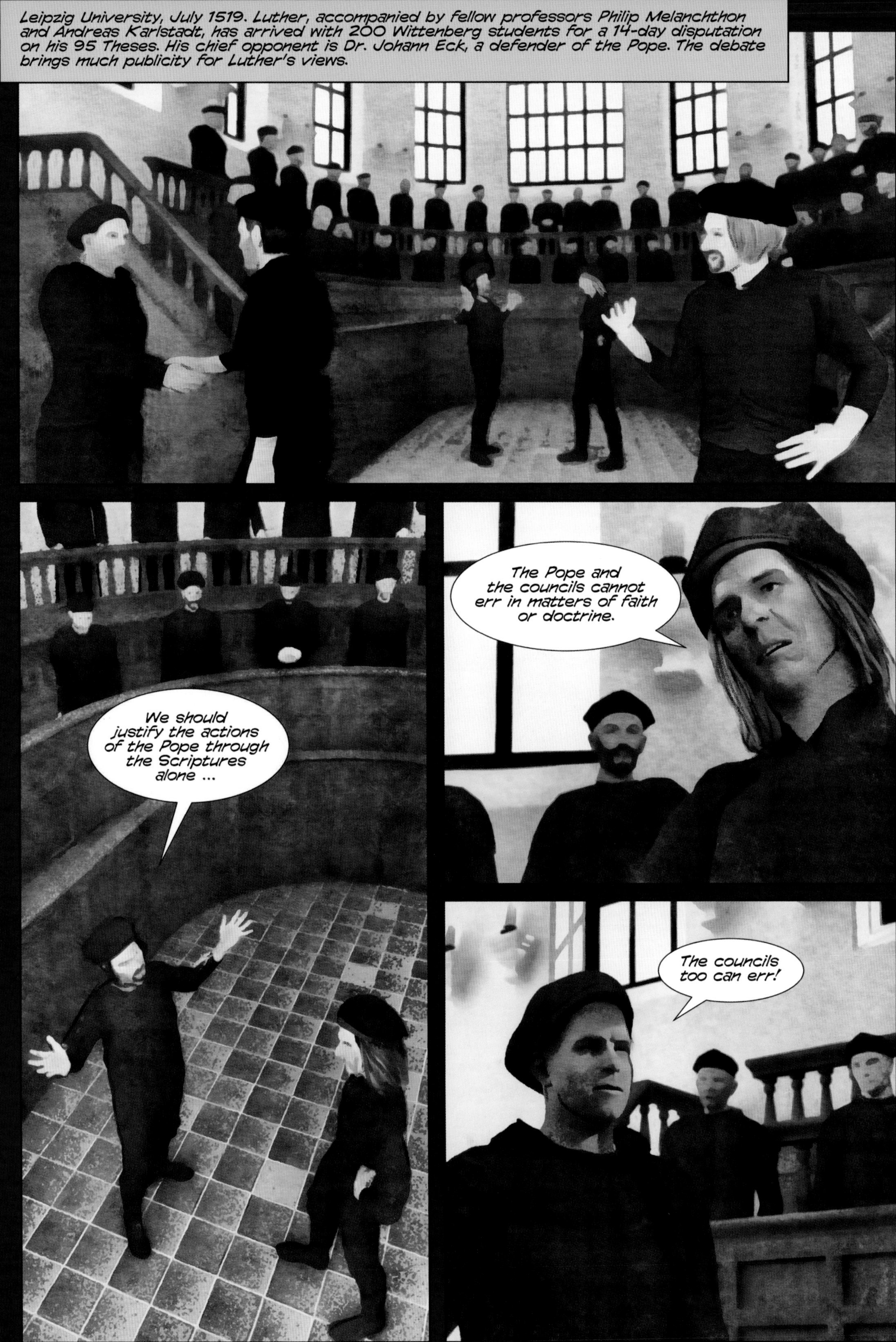
Leipzig University, July 1519. Luther, accompanied by fellow professors Philip Melanchthon and Andreas Karlstadt, has arrived with 200 Wittenberg students for a 14-day disputation on his 95 Theses. His chief opponent is Dr. Johann Eck, a defender of the Pope. The debate brings much publicity for Luther's views.
We should justify the actions of the Pope through the Scriptures alone ...
The Pope and the councils cannot err in matters of faith or doctrine.
The councils too can err!

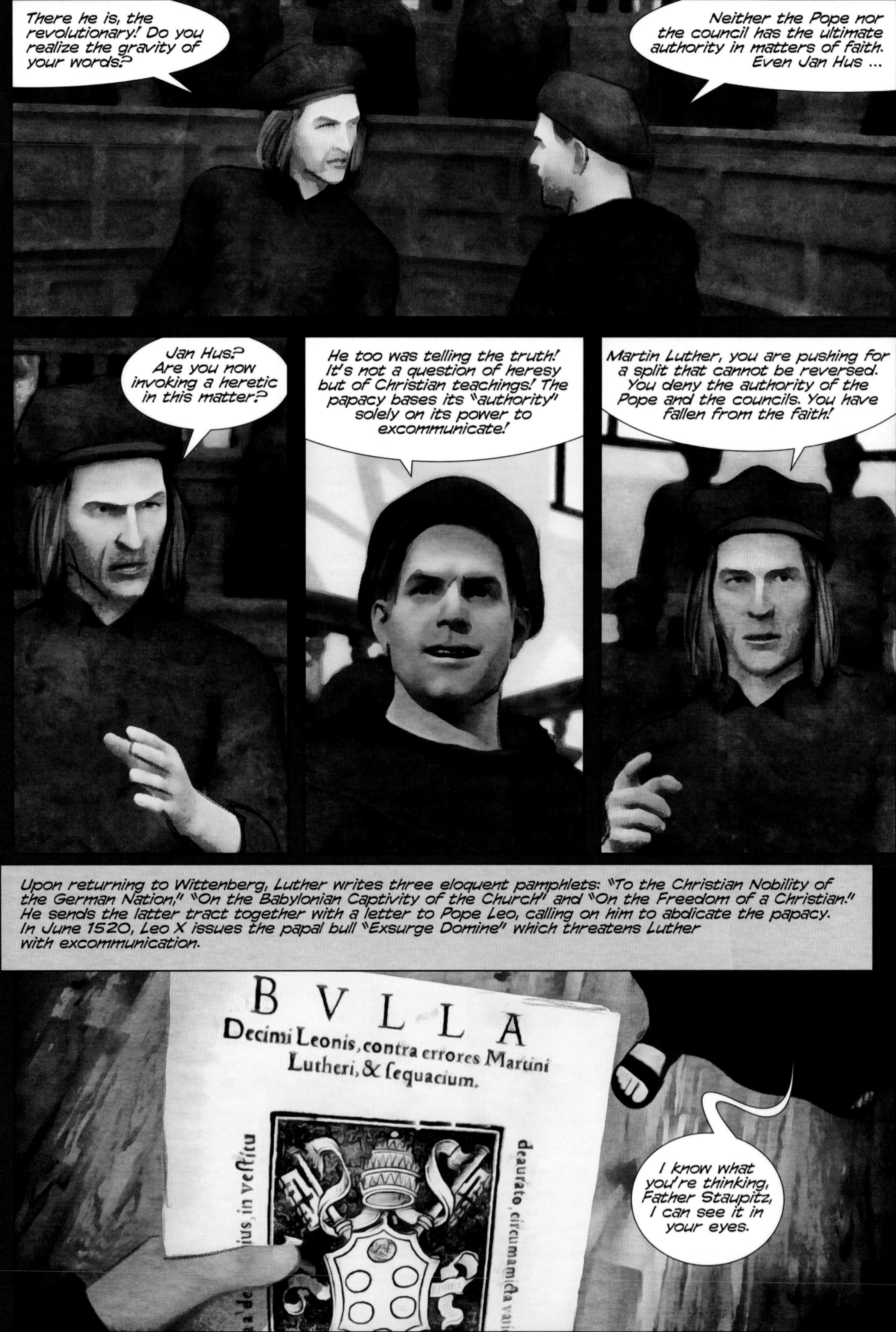
There he is, the revolutionary! Do you realize the gravity of your words?
Neither the Pope nor the council has the ultimate authority in matters of faith. Even Jan Hus ...
Jan Hus? Are you now invoking a heretic in this matter?
He too was telling the truth! It's not a question of heresy but of Christian teachings! The papacy bases its "authority" solely on its power to excommunicate!
Martin Luther, you are pushing for a split that cannot be reversed. You deny the authority of the Pope and the councils. You have fallen from the faith!
Upon returning to Wittenberg, Luther writes three eloquent pamphlets: "To the Christian Nobility of the German Nation," "On the Babylonian Captivity of the Church" and "On the Freedom of a Christian." He sends the latter tract together with a letter to Pope Leo, calling on him to abdicate the papacy. In June 1520, Leo X issues the papal bull "Exsurge Domine" which threatens Luther with excommunication.
BVLLA
Decimi Leonis, contra errores Martini Lutheri, & sequacium.
I know what you're thinking, Father Staupitz, I can see it in your eyes.

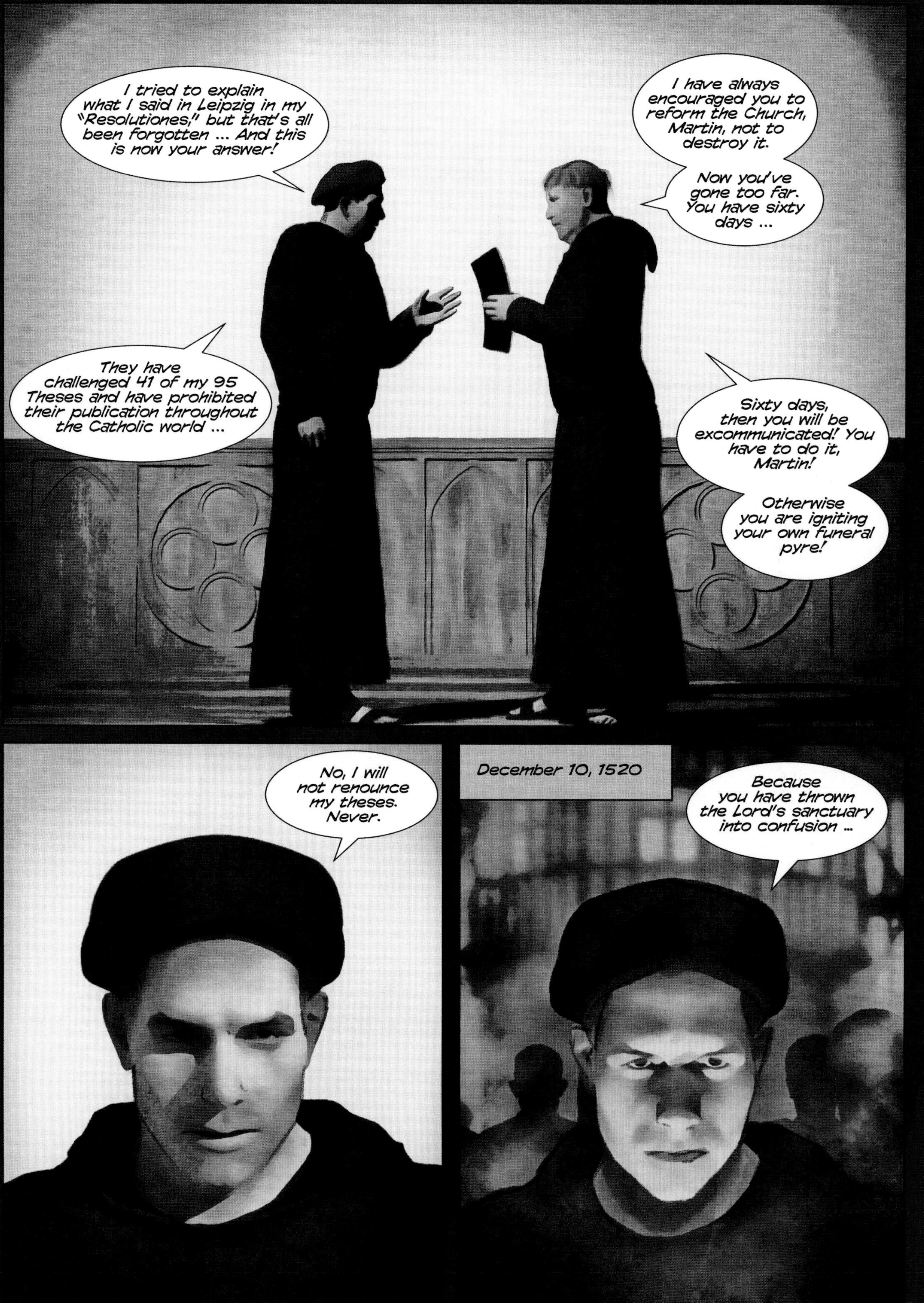
I tried to explain what I said in Leipzig in my "Resolutiones," but that's all been forgotten ... And this is now your answer!
I have always encouraged you to reform the Church, Martin, not to destroy it.
Now you've gone too far. You have sixty days ...
They have challenged 41 of my 95 Theses and have prohibited their publication throughout the Catholic world ...
Sixty days, then you will be excommunicated! You have to do it, Martin!
Otherwise you are igniting your own funeral pyre!
No, I will not renounce my theses. Never.
December 10, 1520
Because you have thrown the Lord's sanctuary into confusion ...

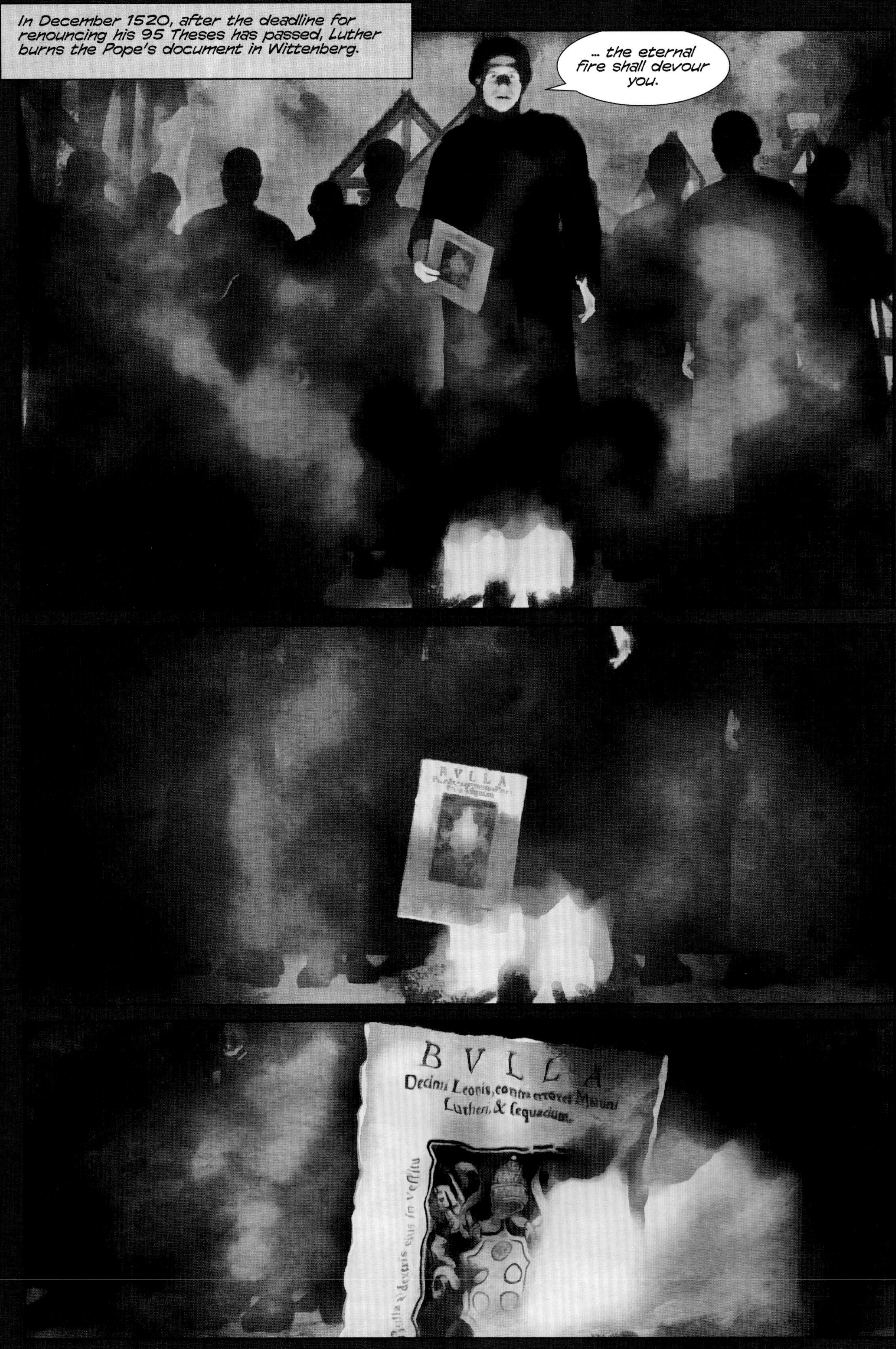
In December 1520, after the deadline for renouncing his 95 Theses has passed, Luther burns the Pope's document in Wittenberg.
... the eternal fire shall devour you.
BVLLA
Decimi Leonis, contra errores
Lutheri, & sequacium.

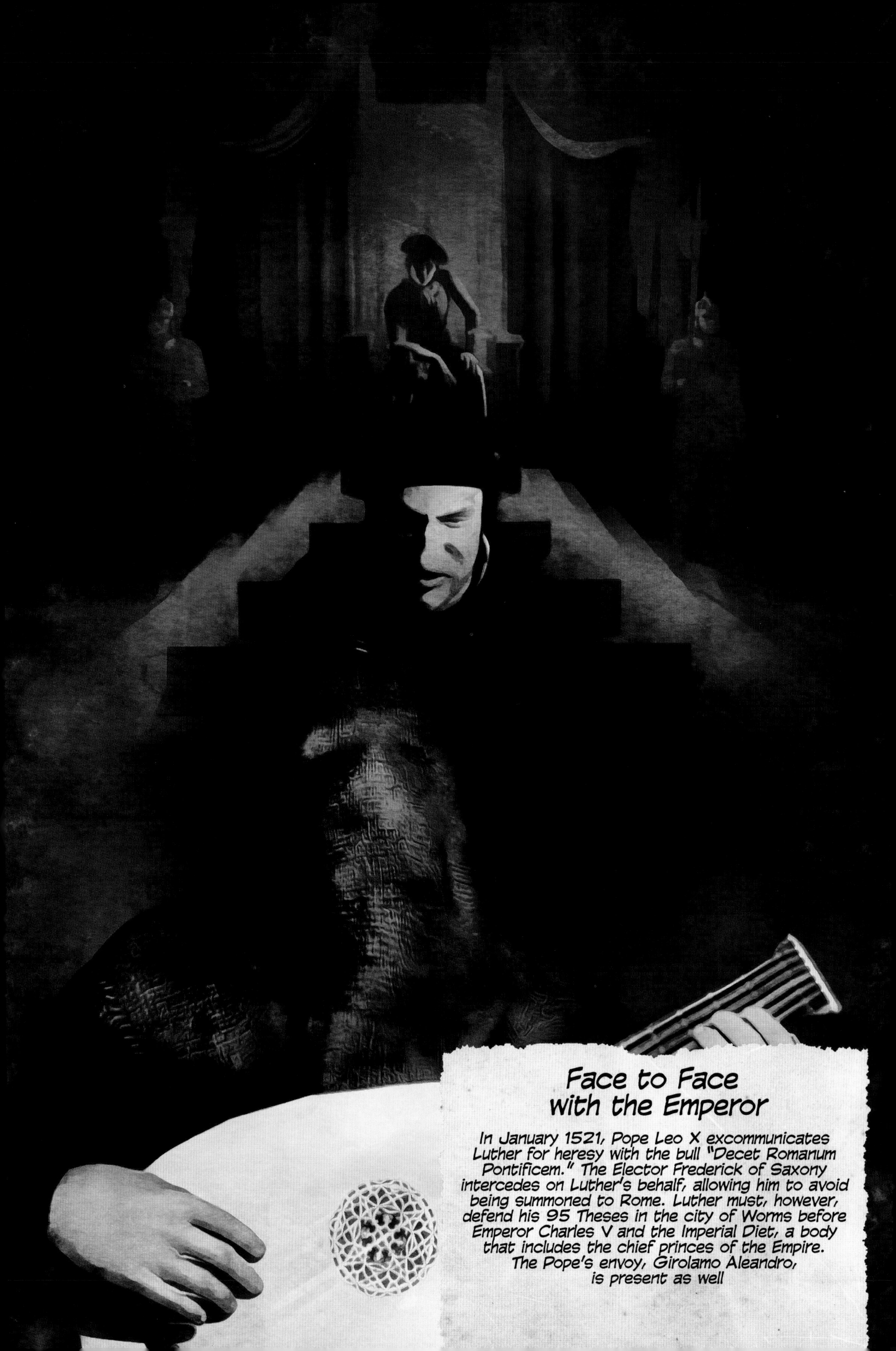
Face to Face
with the Emperor
In January 1521, Pope Leo X excommunicates Luther for heresy with the bull "Decet Romanum Pontificem." The Elector Frederick of Saxony intercedes on Luther's behalf, allowing him to avoid being summoned to Rome. Luther must, however, defend his 95 Theses in the city of Worms before Emperor Charles V and the Imperial Diet, a body that includes the chief princes of the Empire. The Pope's envoy, Girolamo Aleandro, is present as well

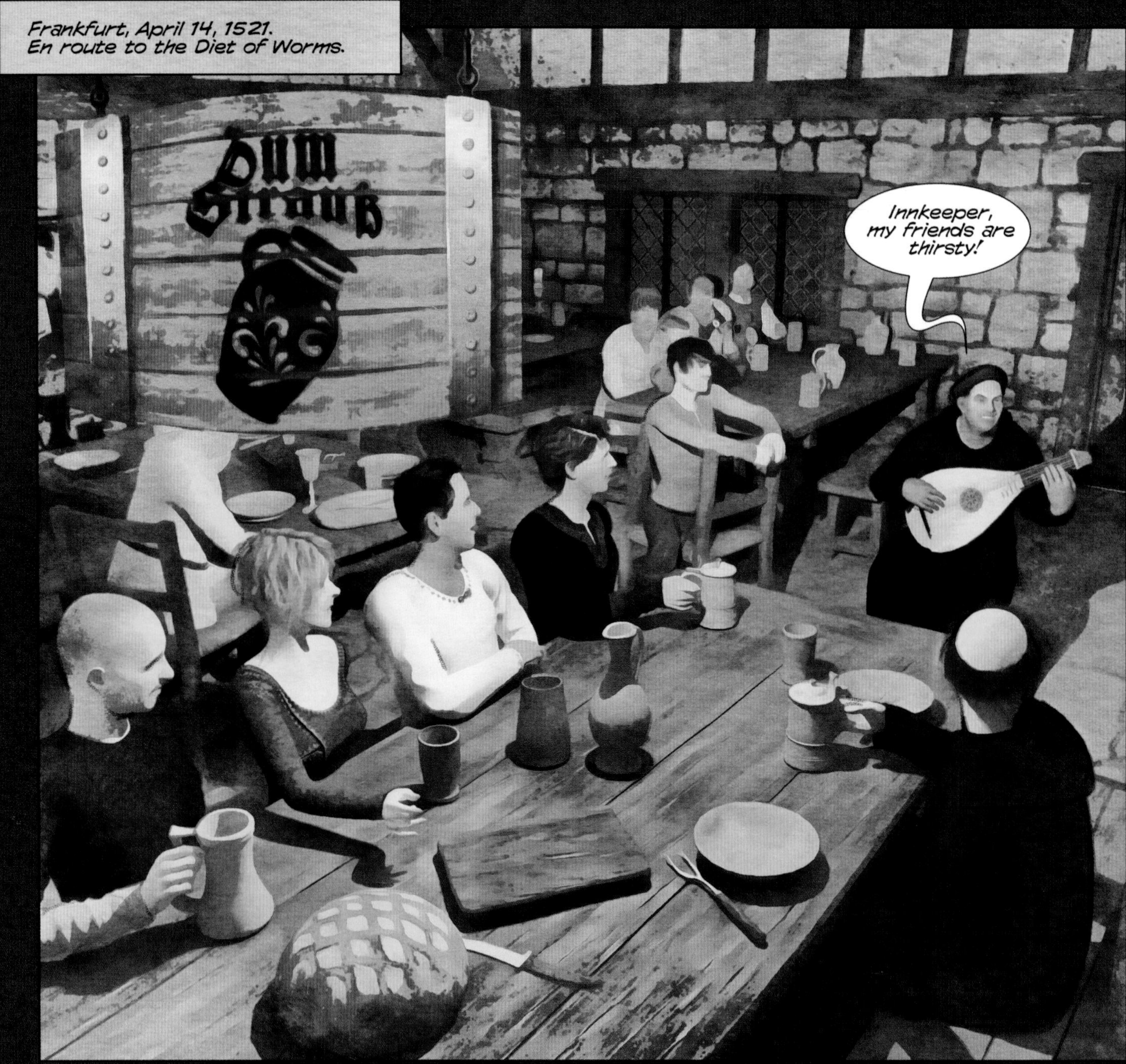
Frankfurt, April 14, 1521.
En route to the Diet of Worms.
Zum Strauß
Innkeeper, my friends are thirsty!

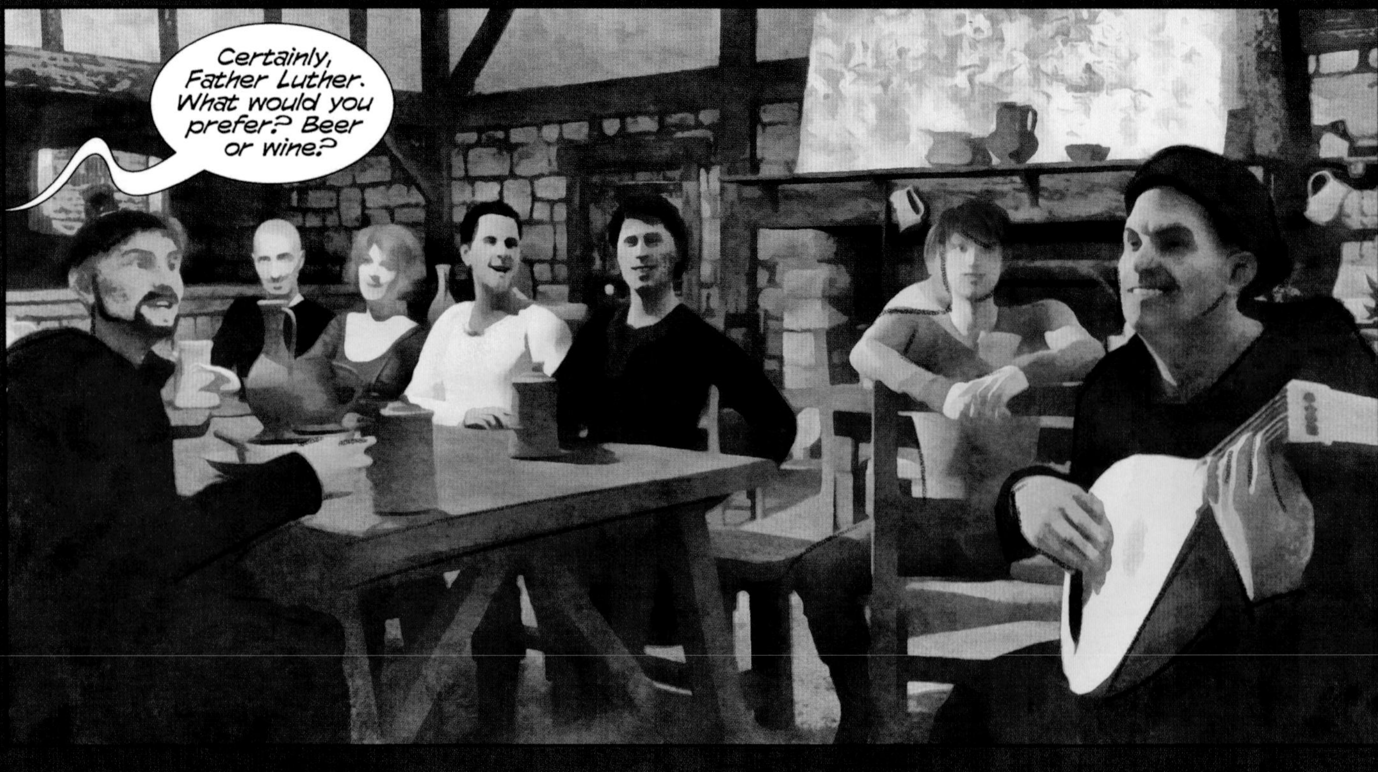
Certainly, Father Luther. What would you prefer? Beer or wine?

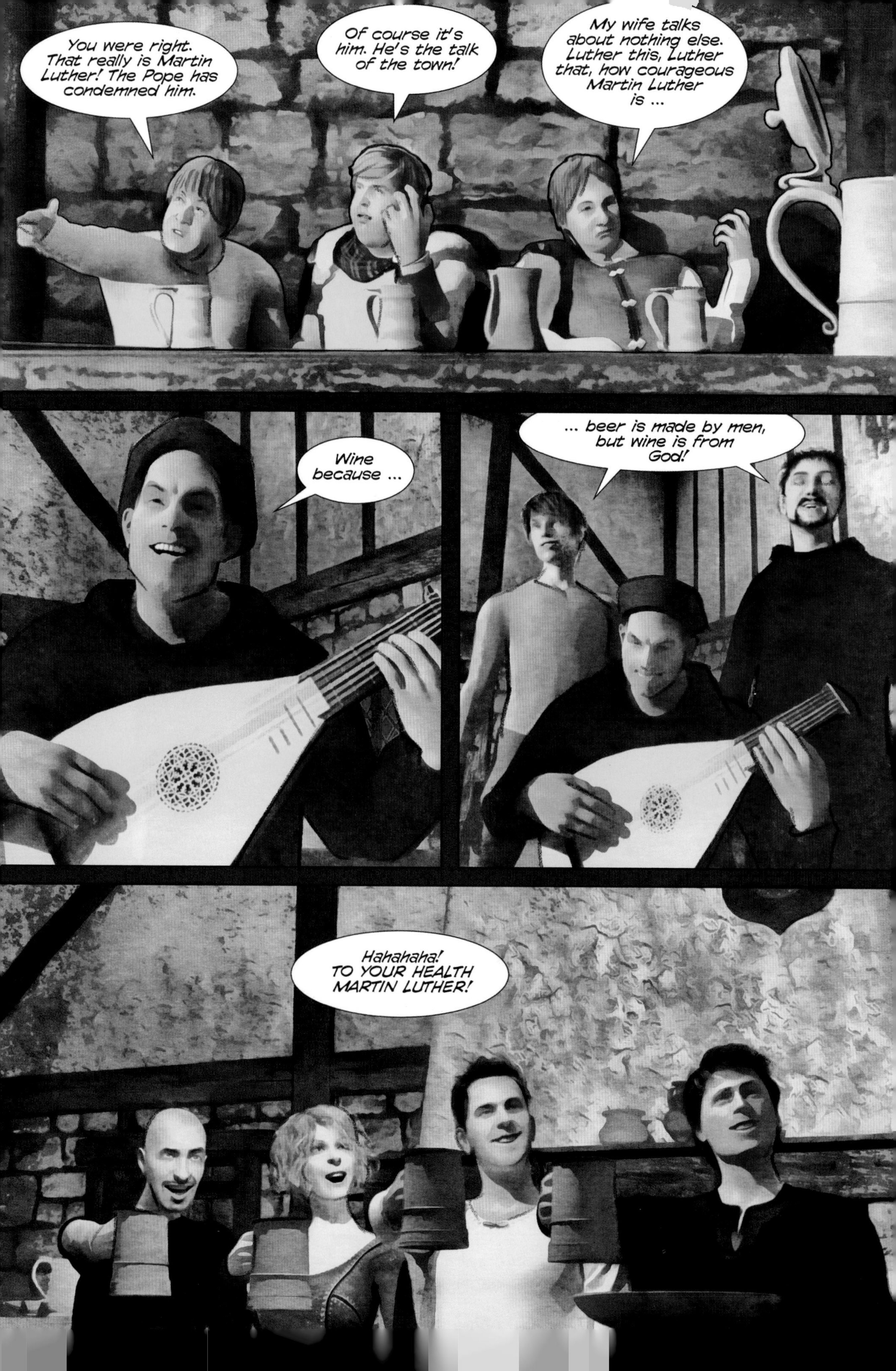
You were right. That really is Martin Luther! The Pope has condemned him.
Of course it's him. He's the talk of the town!
My wife talks about nothing else. Luther this, Luther that, how courageous Martin Luther is ...
Wine because ...
... beer is made by men, but wine is from God!
Hahahaha! TO YOUR HEALTH MARTIN LUTHER!

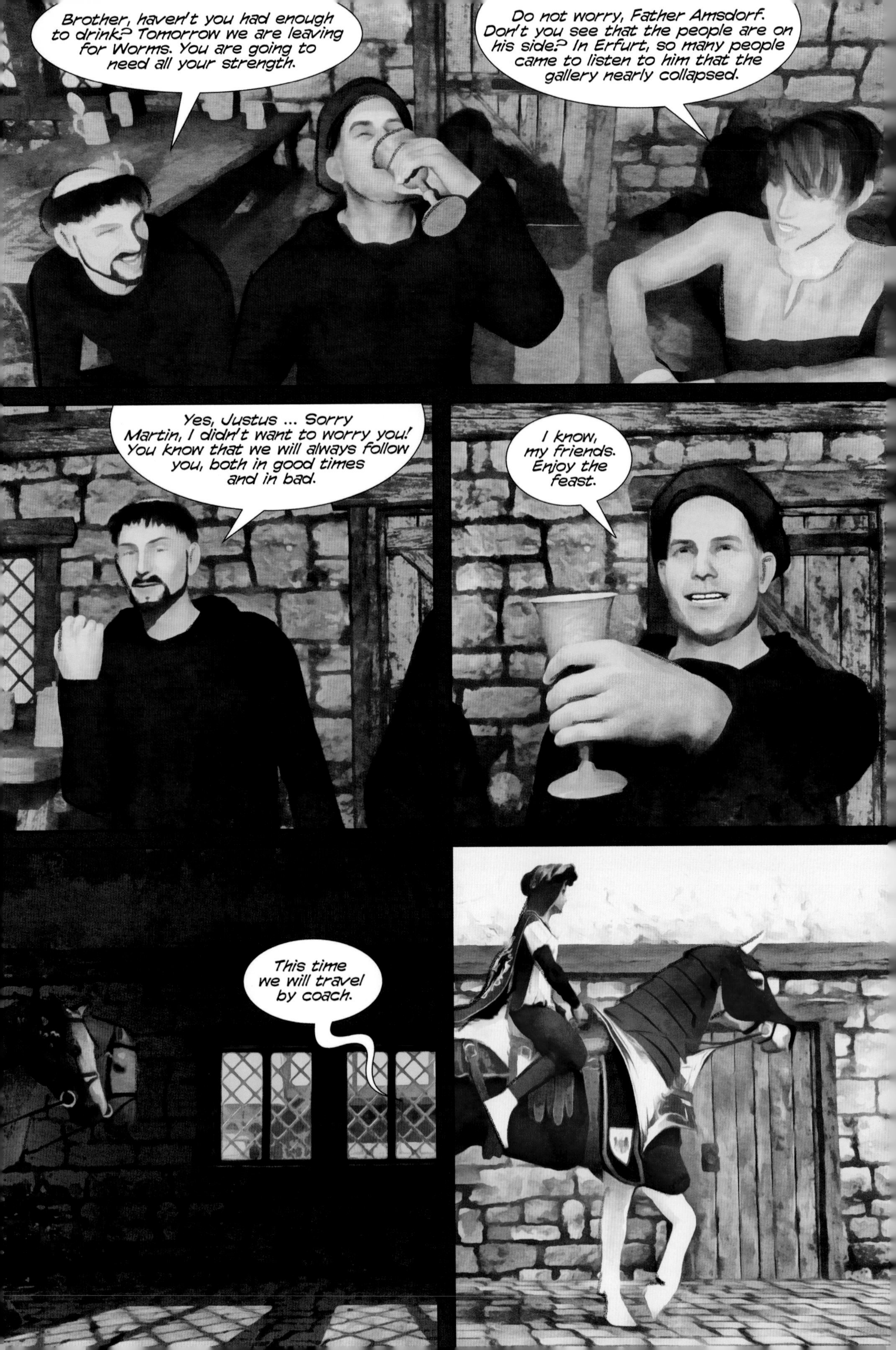
Brother, haven't you had enough to drink? Tomorrow we are leaving for Worms. You are going to need all your strength.
Do not worry, Father Amsdorf. Don't you see that the people are on his side? In Erfurt, so many people came to listen to him that the gallery nearly collapsed.
Yes, Justus ... Sorry Martin, I didn't want to worry you! You know that we will always follow you, both in good times and in bad.
I know, my friends. Enjoy the feast.
This time we will travel by coach.

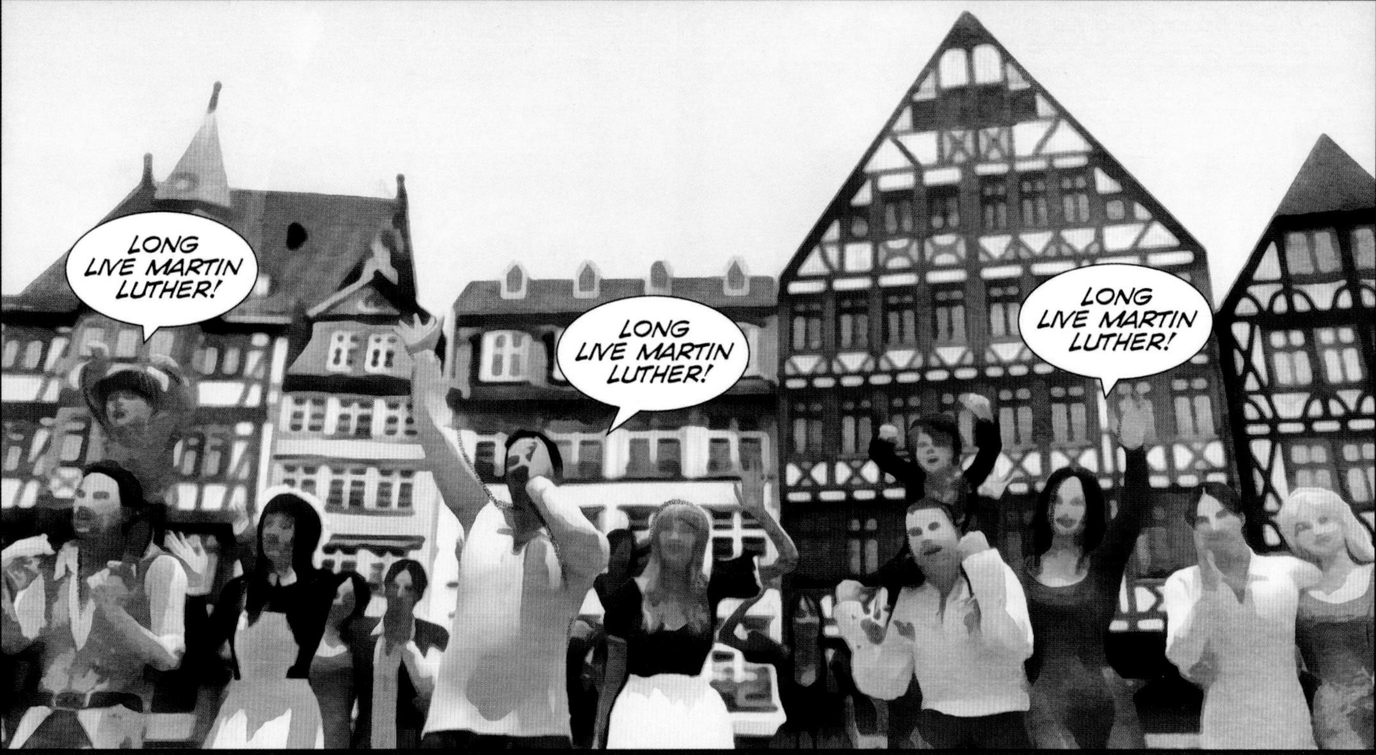
LONG LIVE MARTIN LUTHER!
LONG LIVE MARTIN LUTHER!
LONG LIVE MARTIN LUTHER!

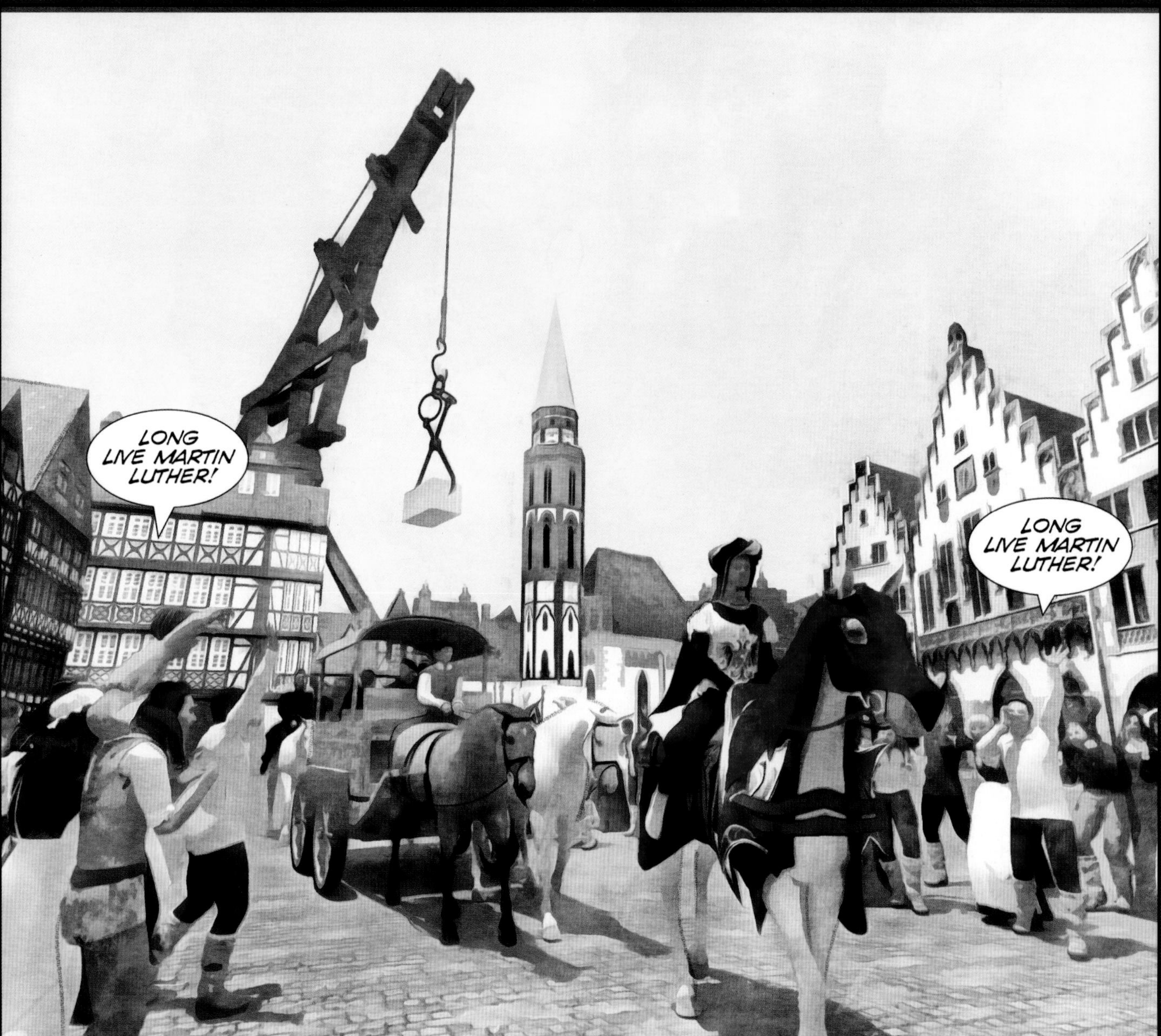
LONG LIVE MARTIN LUTHER!
LONG LIVE MARTIN LUTHER!

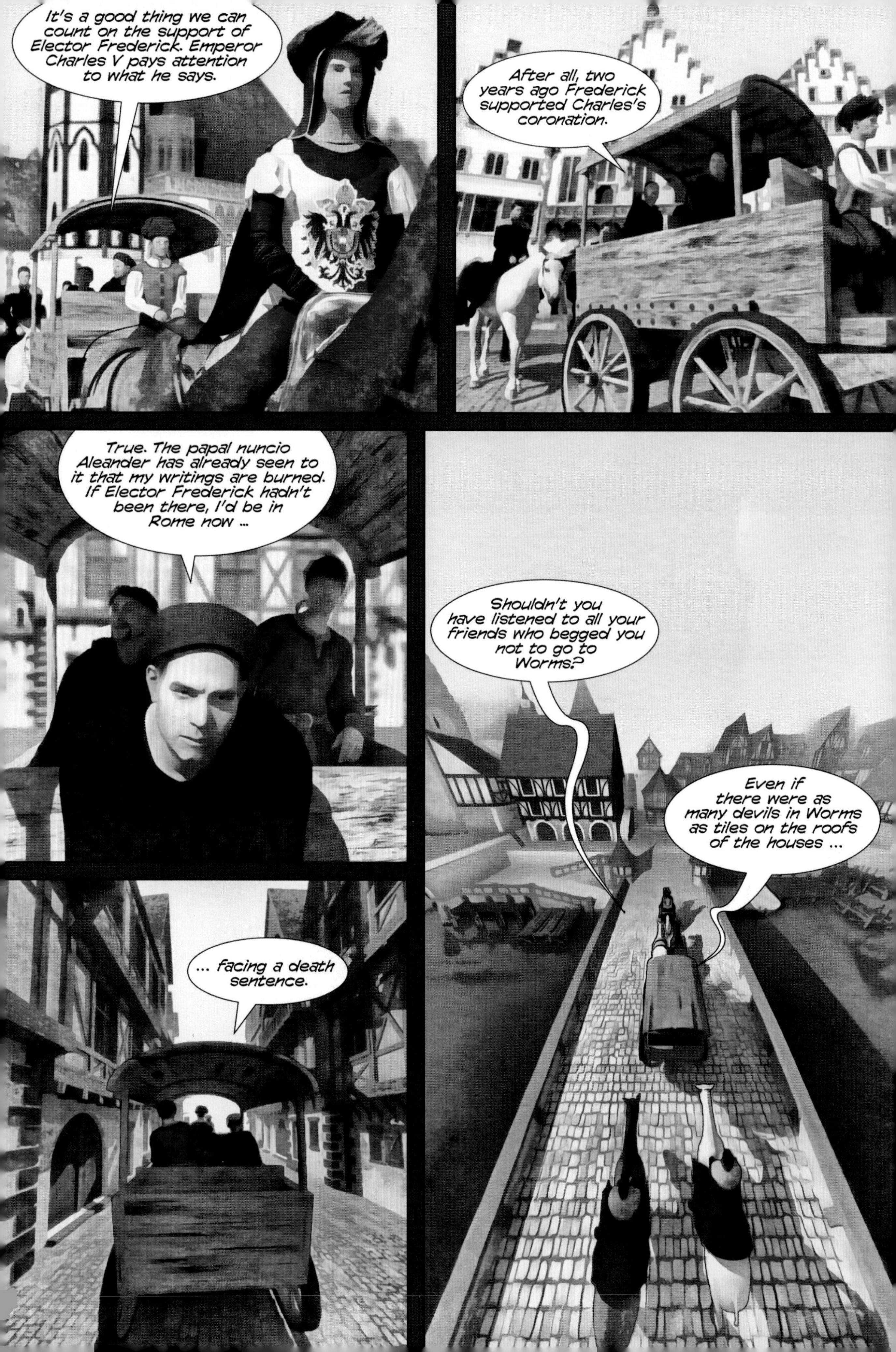
It's a good thing we can count on the support of Elector Frederick. Emperor Charles V pays attention to what he says.
After all, two years ago Frederick supported Charles's coronation.
True. The papal nuncio Aleander has already seen to it that my writings are burned. If Elector Frederick hadn't been there, I'd be in Rome now ...
... facing a death sentence.
Shouldn't you have listened to all your friends who begged you not to go to Worms?
Even if there were as many devils in Worms as tiles on the roofs of the houses ...

... I would still go!

Diet of Worms, April 1521
The Imperial Diet has been meeting since January, with the 21-year-old Emperor Charles V presiding. At the urging of the German princes, Martin Luther is summoned to the Diet to defend himself on April 21. The Emperor guarantees him safe passage to and from Worms.

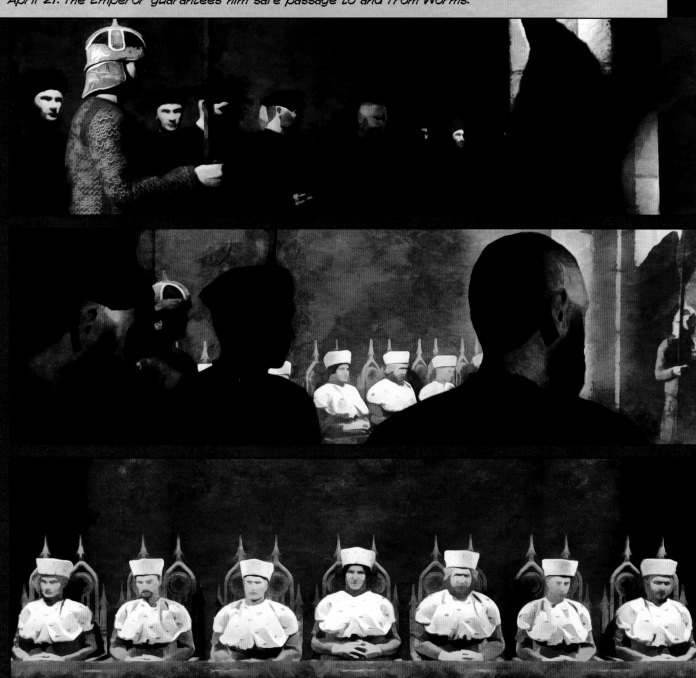

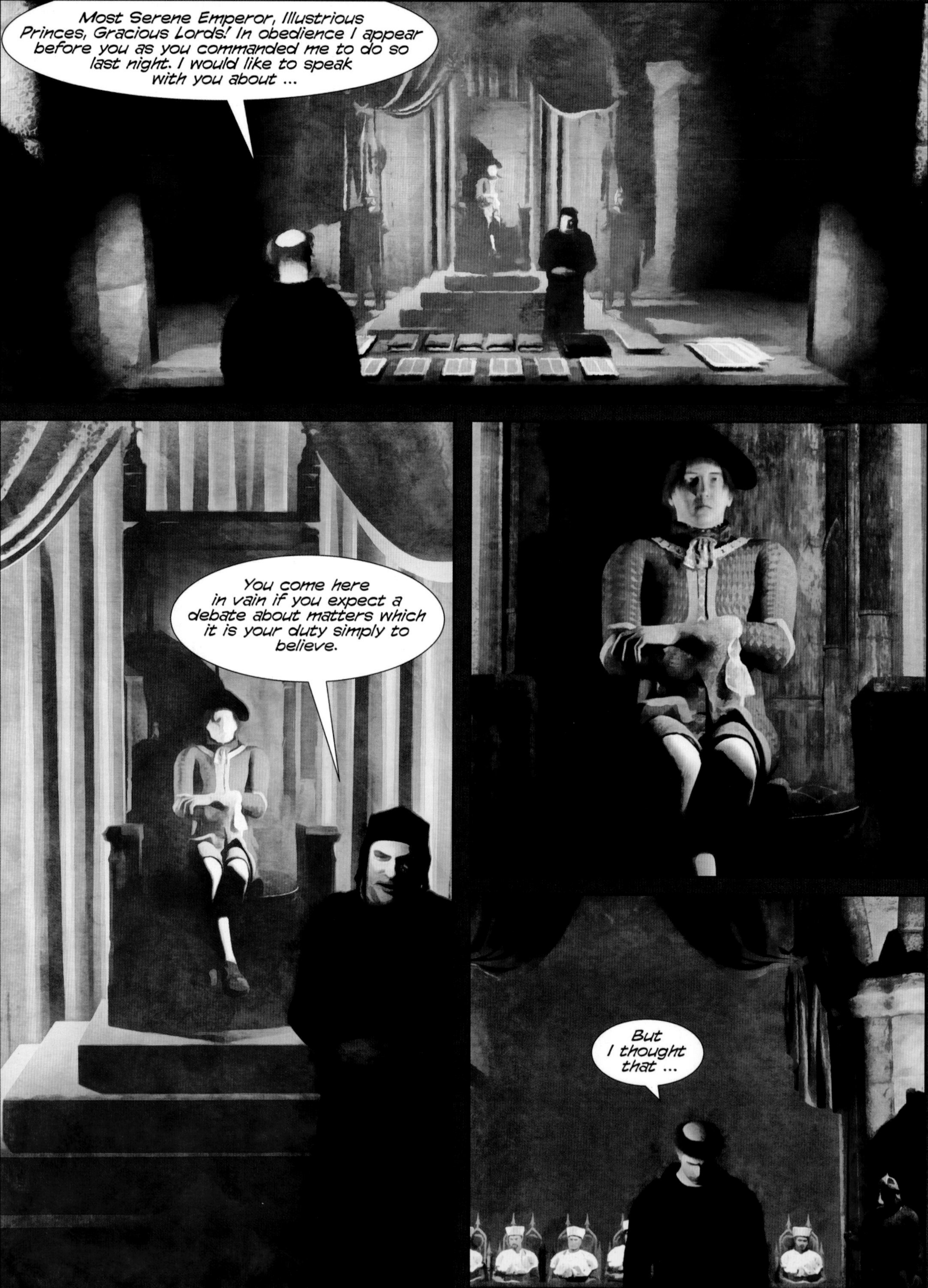
Most Serene Emperor, Illustrious Princes, Gracious Lords! In obedience I appear before you as you commanded me to do so last night. I would like to speak with you about ...
You come here in vain if you expect a debate about matters which it is your duty simply to believe.
But I thought that ...

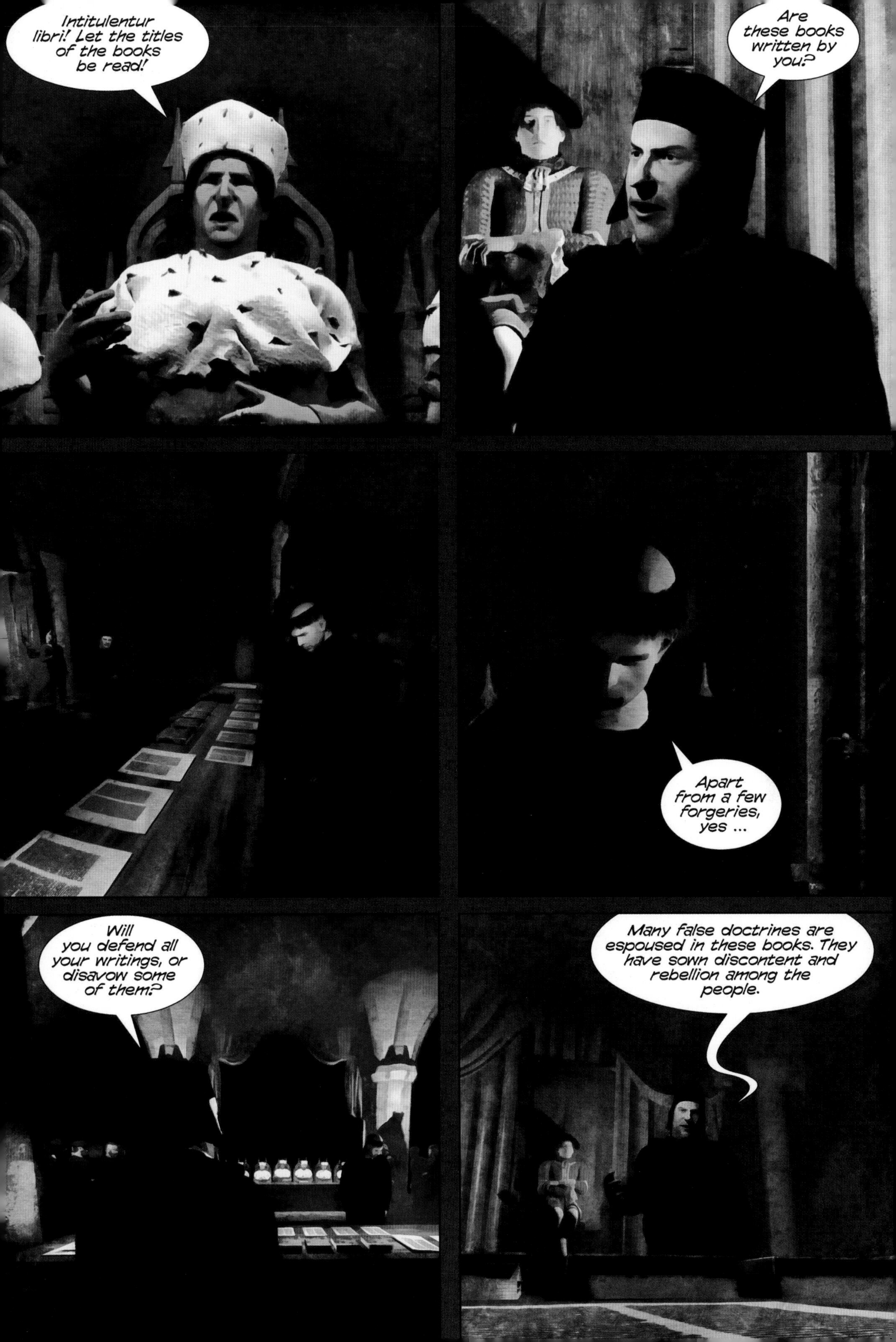
Intitulentur libri! Let the titles of the books be read!
Are these books written by you?
Apart from a few forgeries, yes ...
Will you defend all your writings, or disavow some of them?
Many false doctrines are espoused in these books. They have sown discontent and rebellion among the people.

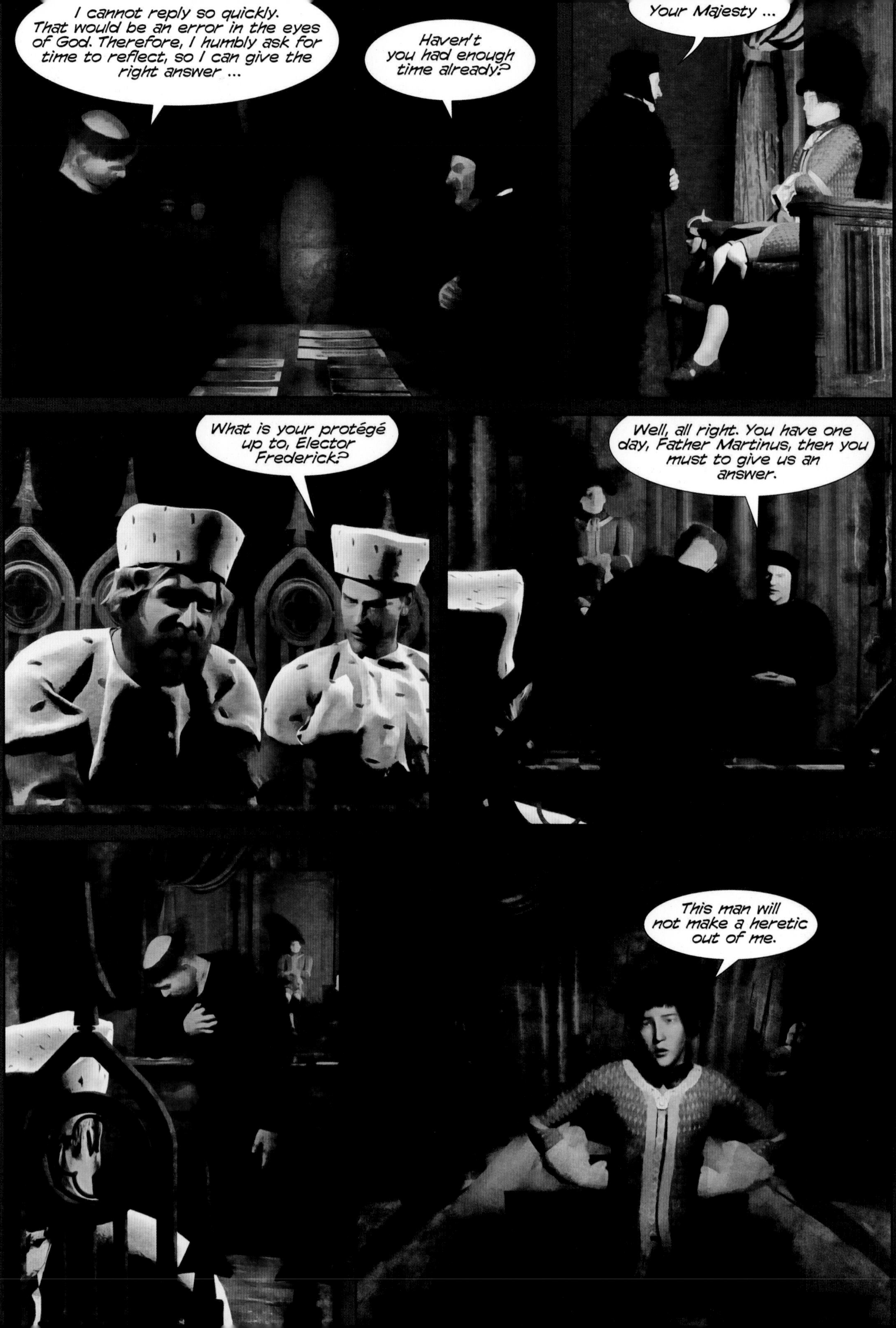
I cannot reply so quickly. That would be an error in the eyes of God. Therefore, I humbly ask for time to reflect, so I can give the right answer ...
Haven't you had enough time already?
Your Majesty ...
What is your protégé up to, Elector Frederick?
Well, all right. You have one day, Father Martinus, then you must to give us an answer.
This man will not make a heretic out of me.

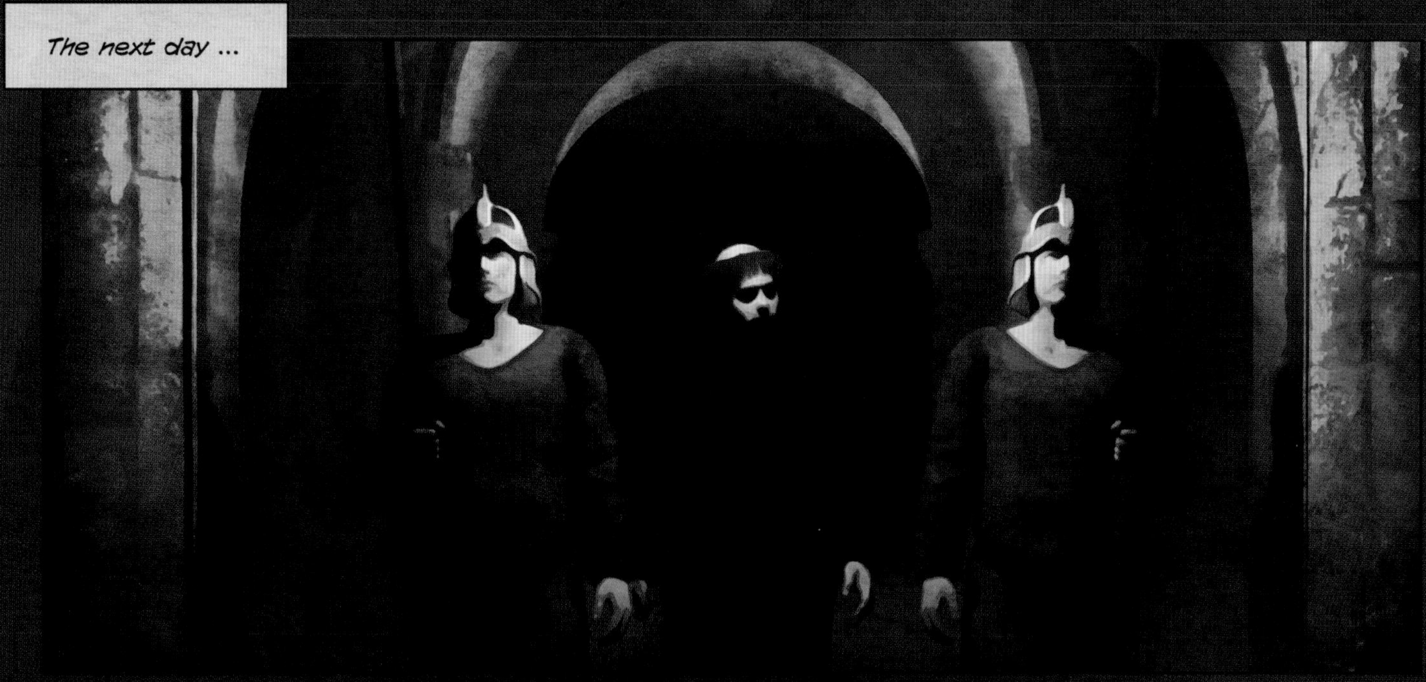
The next day ...

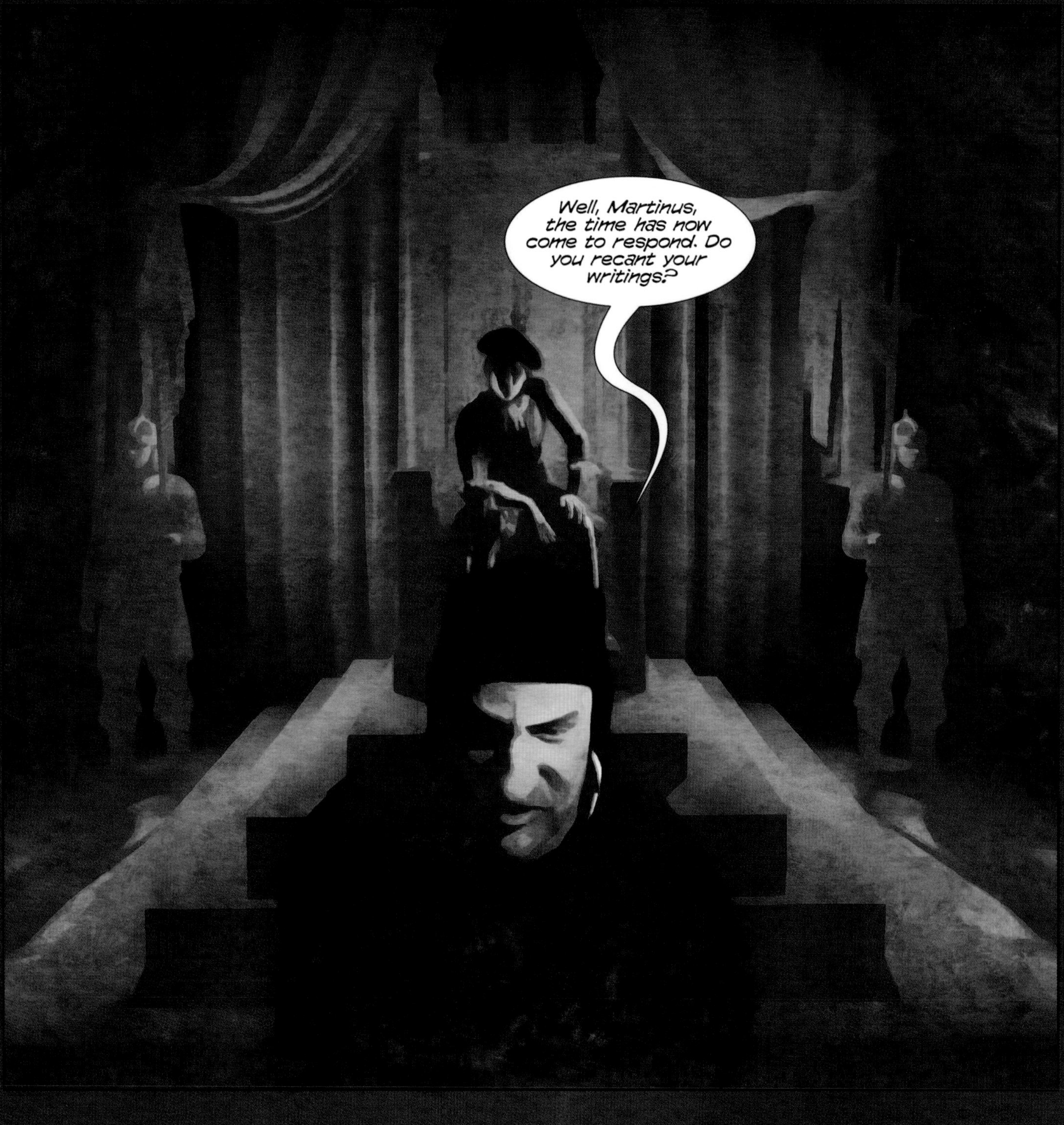
Well, Martinus, the time has now come to respond. Do you recant your writings?

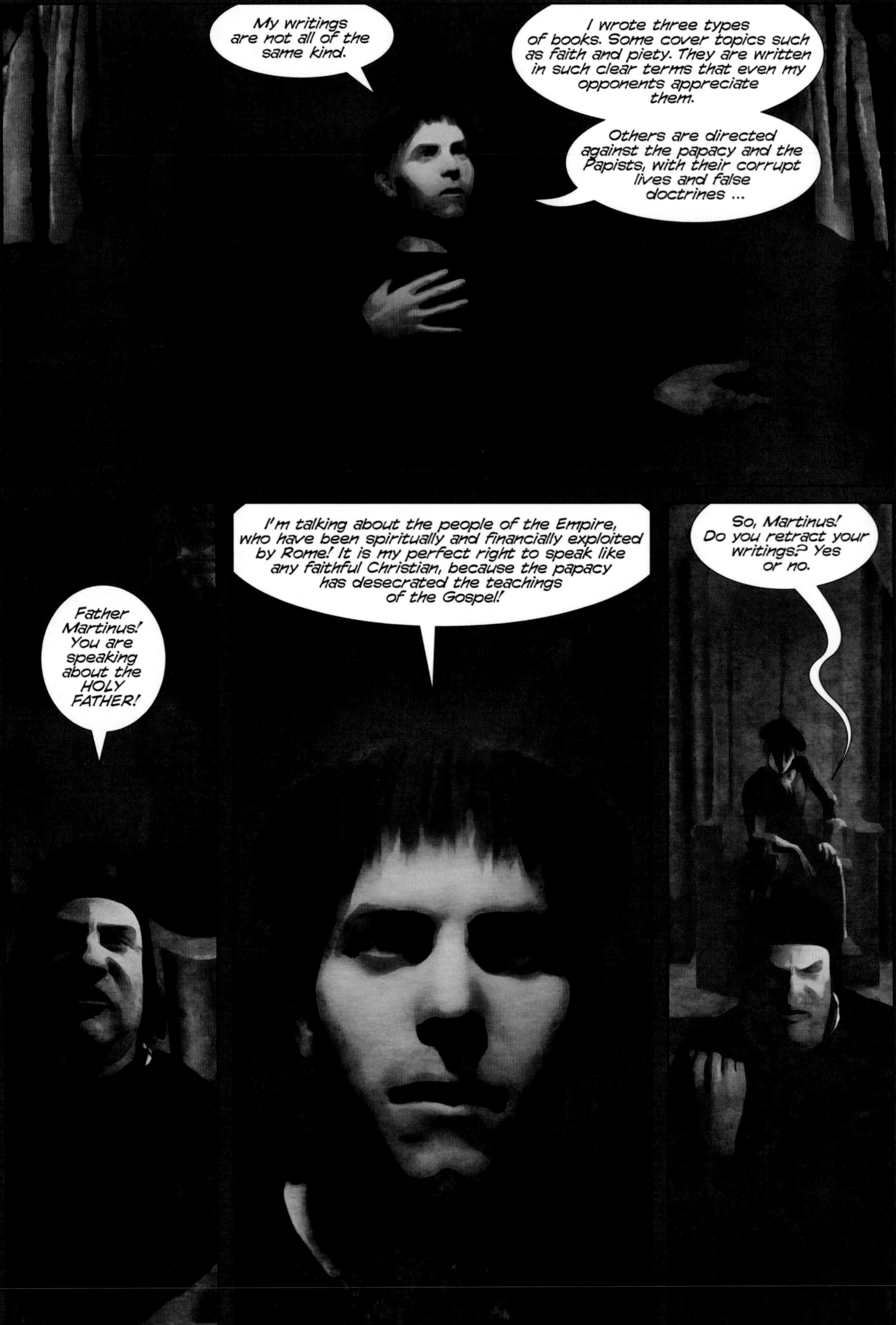
My writings are not all of the same kind.
I wrote three types of books. Some cover topics such as faith and piety. They are written in such clear terms that even my opponents appreciate them.
Others are directed against the papacy and the Papists, with their corrupt lives and false doctrines ...
Father Martinus! You are speaking about the HOLY FATHER!
I'm talking about the people of the Empire, who have been spiritually and financially exploited by Rome! It is my perfect right to speak like any faithful Christian, because the papacy has desecrated the teachings of the Gospel!
So, Martinus! Do you retract your writings? Yes or no.

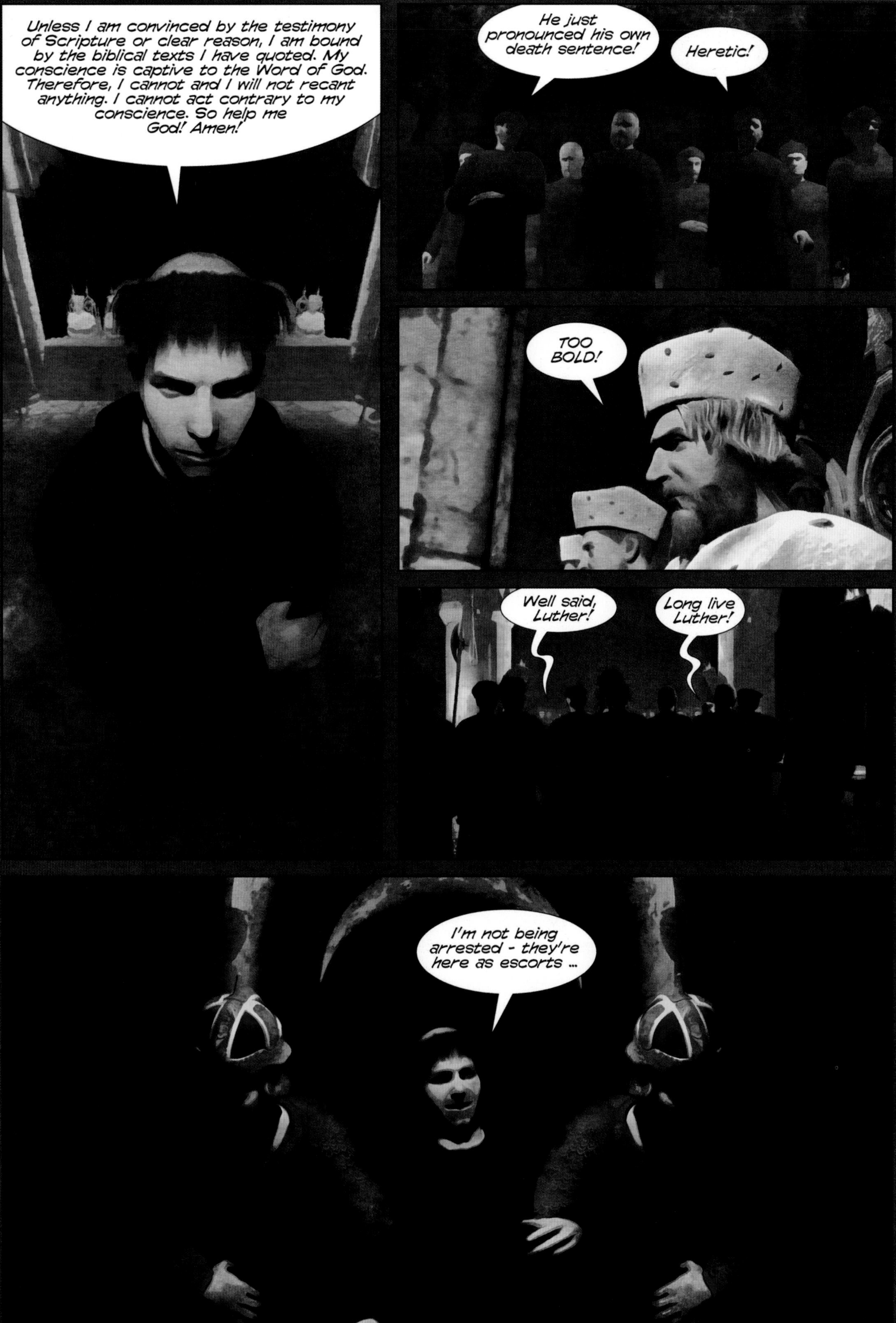
Unless I am convinced by the testimony of Scripture or clear reason, I am bound by the biblical texts I have quoted. My conscience is captive to the Word of God. Therefore, I cannot and I will not recant anything. I cannot act contrary to my conscience. So help me God! Amen!
He just pronounced his own death sentence!
Heretic!
TOO BOLD!
Well said, Luther!
Long live Luther!
I'm not being arrested - they're here as escorts ...

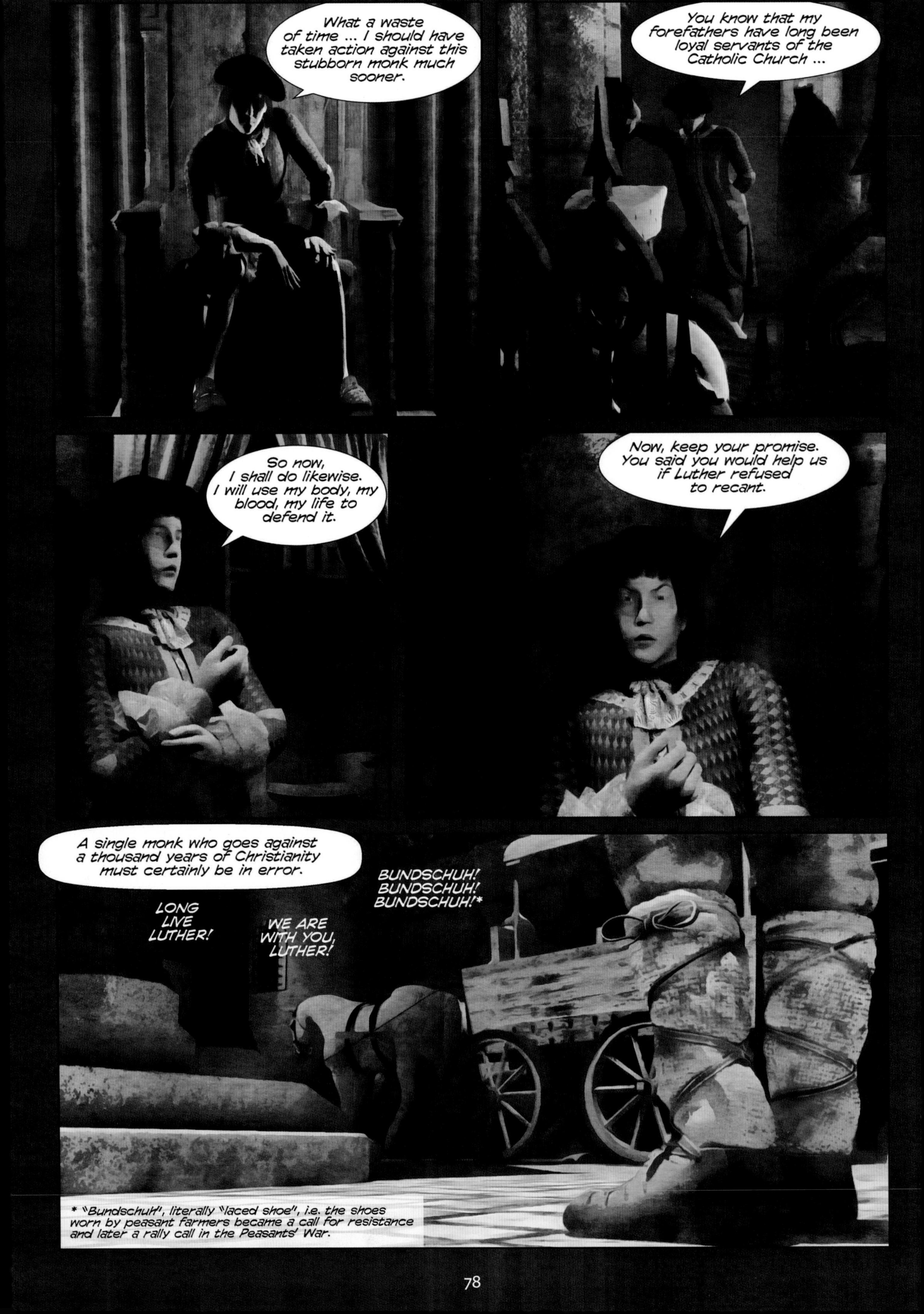
What a waste of time ... I should have taken action against this stubborn monk much sooner.
You know that my forefathers have long been loyal servants of the Catholic Church ...
So now, I shall do likewise. I will use my body, my blood, my life to defend it.
Now, keep your promise. You said you would help us if Luther refused to recant.
A single monk who goes against a thousand years of Christianity must certainly be in error.
LONG LIVE LUTHER!
WE ARE WITH YOU, LUTHER!
BUNDSCHUH! BUNDSCHUH! BUNDSCHUH!*

* "Bundschuh", literally "laced shoe", i.e. the shoes worn by peasant farmers became a call for resistance and later a rally call in the Peasants' War.

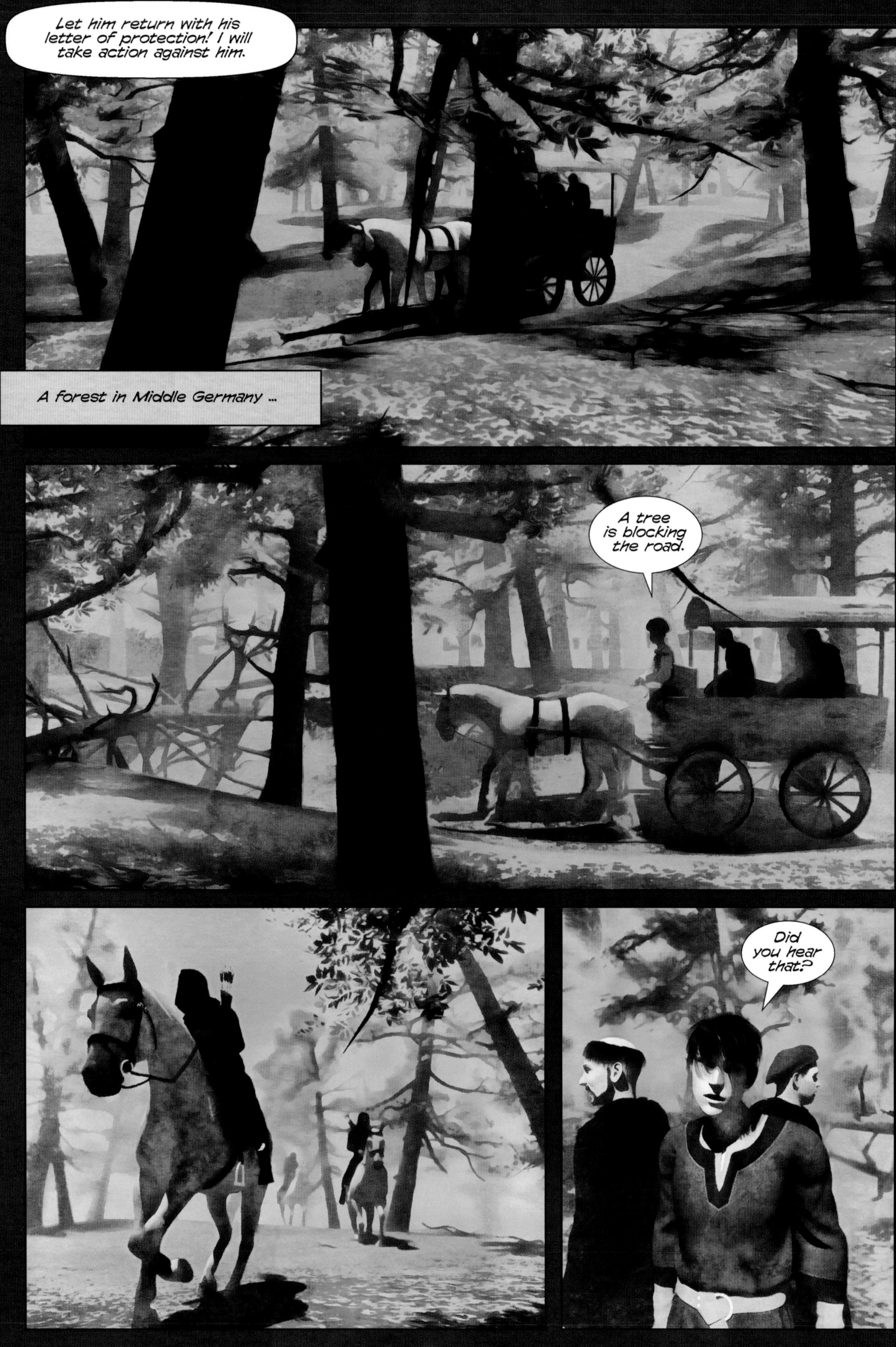
Let him return with his letter of protection! I will take action against him.
A forest in Middle Germany ...
A tree is blocking the road.
Did you hear that?

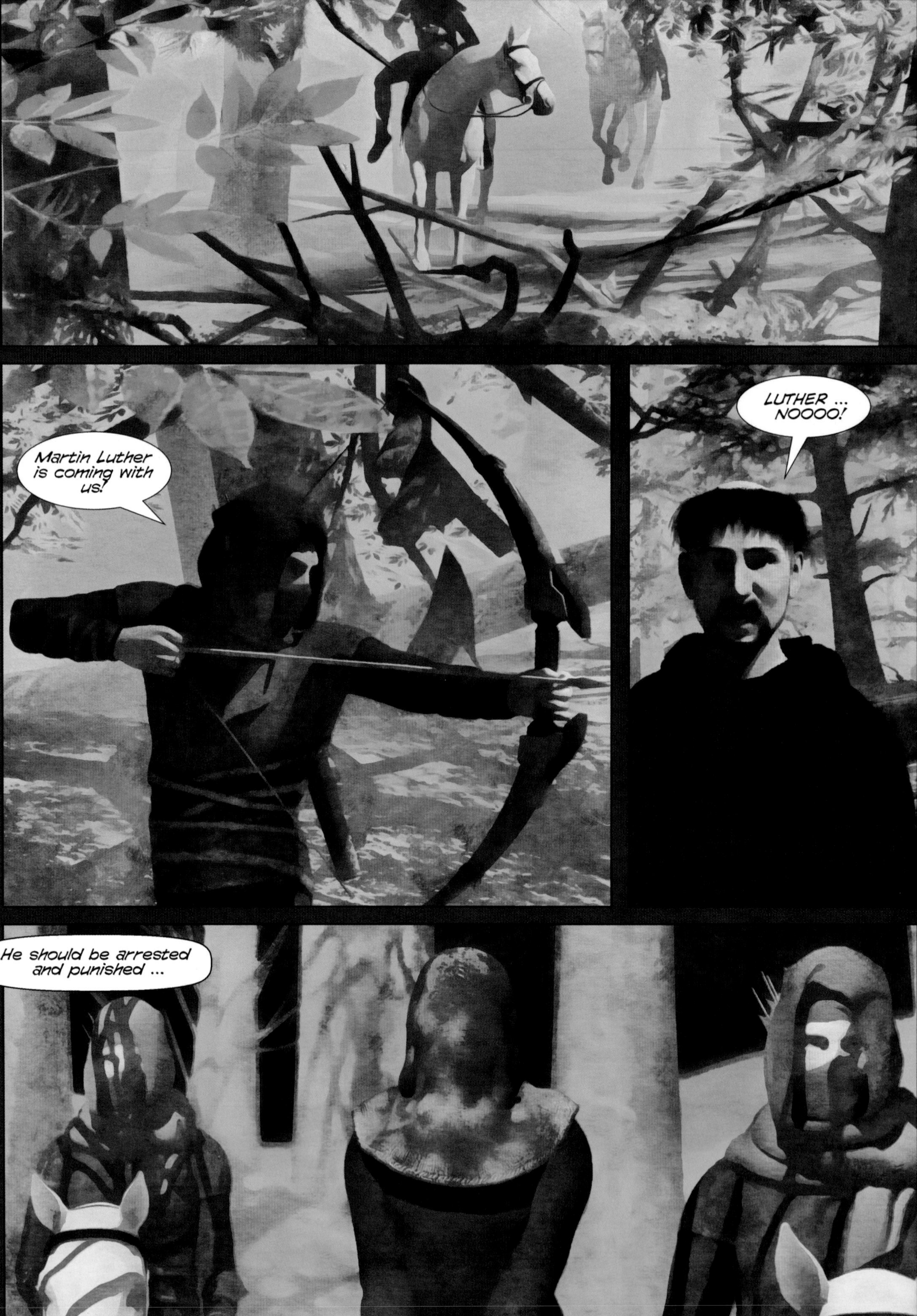
Martin Luther is coming with us!
LUTHER ... NOOOO!
He should be arrested and punished ...

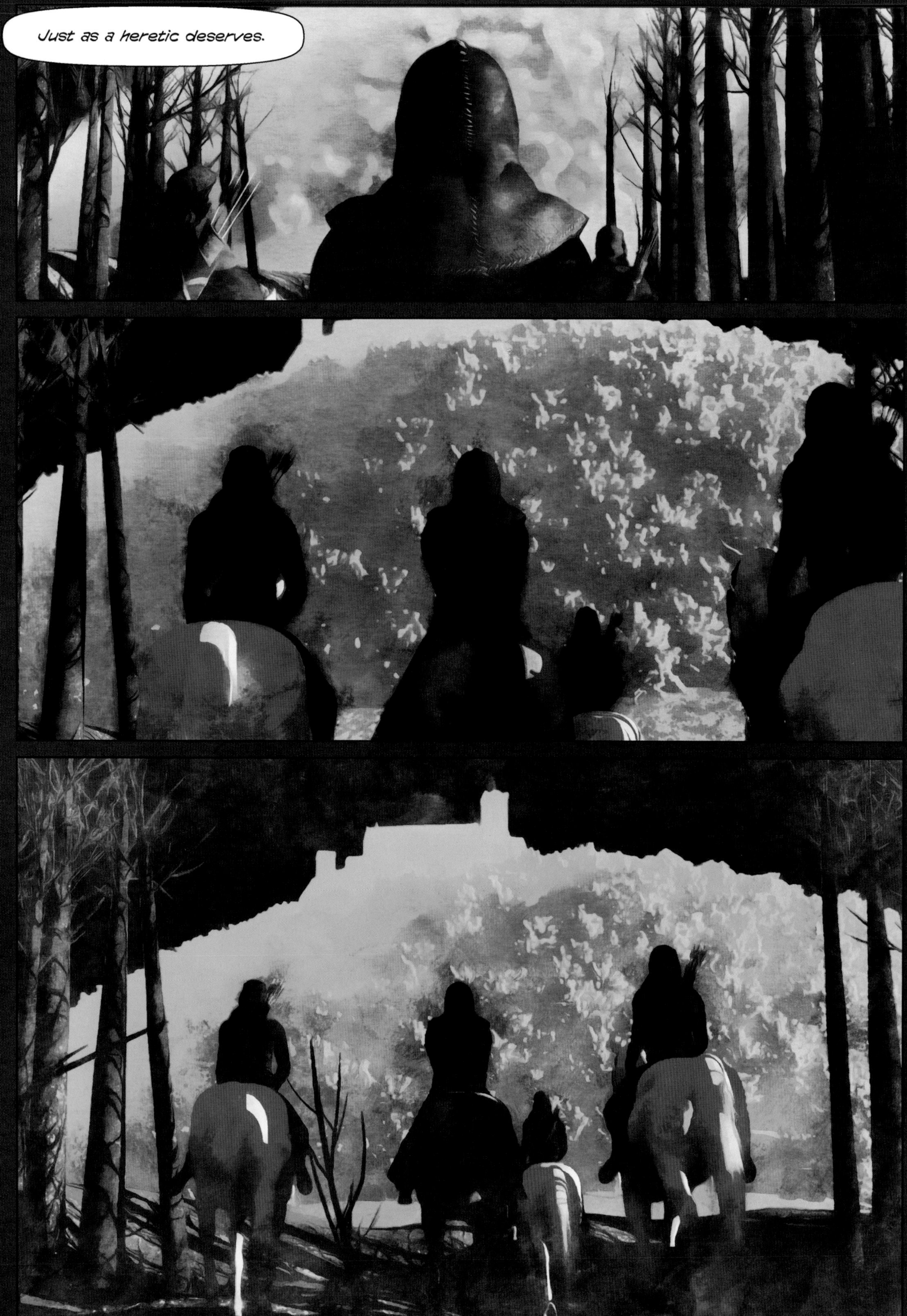
Just as a heretic deserves.

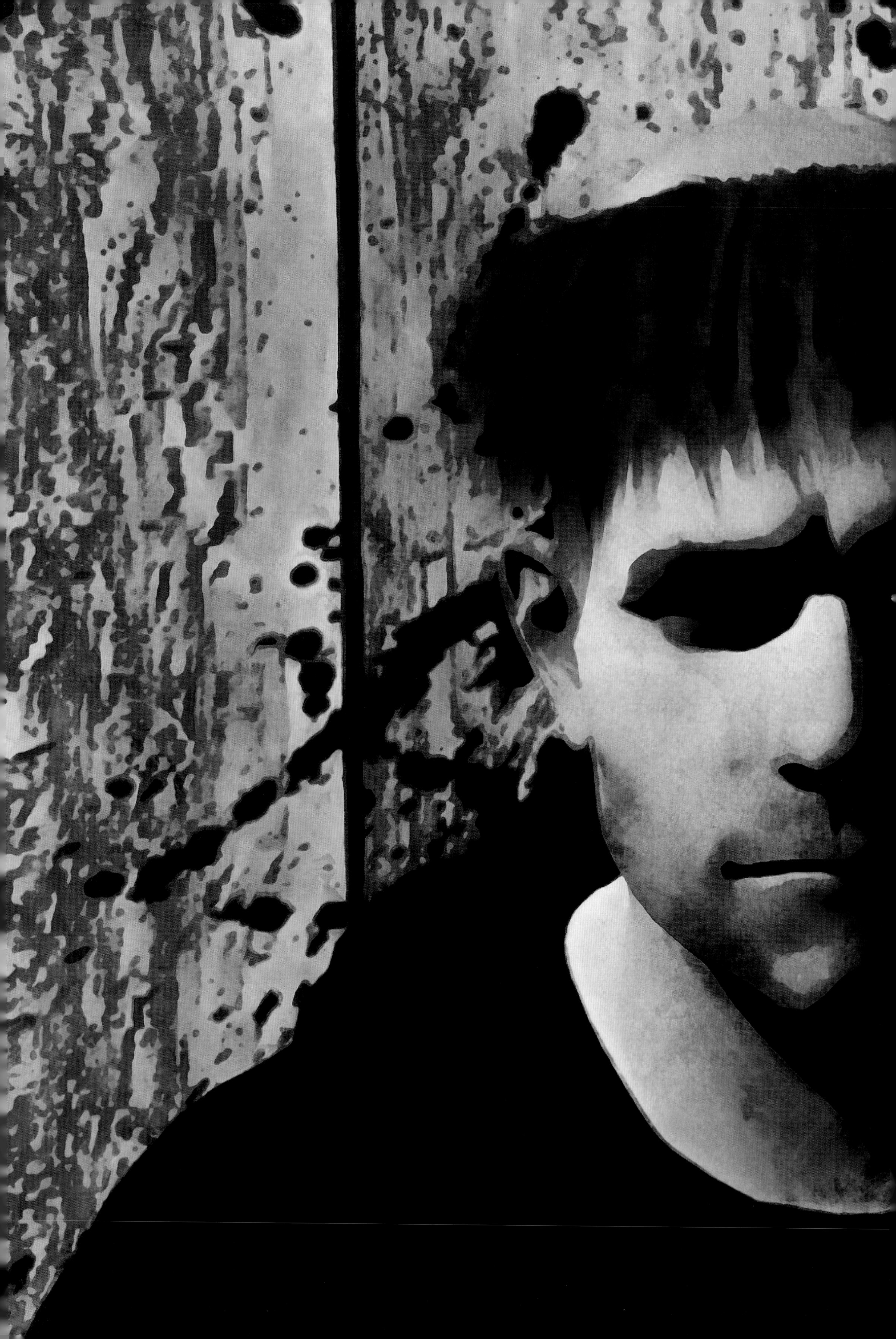

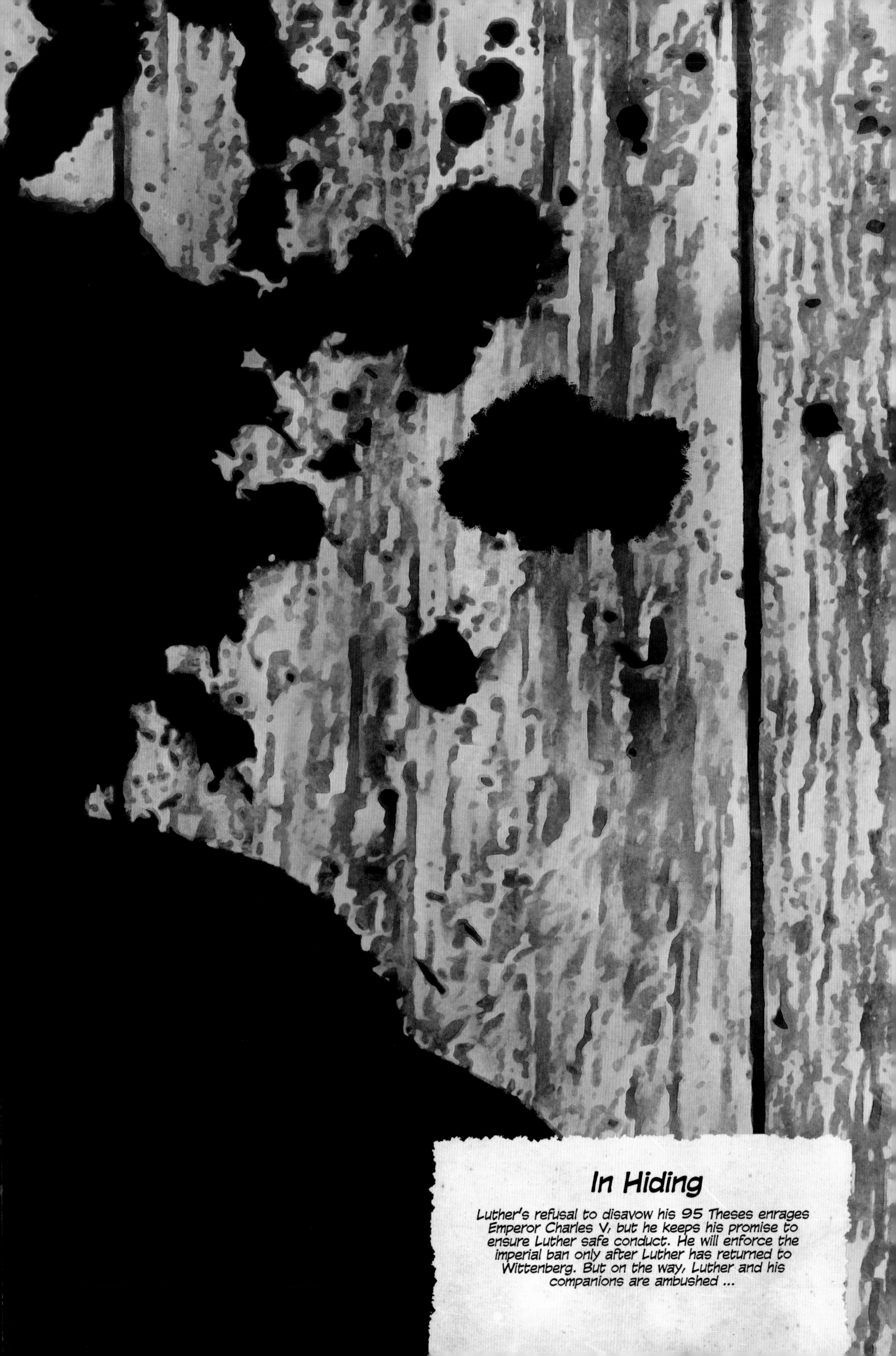

In Hiding

Luther's refusal to disavow his 95 Theses enrages Emperor Charles V, but he keeps his promise to ensure Luther safe conduct. He will enforce the imperial ban only after Luther has returned to Wittenberg. But on the way, Luther and his companions are ambushed ...

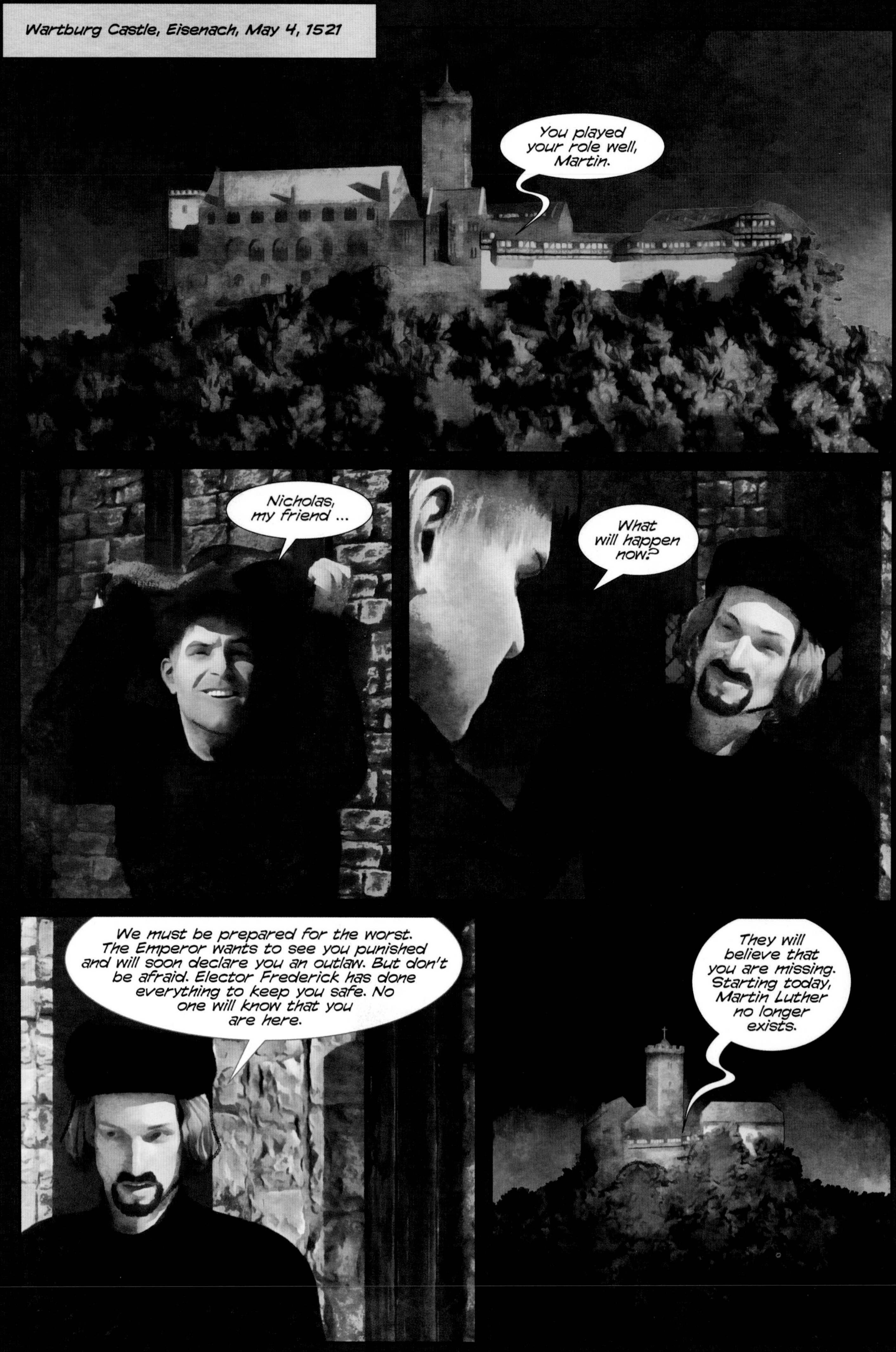

Wartburg Castle, Eisenach, May 4, 1521
You played your role well, Martin.
Nicholas, my friend ...
What will happen now?
We must be prepared for the worst. The Emperor wants to see you punished and will soon declare you an outlaw. But don't be afraid. Elector Frederick has done everything to keep you safe. No one will know that you are here.
They will believe that you are missing. Starting today, Martin Luther no longer exists.

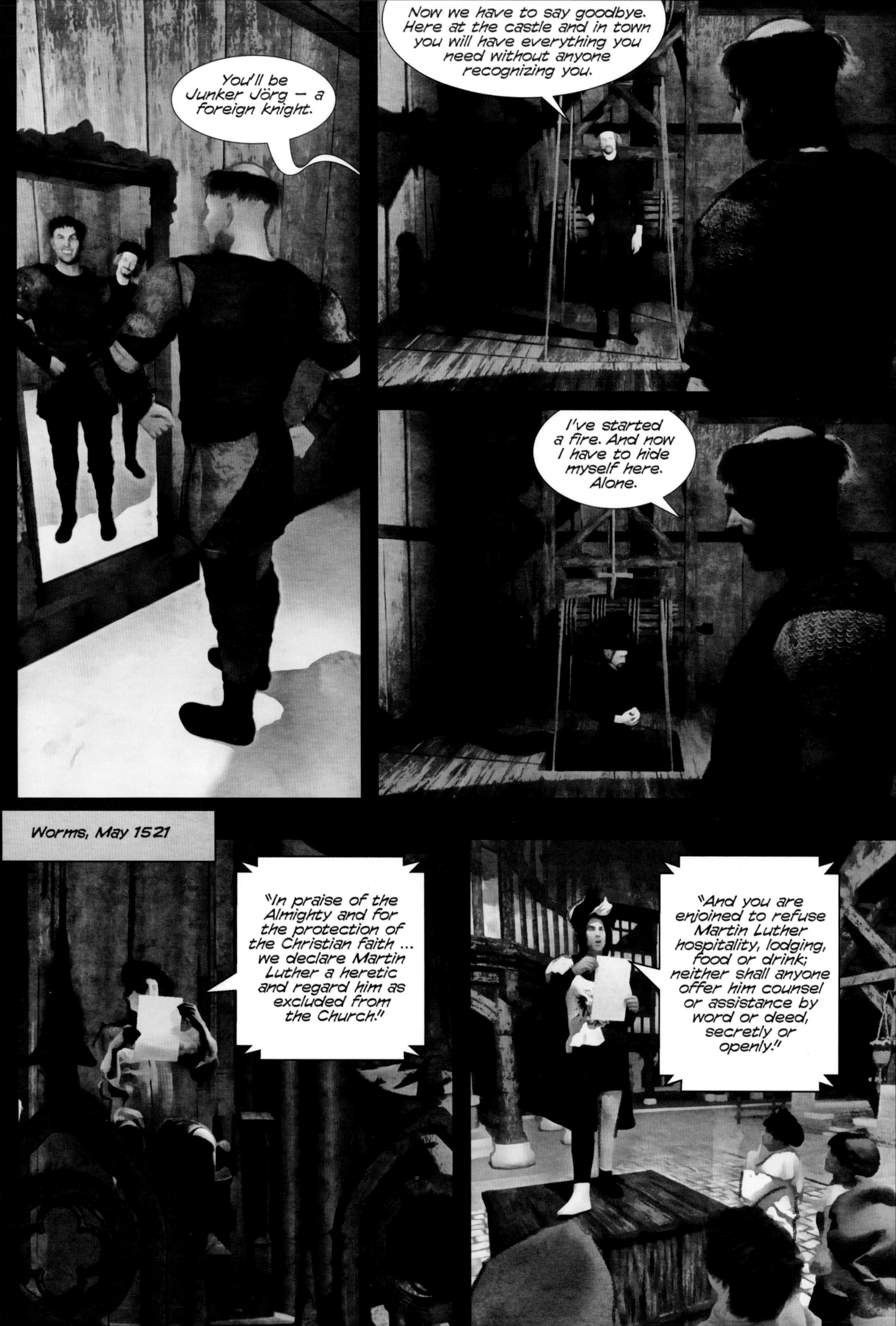
You'll be Junker Jörg — a foreign knight.
Now we have to say goodbye. Here at the castle and in town you will have everything you need without anyone recognizing you.
I've started a fire. And now I have to hide myself here. Alone.
Worms, May 1521
"In praise of the Almighty and for the protection of the Christian faith ... we declare Martin Luther a heretic and regard him as excluded from the Church."
"And you are enjoined to refuse Martin Luther hospitality, lodging, food or drink; neither shall anyone offer him counsel or assistance by word or deed, secretly or openly."

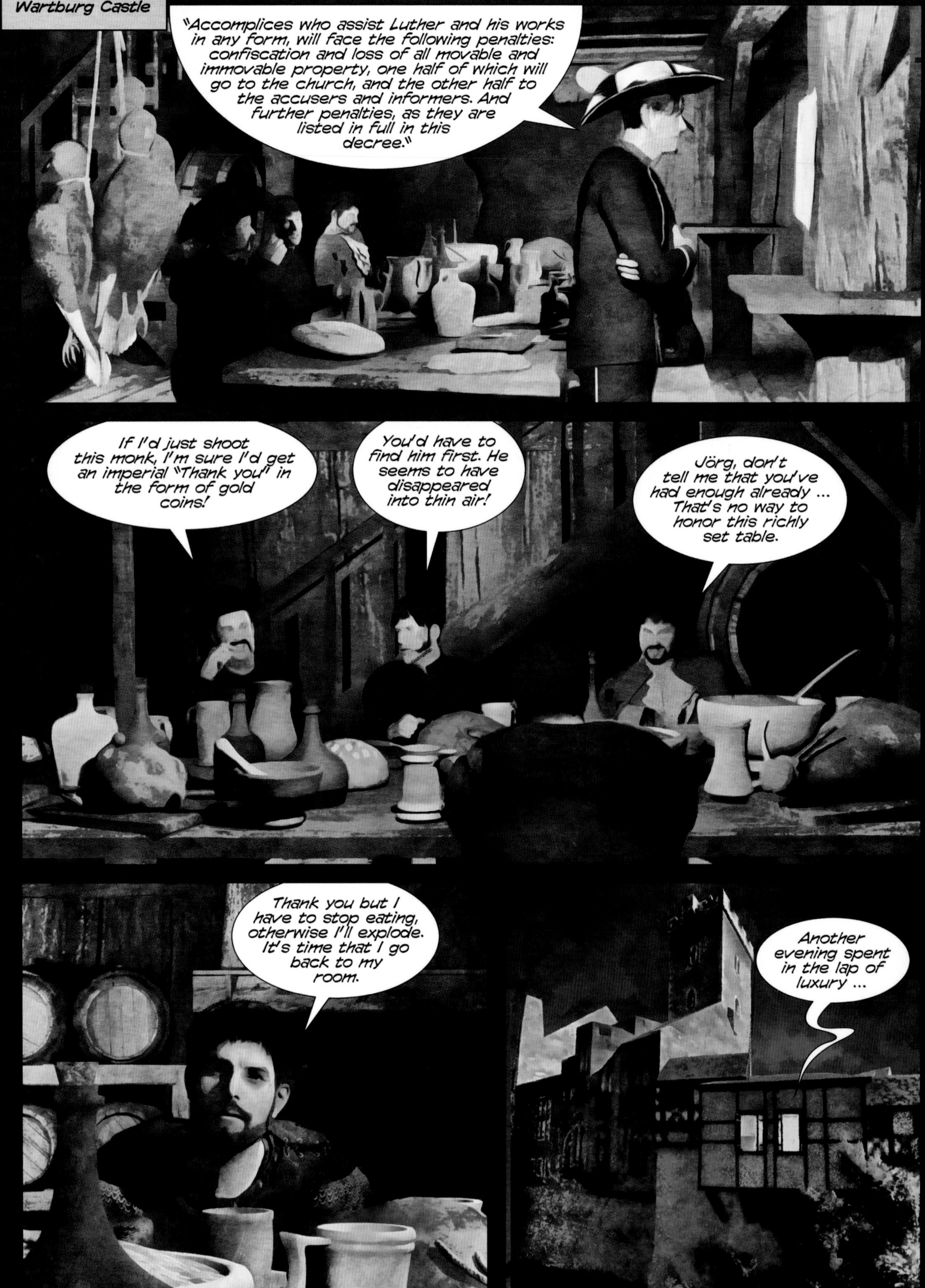
Wartburg Castle
"Accomplices who assist Luther and his works in any form, will face the following penalties: confiscation and loss of all movable and immovable property, one half of which will go to the church, and the other half to the accusers and informers. And further penalties, as they are listed in full in this decree."
If I'd just shoot this monk, I'm sure I'd get an imperial "Thank you" in the form of gold coins!
You'd have to find him first. He seems to have disappeared into thin air!
Jörg, don't tell me that you've had enough already ... That's no way to honor this richly set table.
Thank you but I have to stop eating, otherwise I'll explode. It's time that I go back to my room.
Another evening spent in the lap of luxury ...

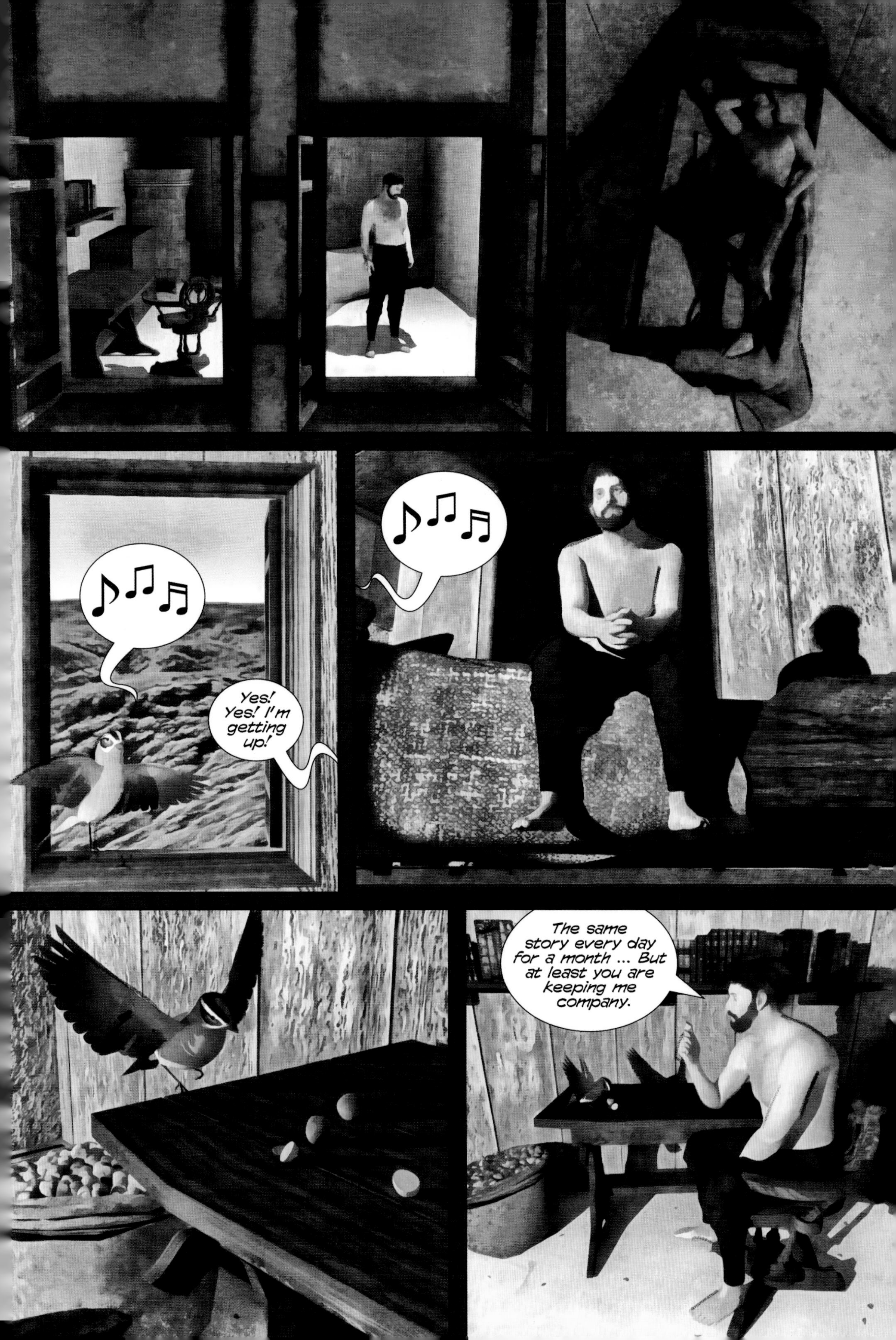
♪♫♬
♪♫♬
Yes! Yes! I'm getting up!
The same story every day for a month ... But at least you are keeping me company.

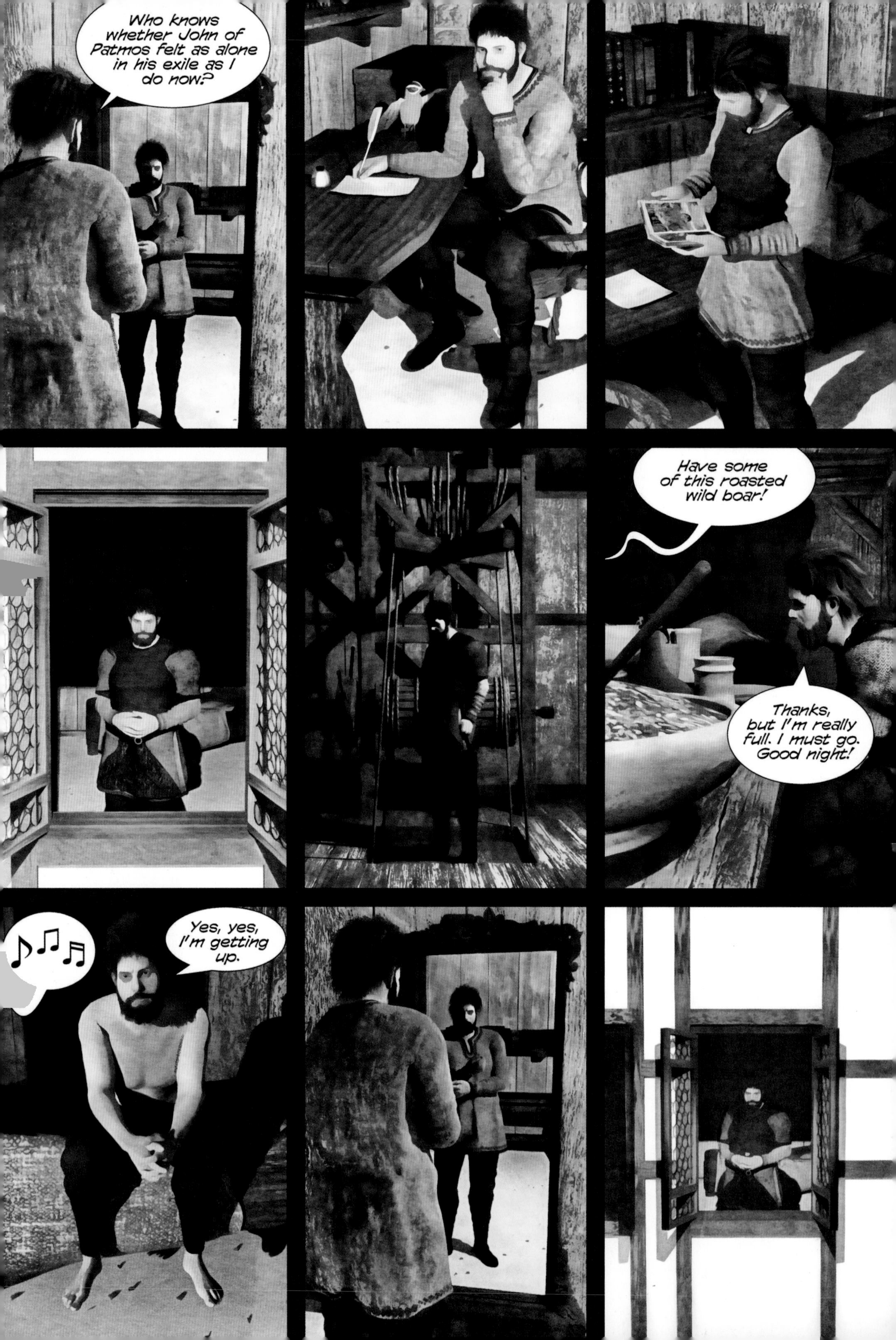
Who knows whether John of Patmos felt as alone in his exile as I do now?
Have some of this roasted wild boar!
Thanks, but I'm really full. I must go. Good night!
Yes, yes, I'm getting up.

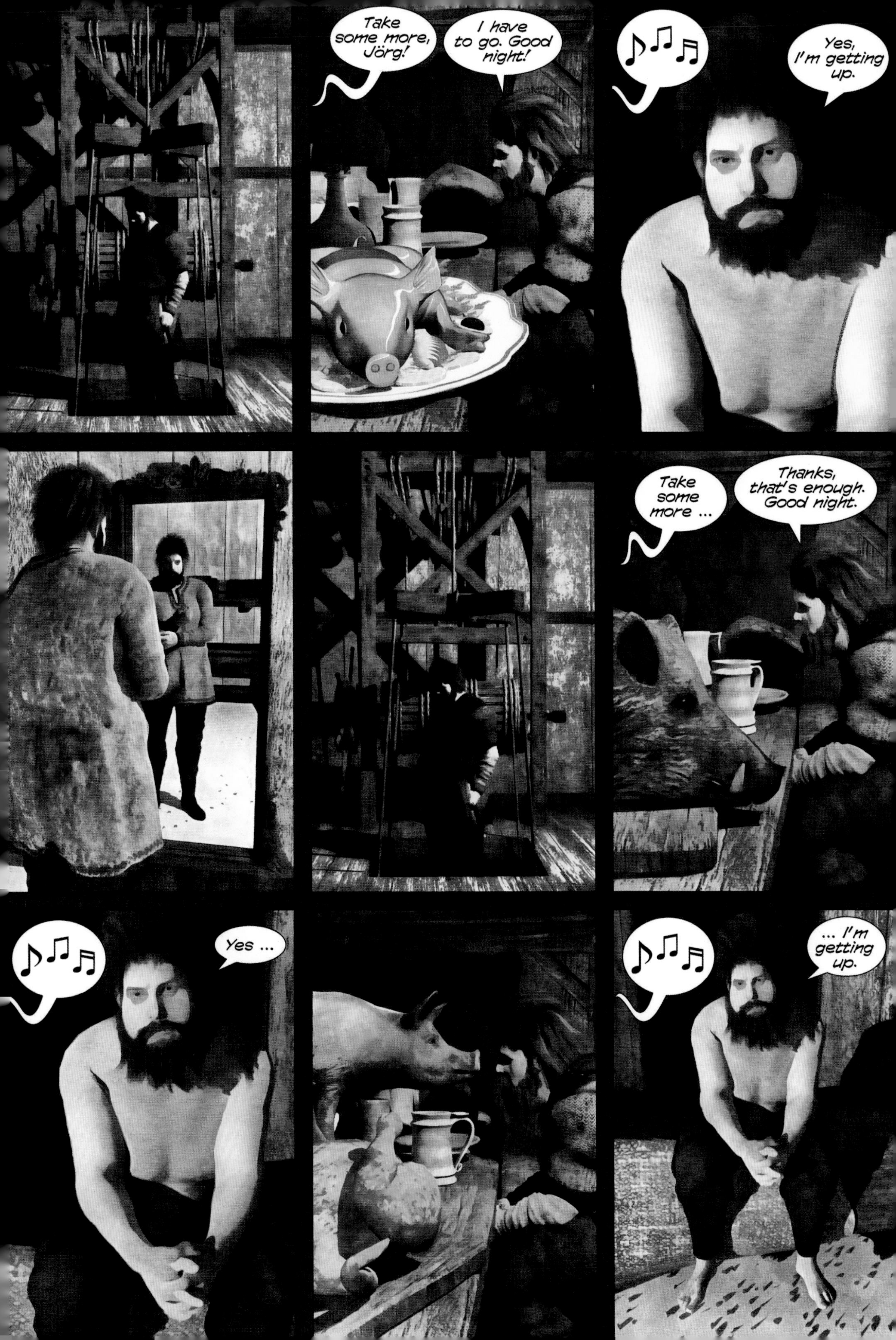
Take some more, Jörg!
I have to go. Good night!
Yes, I'm getting up.
Take some more ...
Thanks, that's enough. Good night.
Yes ...
... I'm getting up.

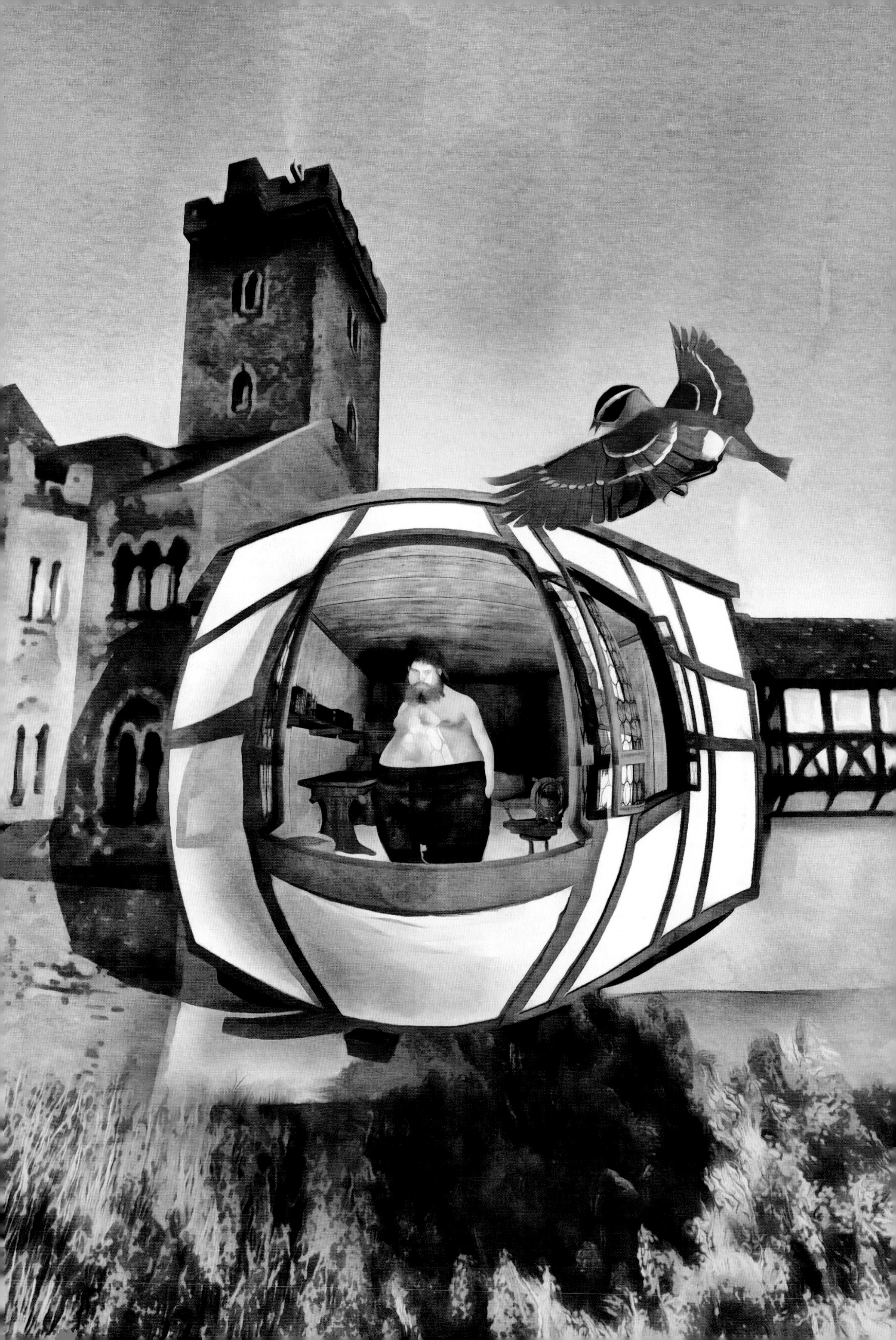

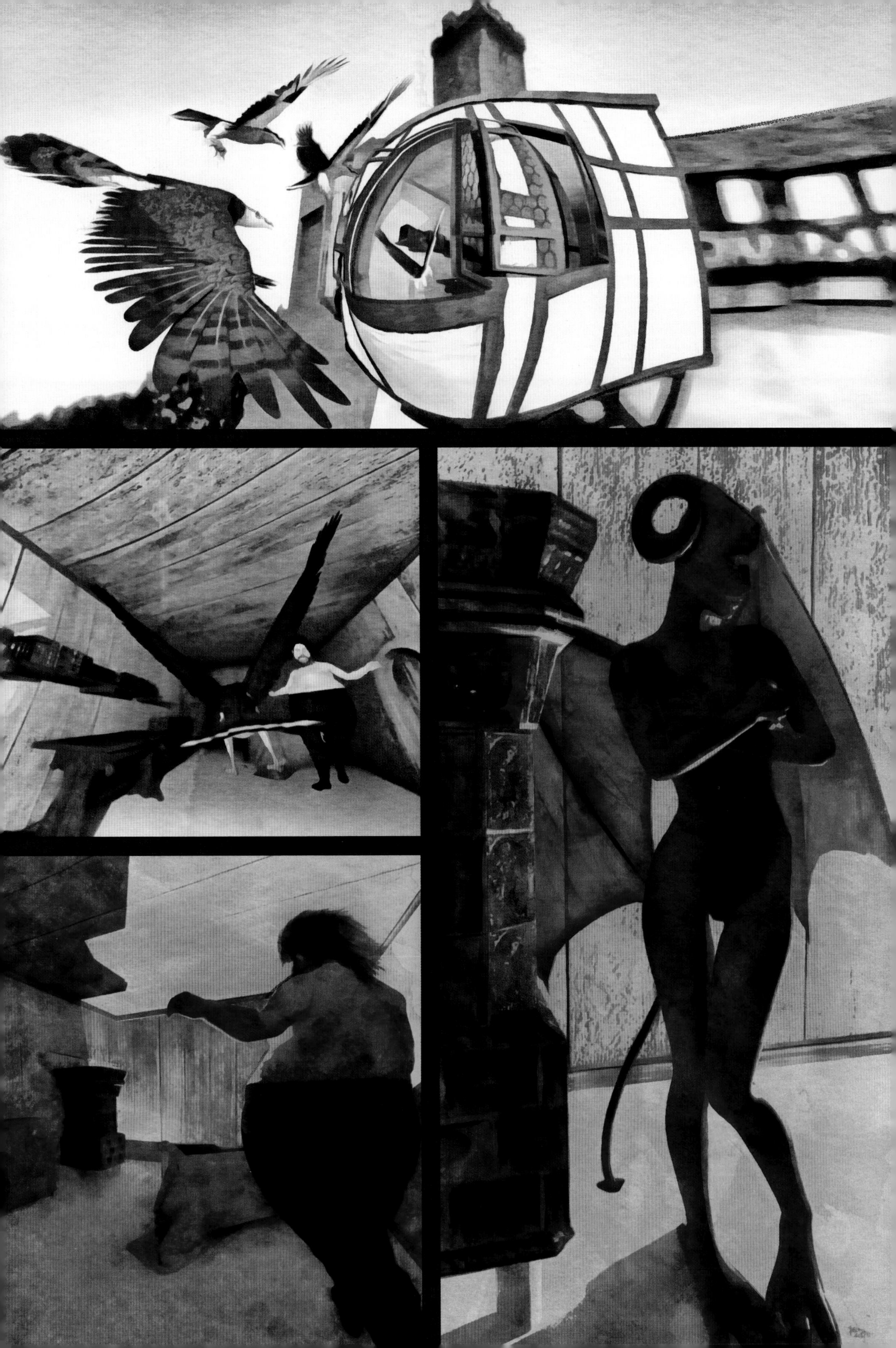

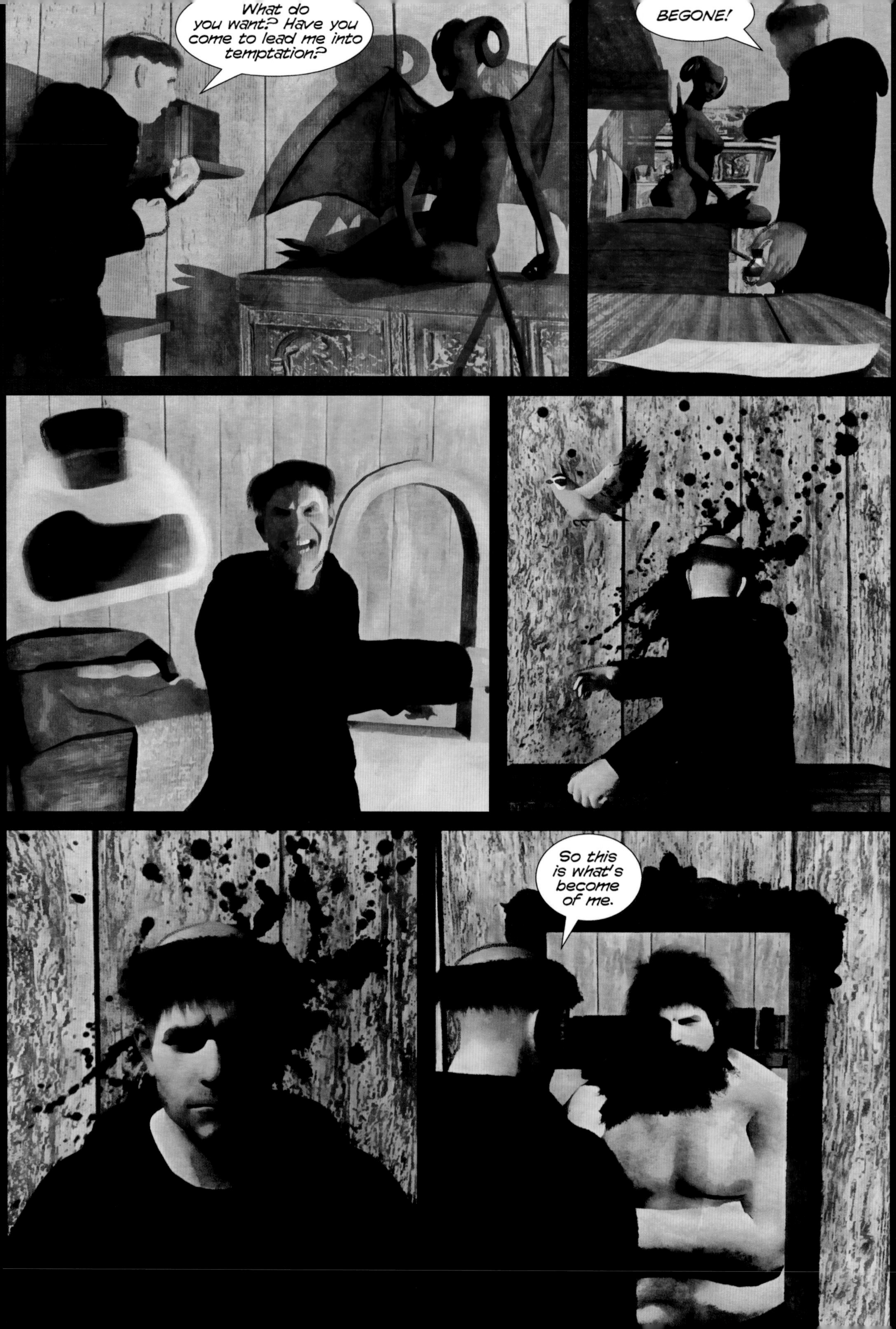
What do you want? Have you come to lead me into temptation?
BEGONE!
So this is what's become of me.

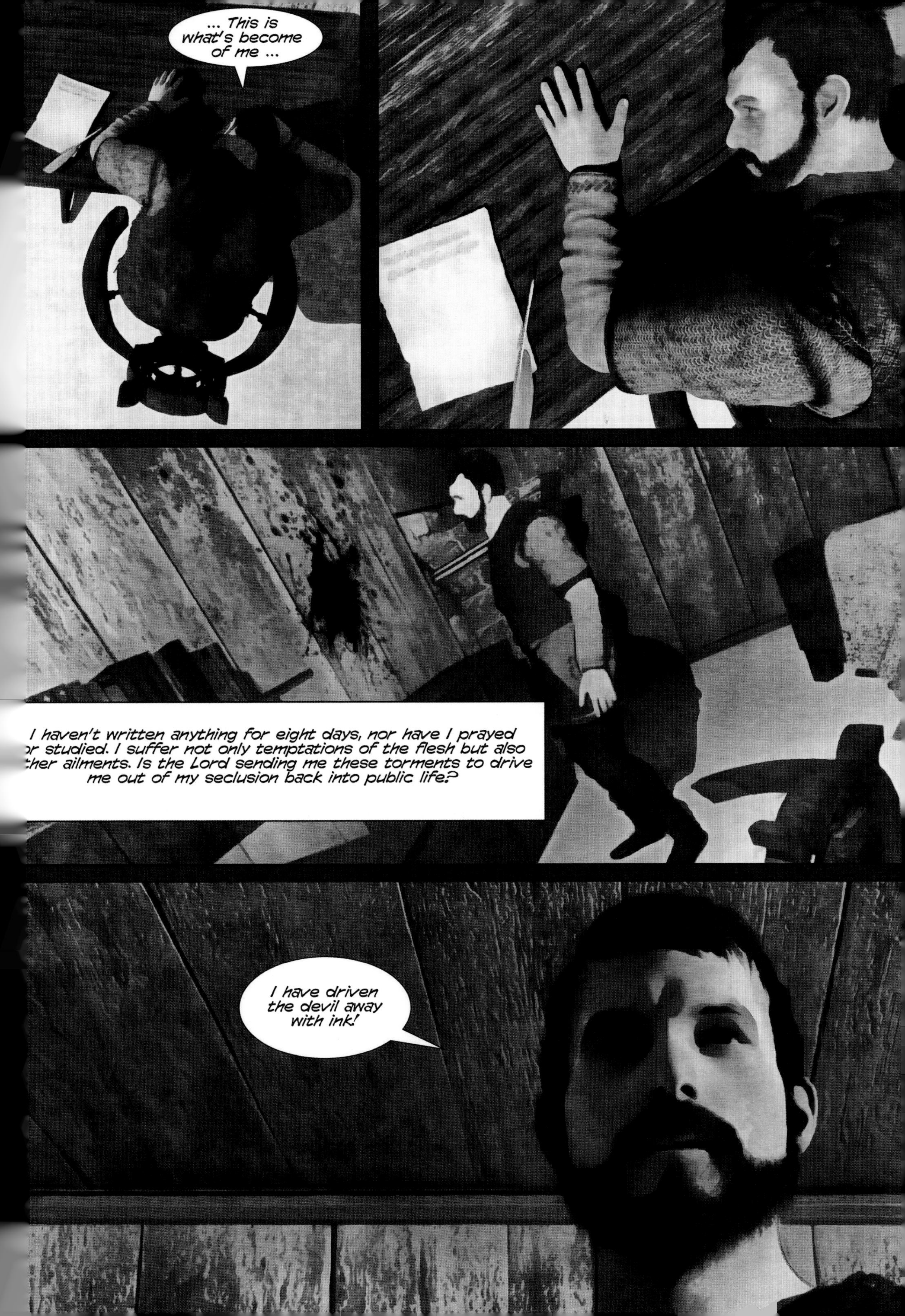
... This is what's become of me ...
I haven't written anything for eight days, nor have I prayed or studied. I suffer not only temptations of the flesh but also other ailments. Is the Lord sending me these torments to drive me out of my seclusion back into public life?
I have driven the devil away with ink!

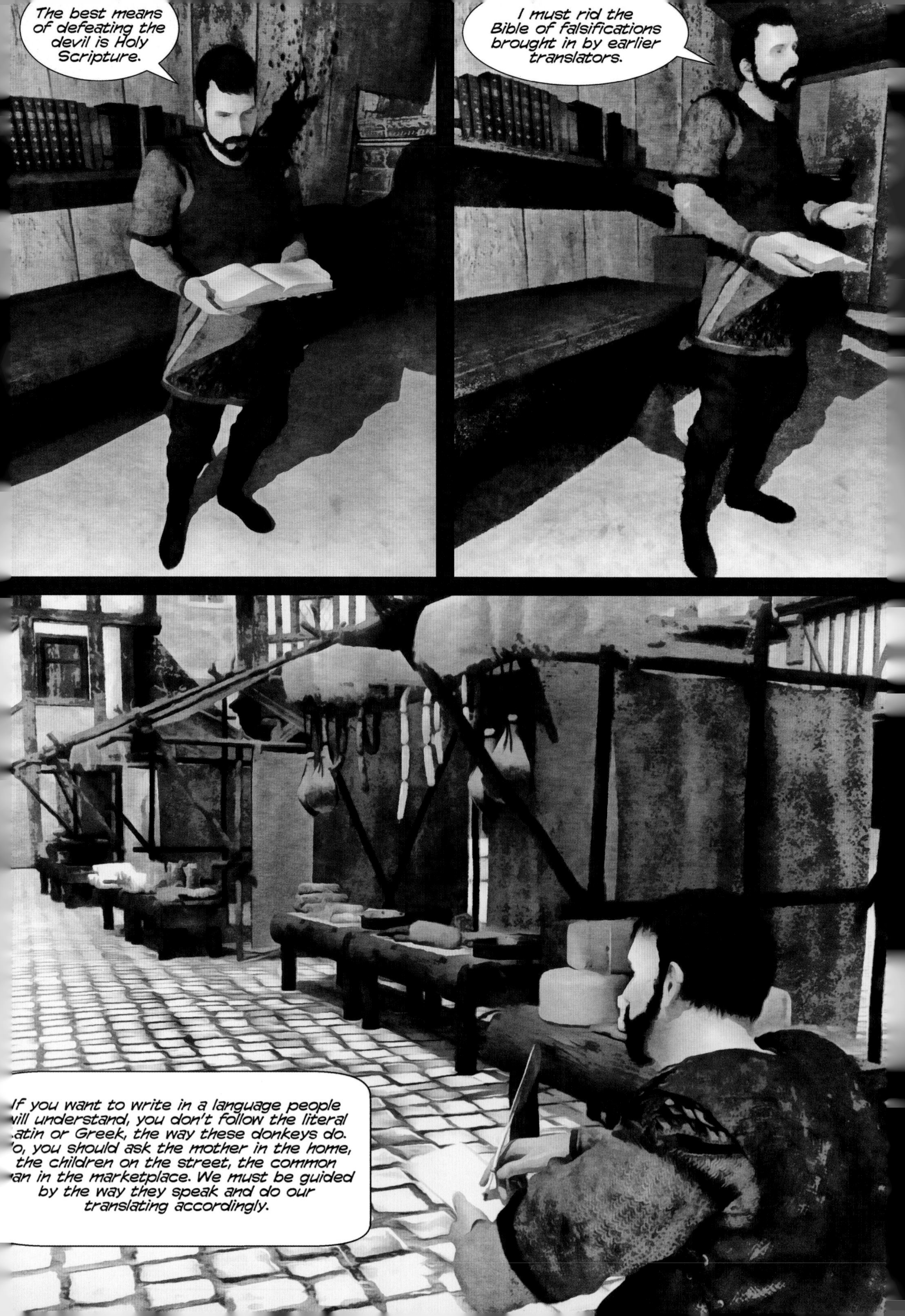
The best means of defeating the devil is Holy Scripture.
I must rid the Bible of falsifications brought in by earlier translators.
If you want to write in a language people
ill understand, you don't follow the literal
atin or Greek, the way these donkeys do.
o, you should ask the mother in the home,
the children on the street, the common
an in the marketplace. We must be guided
by the way they speak and do our
translating accordingly.

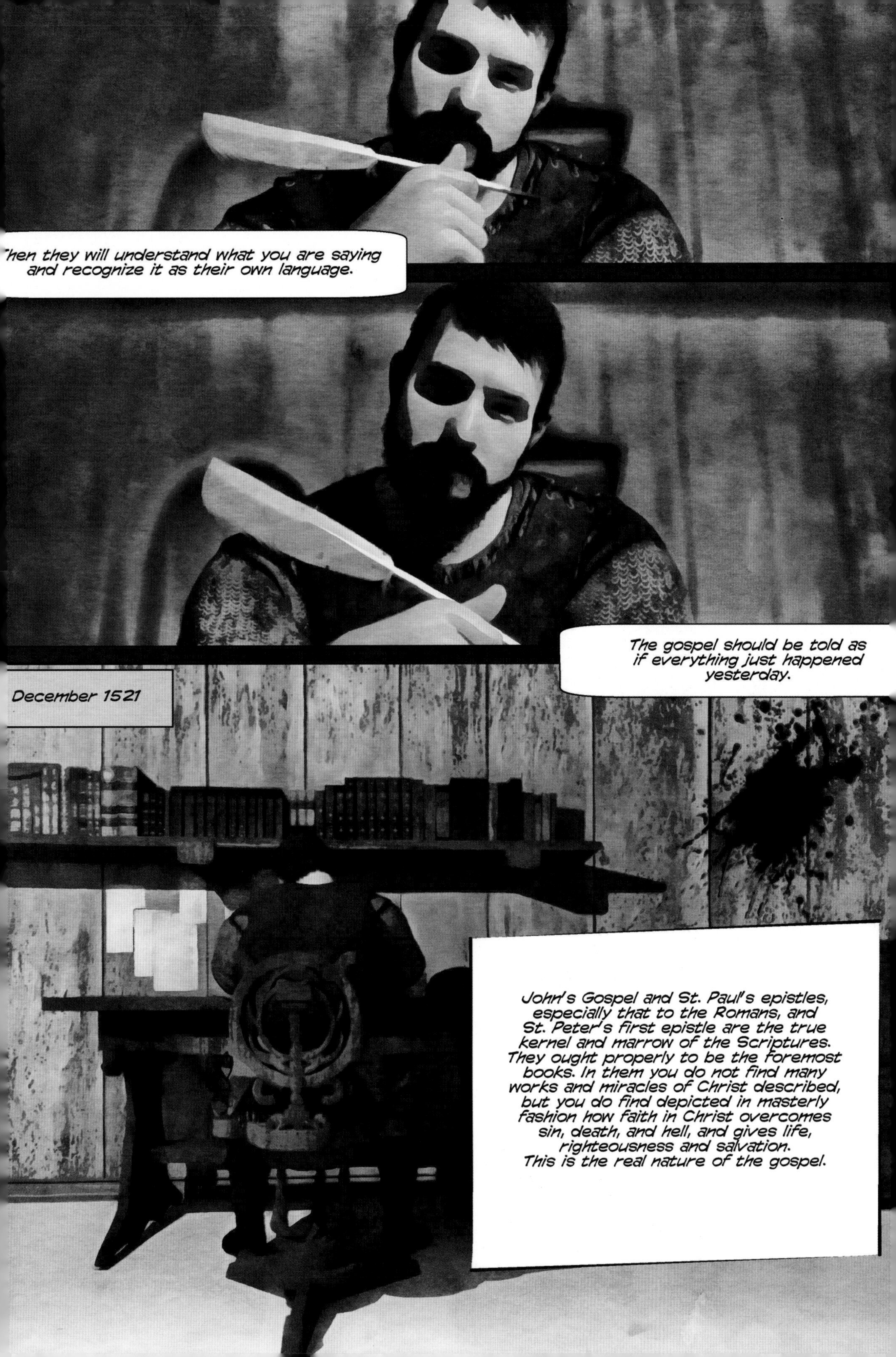
Then they will understand what you are saying and recognize it as their own language.
The gospel should be told as if everything just happened yesterday.
December 1521
John's Gospel and St. Paul's epistles, especially that to the Romans, and St. Peter's first epistle are the true kernel and marrow of the Scriptures. They ought properly to be the foremost books. In them you do not find many works and miracles of Christ described, but you do find depicted in masterly fashion how faith in Christ overcomes sin, death, and hell, and gives life, righteousness and salvation. This is the real nature of the gospel.

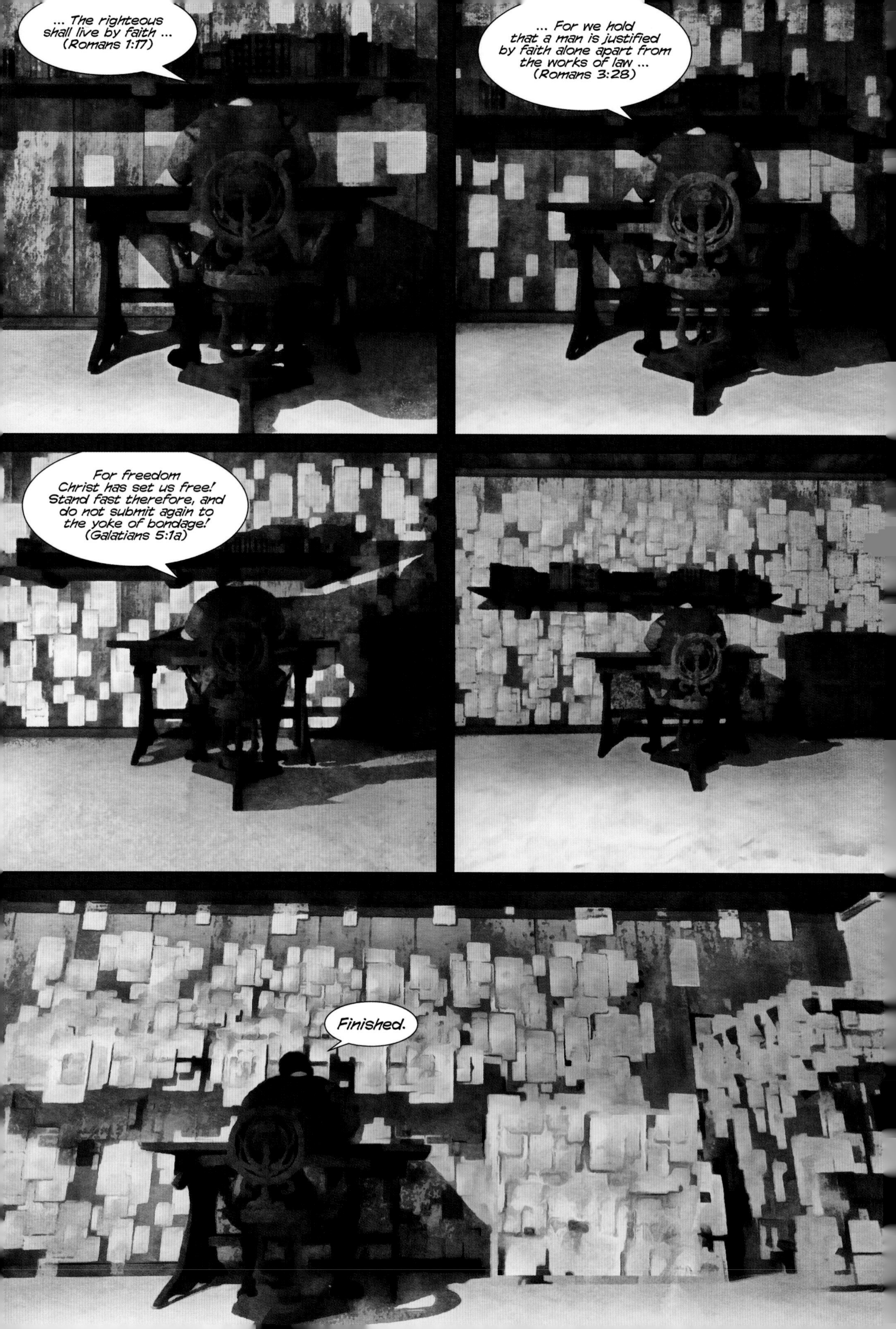
... The righteous shall live by faith ... (Romans 1:17)
... For we hold that a man is justified by faith alone apart from the works of law ... (Romans 3:28)
For freedom Christ has set us free! Stand fast therefore, and do not submit again to the yoke of bondage! (Galatians 5:1a)
Finished.

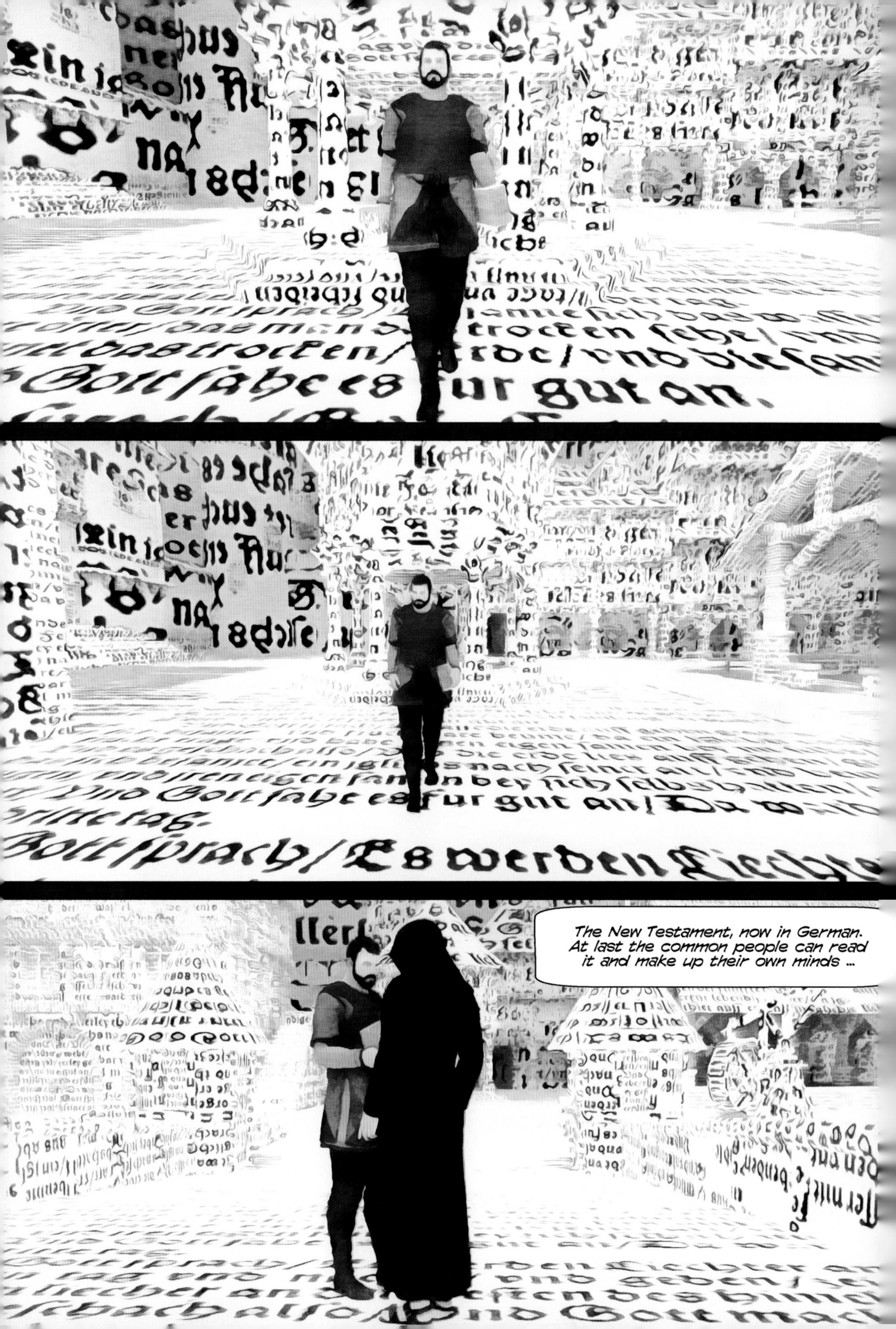
The New Testament, now in German. At last the common people can read it and make up their own minds ...

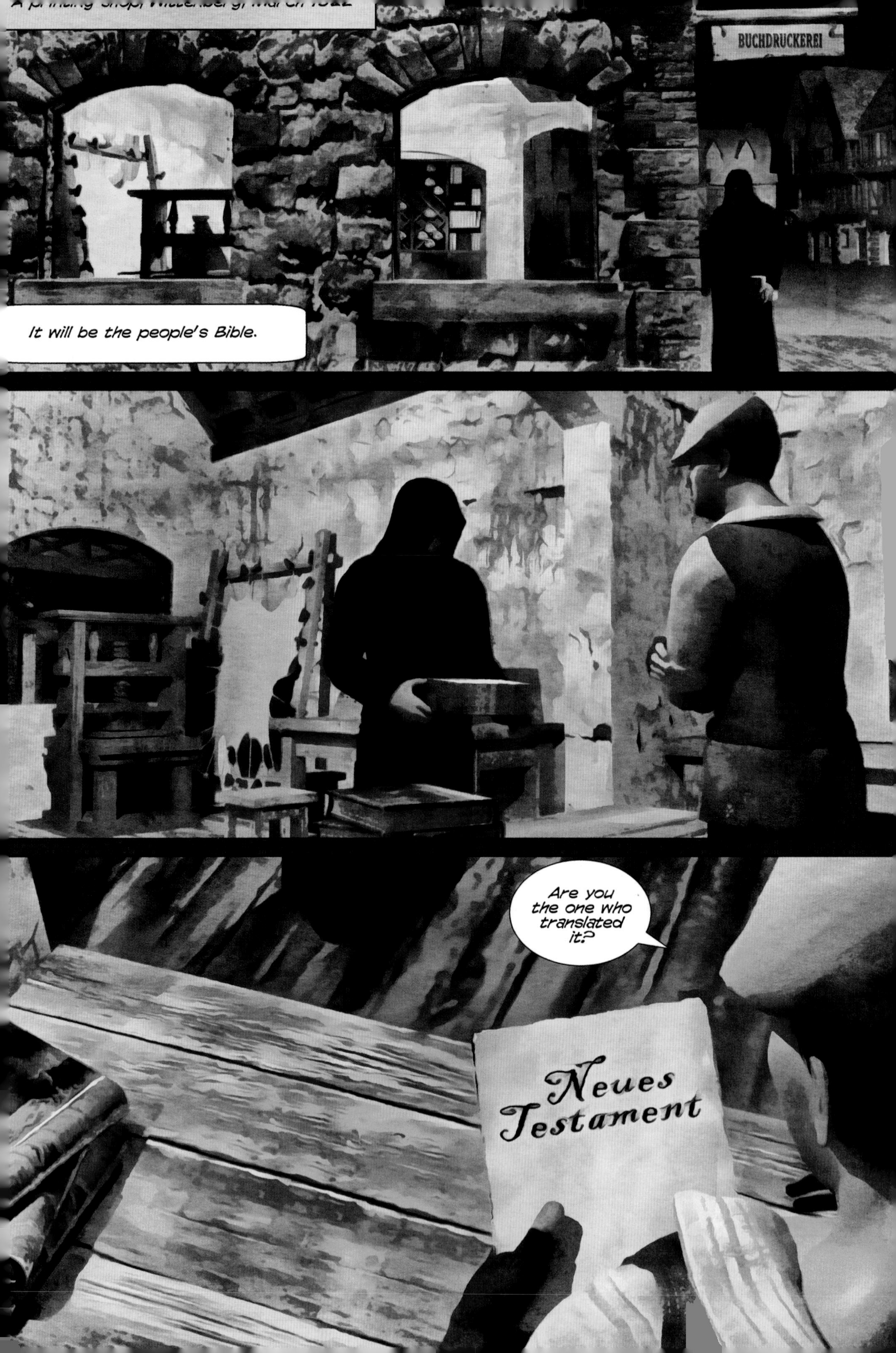
A printing shop, Wittenberg, March 1522
BUCHDRUCKEREI
It will be the people's Bible.
Are you the one who translated it?
Neues Testament

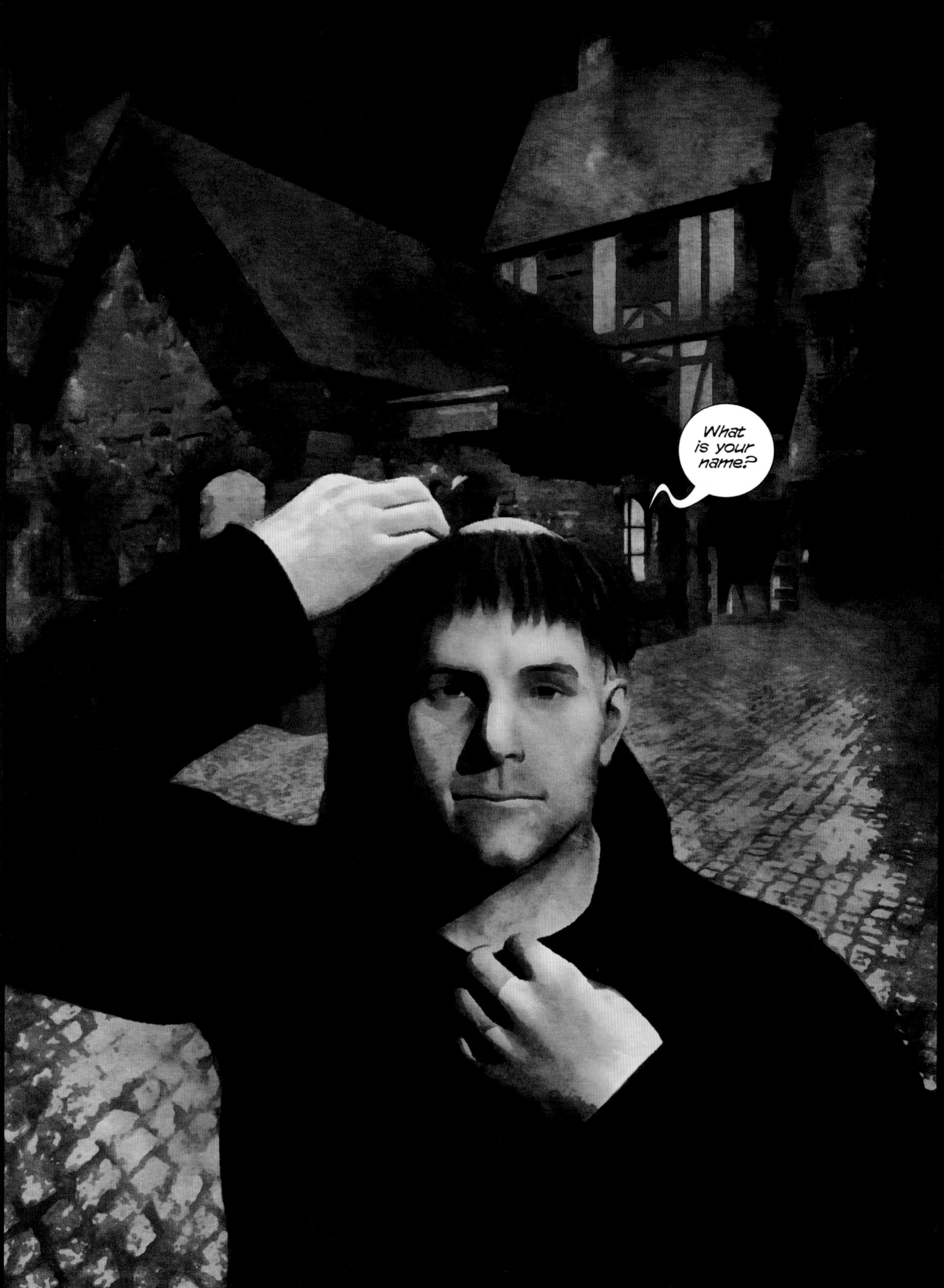
What is your name?

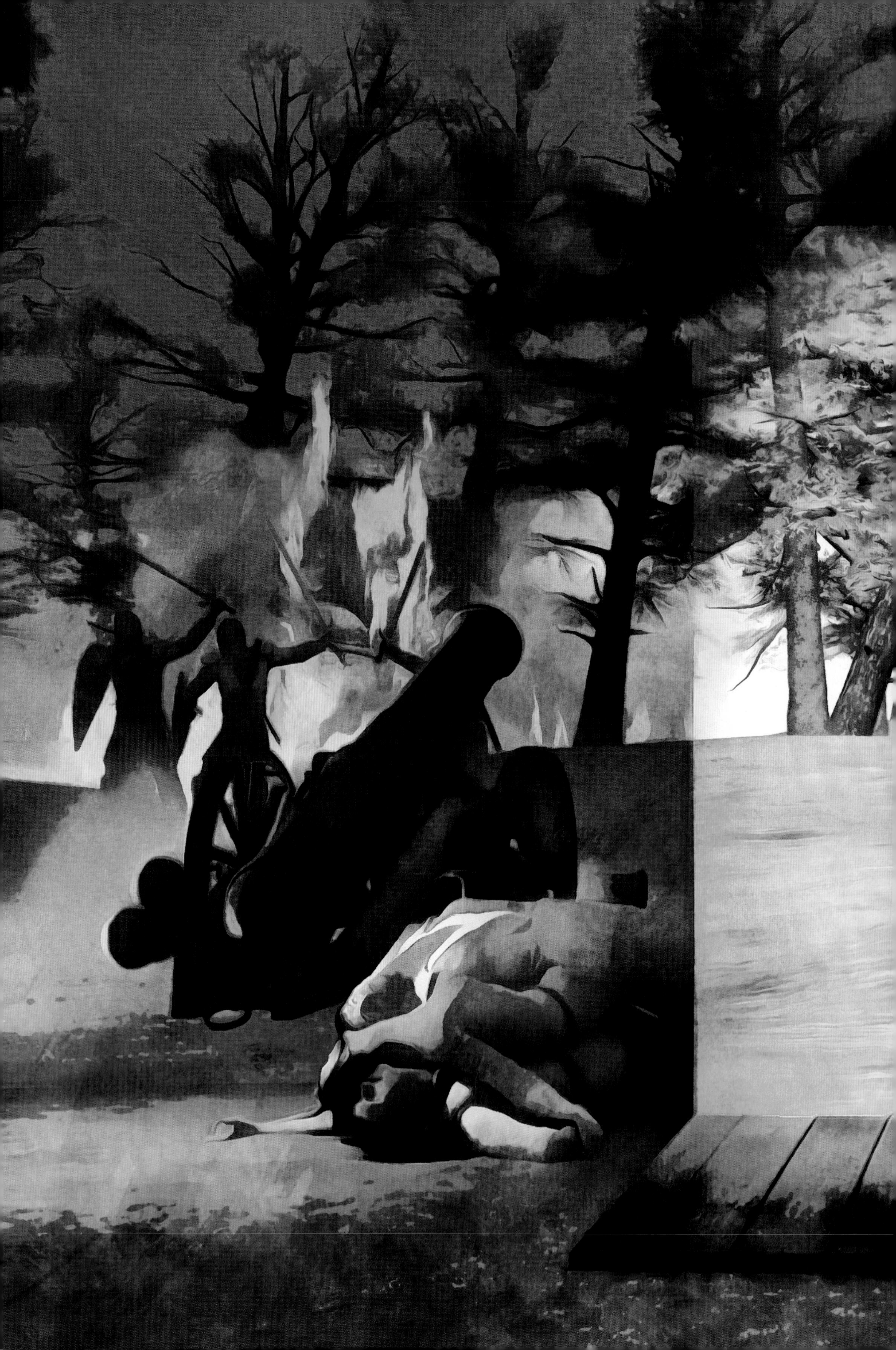

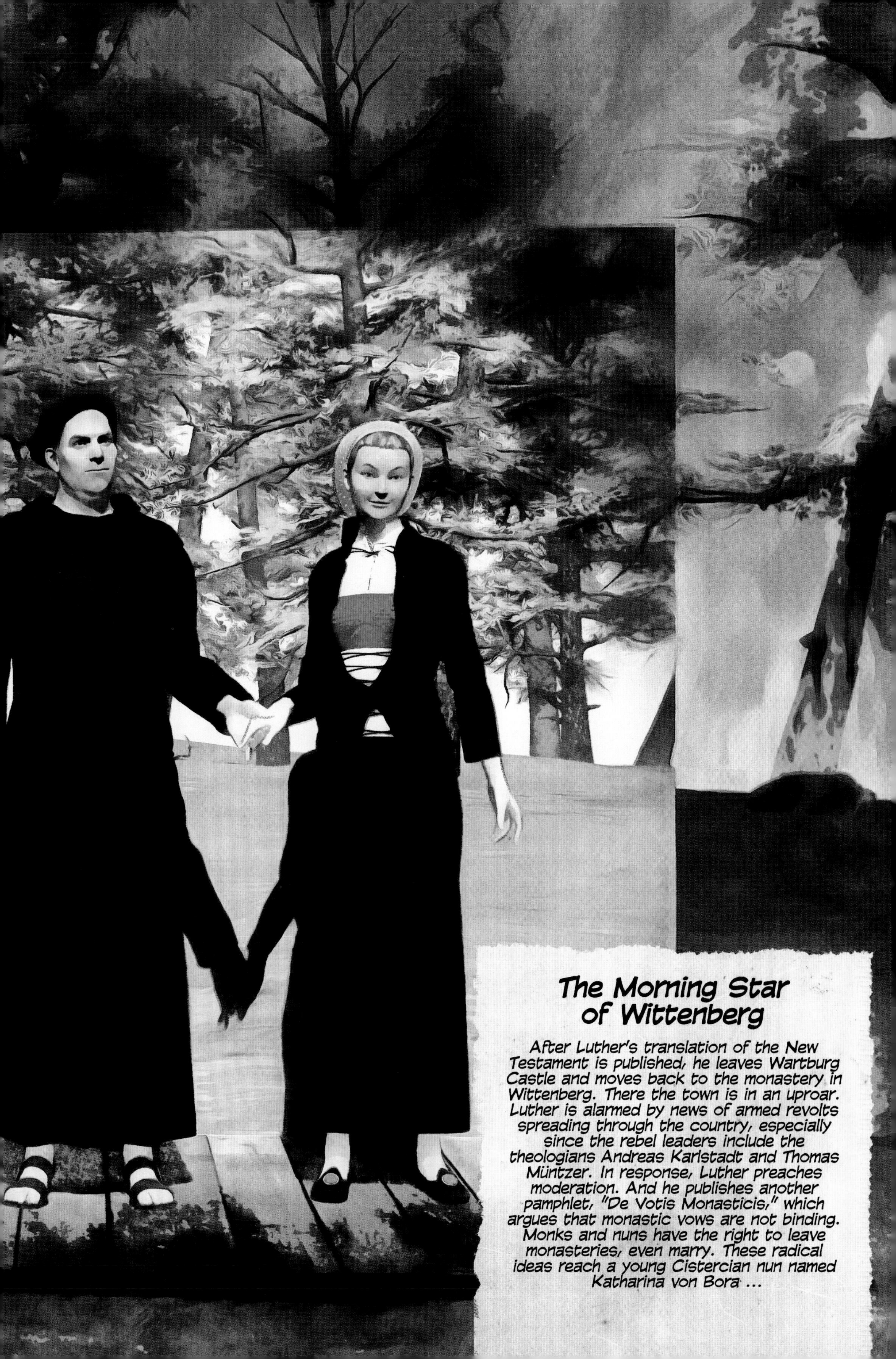
The Morning Star of Wittenberg
After Luther's translation of the New Testament is published, he leaves Wartburg Castle and moves back to the monastery in Wittenberg. There the town is in an uproar. Luther is alarmed by news of armed revolts spreading through the country, especially since the rebel leaders include the theologians Andreas Karlstadt and Thomas Müntzer. In response, Luther preaches moderation. And he publishes another pamphlet, "De Votis Monasticis," which argues that monastic vows are not binding. Monks and nuns have the right to leave monasteries, even marry. These radical ideas reach a young Cistercian nun named Katharina von Bora ...

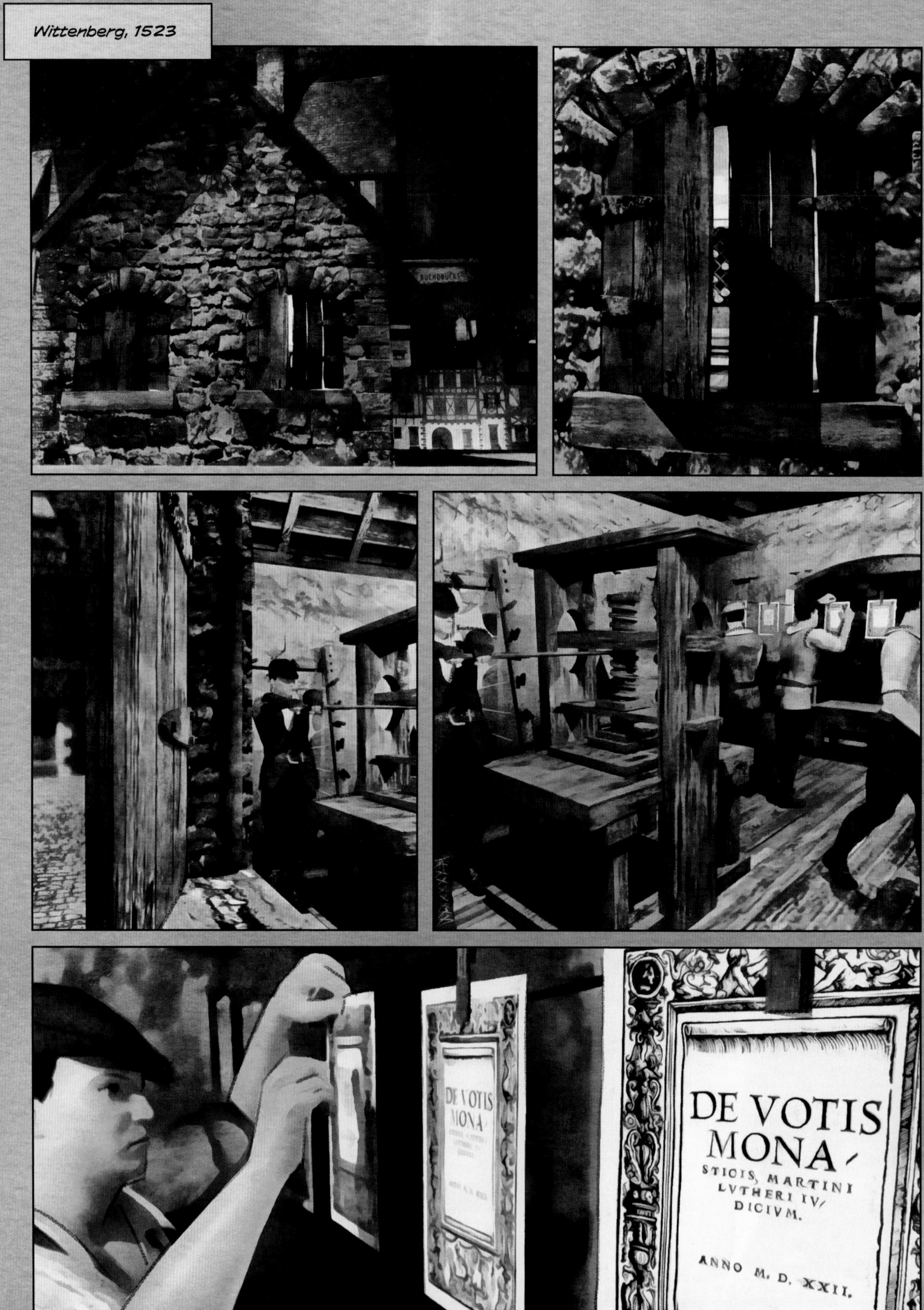
Wittenberg, 1523
DE VOTIS MONA/
STICIS, MARTINI
LVTHERI IV/
DICIVM.
ANNO M. D. XXII.

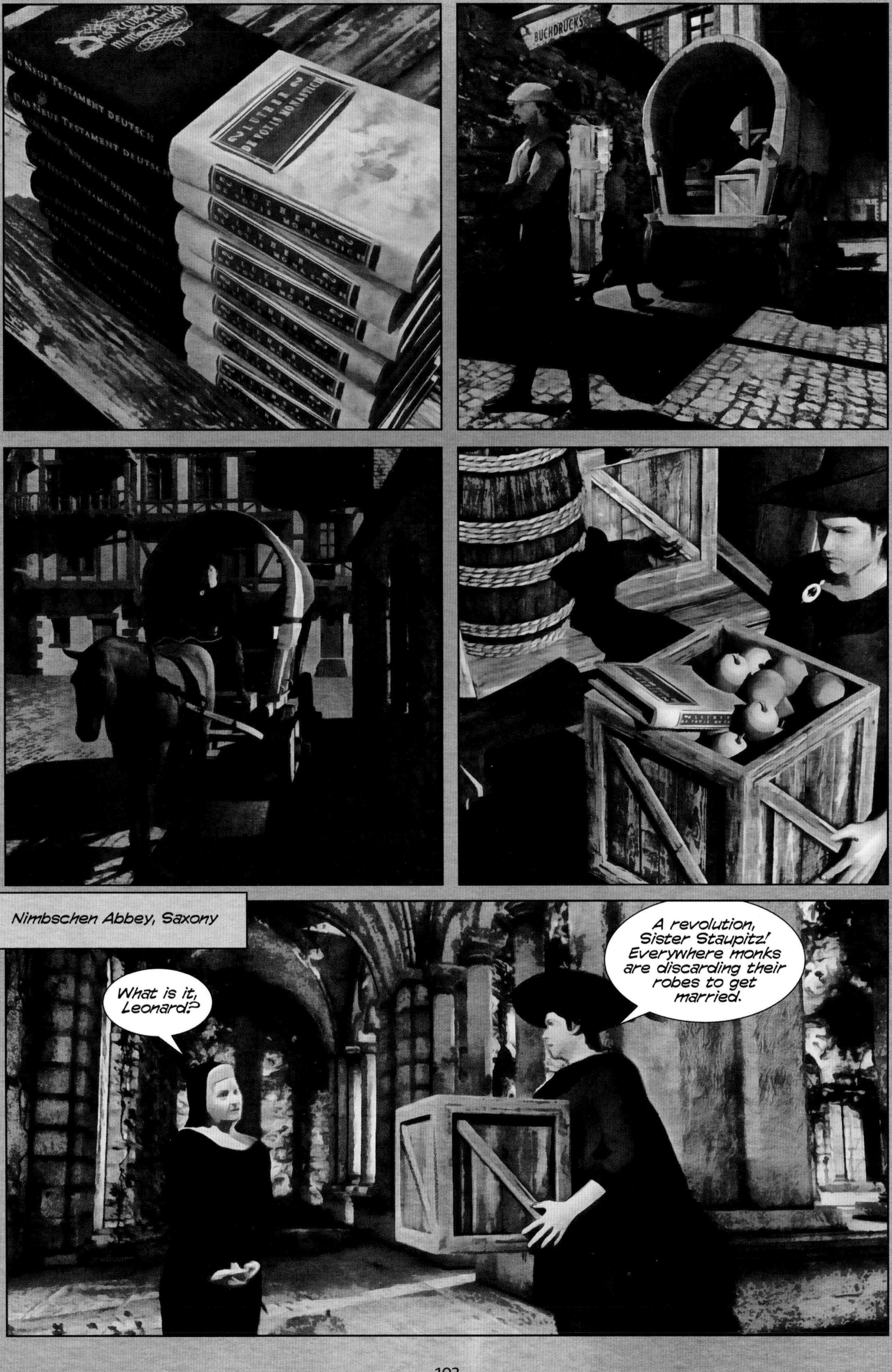
Das Neue Testament Deutsch
BUCHDRUCKS
Nimbschen Abbey, Saxony
What is it, Leonard?
A revolution, Sister Staupitz! Everywhere monks are discarding their robes to get married.

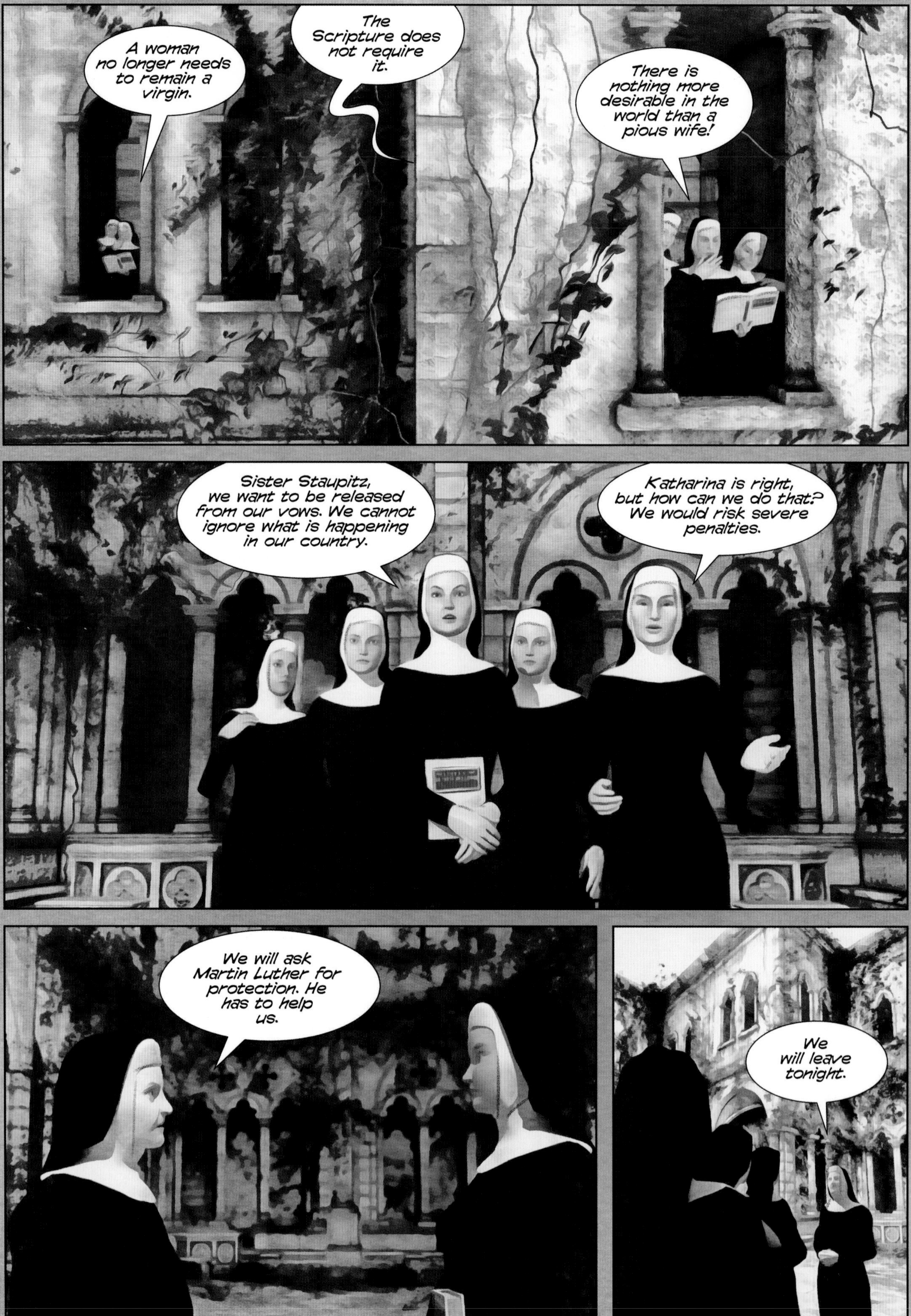
A woman no longer needs to remain a virgin.
The Scripture does not require it.
There is nothing more desirable in the world than a pious wife!
Sister Staupitz, we want to be released from our vows. We cannot ignore what is happening in our country.
Katharina is right, but how can we do that? We would risk severe penalties.
We will ask Martin Luther for protection. He has to help us.
We will leave tonight.

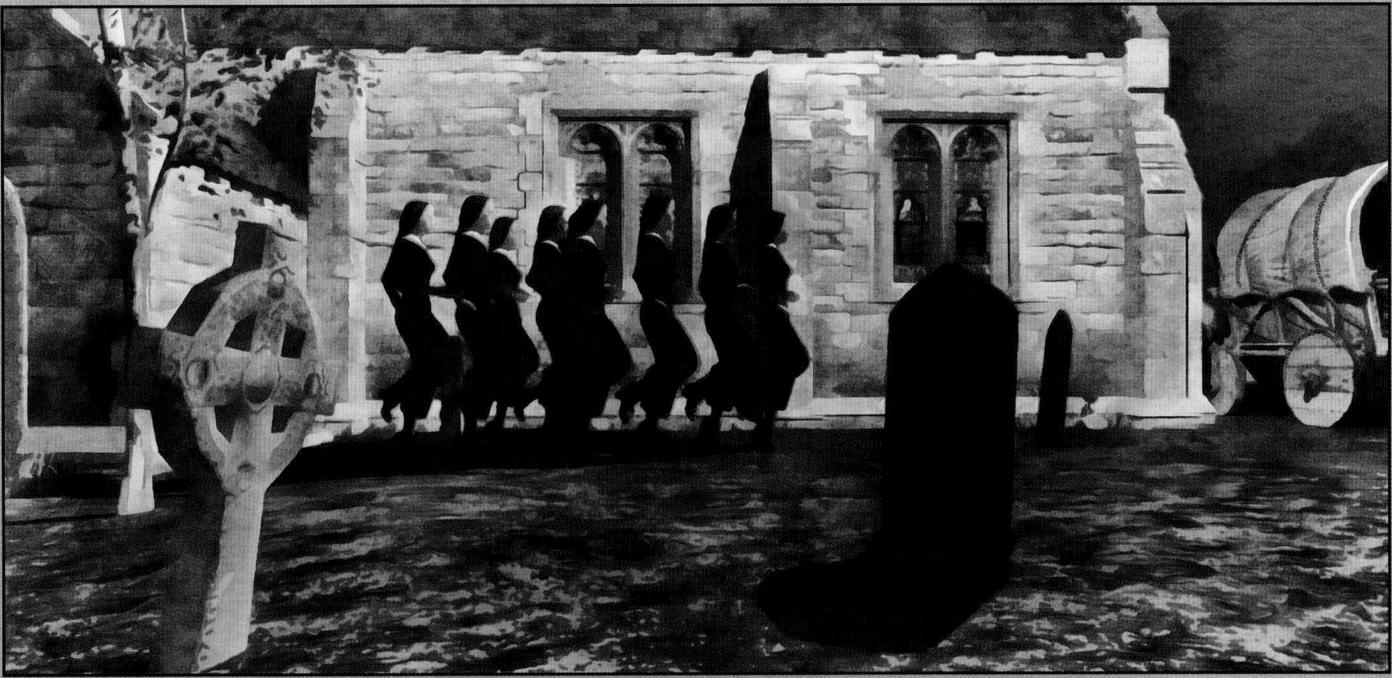

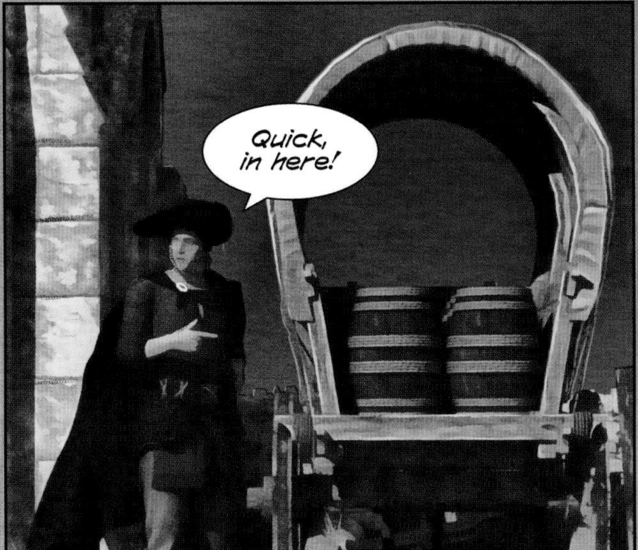
Quick, in here!

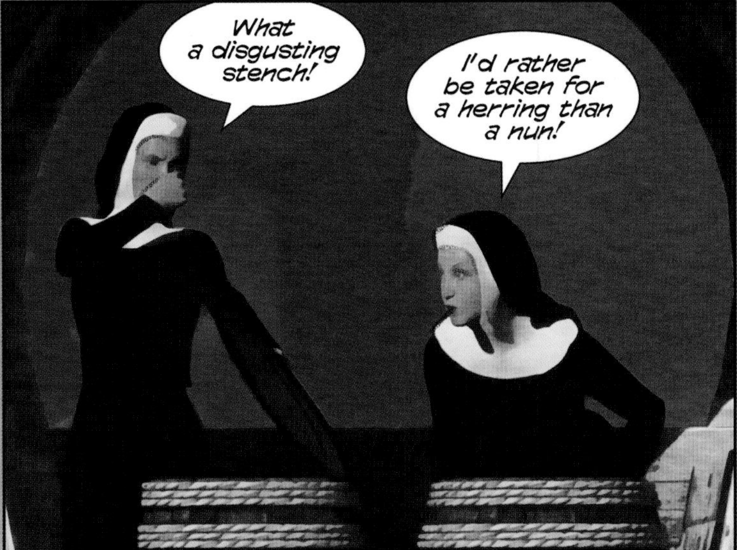
What a disgusting stench!
I'd rather be taken for a herring than a nun!

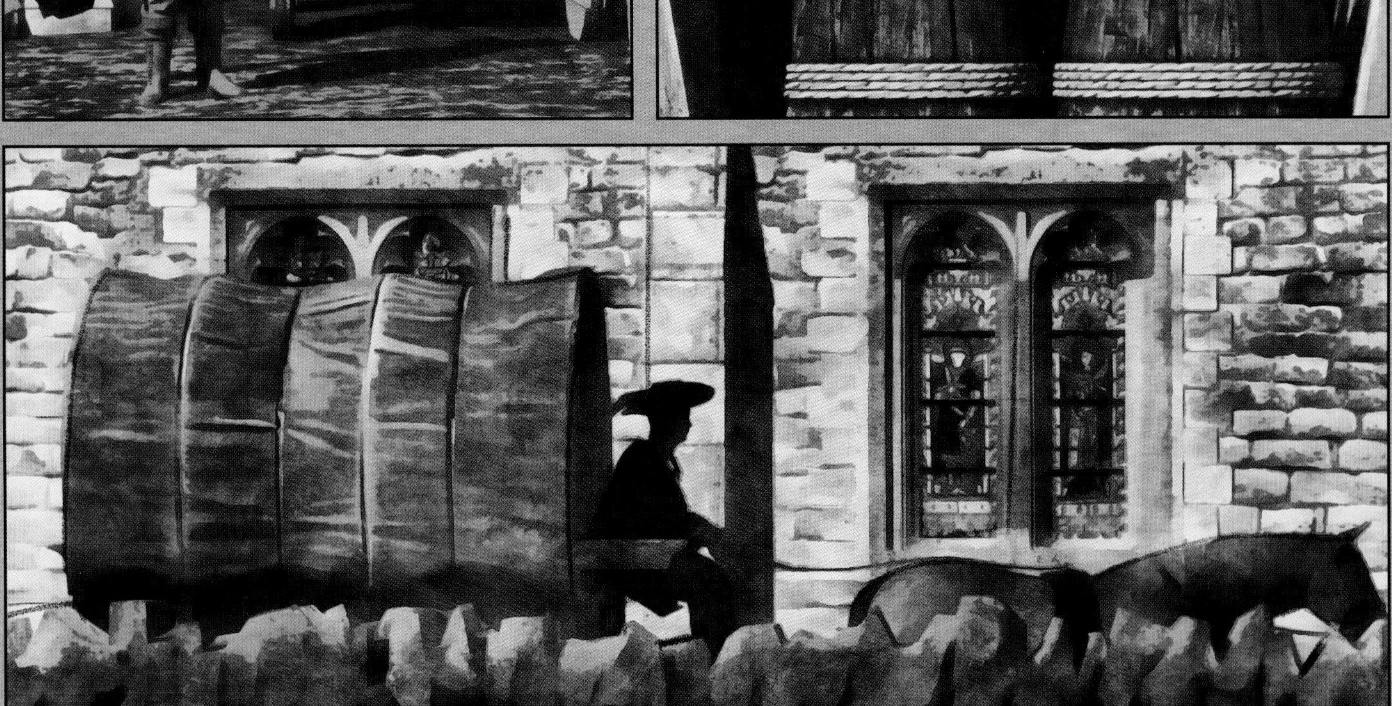

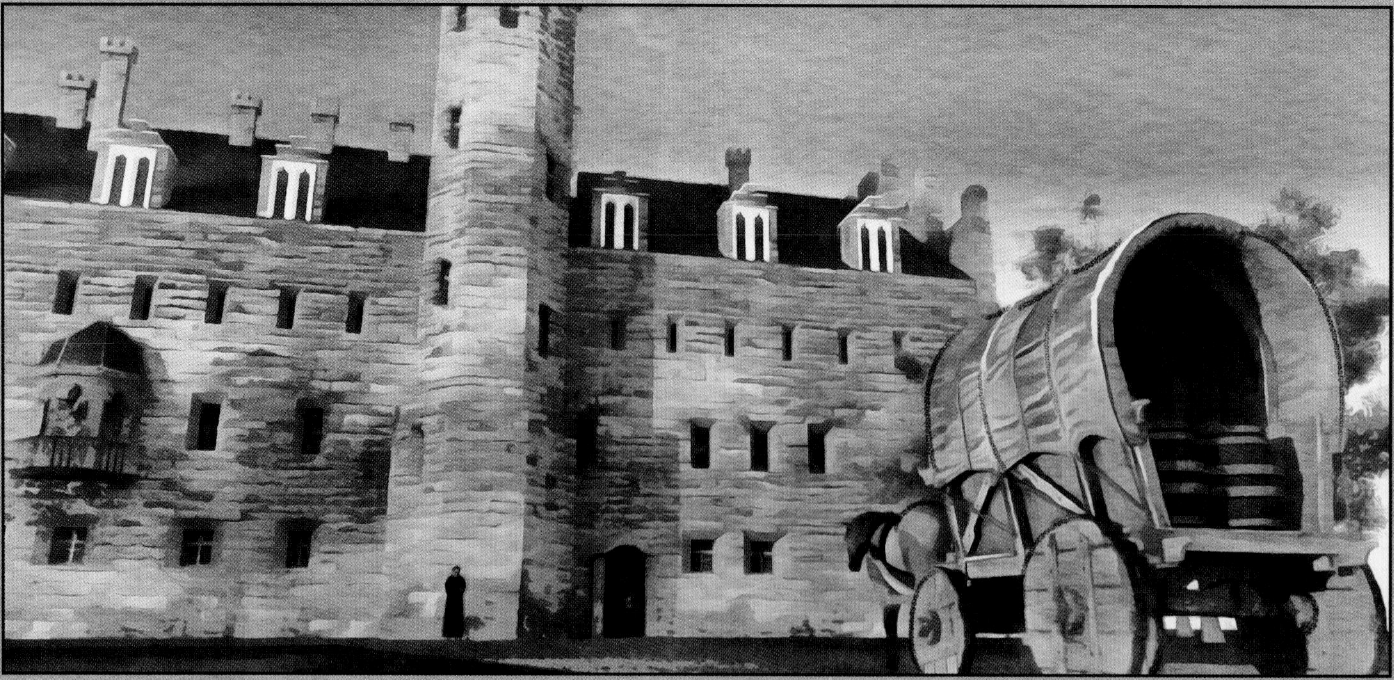

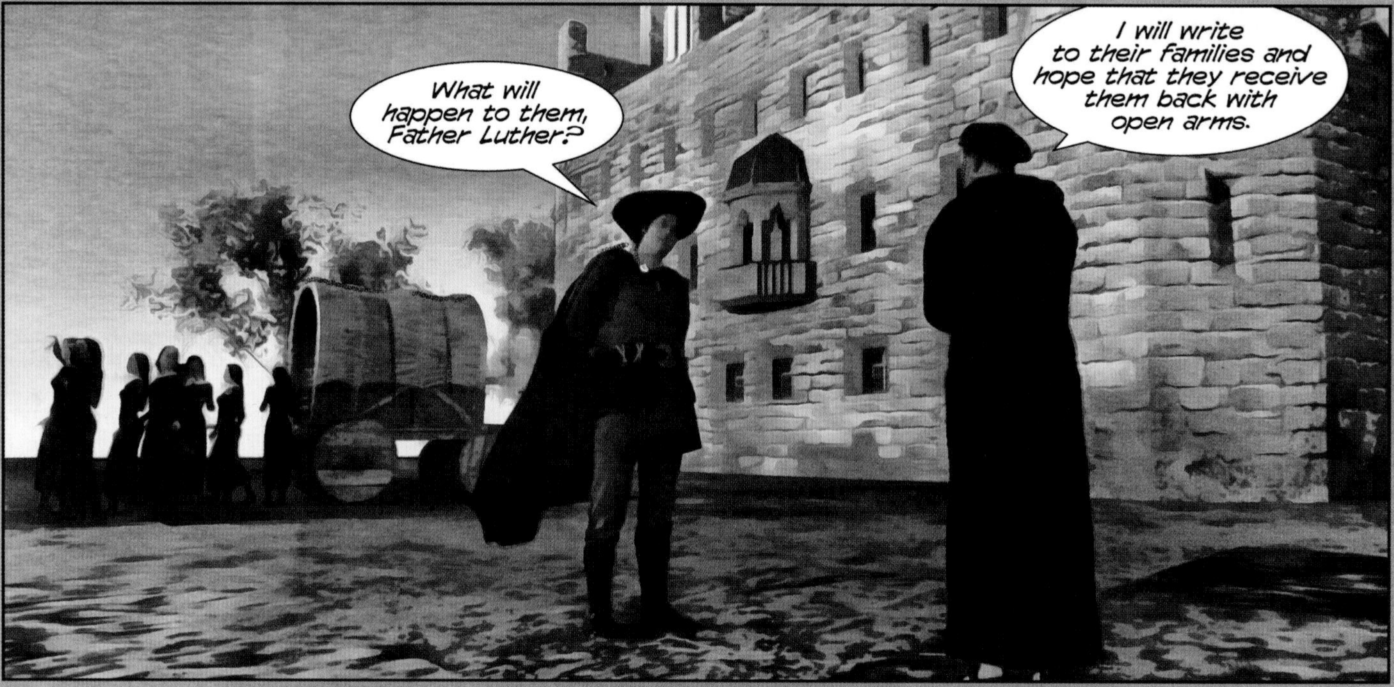
What will happen to them, Father Luther?
I will write to their families and hope that they receive them back with open arms.

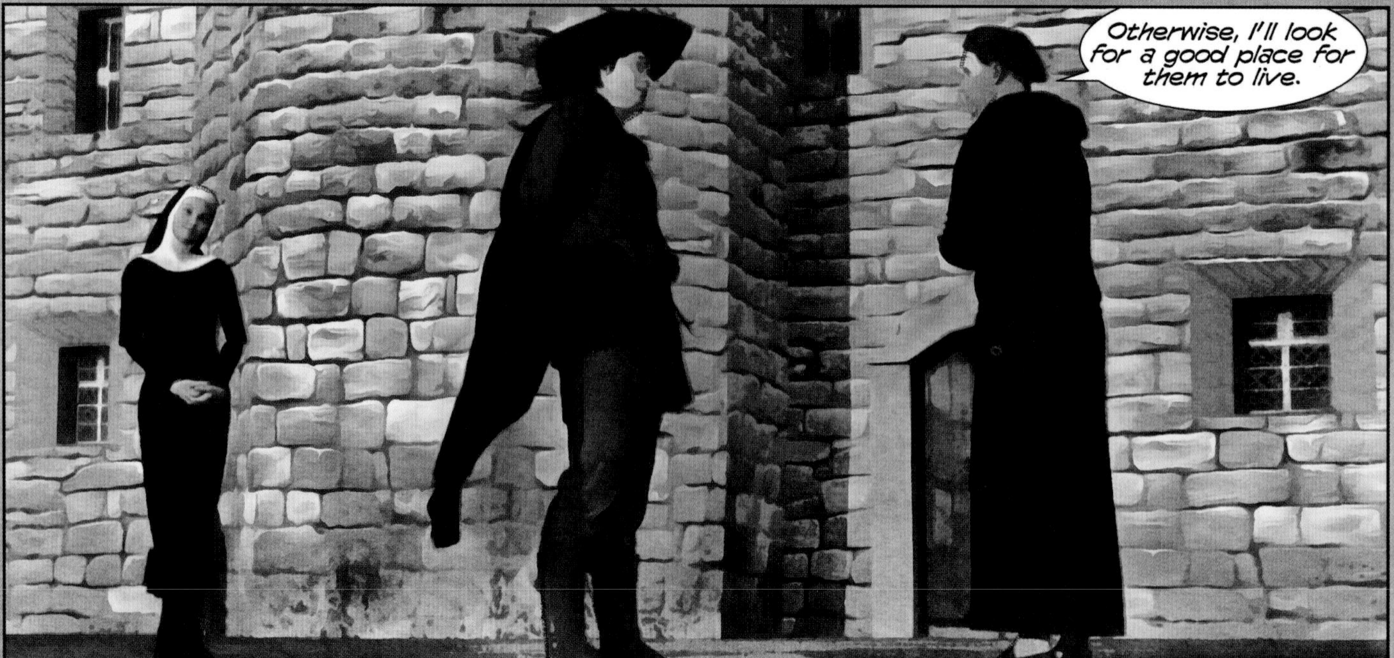
Otherwise, I'll look for a good place for them to live.

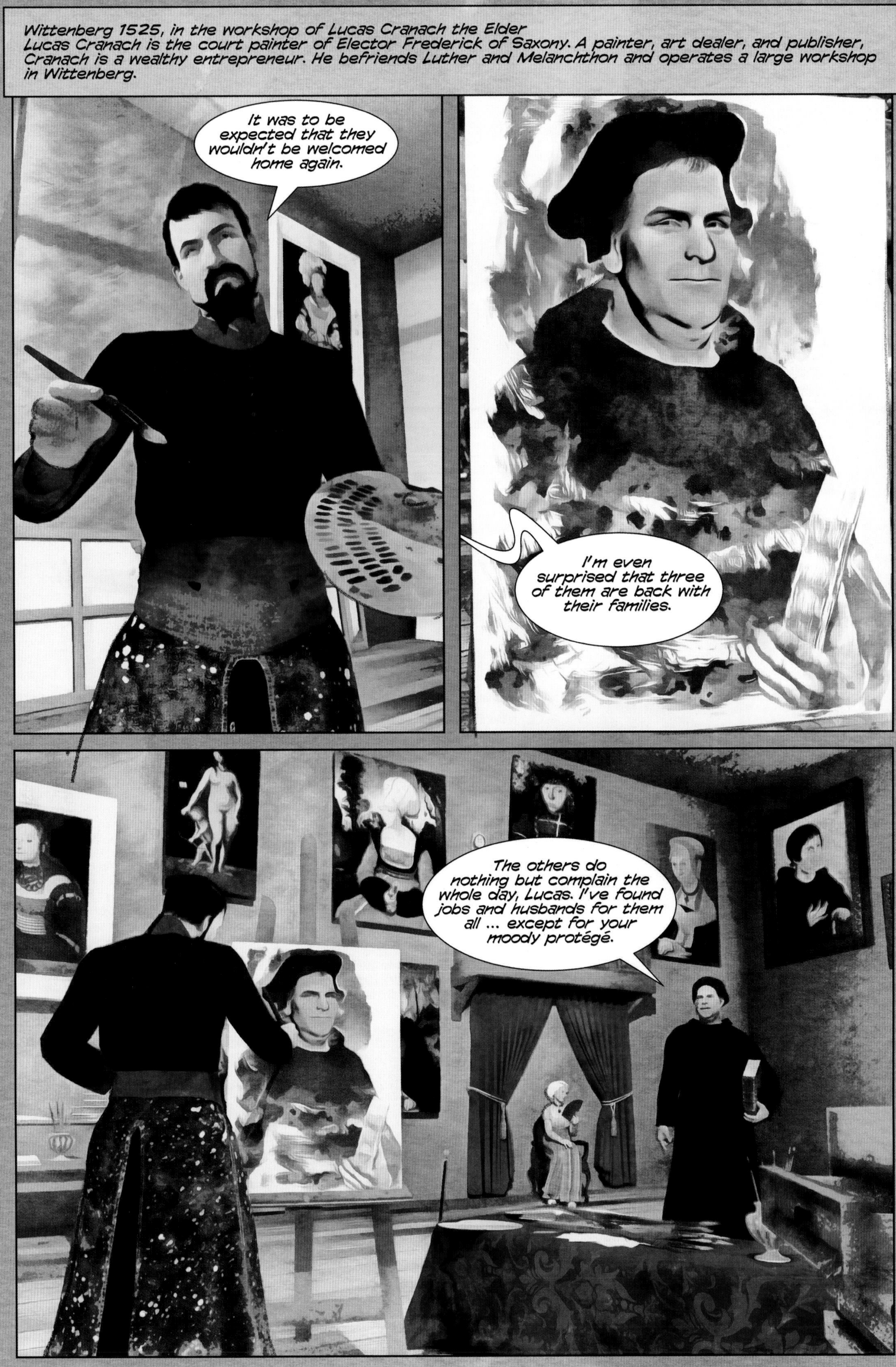
Wittenberg 1525, in the workshop of Lucas Cranach the Elder
Lucas Cranach is the court painter of Elector Frederick of Saxony. A painter, art dealer, and publisher, Cranach is a wealthy entrepreneur. He befriends Luther and Melanchthon and operates a large workshop in Wittenberg.
It was to be expected that they wouldn't be welcomed home again.
I'm even surprised that three of them are back with their families.
The others do nothing but complain the whole day, Lucas. I've found jobs and husbands for them all ... except for your moody protégé.

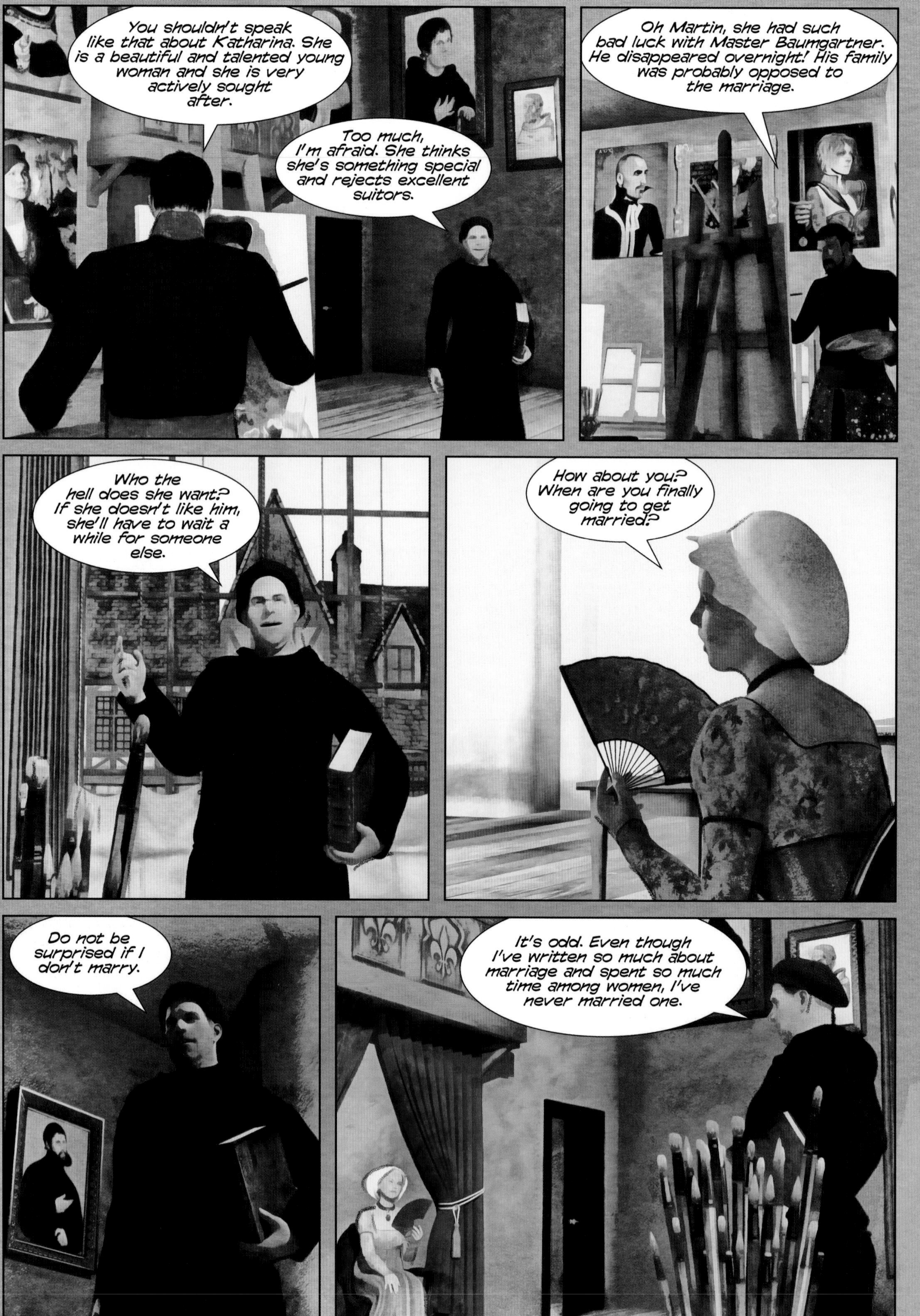
You shouldn't speak like that about Katharina. She is a beautiful and talented young woman and she is very actively sought after.
Too much, I'm afraid. She thinks she's something special and rejects excellent suitors.
Oh Martin, she had such bad luck with Master Baumgartner. He disappeared overnight! His family was probably opposed to the marriage.
Who the hell does she want? If she doesn't like him, she'll have to wait a while for someone else.
How about you? When are you finally going to get married?
Do not be surprised if I don't marry.
It's odd. Even though I've written so much about marriage and spent so much time among women, I've never married one.

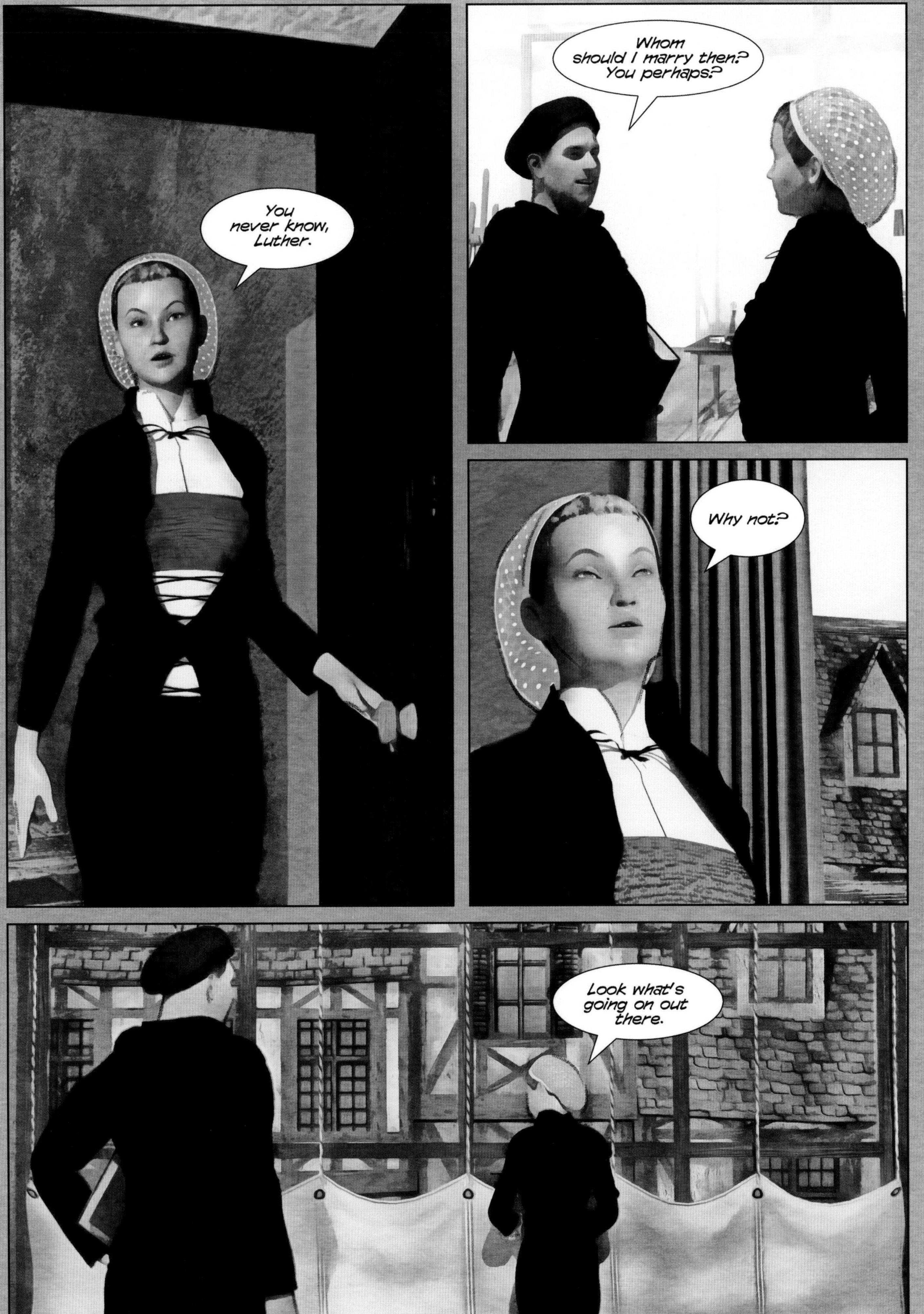
You never know, Luther.
Whom should I marry then? You perhaps?
Why not?
Look what's going on out there.

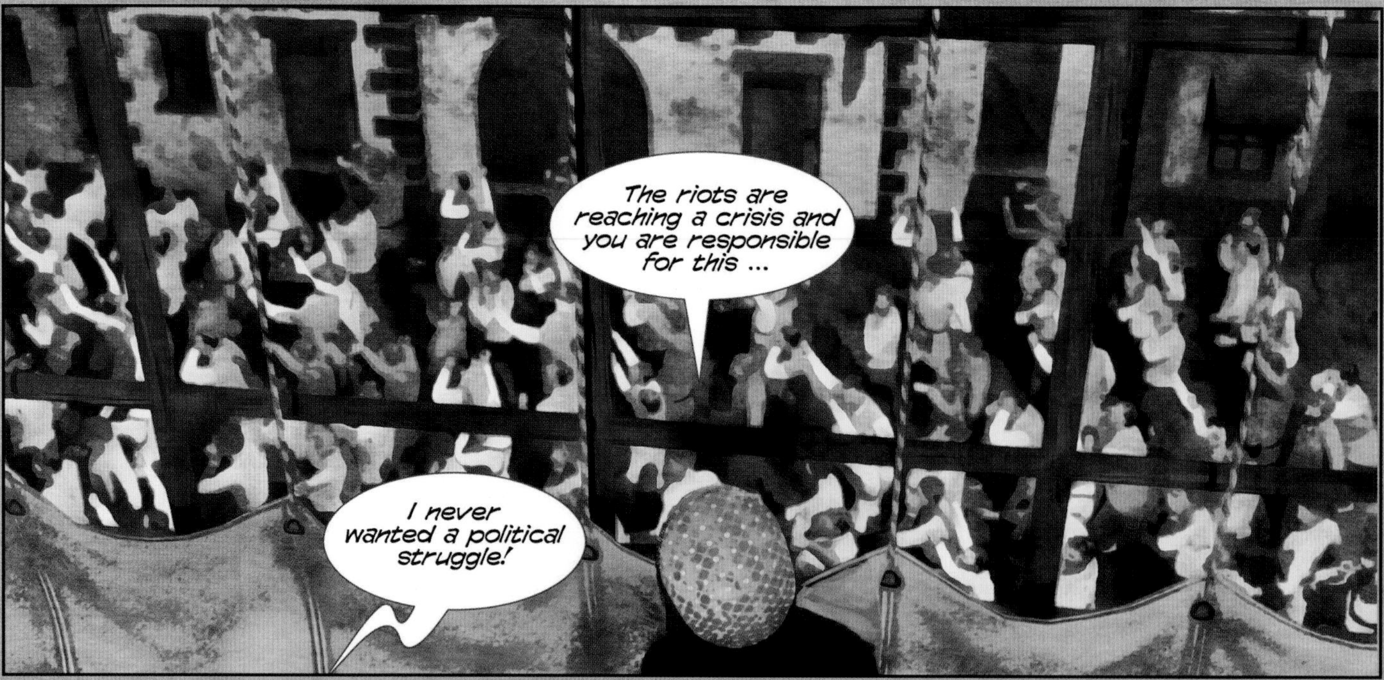
The riots are reaching a crisis and you are responsible for this ...
I never wanted a political struggle!

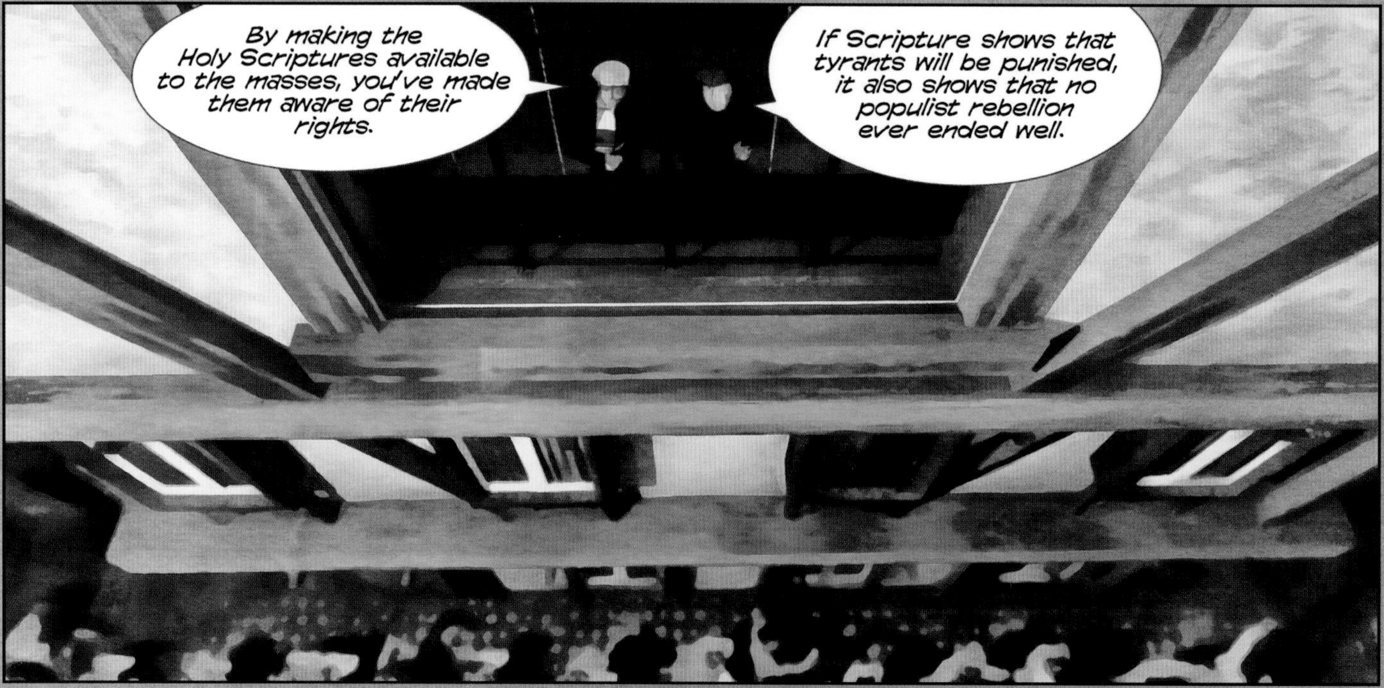
By making the Holy Scriptures available to the masses, you've made them aware of their rights.
If Scripture shows that tyrants will be punished, it also shows that no populist rebellion ever ended well.

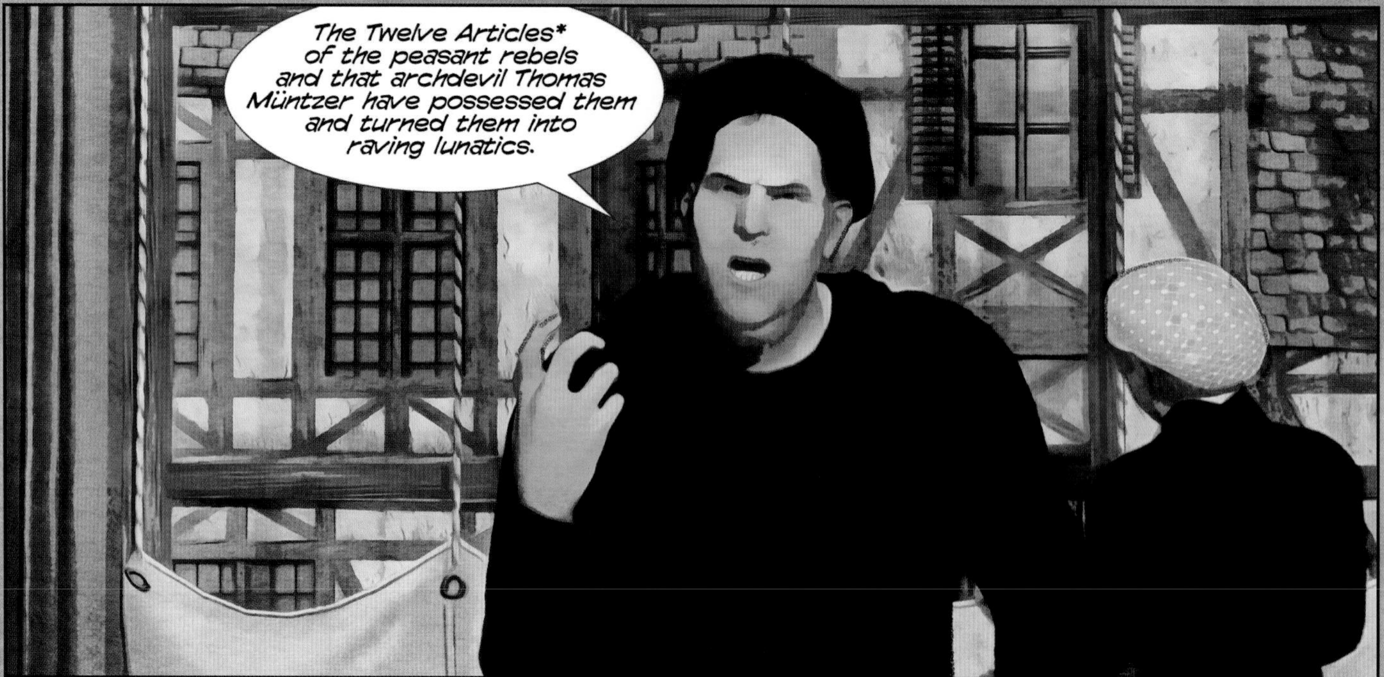
The Twelve Articles* of the peasant rebels and that archdevil Thomas Müntzer have possessed them and turned them into raving lunatics.

** The Twelve Articles were a list of demands adopted by peasant groups who met in 1525 in the town of Memmingen. They called for the abolition of serfdom, the free election of pastors, and hunting and fishing rights for all.*

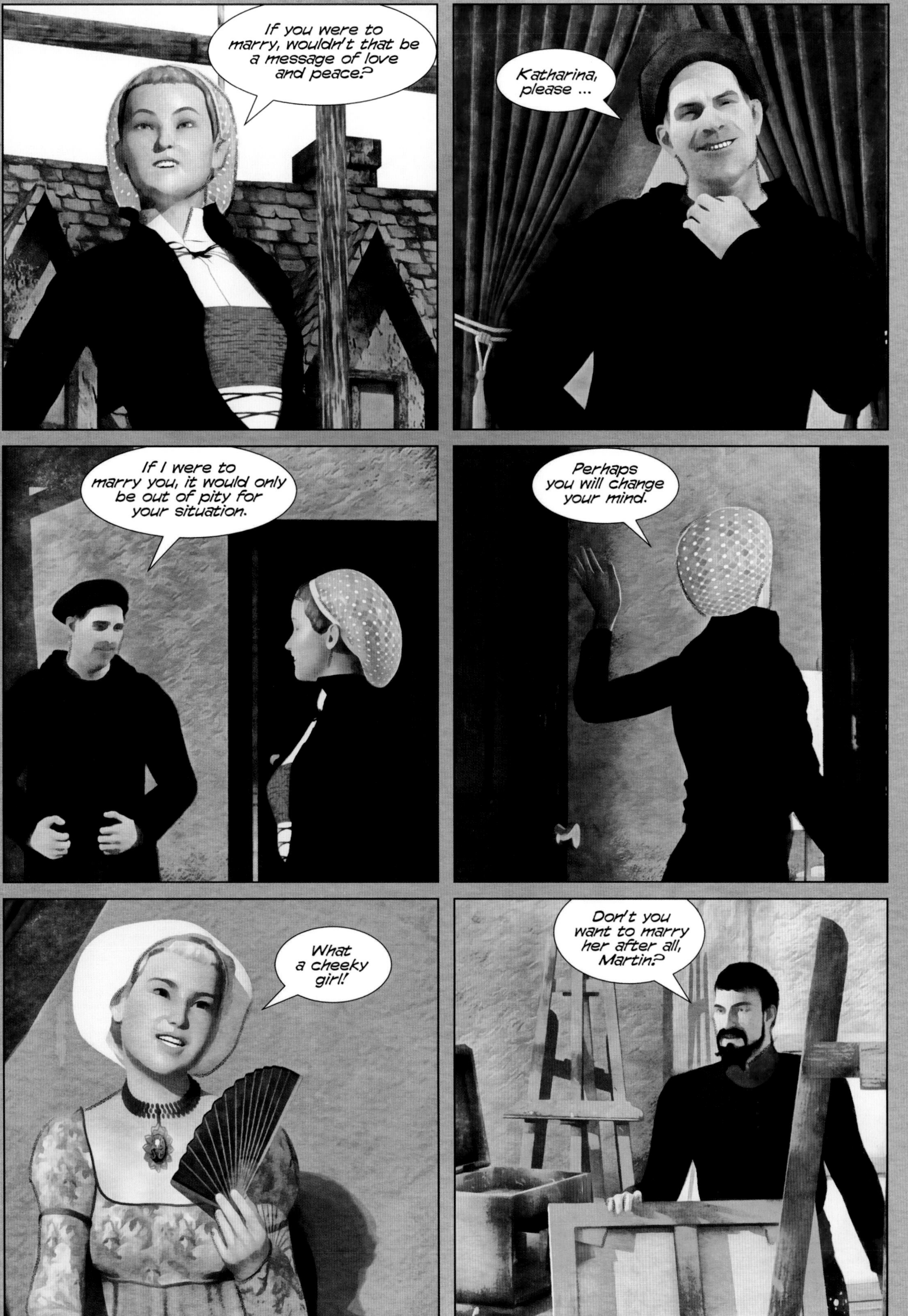
If you were to marry, wouldn't that be a message of love and peace?
Katharina, please ...
If I were to marry you, it would only be out of pity for your situation.
Perhaps you will change your mind.
What a cheeky girl!
Don't you want to marry her after all, Martin?

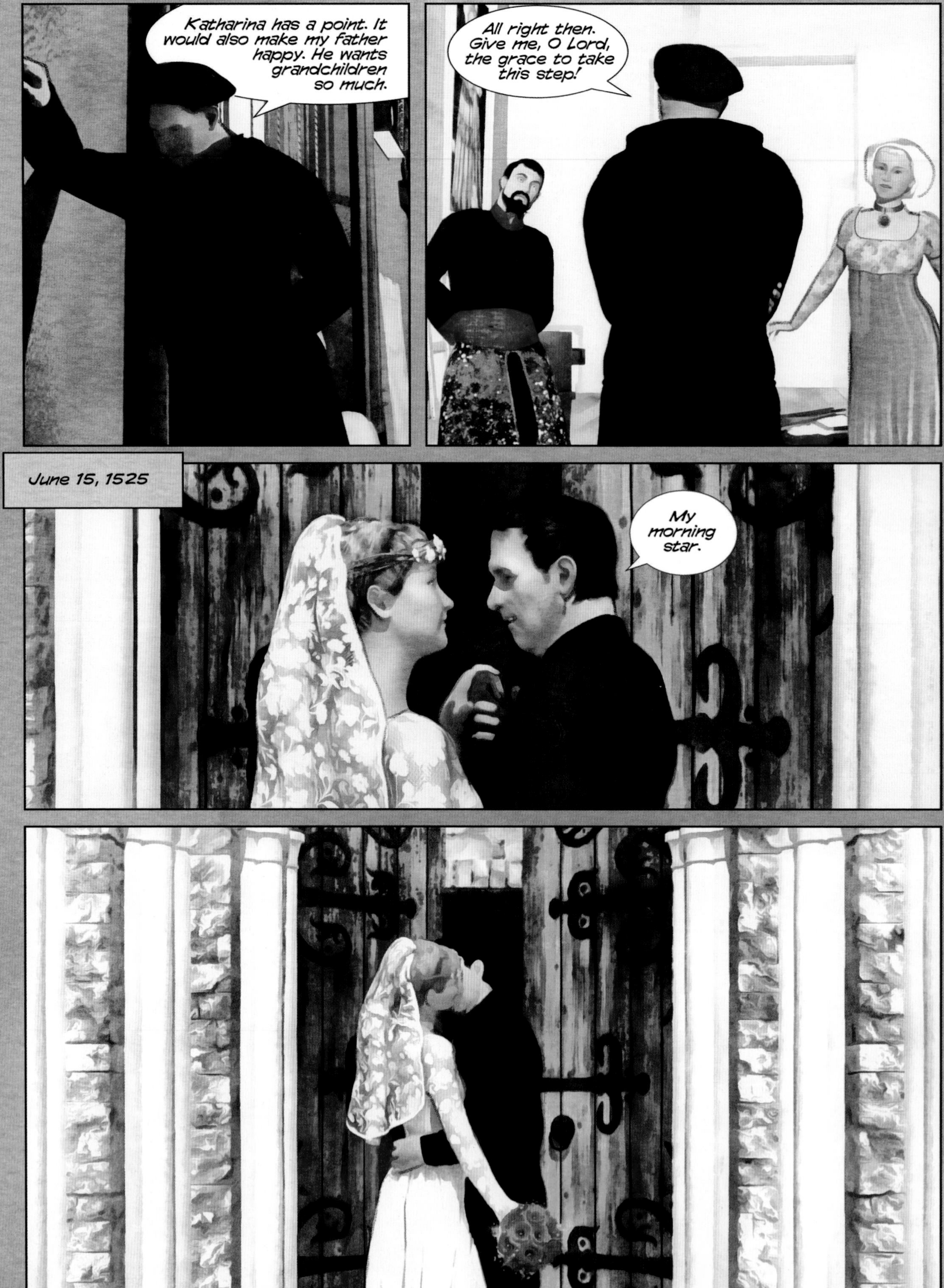
Katharina has a point. It would also make my father happy. He wants grandchildren so much.
All right then. Give me, O Lord, the grace to take this step!
June 15, 1525
My morning star.

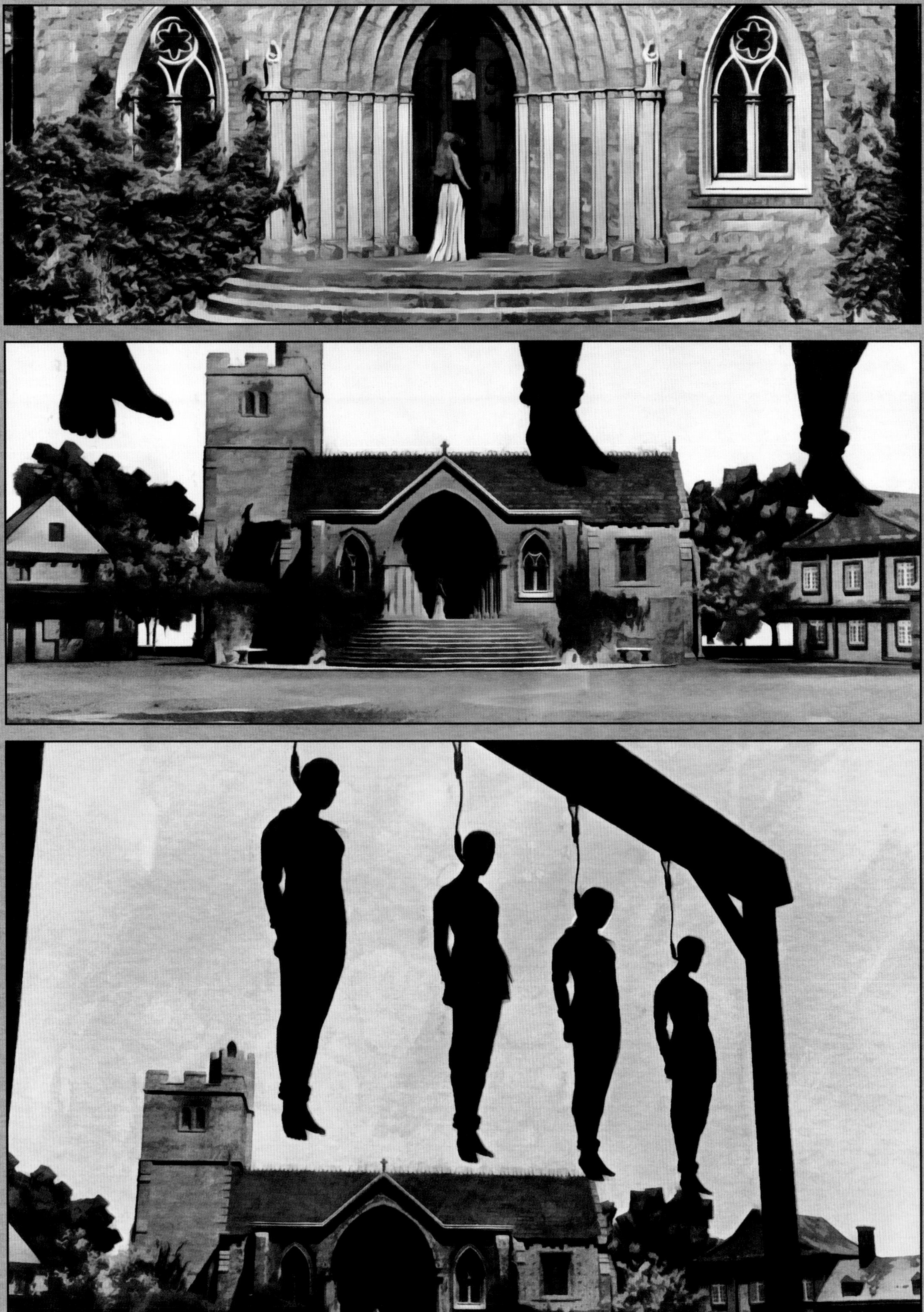

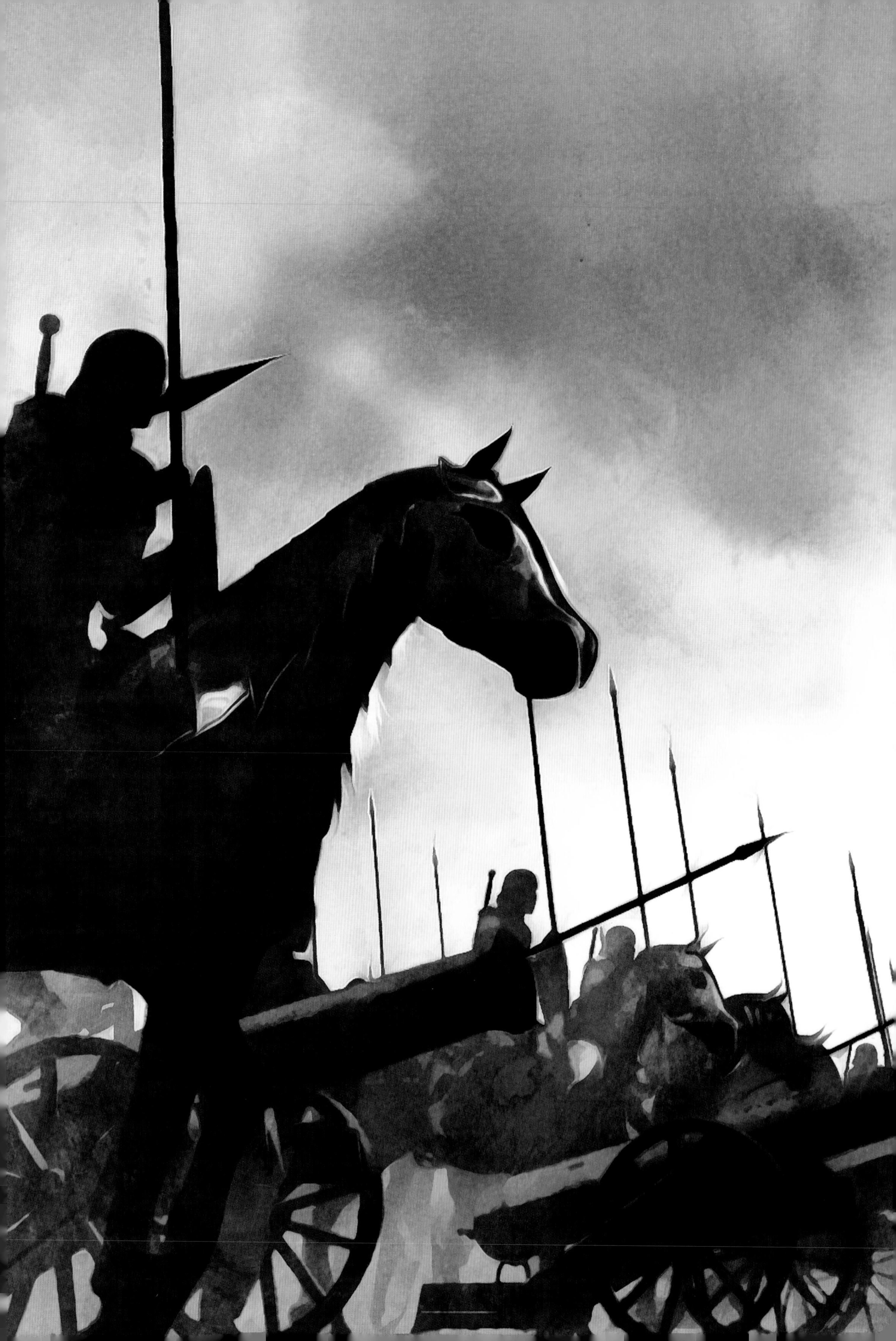

"Their Blood Is on My Hands"

Inspired by Luther's reforms and the Twelve Articles, peasants throughout the country demand radical change. Thomas Müntzer spurs them on with his fiery sermons. The protest movement soon leads to violence against the upper classes and church leaders. Luther condemns the rebellion and calls for a crackdown. The princes will be only too happy to oblige.

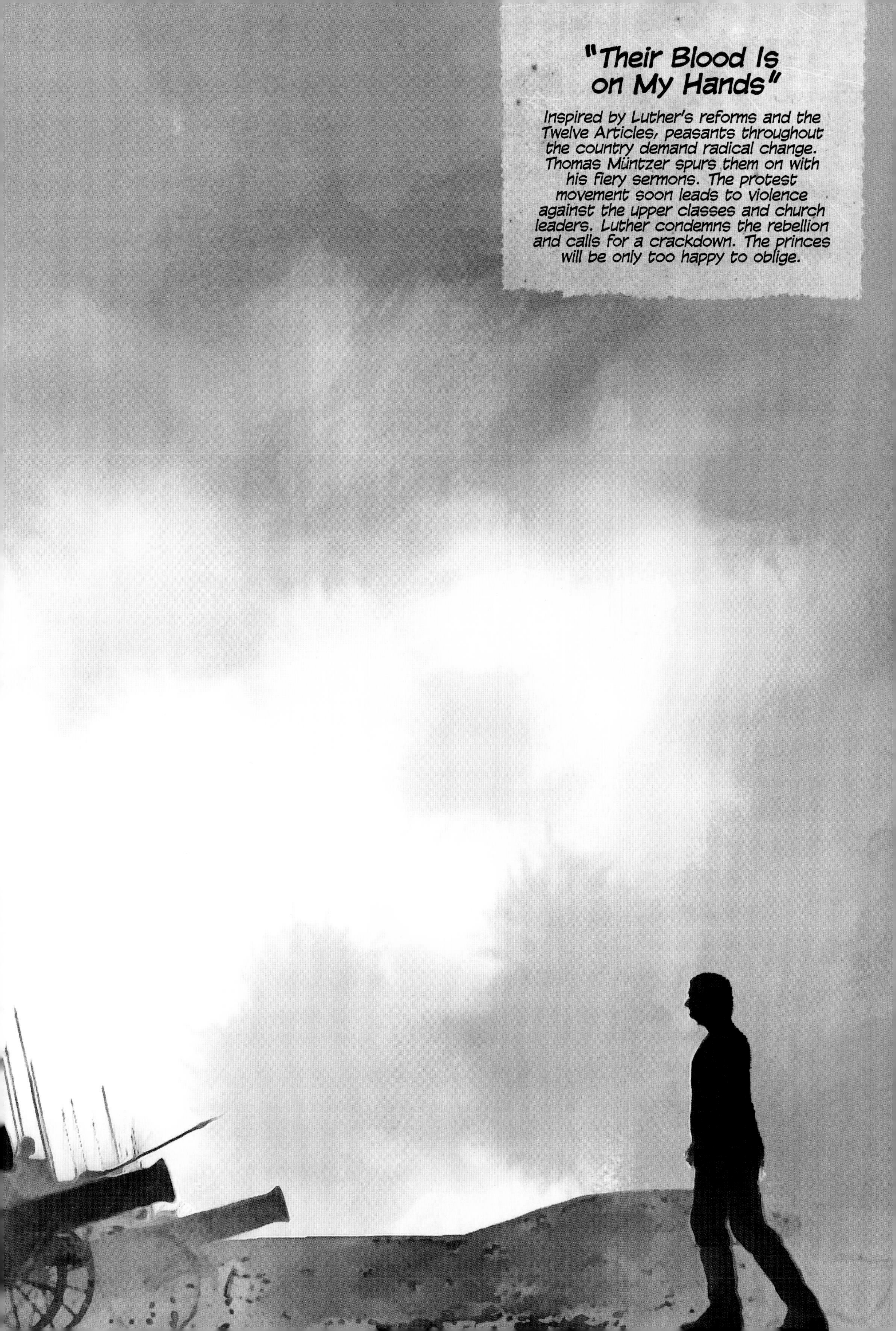

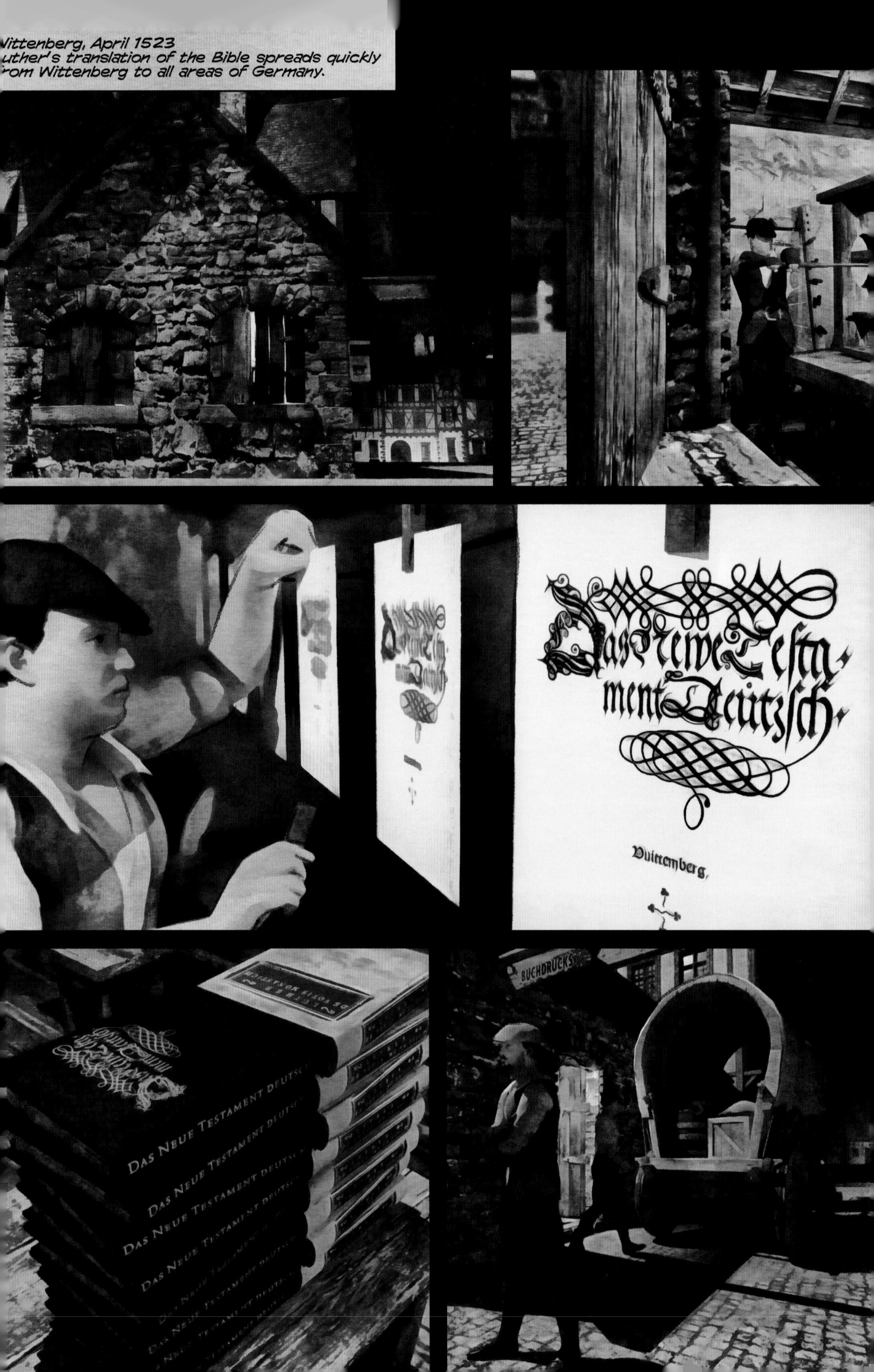
Wittenberg, April 1523
Luther's translation of the Bible spreads quickly from Wittenberg to all areas of Germany.
Das Newe Testament Deützsch.
Vuittemberg.
DAS NEUE TESTAMENT DEUTSCH
BUCHDRUCKS

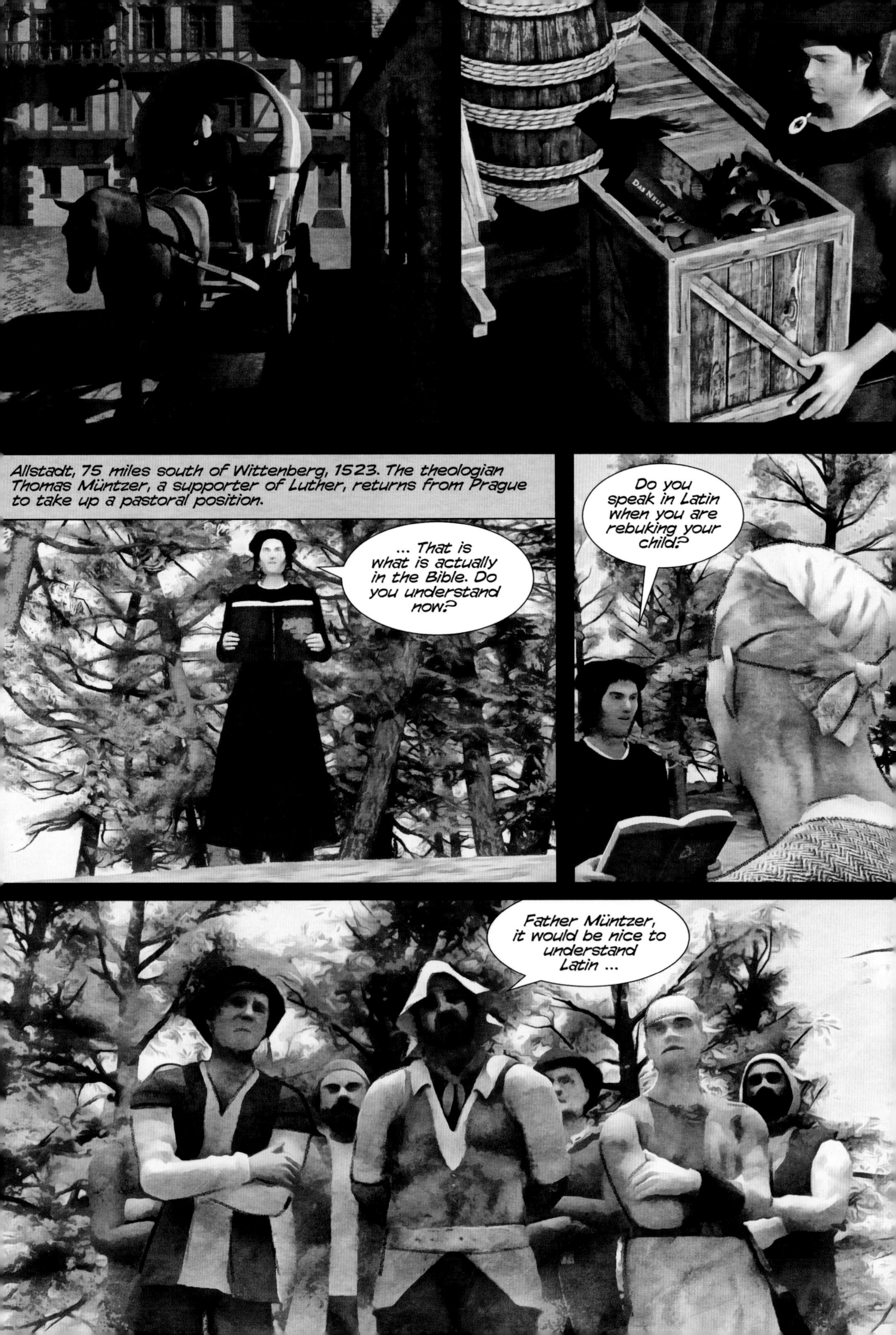
Allstadt, 75 miles south of Wittenberg, 1523. The theologian Thomas Müntzer, a supporter of Luther, returns from Prague to take up a pastoral position.
... That is what is actually in the Bible. Do you understand now?
Do you speak in Latin when you are rebuking your child?
Father Müntzer, it would be nice to understand Latin ...

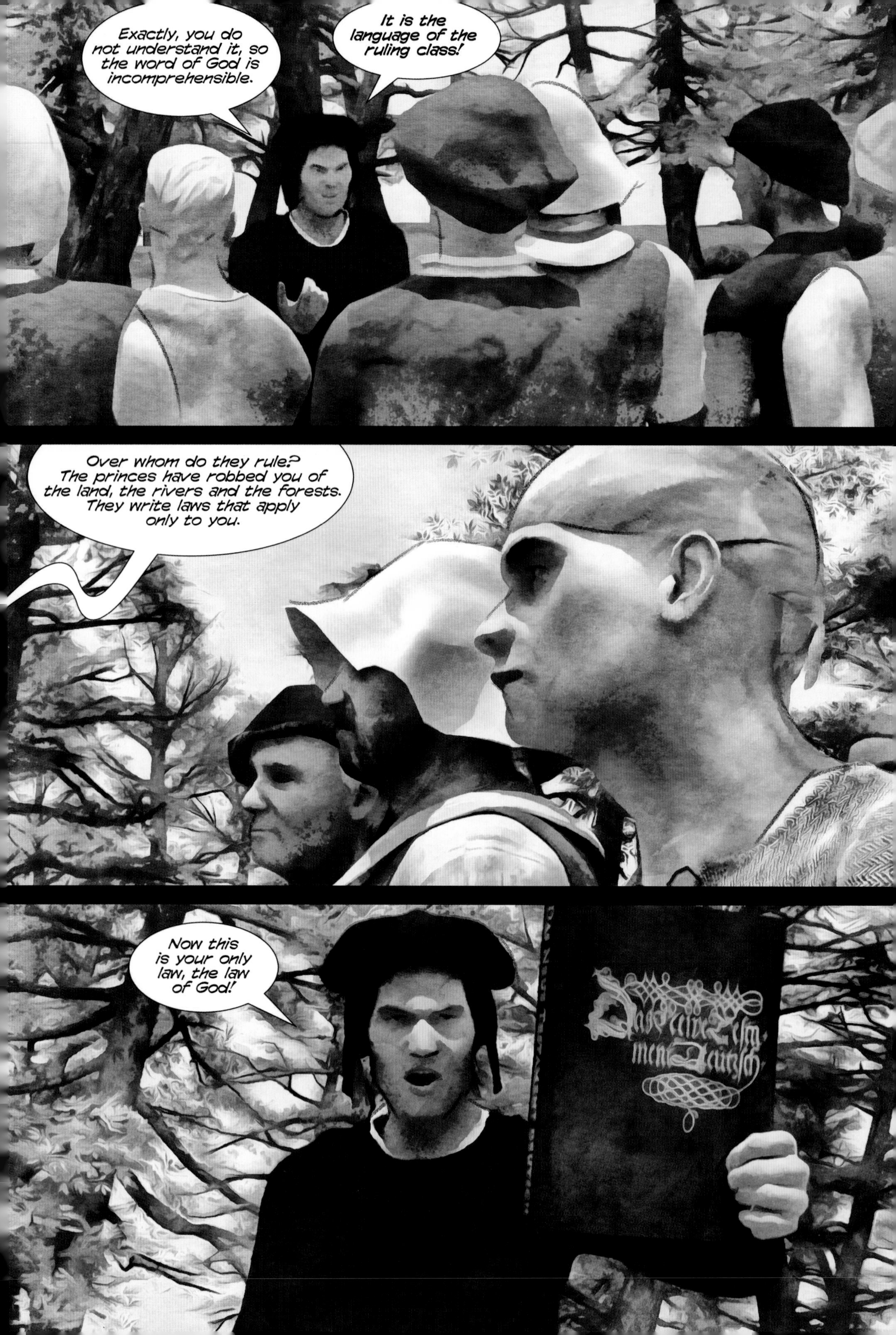
Exactly, you do not understand it, so the word of God is incomprehensible.
It is the language of the ruling class!
Over whom do they rule? The princes have robbed you of the land, the rivers and the forests. They write laws that apply only to you.
Now this is your only law, the law of God!

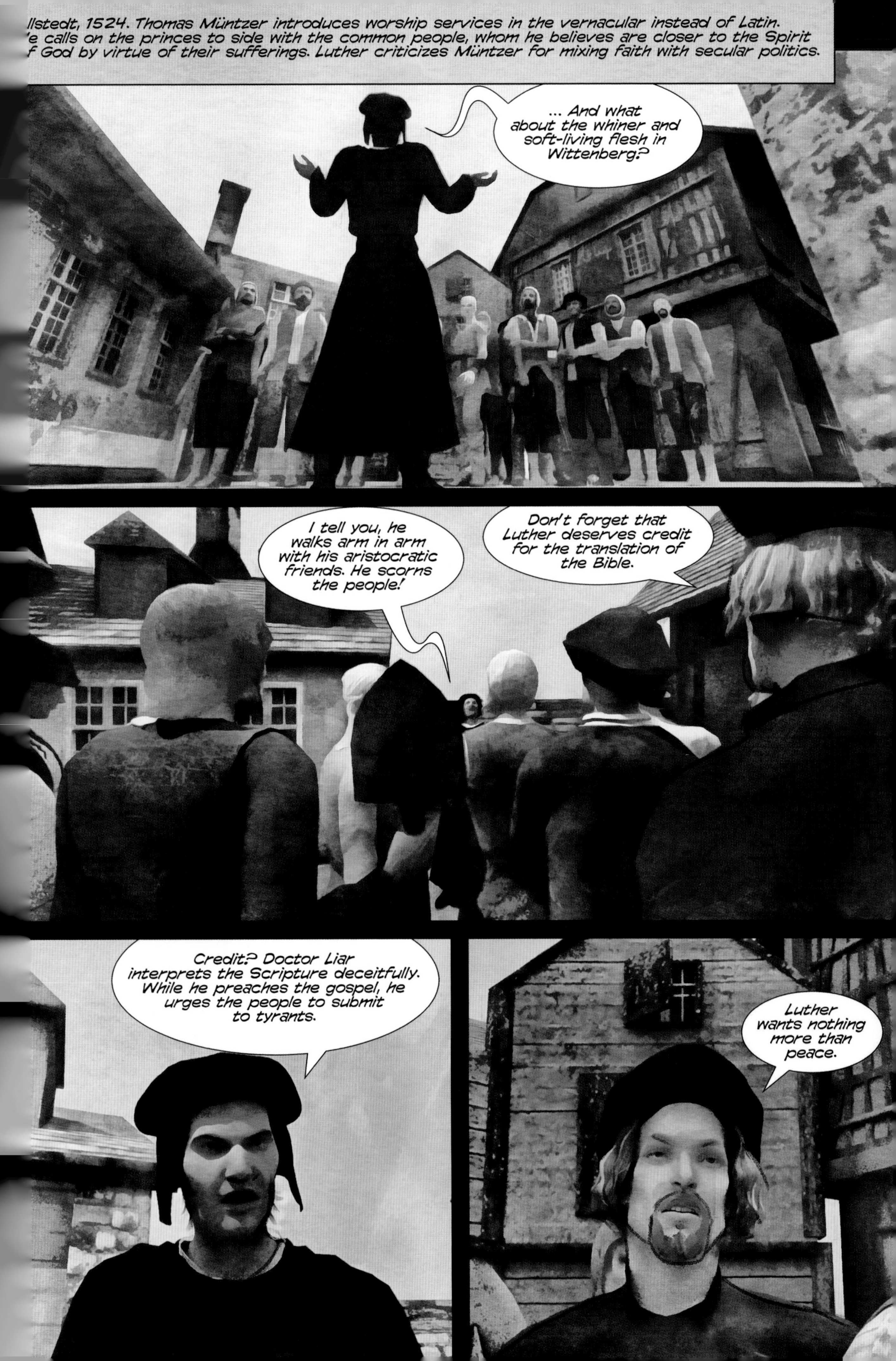
llstedt, 1524. Thomas Müntzer introduces worship services in the vernacular instead of Latin.
e calls on the princes to side with the common people, whom he believes are closer to the Spirit
f God by virtue of their sufferings. Luther criticizes Müntzer for mixing faith with secular politics.
... And what about the whiner and soft-living flesh in Wittenberg?
I tell you, he walks arm in arm with his aristocratic friends. He scorns the people!
Don't forget that Luther deserves credit for the translation of the Bible.
Credit? Doctor Liar interprets the Scripture deceitfully. While he preaches the gospel, he urges the people to submit to tyrants.
Luther wants nothing more than peace.

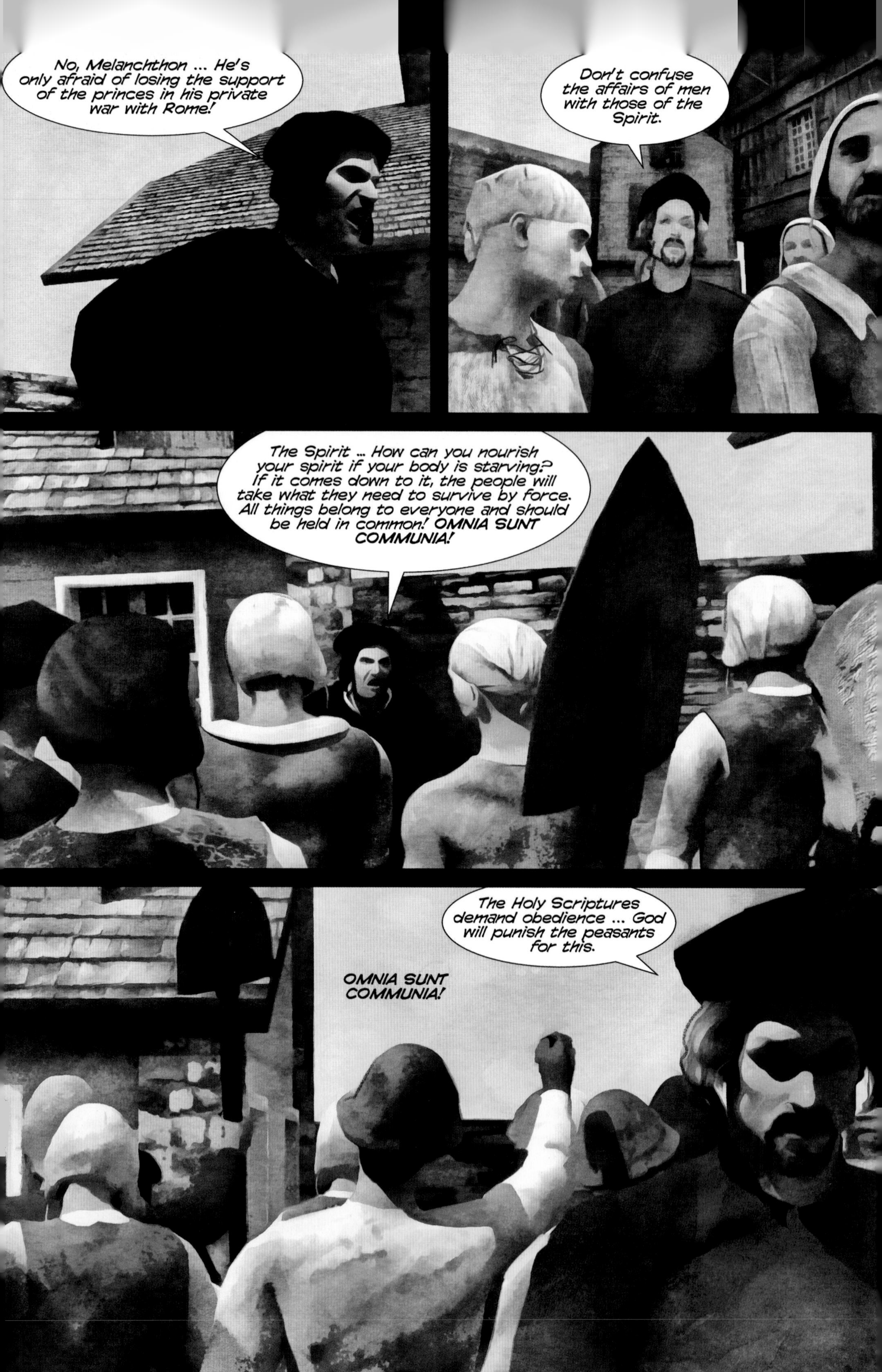
No, Melanchthon ... He's only afraid of losing the support of the princes in his private war with Rome!
Don't confuse the affairs of men with those of the Spirit.
The Spirit ... How can you nourish your spirit if your body is starving? If it comes down to it, the people will take what they need to survive by force. All things belong to everyone and should be held in common! OMNIA SUNT COMMUNIA!
The Holy Scriptures demand obedience ... God will punish the peasants for this.
OMNIA SUNT COMMUNIA!

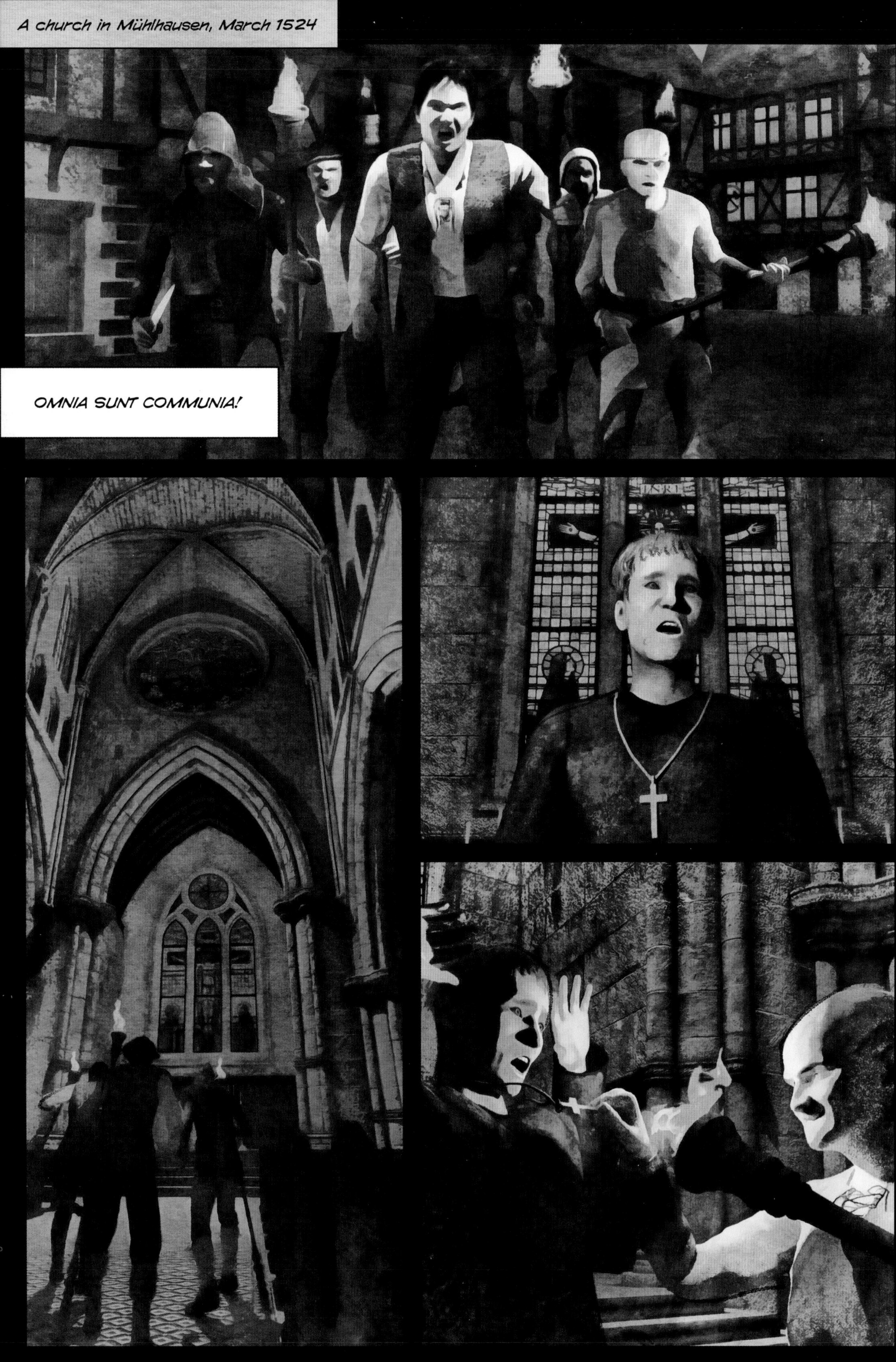
A church in Mühlhausen, March 1524
OMNIA SUNT COMMUNIA!

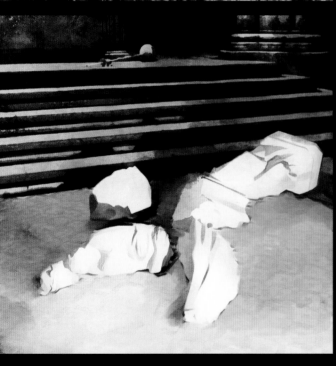

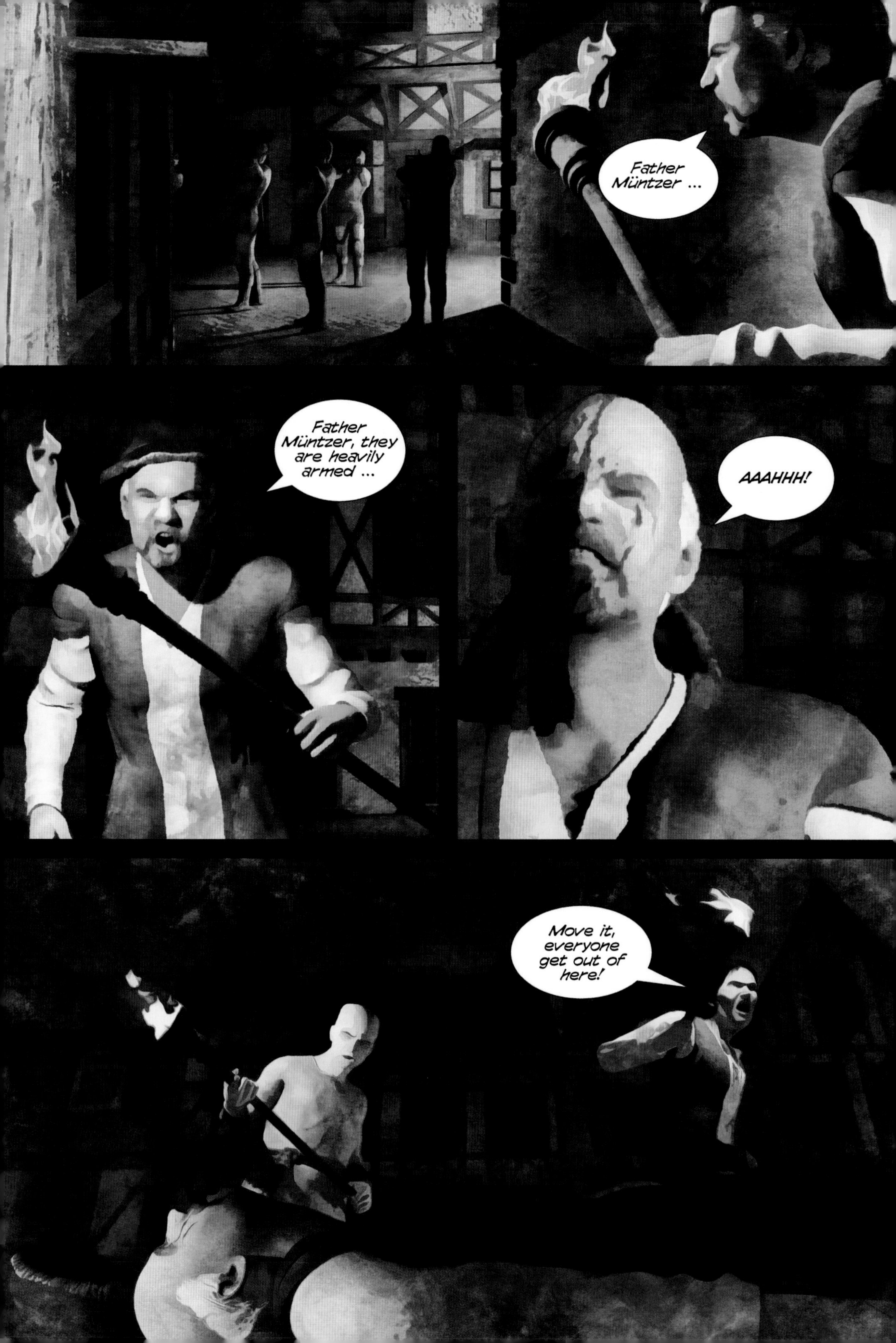
Father Müntzer ...
Father Müntzer, they are heavily armed ...
AAAHHH!
Move it, everyone get out of here!

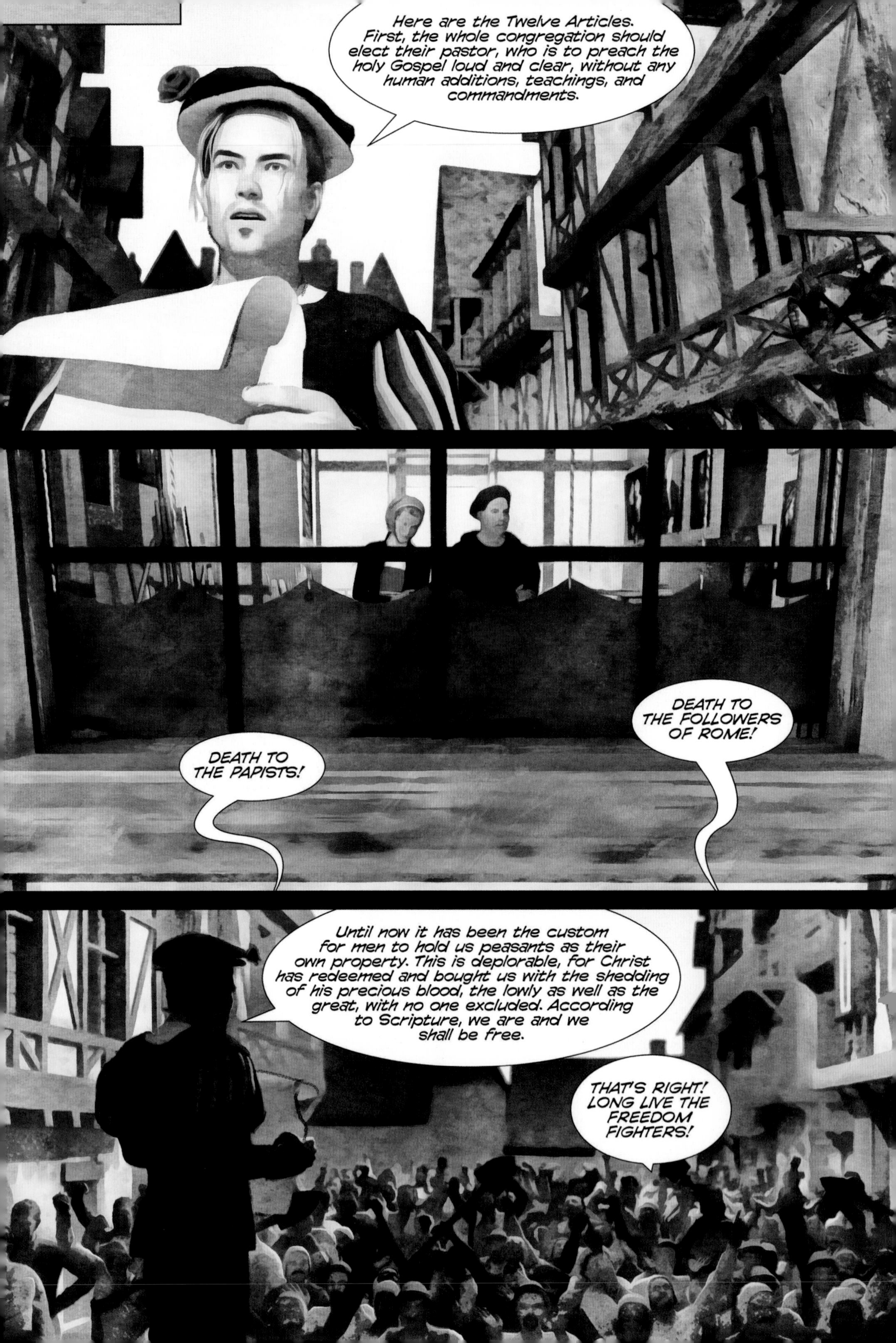
Here are the Twelve Articles. First, the whole congregation should elect their pastor, who is to preach the holy Gospel loud and clear, without any human additions, teachings, and commandments.
DEATH TO THE PAPISTS!
DEATH TO THE FOLLOWERS OF ROME!
Until now it has been the custom for men to hold us peasants as their own property. This is deplorable, for Christ has redeemed and bought us with the shedding of his precious blood, the lowly as well as the great, with no one excluded. According to Scripture, we are and we shall be free.
THAT'S RIGHT! LONG LIVE THE FREEDOM FIGHTERS!

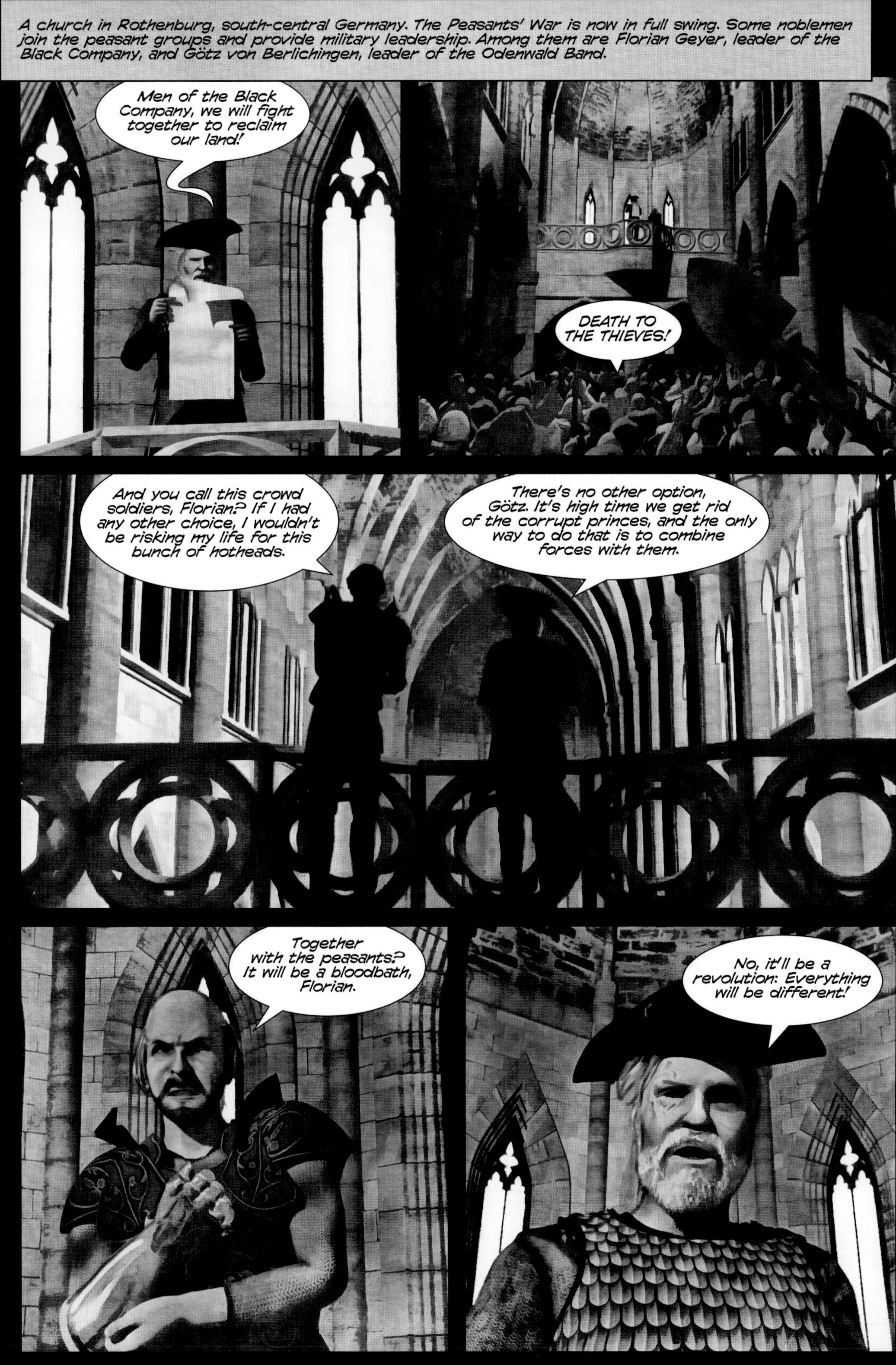
A church in Rothenburg, south-central Germany. The Peasants' War is now in full swing. Some noblemen join the peasant groups and provide military leadership. Among them are Florian Geyer, leader of the Black Company, and Götz von Berlichingen, leader of the Odenwald Band.
Men of the Black Company, we will fight together to reclaim our land!
DEATH TO THE THIEVES!
And you call this crowd soldiers, Florian? If I had any other choice, I wouldn't be risking my life for this bunch of hotheads.
There's no other option, Götz. It's high time we get rid of the corrupt princes, and the only way to do that is to combine forces with them.
Together with the peasants? It will be a bloodbath, Florian.
No, it'll be a revolution: Everything will be different!

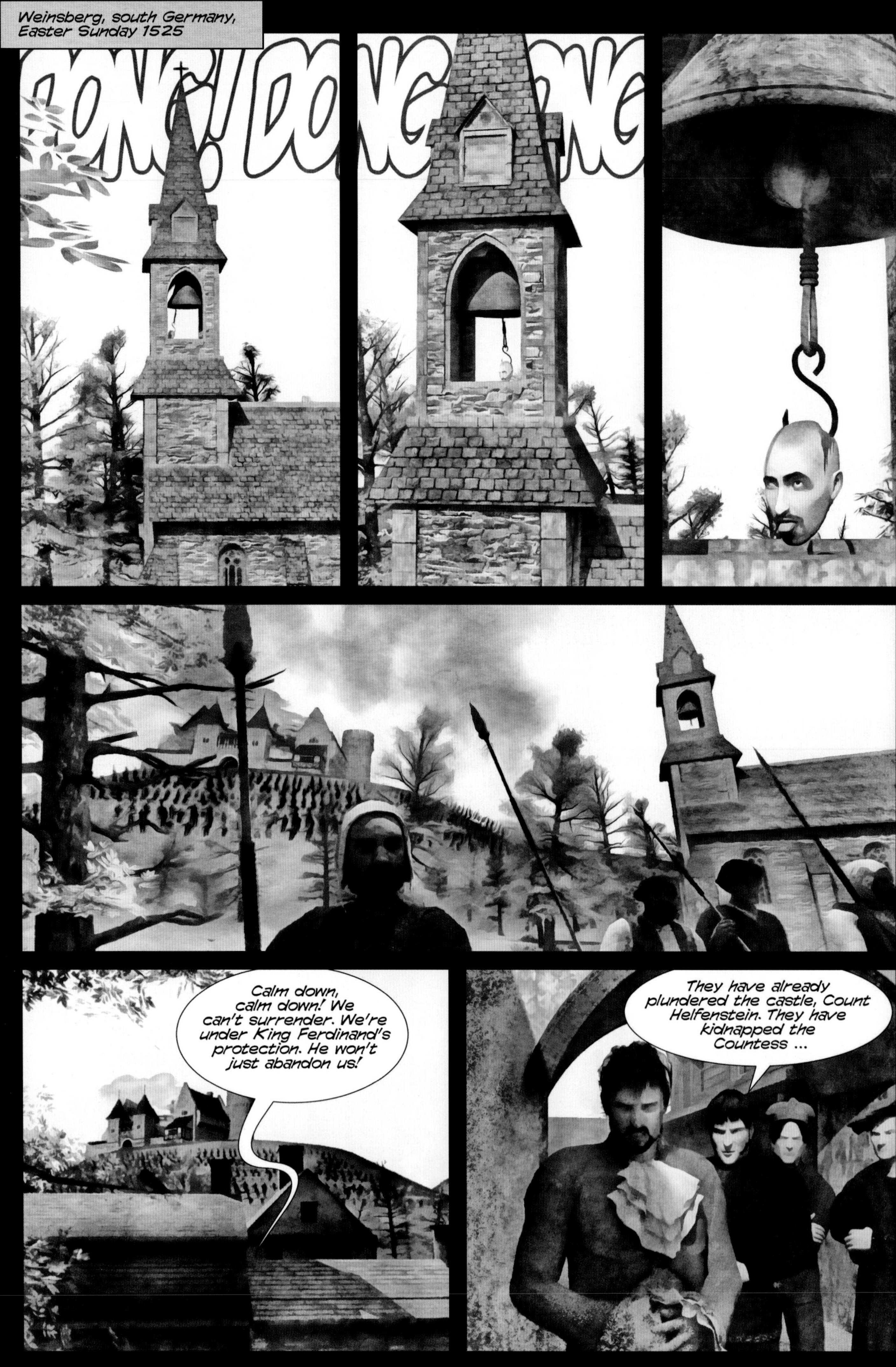

Weinsberg, south Germany, Easter Sunday 1525
DONG! DONG DONG
Calm down, calm down! We can't surrender. We're under King Ferdinand's protection. He won't just abandon us!
They have already plundered the castle, Count Helfenstein. They have kidnapped the Countess ...

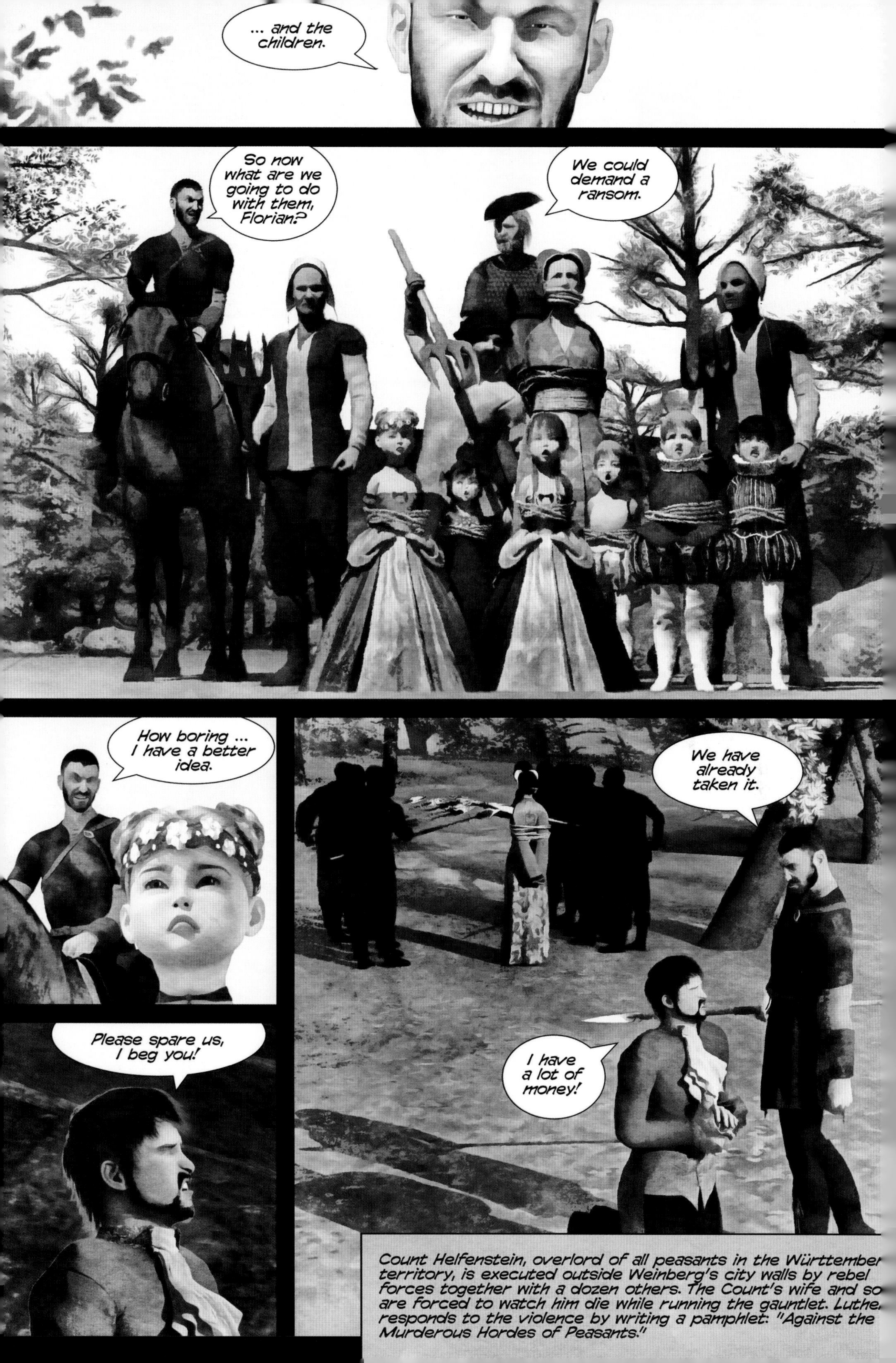
... and the children.
So now what are we going to do with them, Florian?
We could demand a ransom.
How boring ... I have a better idea.
Please spare us, I beg you!
We have already taken it.
I have a lot of money!
Count Helfenstein, overlord of all peasants in the Württember territory, is executed outside Weinberg's city walls by rebel forces together with a dozen others. The Count's wife and so are forced to watch him die while running the gauntlet. Luthe responds to the violence by writing a pamphlet: "Against the Murderous Hordes of Peasants."

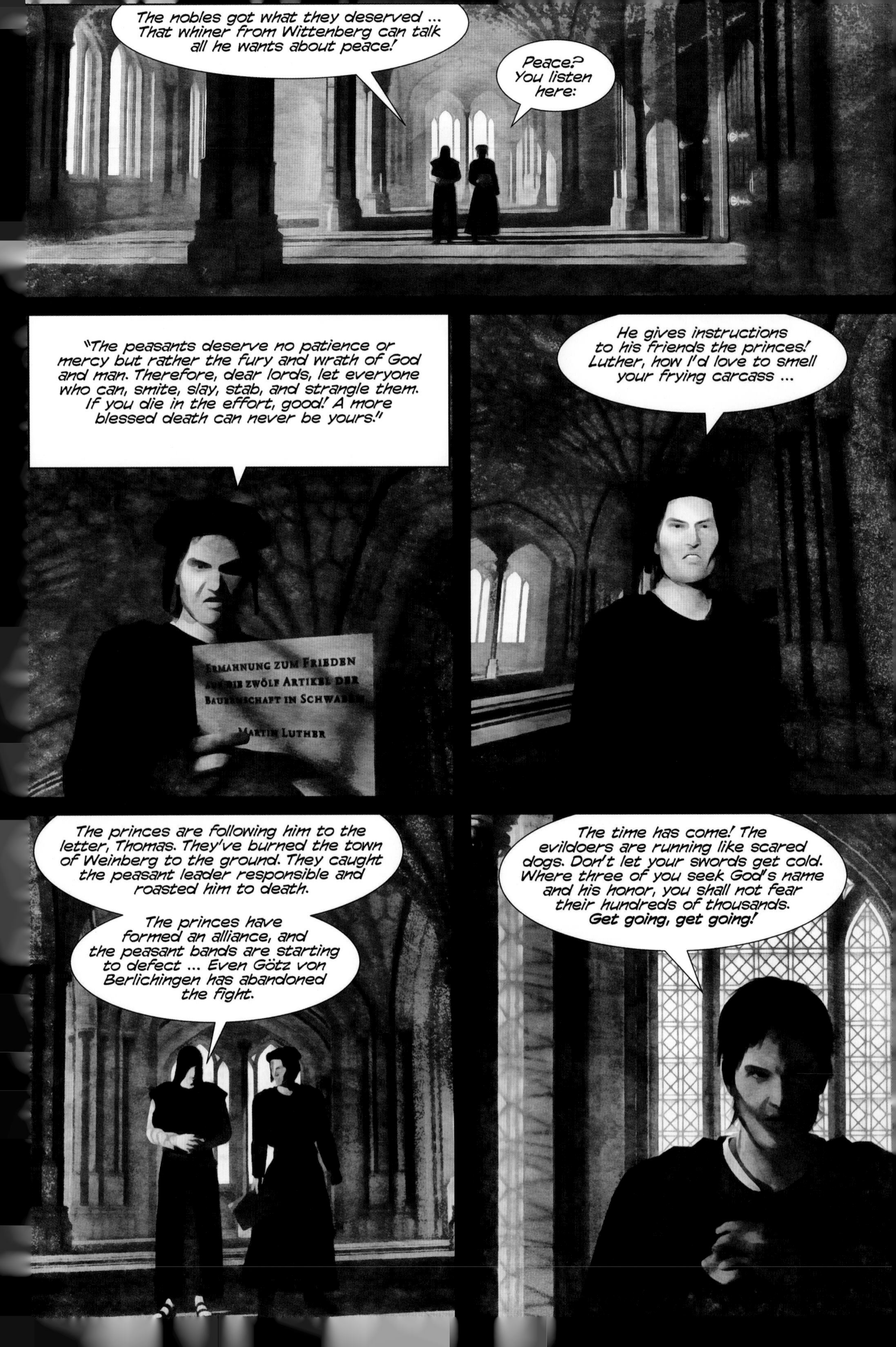

The nobles got what they deserved ... That whiner from Wittenberg can talk all he wants about peace!
Peace? You listen here:
"The peasants deserve no patience or mercy but rather the fury and wrath of God and man. Therefore, dear lords, let everyone who can, smite, slay, stab, and strangle them. If you die in the effort, good! A more blessed death can never be yours."
ERMAHNUNG ZUM FRIEDEN
He gives instructions to his friends the princes! Luther, how I'd love to smell your frying carcass ...
The princes are following him to the letter, Thomas. They've burned the town of Weinberg to the ground. They caught the peasant leader responsible and roasted him to death.
The princes have formed an alliance, and the peasant bands are starting to defect ... Even Götz von Berlichingen has abandoned the fight.
The time has come! The evildoers are running like scared dogs. Don't let your swords get cold. Where three of you seek God's name and his honor, you shall not fear their hundreds of thousands. **Get going, get going!**

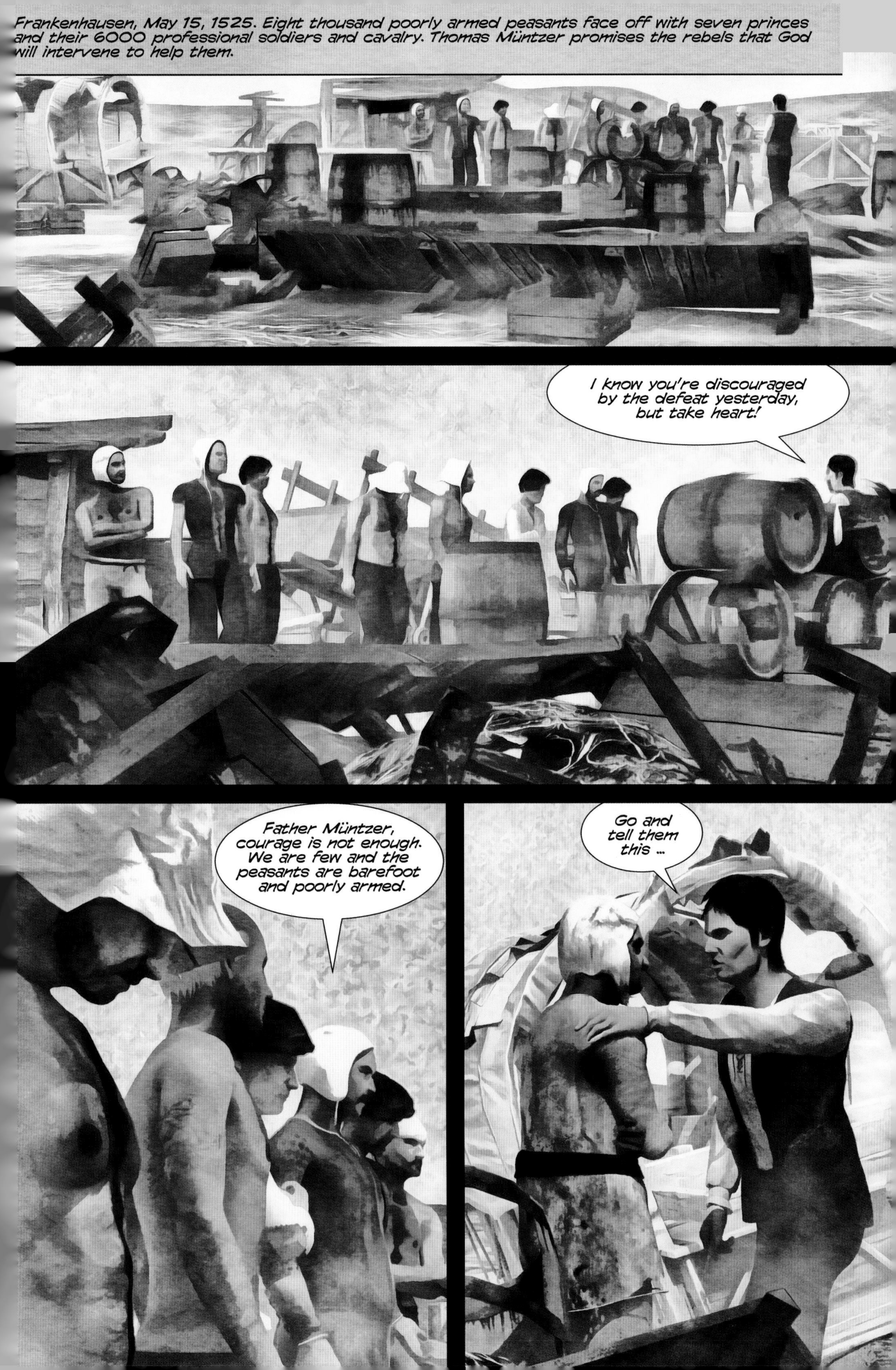
Frankenhausen, May 15, 1525. Eight thousand poorly armed peasants face off with seven princes and their 6000 professional soldiers and cavalry. Thomas Müntzer promises the rebels that God will intervene to help them.
I know you're discouraged by the defeat yesterday, but take heart!
Father Müntzer, courage is not enough. We are few and the peasants are barefoot and poorly armed.
Go and tell them this ...

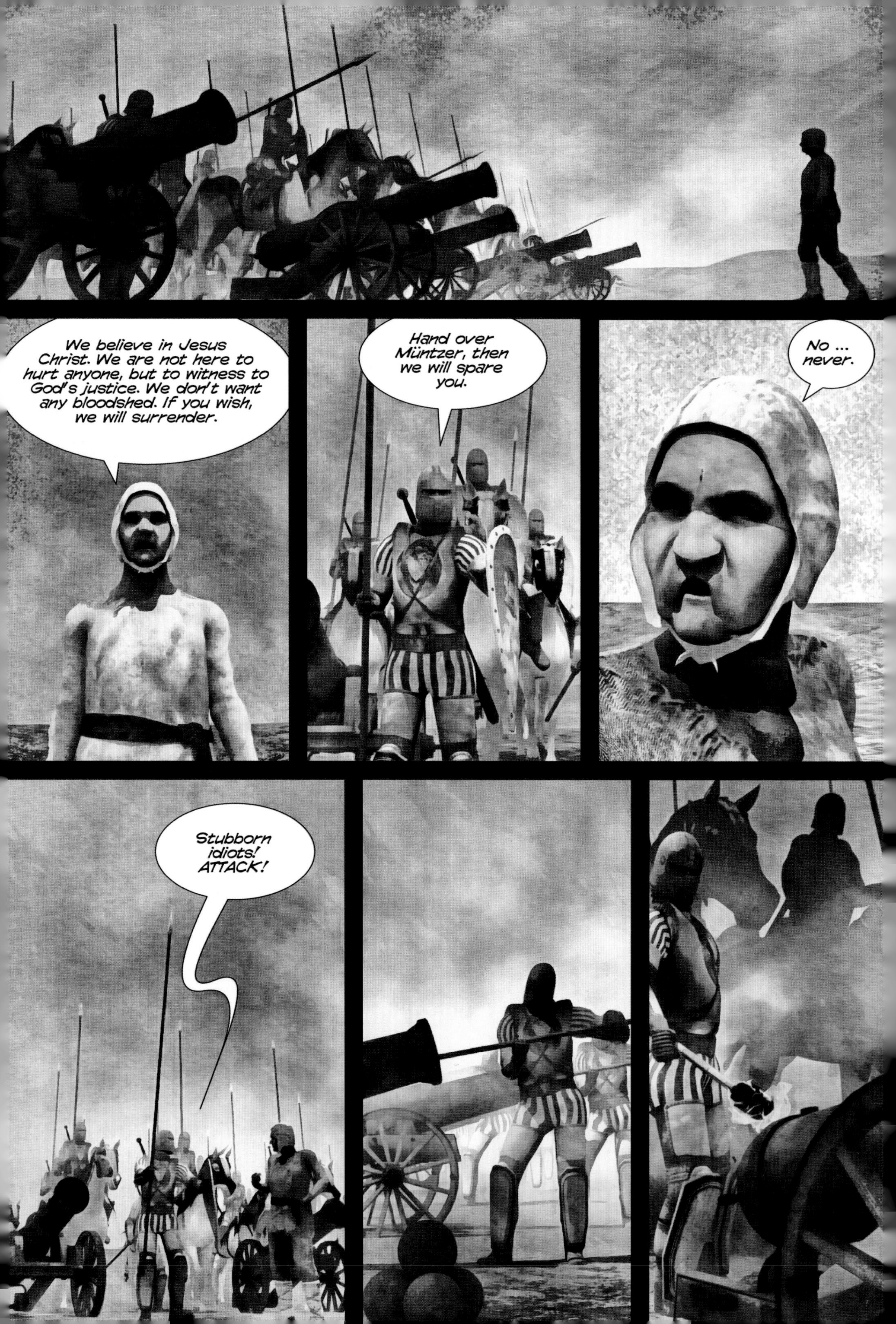
We believe in Jesus Christ. We are not here to hurt anyone, but to witness to God's justice. We don't want any bloodshed. If you wish, we will surrender.
Hand over Müntzer, then we will spare you.
No ... never.
Stubborn idiots! ATTACK!

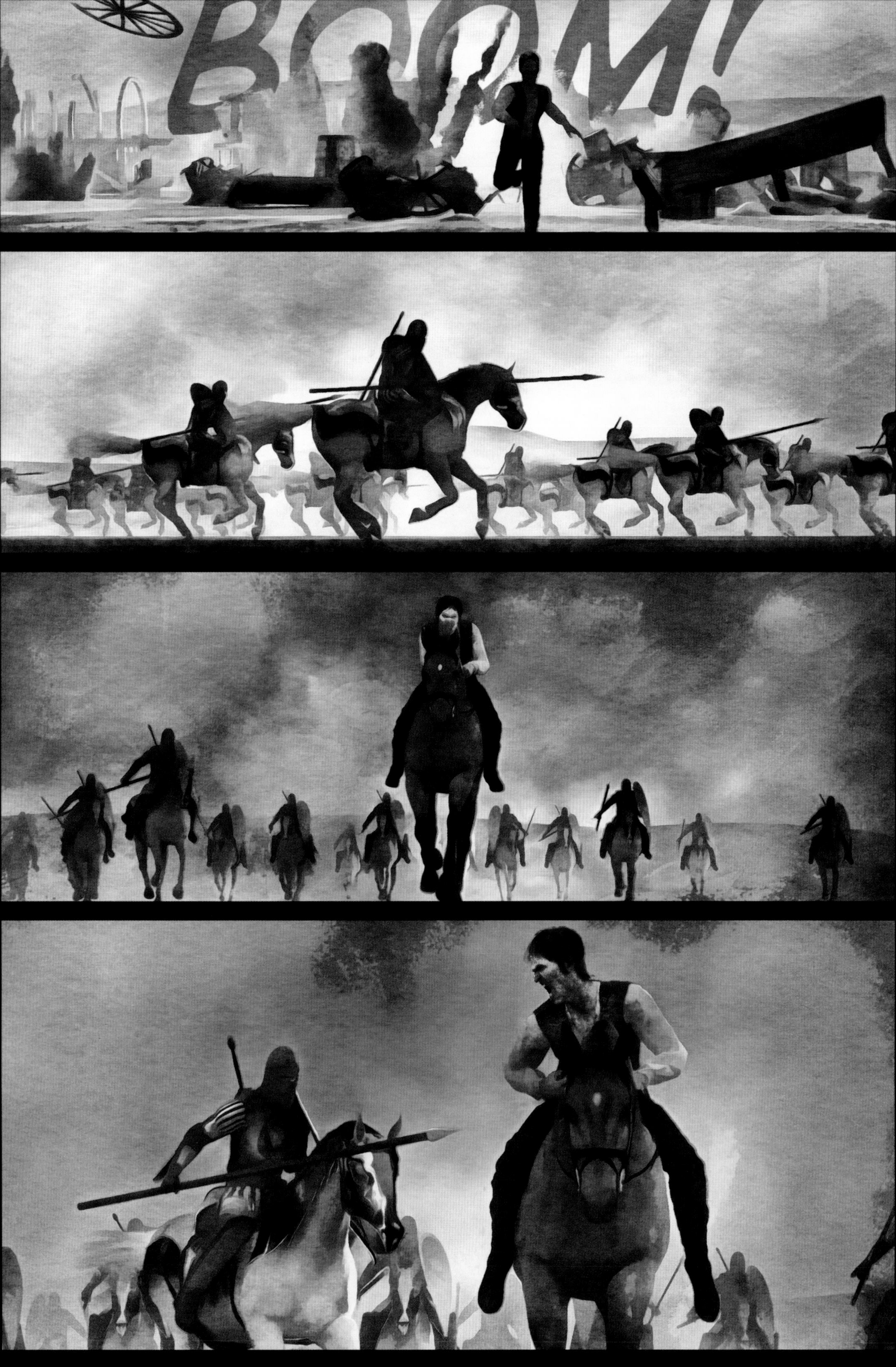
BOOM!

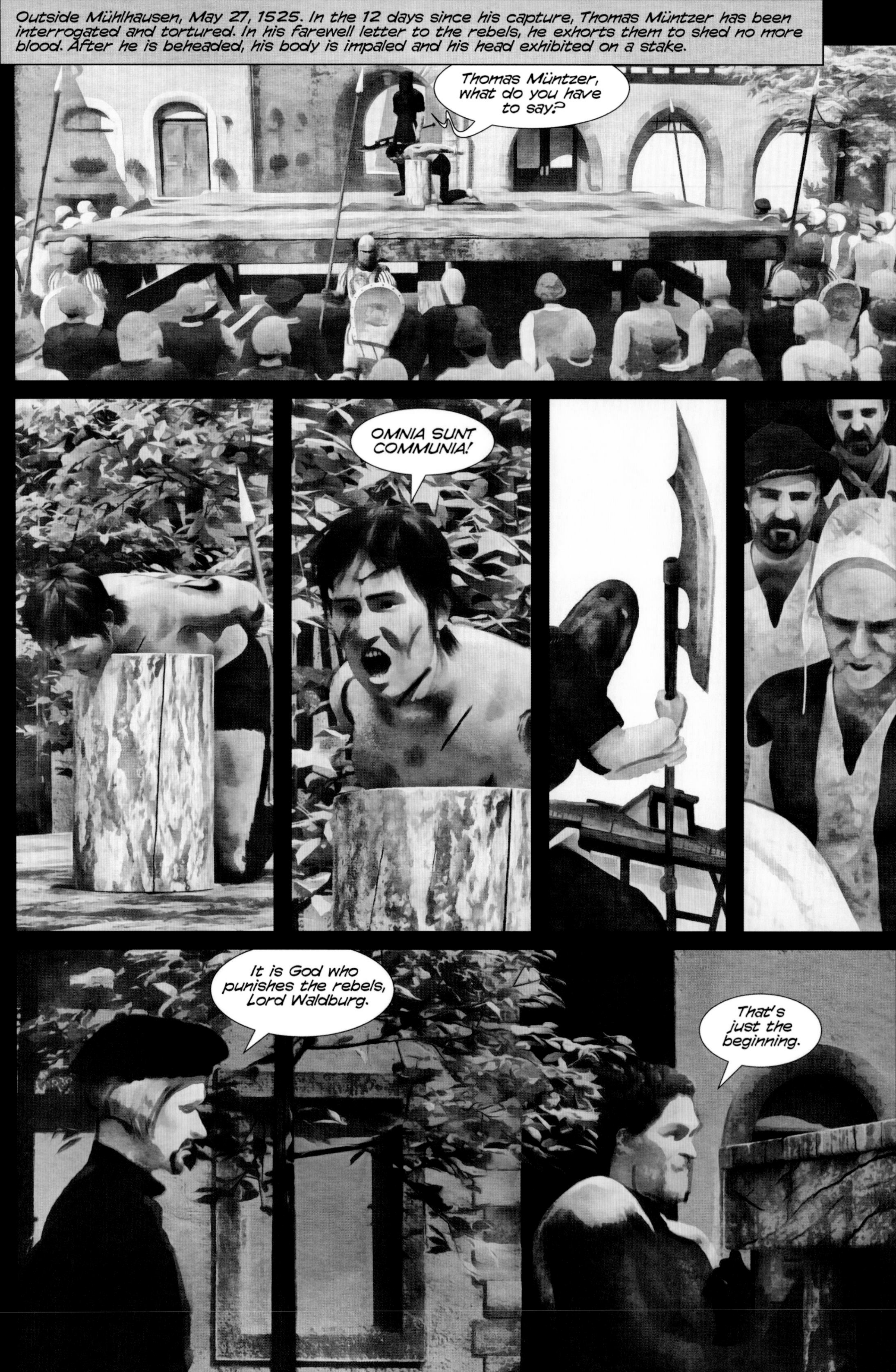
Outside Mühlhausen, May 27, 1525. In the 12 days since his capture, Thomas Müntzer has been interrogated and tortured. In his farewell letter to the rebels, he exhorts them to shed no more blood. After he is beheaded, his body is impaled and his head exhibited on a stake.
Thomas Müntzer, what do you have to say?
OMNIA SUNT COMMUNIA!
It is God who punishes the rebels, Lord Waldburg.
That's just the beginning.

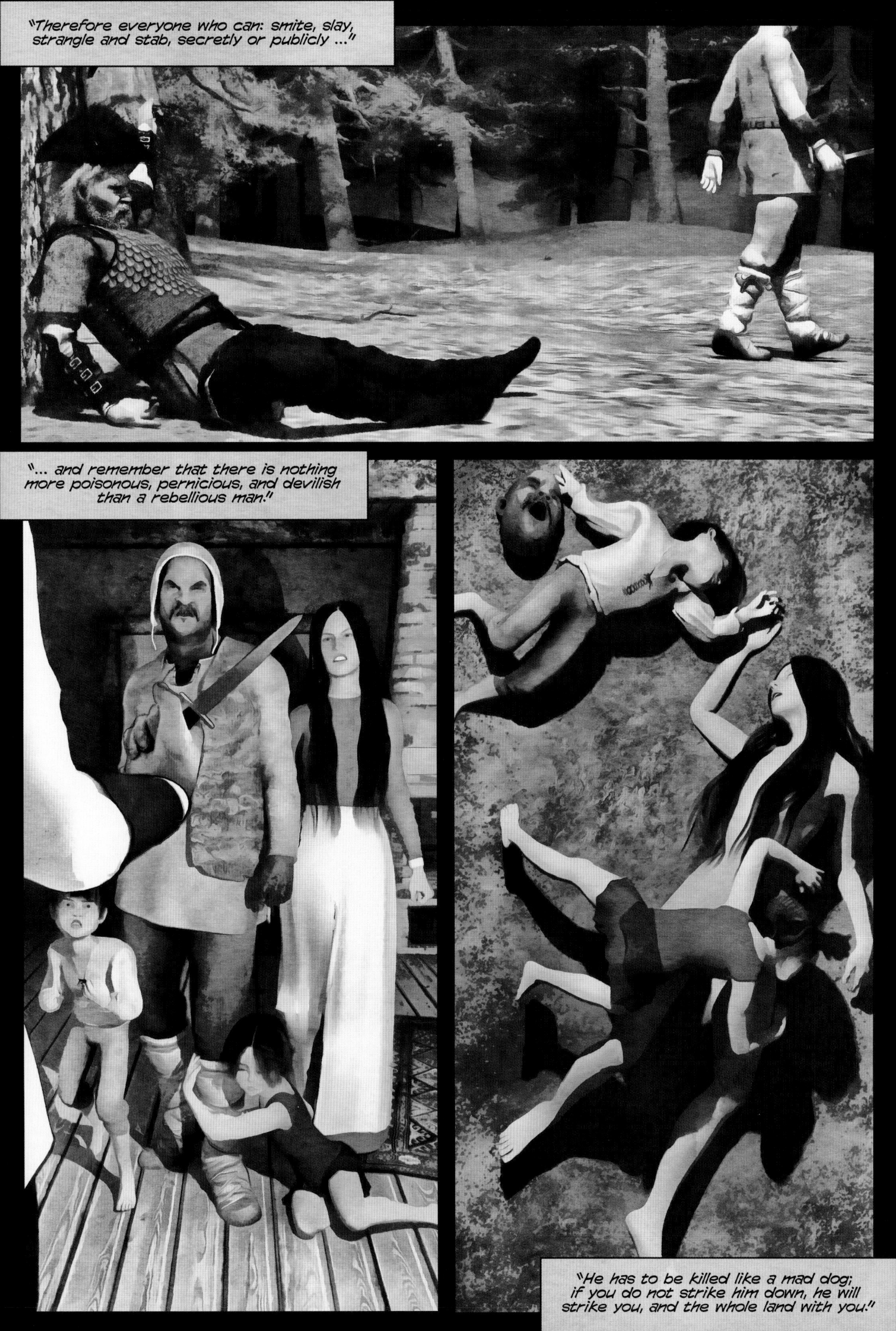
"Therefore everyone who can: smite, slay, strangle and stab, secretly or publicly ..."
"... and remember that there is nothing more poisonous, pernicious, and devilish than a rebellious man."
"He has to be killed like a mad dog; if you do not strike him down, he will strike you, and the whole land with you."

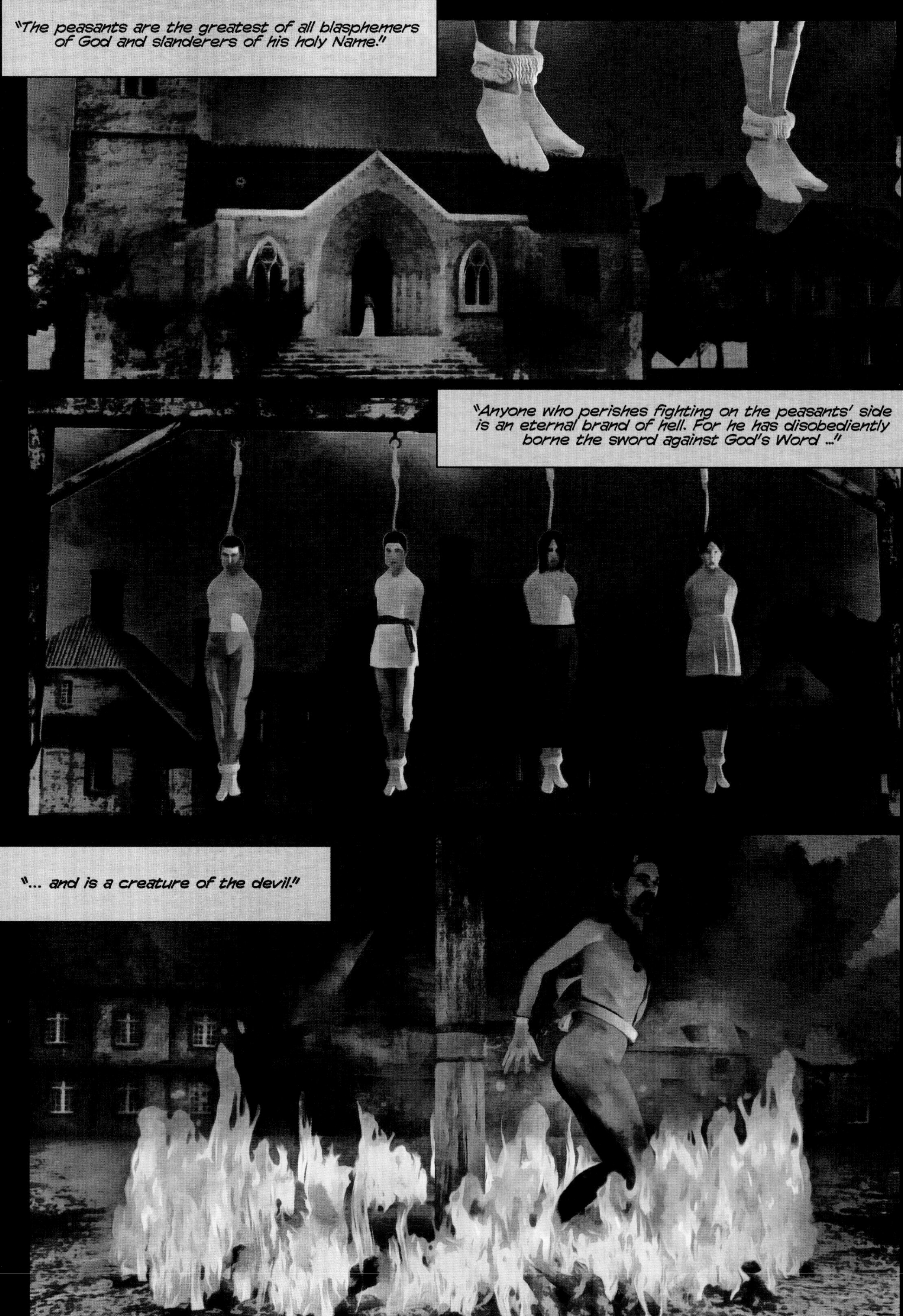
"The peasants are the greatest of all blasphemers of God and slanderers of his holy Name."
"Anyone who perishes fighting on the peasants' side is an eternal brand of hell. For he has disobediently borne the sword against God's Word ..."
"... and is a creature of the devil!"

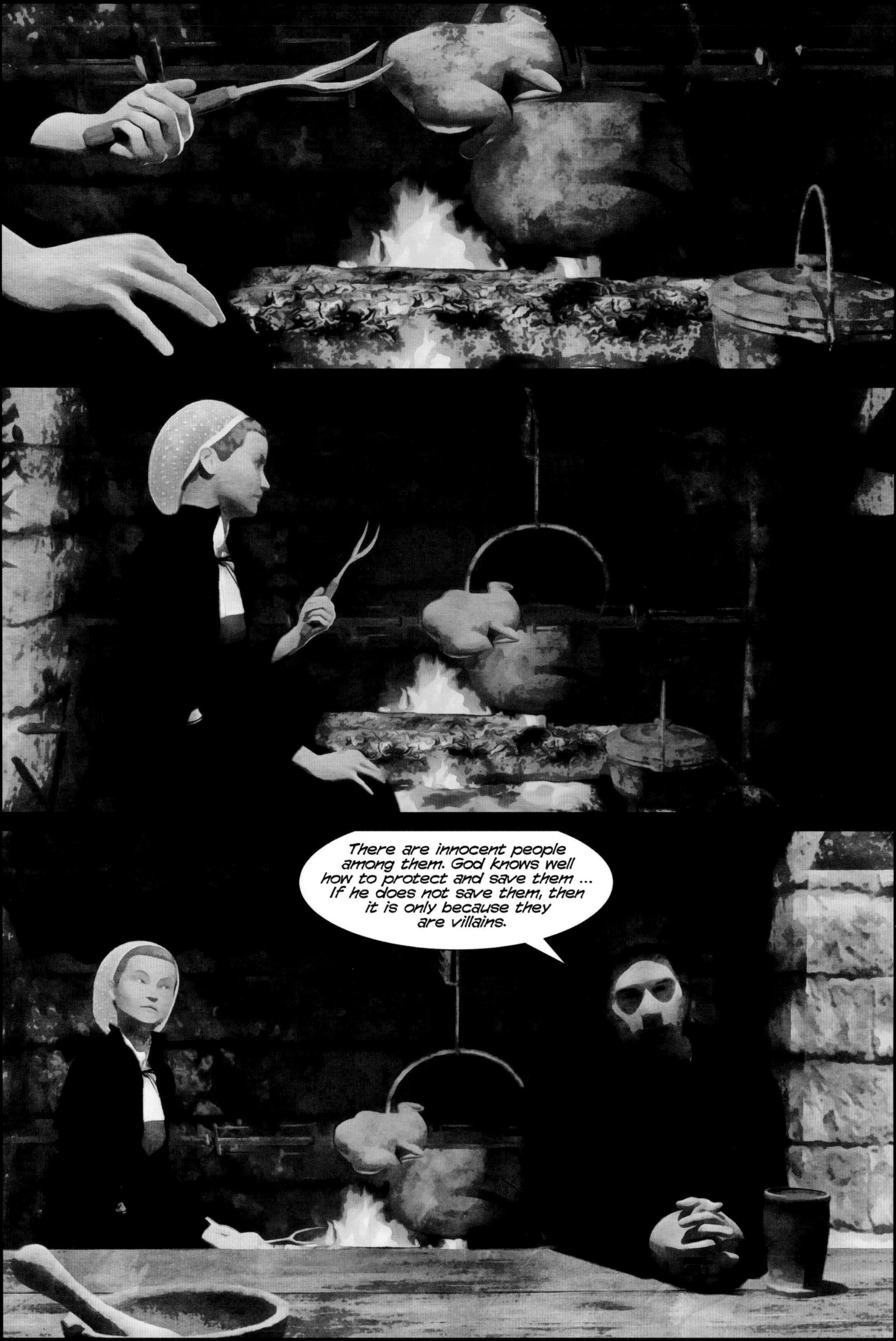
There are innocent people among them. God knows well how to protect and save them ... If he does not save them, then it is only because they are villains.

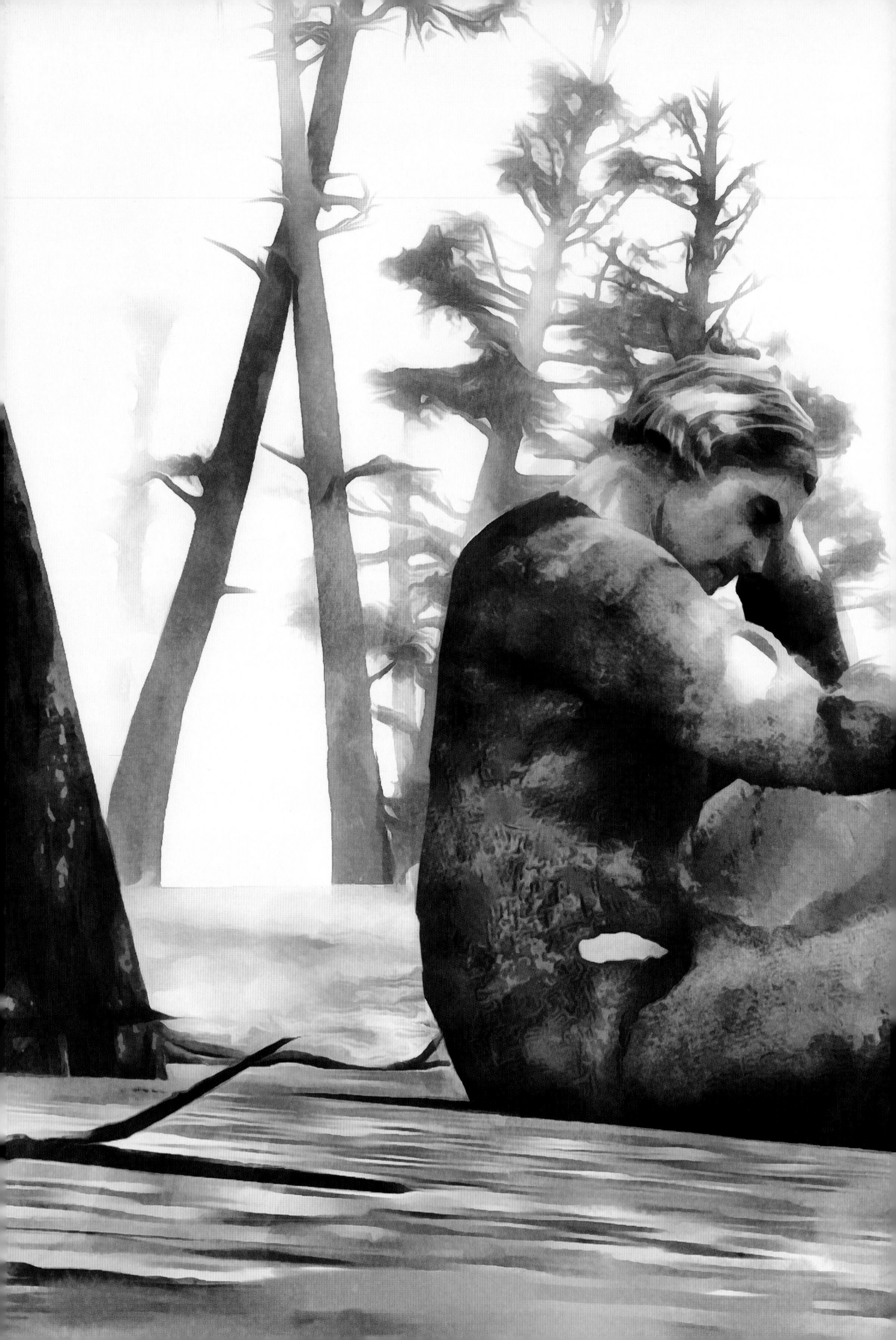

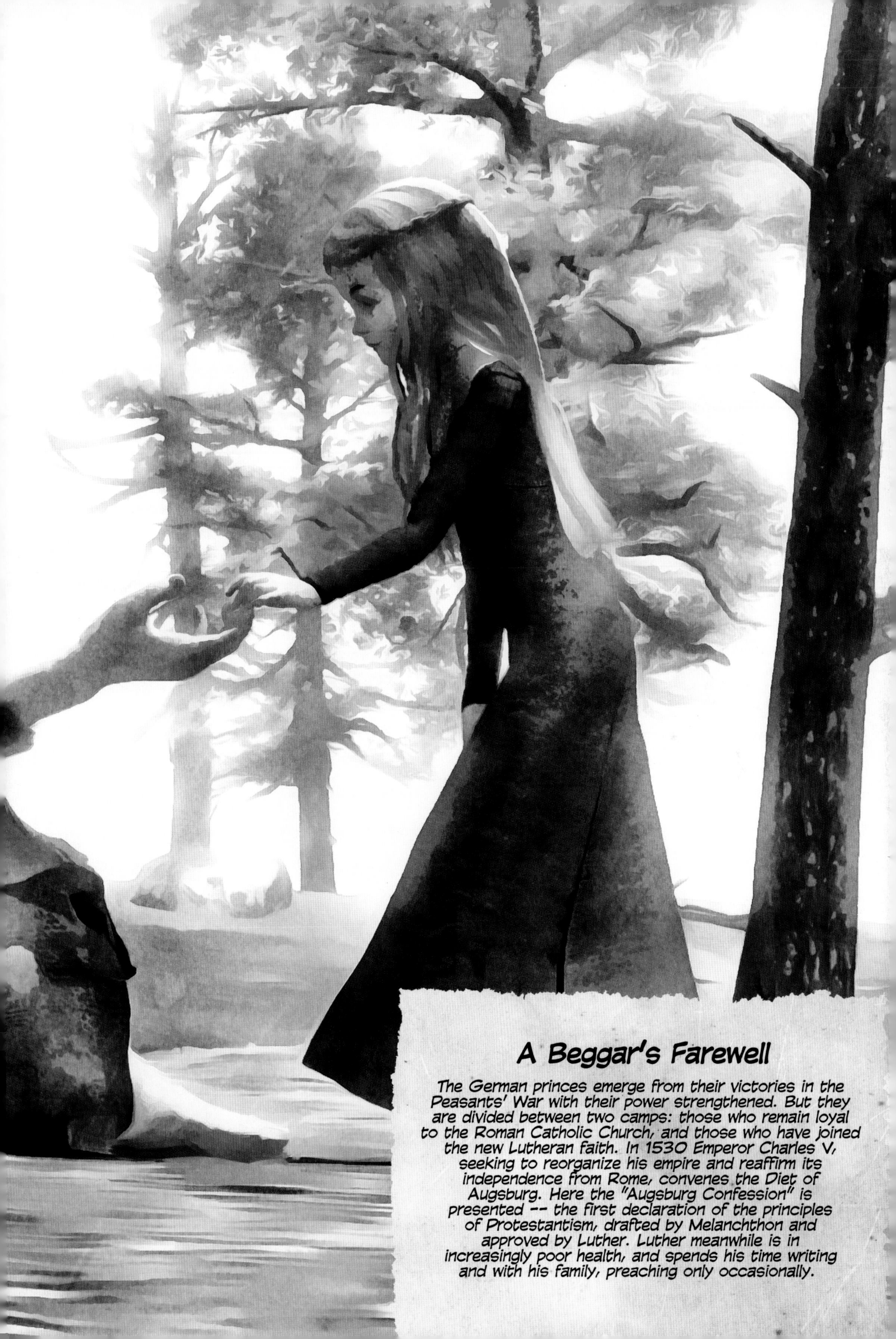

A Beggar's Farewell

The German princes emerge from their victories in the Peasants' War with their power strengthened. But they are divided between two camps: those who remain loyal to the Roman Catholic Church, and those who have joined the new Lutheran faith. In 1530 Emperor Charles V, seeking to reorganize his empire and reaffirm its independence from Rome, convenes the Diet of Augsburg. Here the "Augsburg Confession" is presented -- the first declaration of the principles of Protestantism, drafted by Melanchthon and approved by Luther. Luther meanwhile is in increasingly poor health, and spends his time writing and with his family, preaching only occasionally.

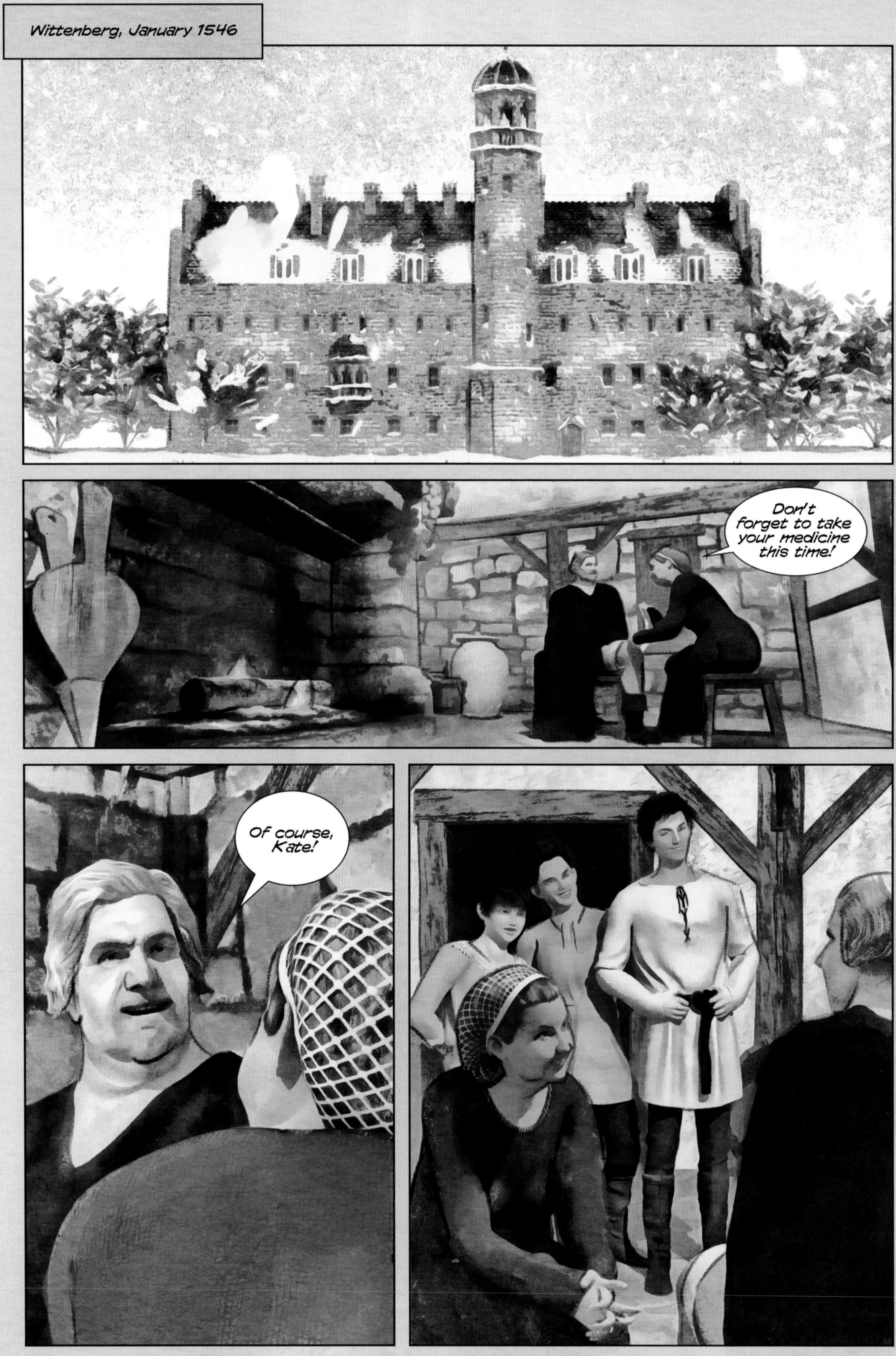
Wittenberg, January 1546
Don't forget to take your medicine this time!
Of course, Kate!

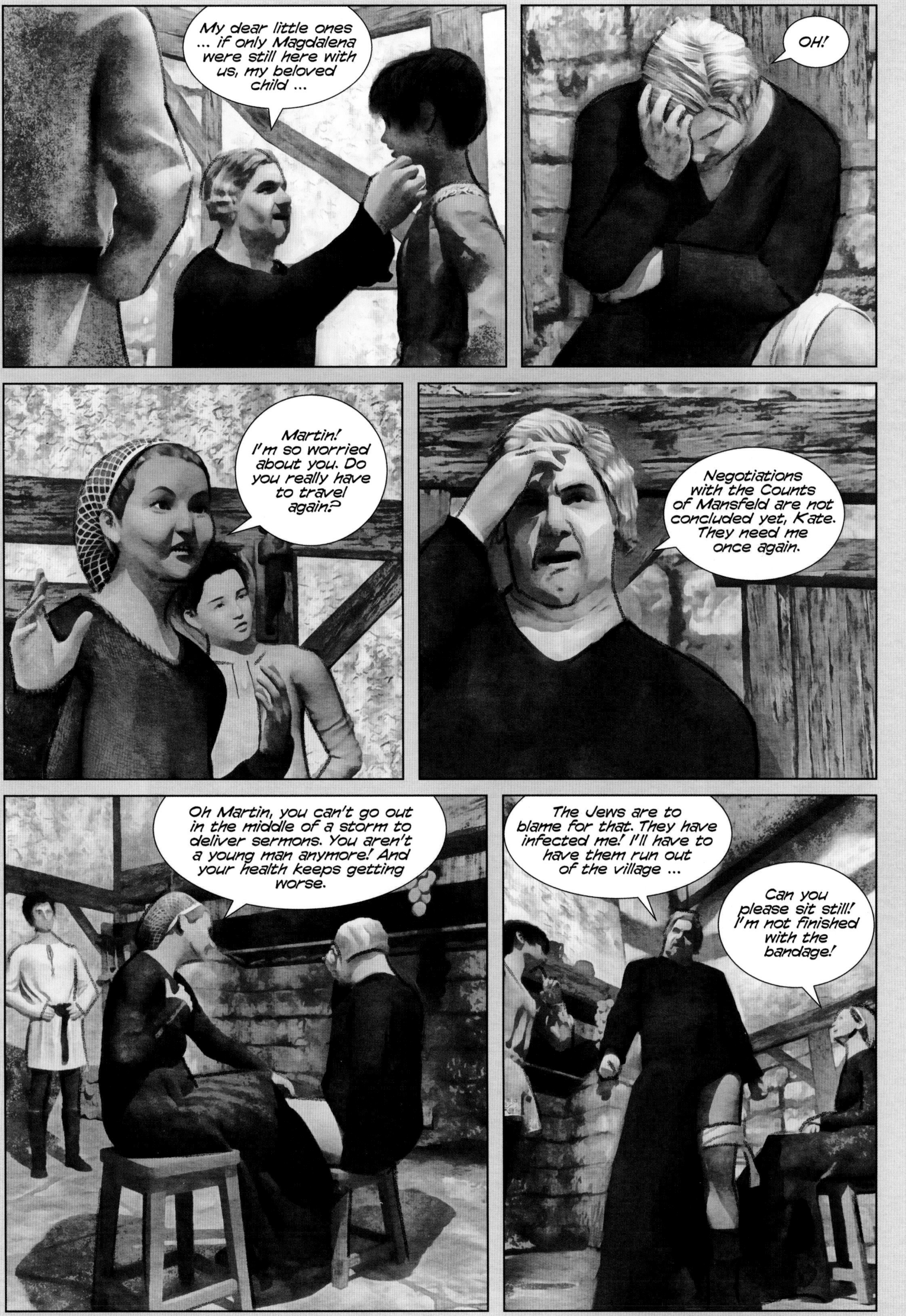
My dear little ones ... if only Magdalena were still here with us, my beloved child ...
OH!
Martin! I'm so worried about you. Do you really have to travel again?
Negotiations with the Counts of Mansfeld are not concluded yet, Kate. They need me once again.
Oh Martin, you can't go out in the middle of a storm to deliver sermons. You aren't a young man anymore! And your health keeps getting worse.
The Jews are to blame for that. They have infected me! I'll have to have them run out of the village ...
Can you please sit still! I'm not finished with the bandage!

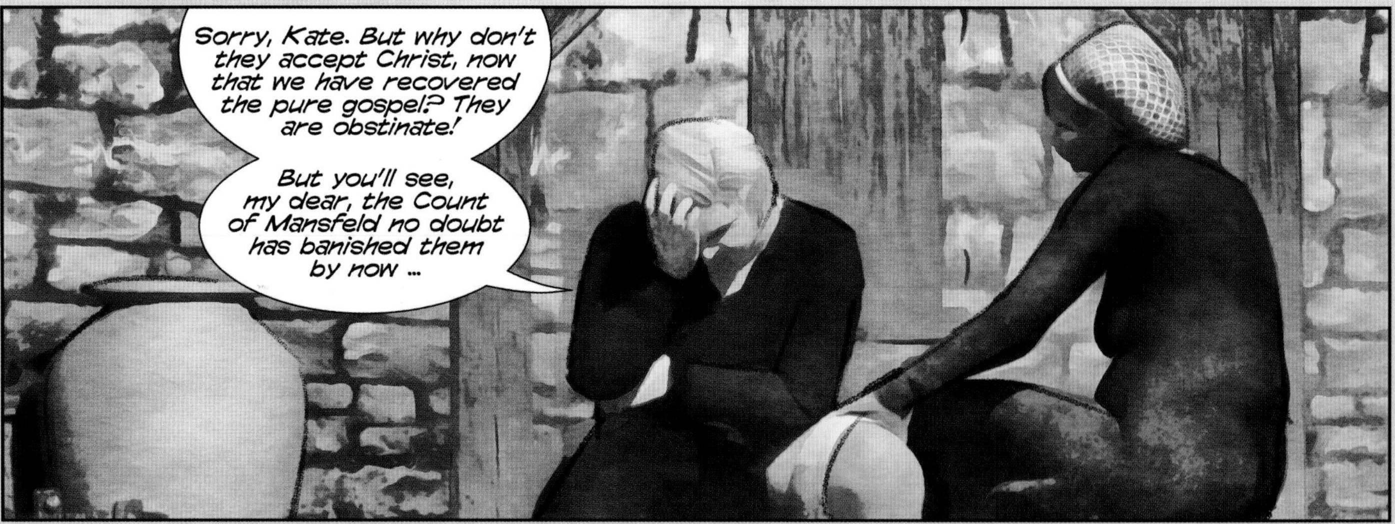
Sorry, Kate. But why don't they accept Christ, now that we have recovered the pure gospel? They are obstinate!
But you'll see, my dear, the Count of Mansfeld no doubt has banished them by now ...

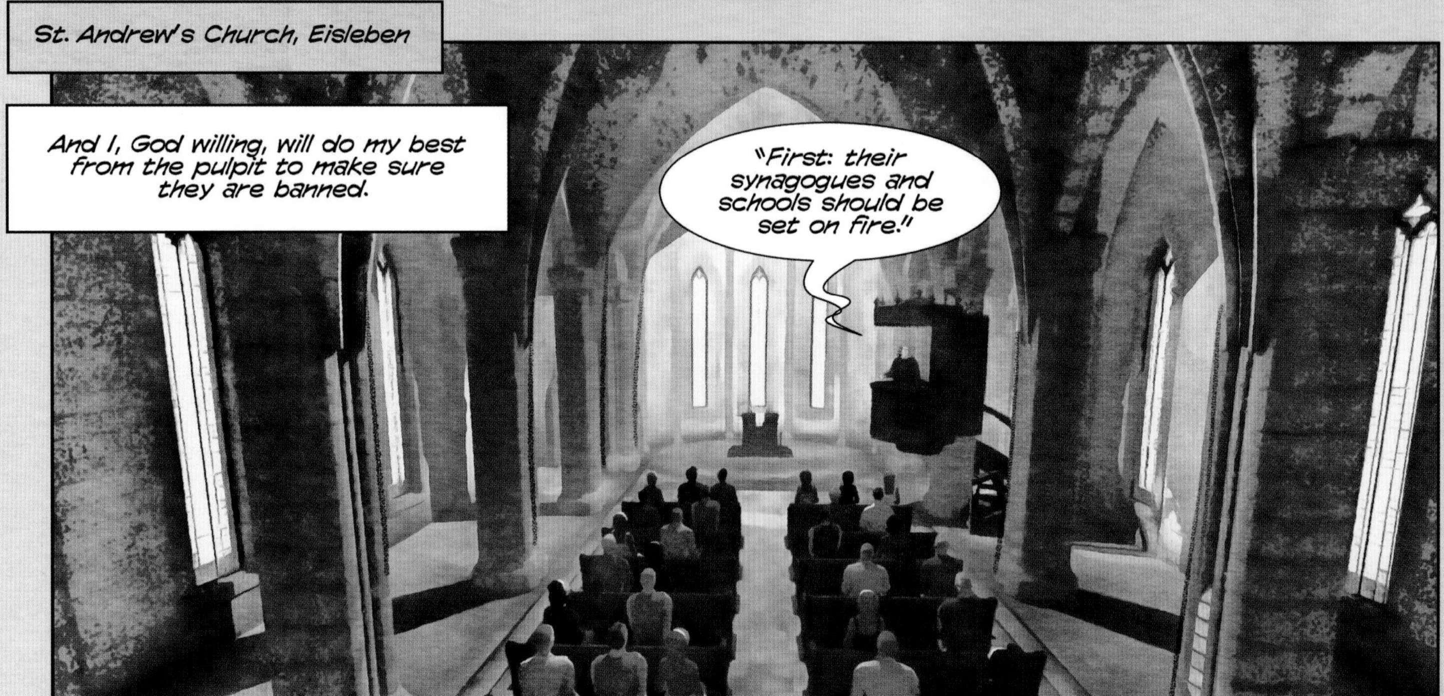
St. Andrew's Church, Eisleben
And I, God willing, will do my best from the pulpit to make sure they are banned.
"First: their synagogues and schools should be set on fire."

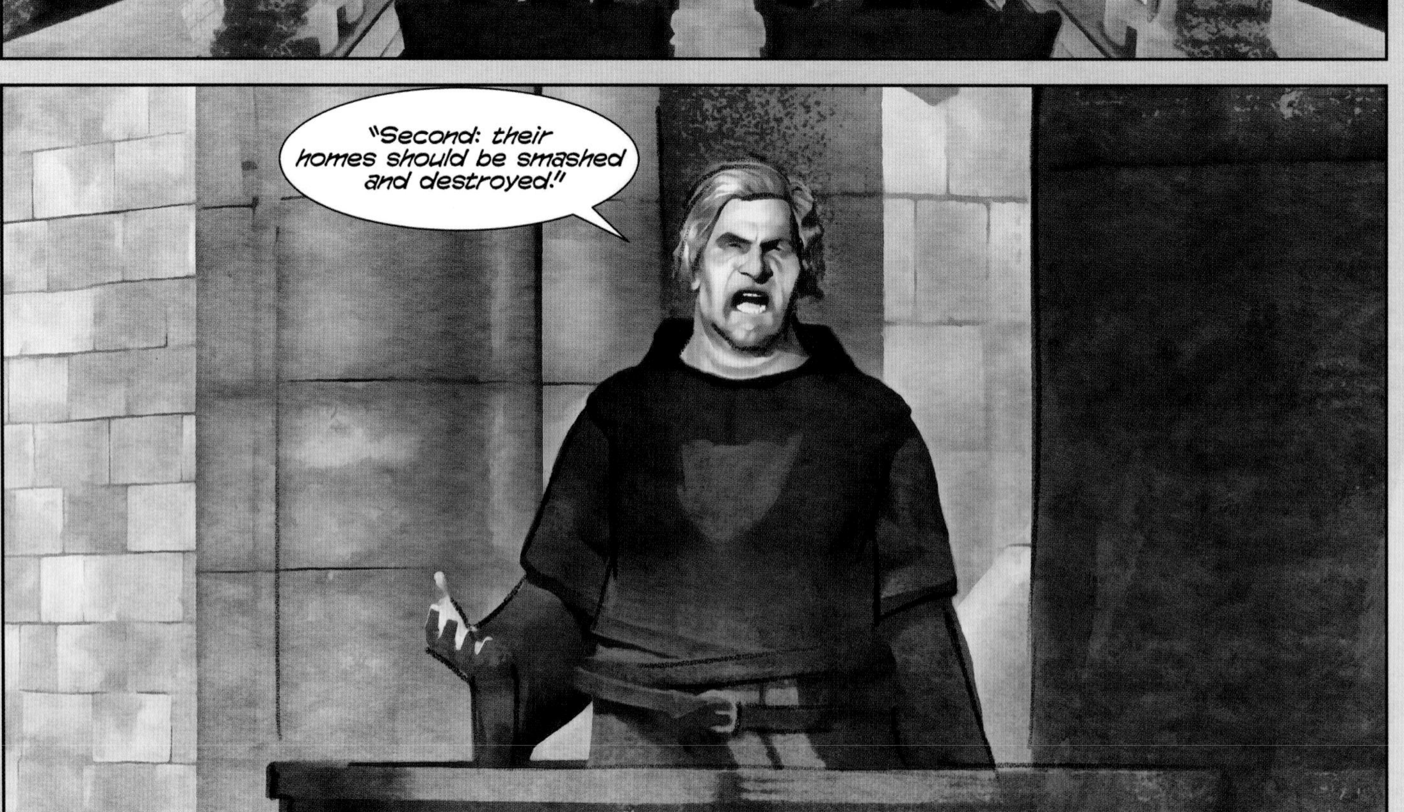
"Second: their homes should be smashed and destroyed."

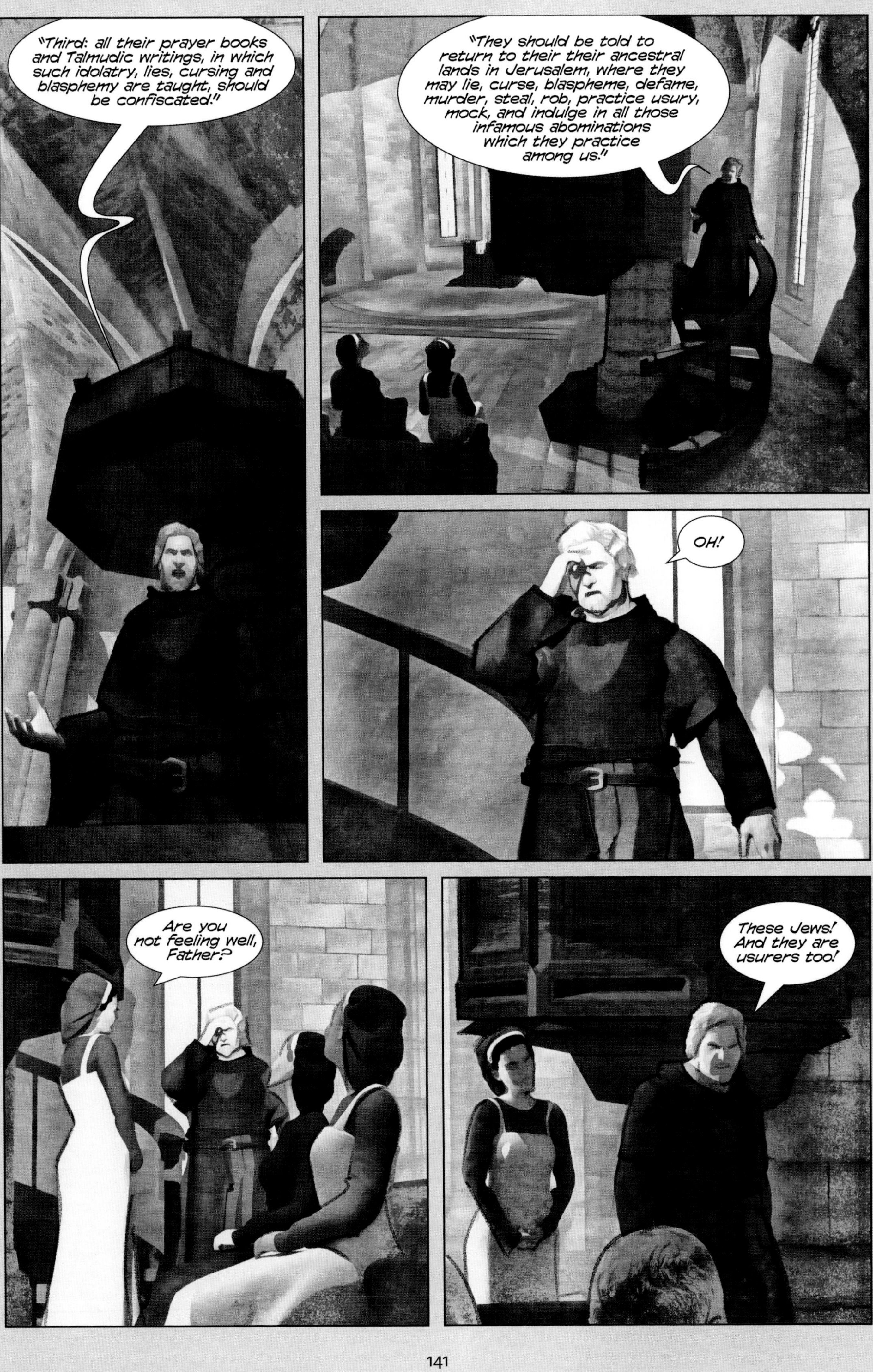
"Third: all their prayer books and Talmudic writings, in which such idolatry, lies, cursing and blasphemy are taught, should be confiscated!"
"They should be told to return to their their ancestral lands in Jerusalem, where they may lie, curse, blaspheme, defame, murder, steal, rob, practice usury, mock, and indulge in all those infamous abominations which they practice among us."
OH!
Are you not feeling well, Father?
These Jews! And they are usurers too!

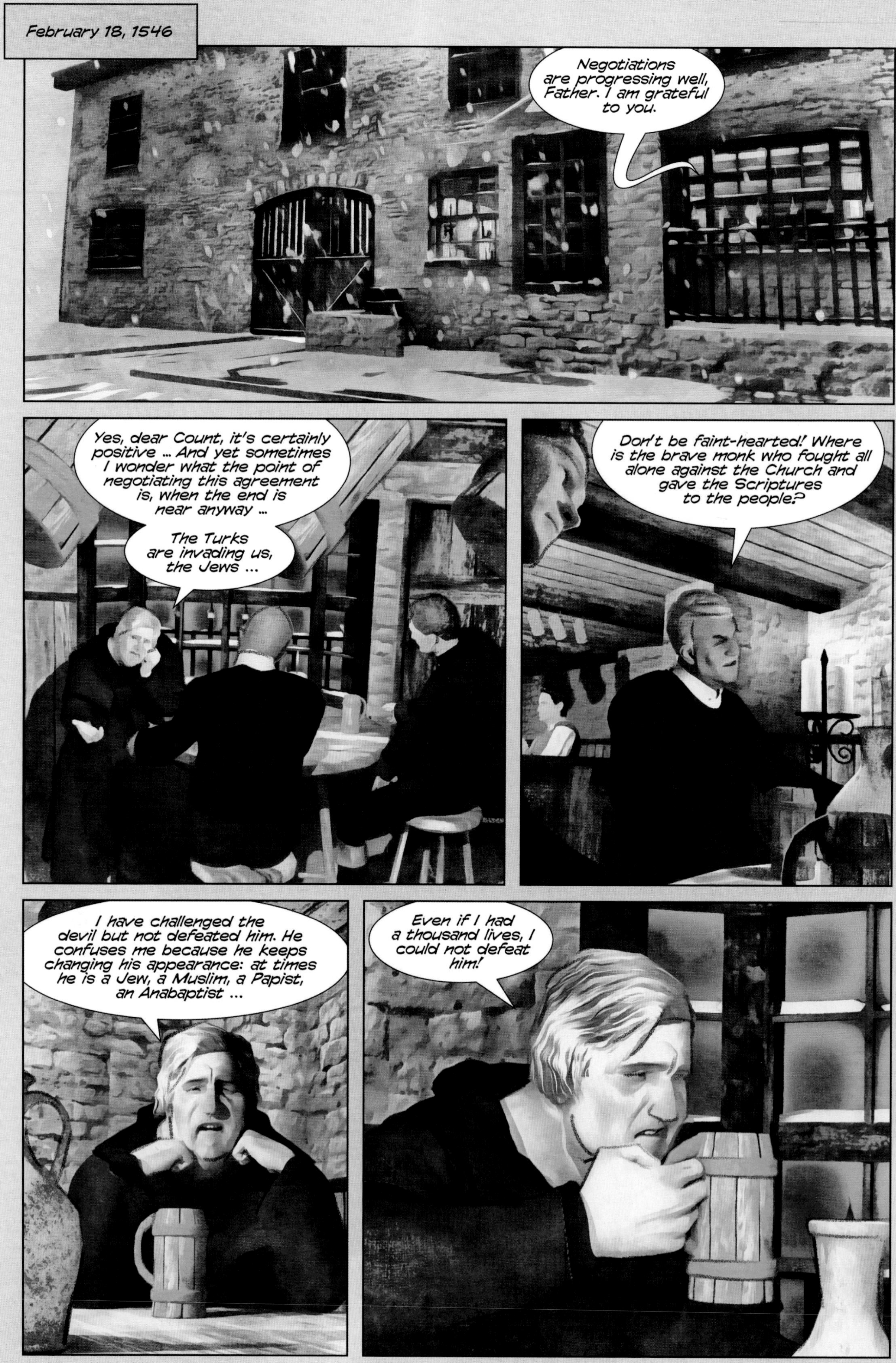
February 18, 1546
Negotiations are progressing well, Father. I am grateful to you.
Yes, dear Count, it's certainly positive ... And yet sometimes I wonder what the point of negotiating this agreement is, when the end is near anyway ...
The Turks are invading us, the Jews ...
Don't be faint-hearted! Where is the brave monk who fought all alone against the Church and gave the Scriptures to the people?
I have challenged the devil but not defeated him. He confuses me because he keeps changing his appearance: at times he is a Jew, a Muslim, a Papist, an Anabaptist ...
Even if I had a thousand lives, I could not defeat him!

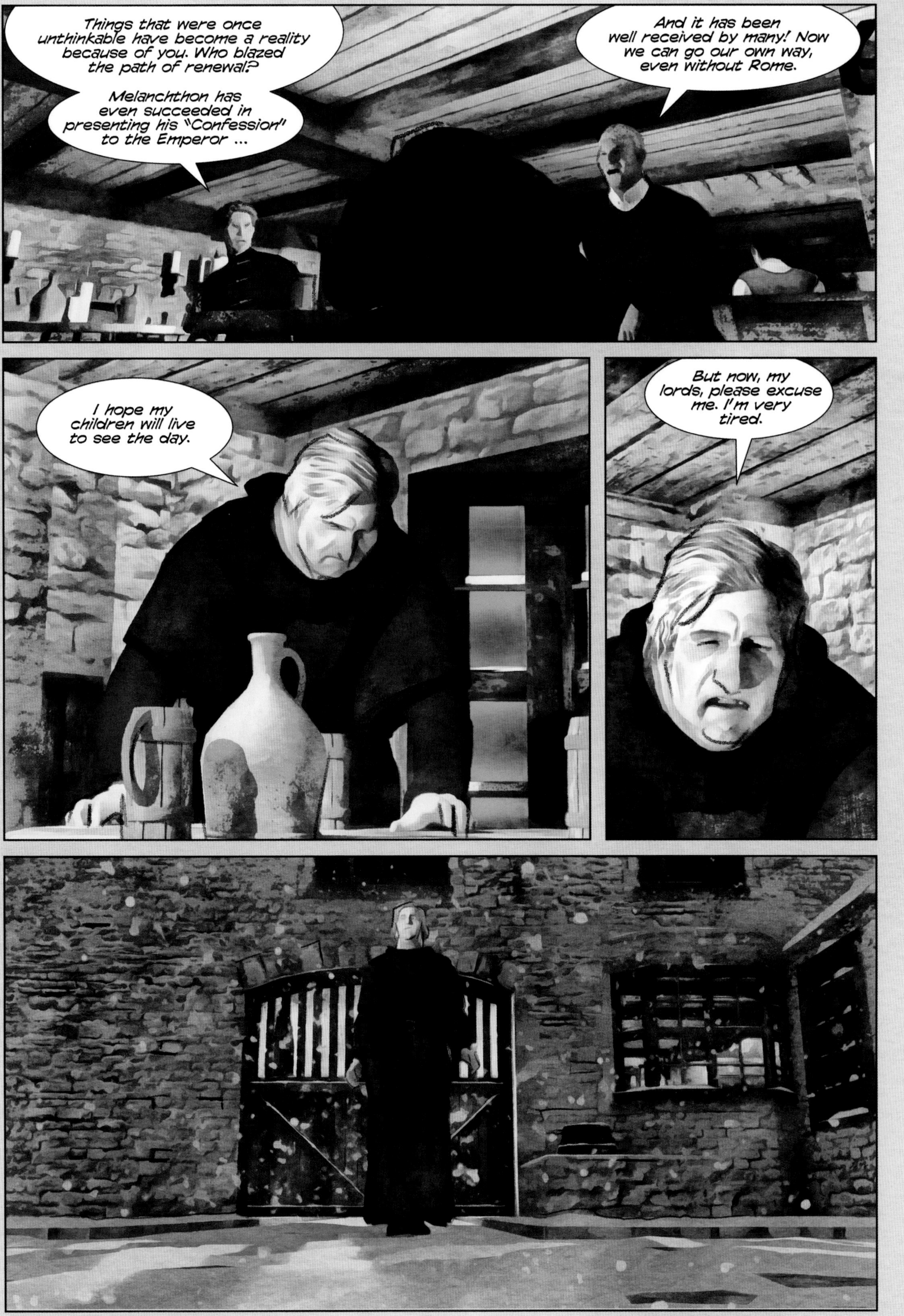
Things that were once unthinkable have become a reality because of you. Who blazed the path of renewal?
Melanchthon has even succeeded in presenting his "Confession" to the Emperor ...
And it has been well received by many! Now we can go our own way, even without Rome.
I hope my children will live to see the day.
But now, my lords, please excuse me. I'm very tired.

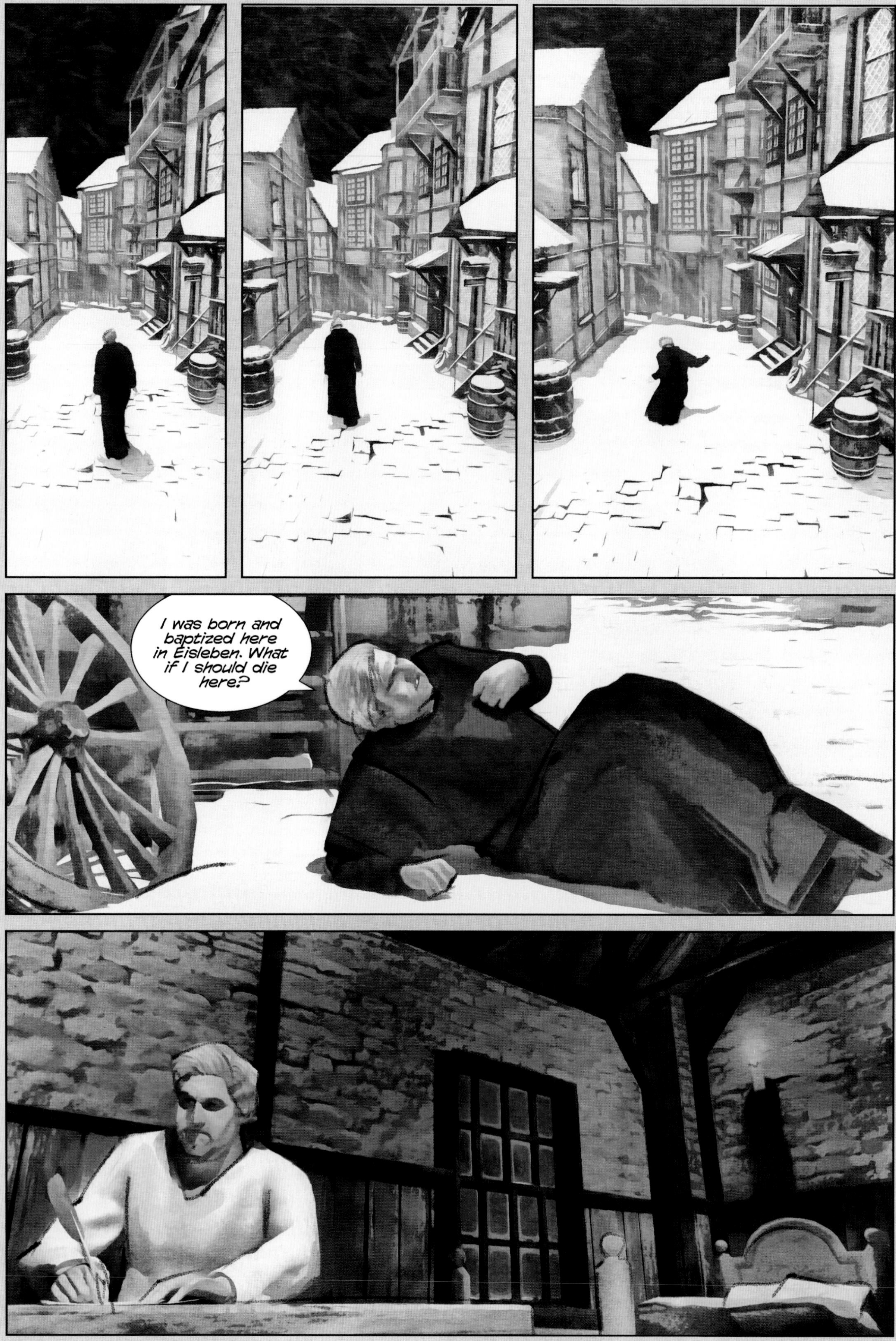
I was born and baptized here in Eisleben. What if I should die here?

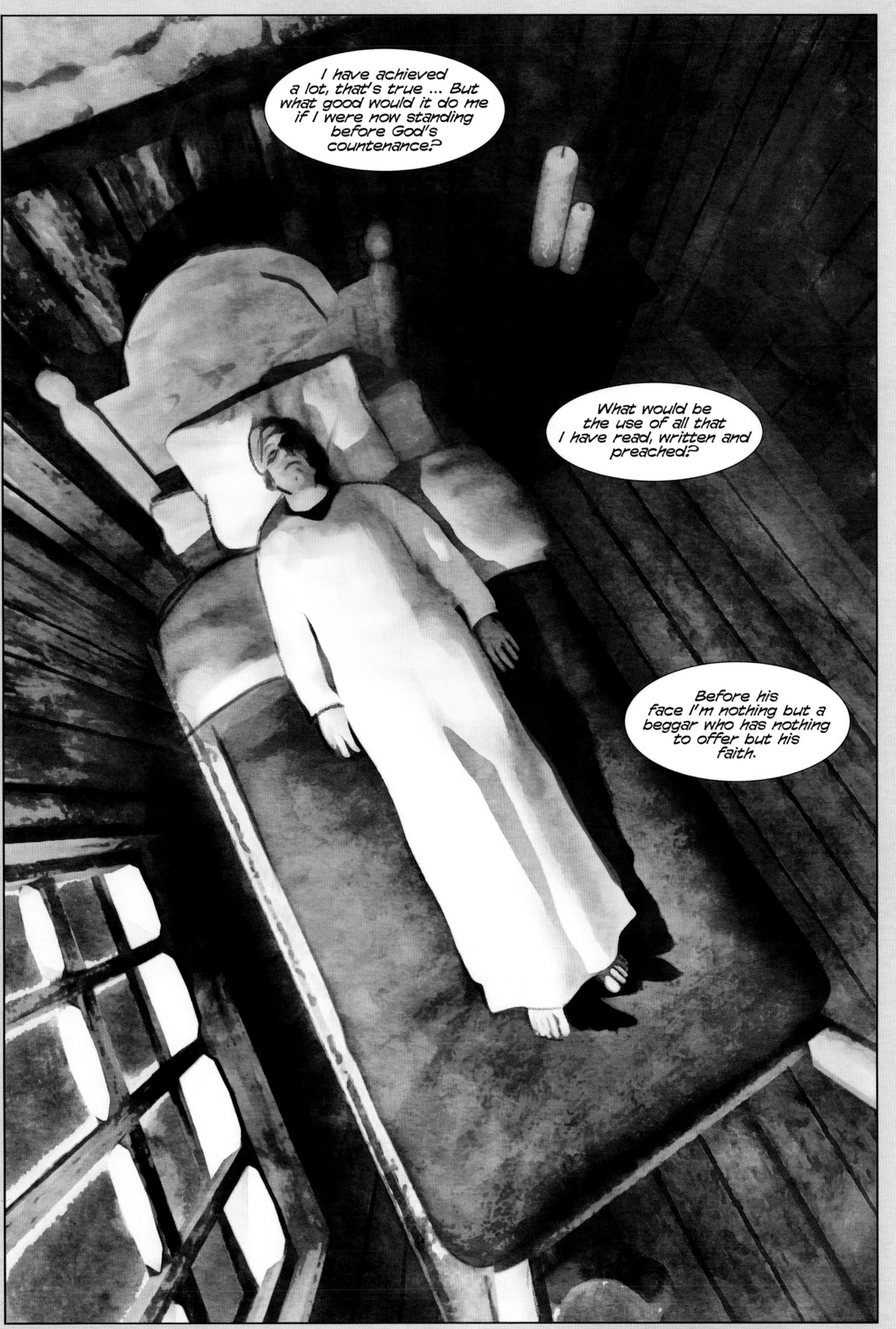
I have achieved a lot, that's true ... But what good would it do me if I were now standing before God's countenance?
What would be the use of all that I have read, written and preached?
Before his face I'm nothing but a beggar who has nothing to offer but his faith.

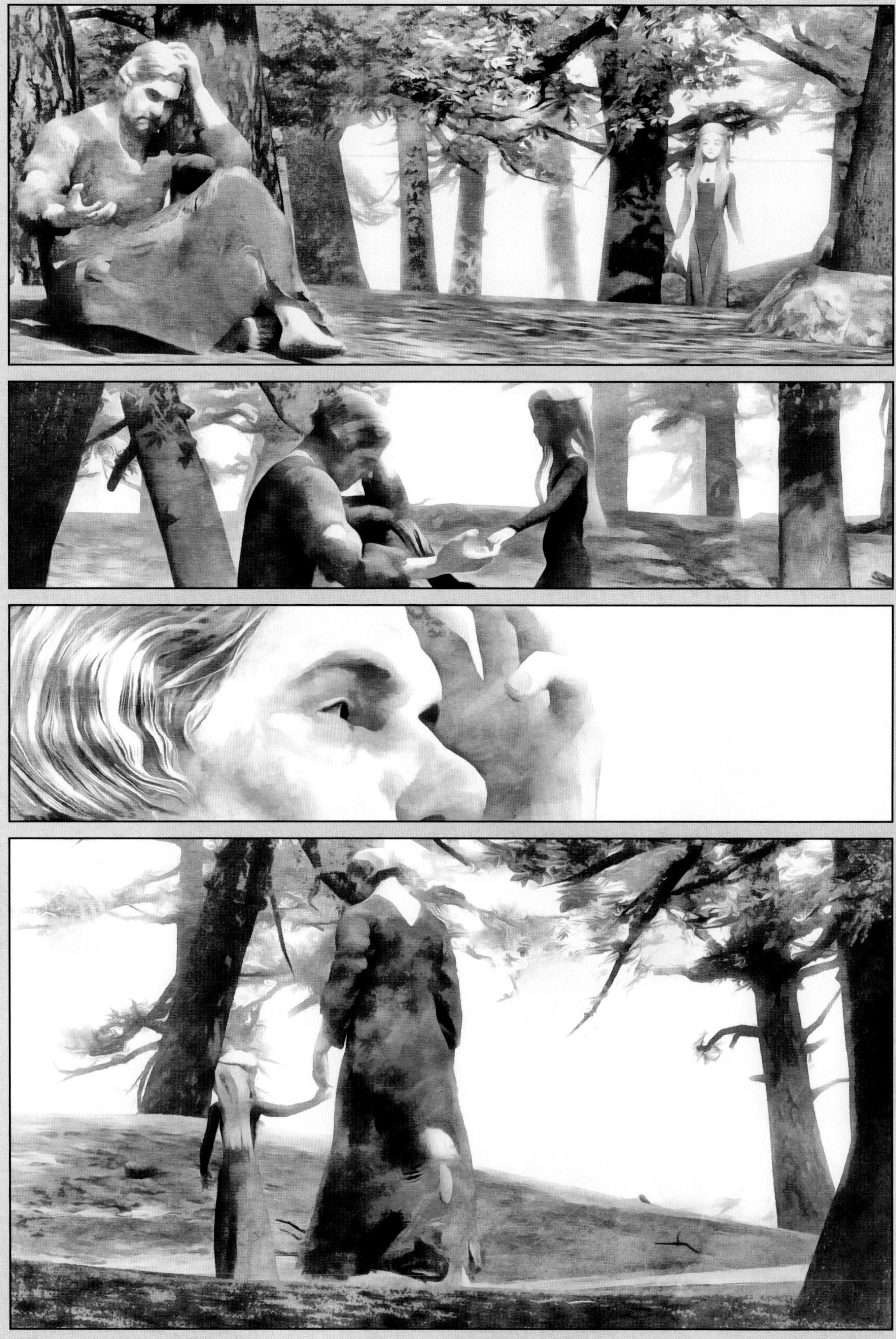

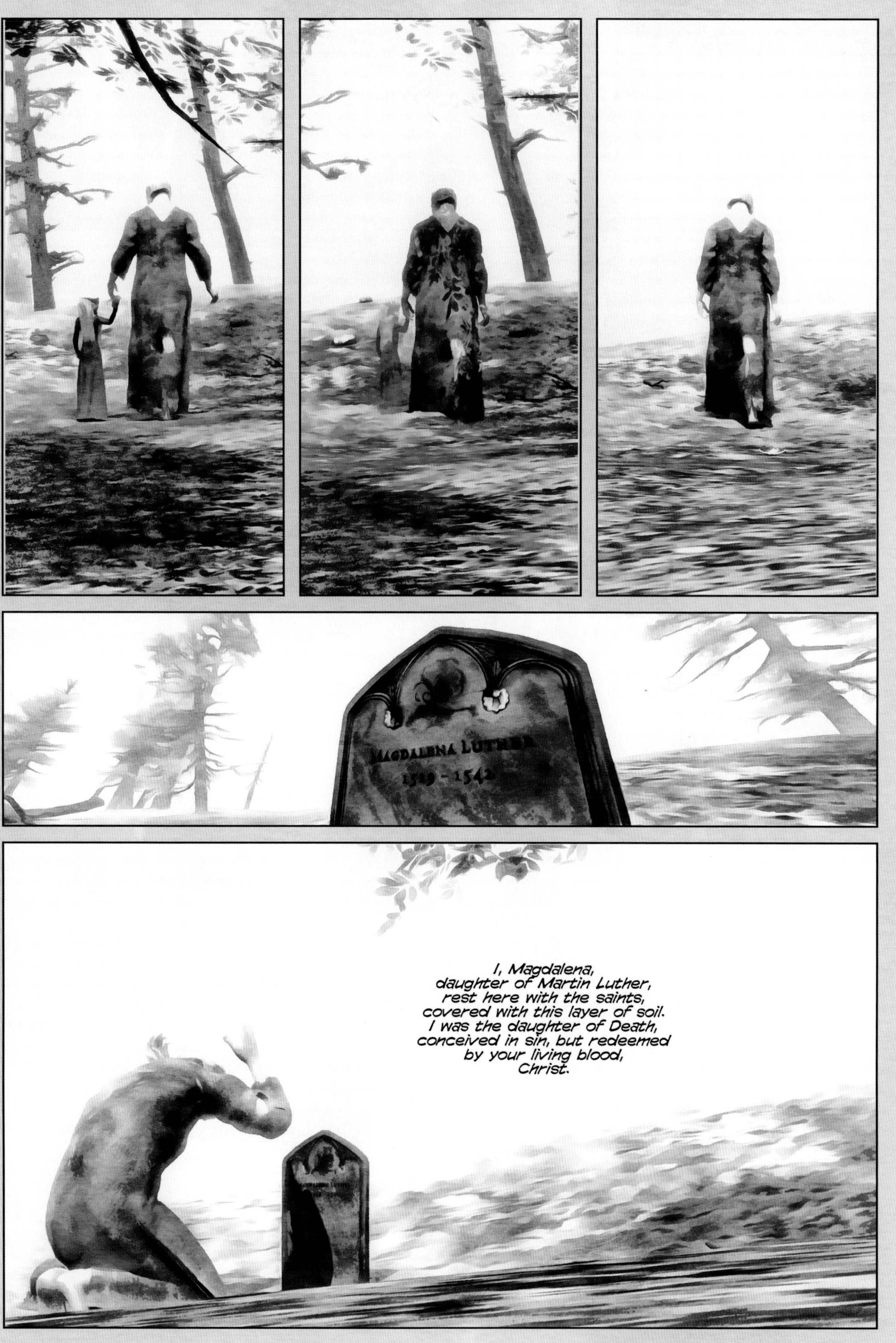
MAGDALENA LUTHER
1529 - 1542
I, Magdalena,
daughter of Martin Luther,
rest here with the saints,
covered with this layer of soil.
I was the daughter of Death,
conceived in sin, but redeemed
by your living blood,
Christ.

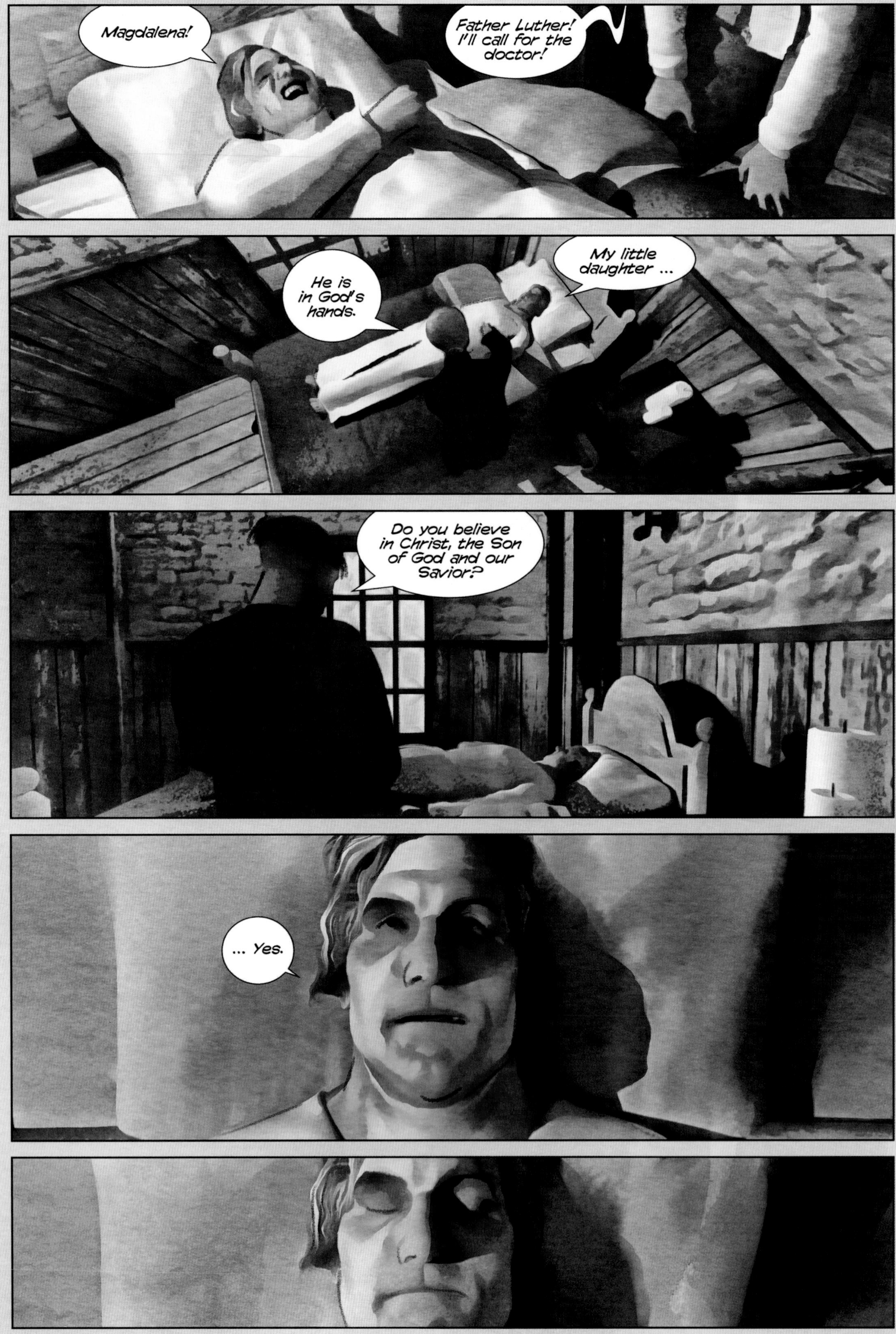
Magdalena!
Father Luther! I'll call for the doctor!
My little daughter ...
He is in God's hands.
Do you believe in Christ, the Son of God and our Savior?
... Yes.

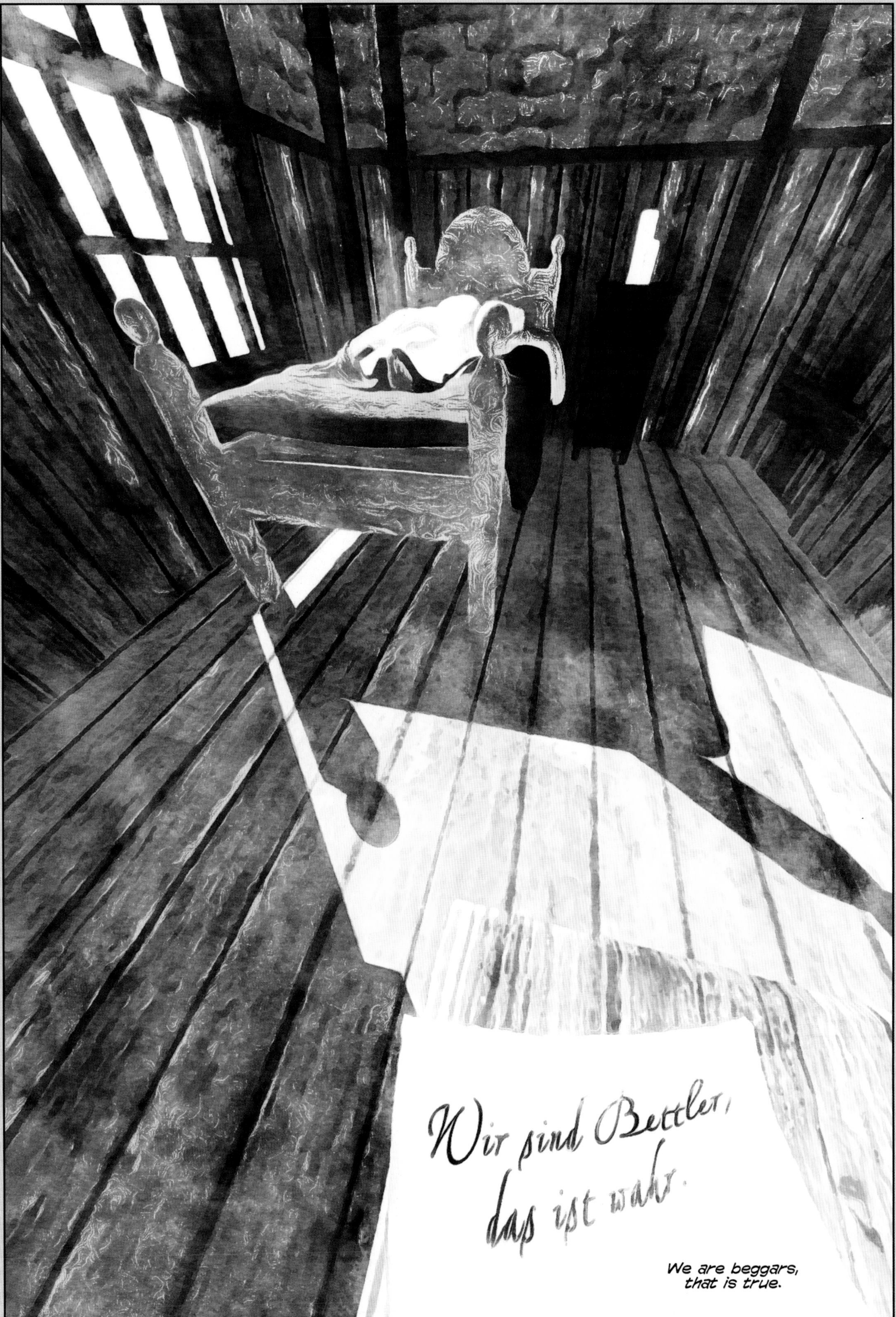
Wir sind Bettler, das ist wahr.
We are beggars, that is true.

EPILOGUE: Augsburg, 1555

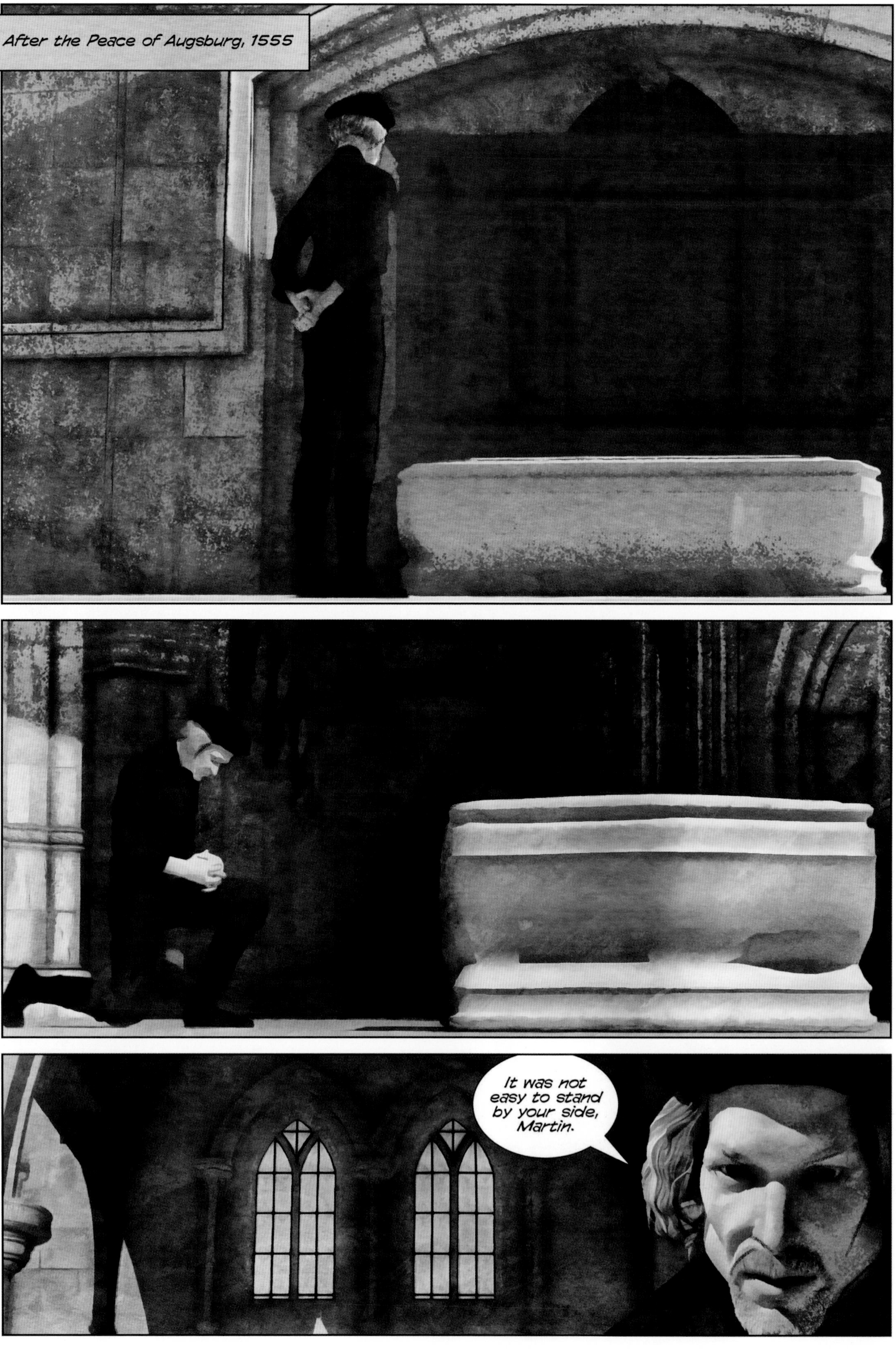
After the Peace of Augsburg, 1555
It was not easy to stand by your side, Martin.

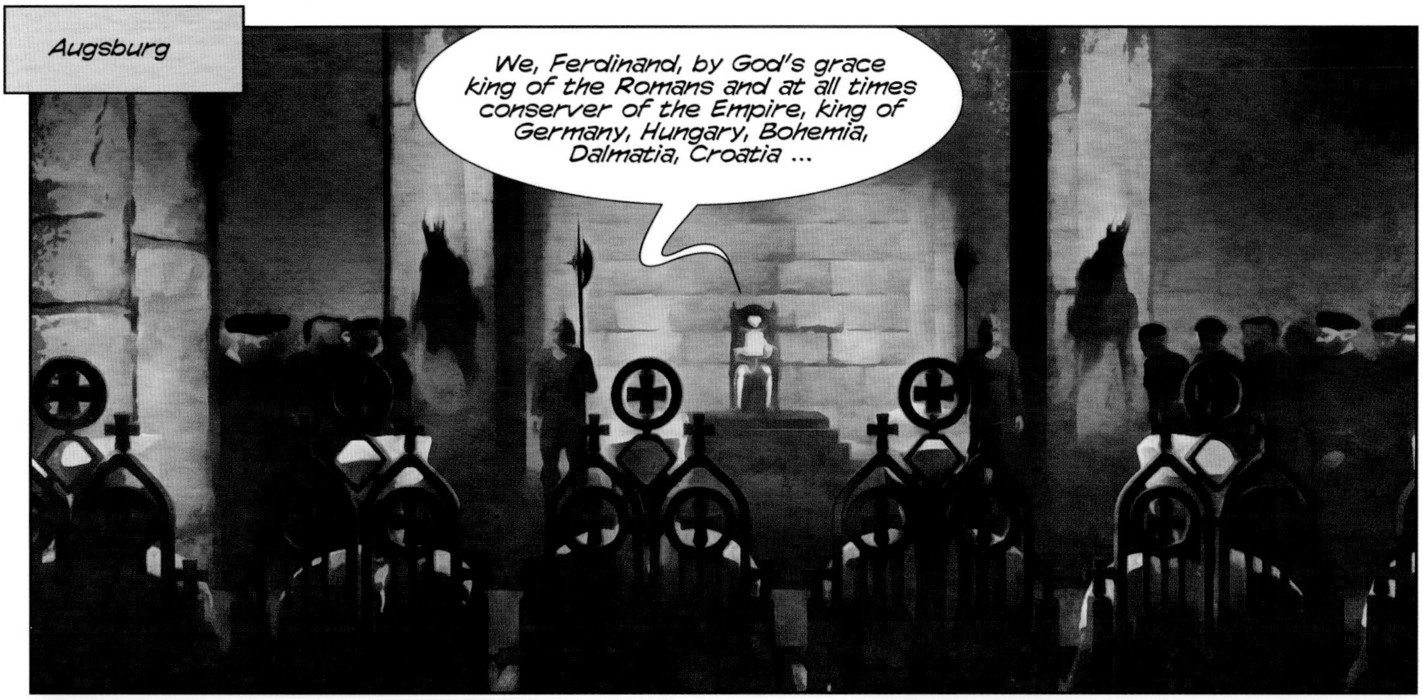
Augsburg
We, Ferdinand, by God's grace king of the Romans and at all times conserver of the Empire, king of Germany, Hungary, Bohemia, Dalmatia, Croatia ...

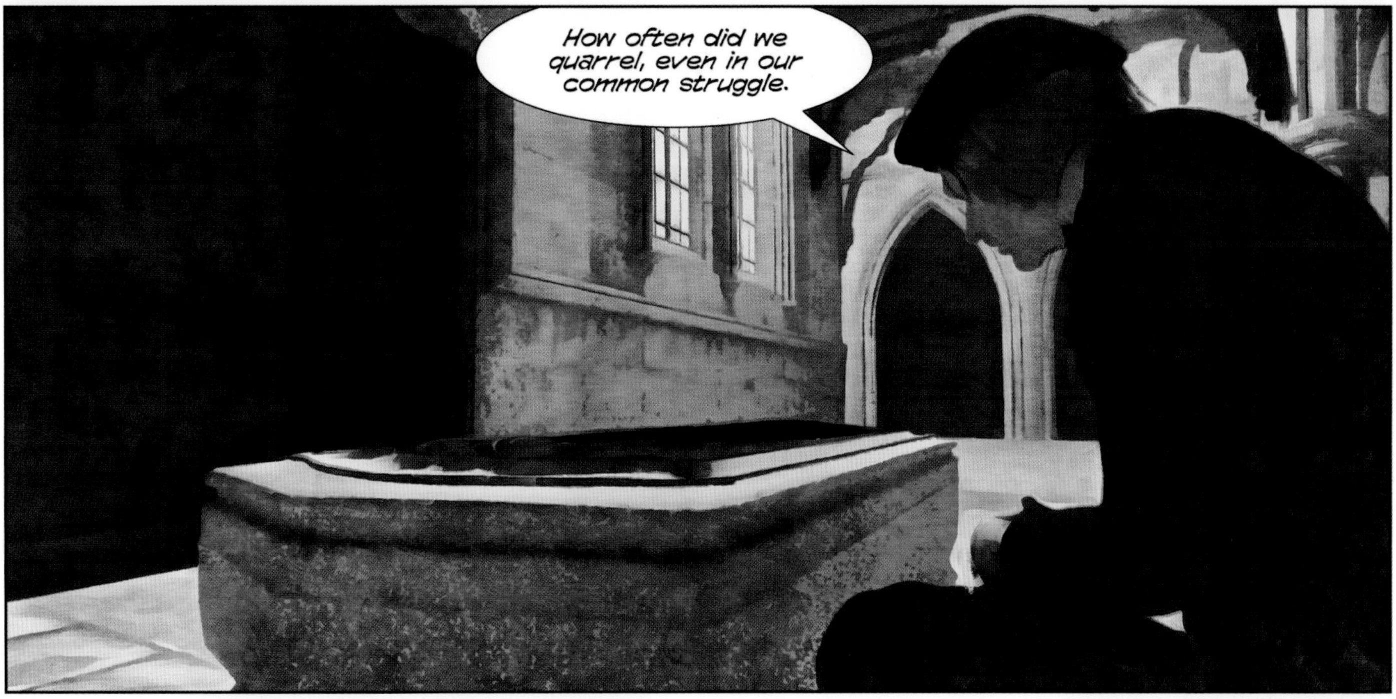
How often did we quarrel, even in our common struggle.

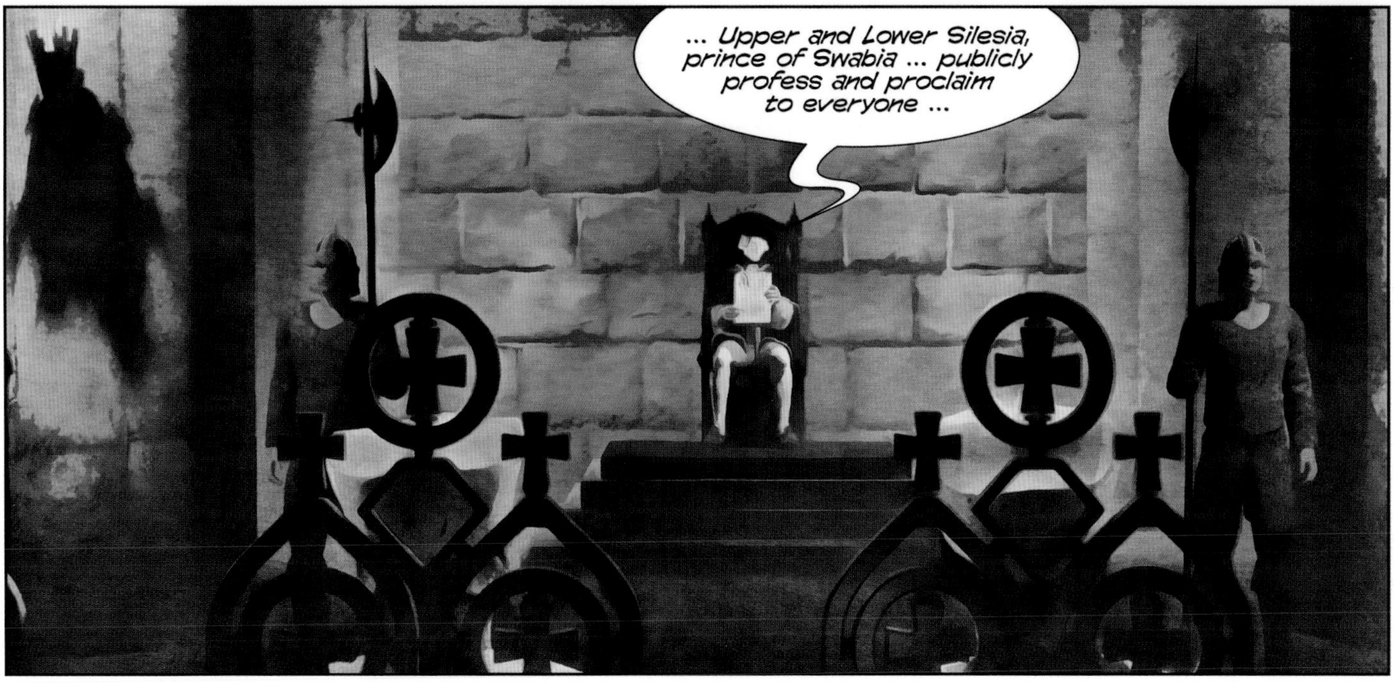
... Upper and Lower Silesia, prince of Swabia ... publicly profess and proclaim to everyone ...

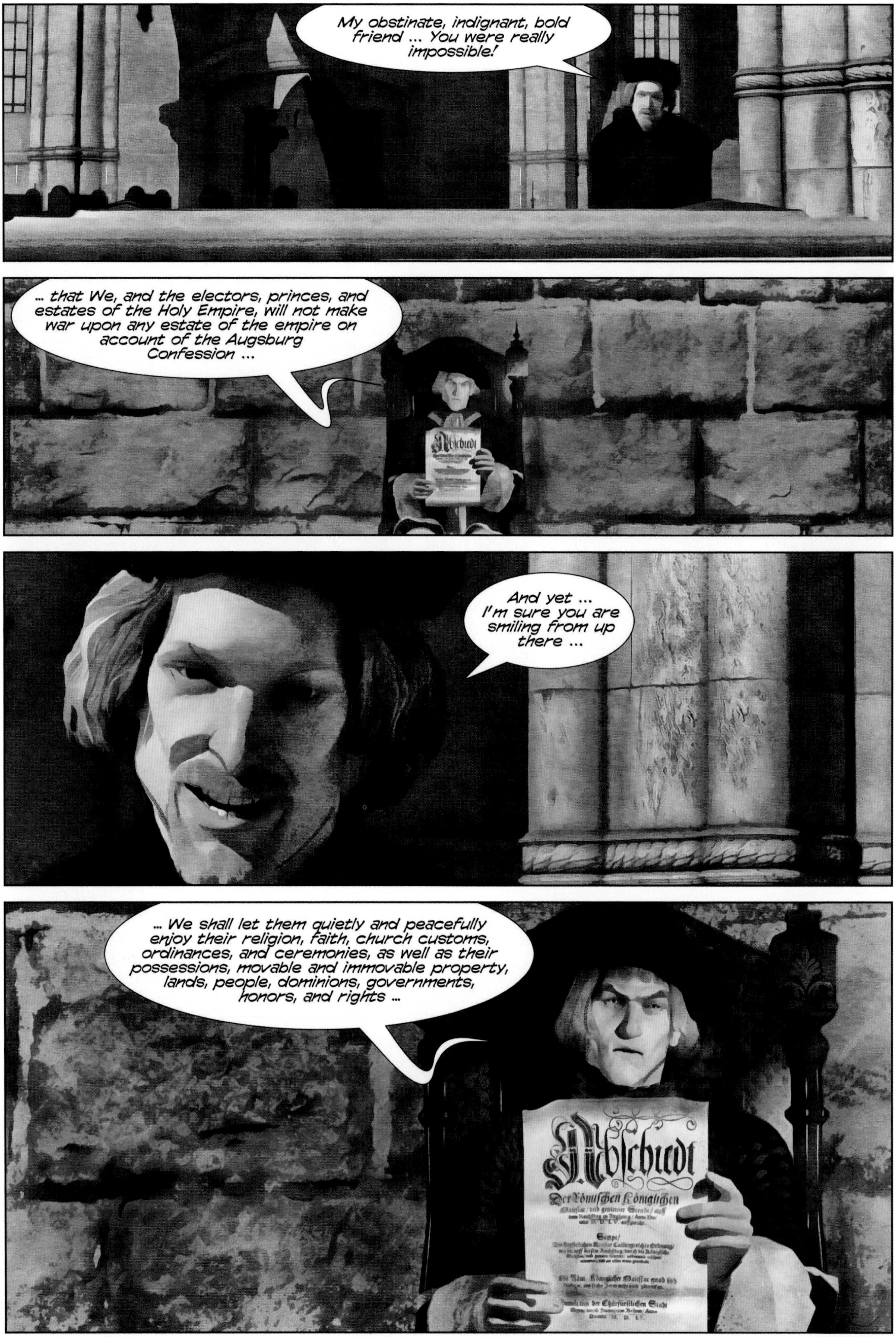
My obstinate, indignant, bold friend ... You were really impossible!
... that We, and the electors, princes, and estates of the Holy Empire, will not make war upon any estate of the empire on account of the Augsburg Confession ...
And yet ... I'm sure you are smiling from up there ...
... We shall let them quietly and peacefully enjoy their religion, faith, church customs, ordinances, and ceremonies, as well as their possessions, movable and immovable property, lands, people, dominions, governments, honors, and rights ...
Abschiedt
Der Römischen Königlichen

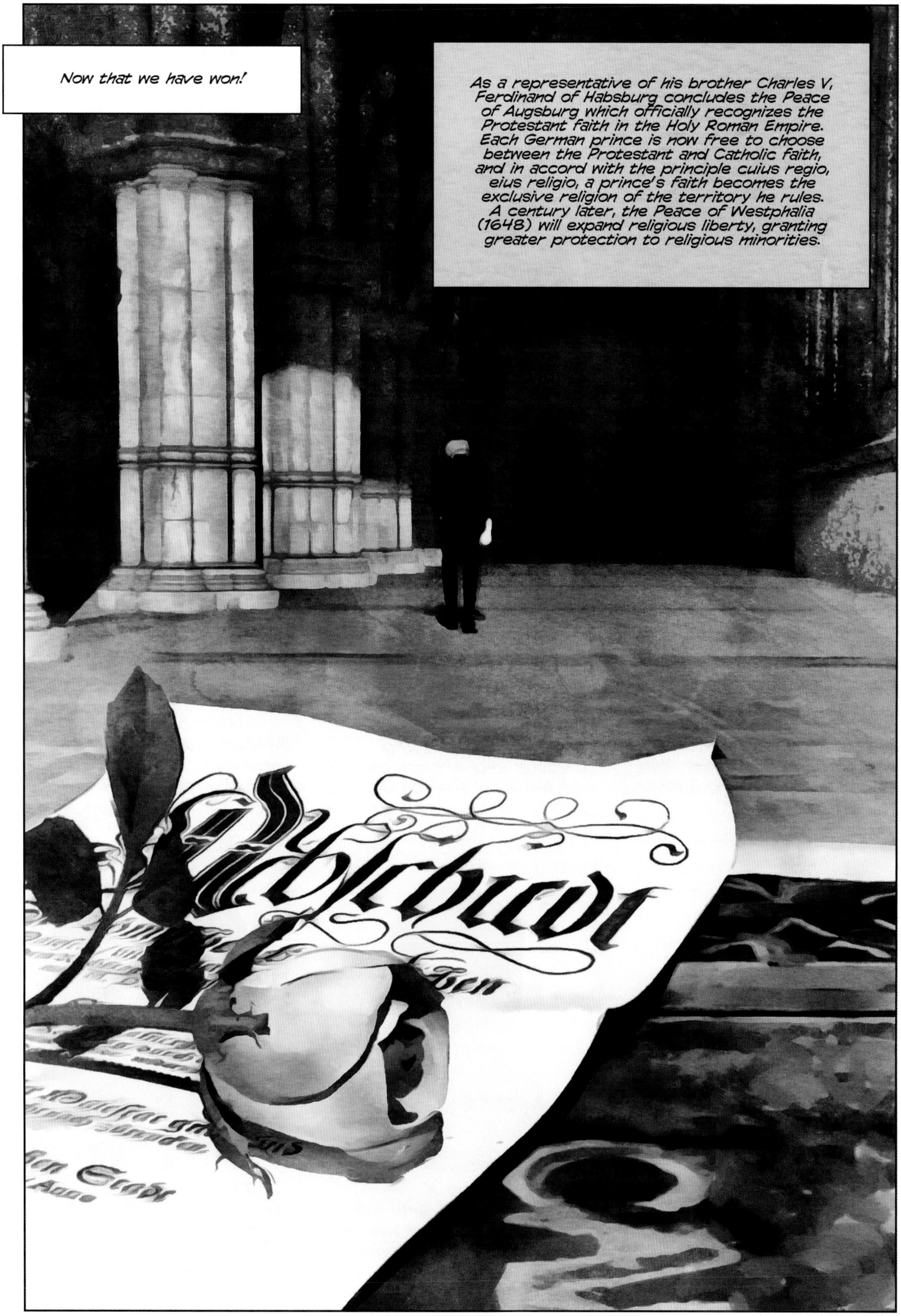
Now that we have won!
As a representative of his brother Charles V, Ferdinand of Habsburg concludes the Peace of Augsburg which officially recognizes the Protestant faith in the Holy Roman Empire. Each German prince is now free to choose between the Protestant and Catholic faith, and in accord with the principle cuius regio, eius religio, a prince's faith becomes the exclusive religion of the territory he rules. A century later, the Peace of Westphalia (1648) will expand religious liberty, granting greater protection to religious minorities.

THE END

Martin Luther
Reformer, translator of the Bible into German, preacher and founder of the Protestant faith.

Katharina von Bora
Left the convent and became Luther's wife.

Philip Melanchthon
Humanist scholar and companion of Luther.

Johann von Staupitz
Theologian, Vicar General of the Augustinian Order and patron of the young Luther.

Albert of Brandenburg
Elector and Archchancellor of the Holy Roman Empire and Cardinal Archbishop of Mainz.

Jakob Fugger
Banker and mining entrepreneur from Augsburg called "Fugger the Rich." He was a maker of kings, emperors, and cardinals.

Johann Tetzel
Dominican friar. As a licensed seller of indulgences under Albert of Brandenburg, he incurred the wrath of Luther, precipitating his 95 Theses.

Leo X
Born as Giovanni de' Medici, in 1513 he was enthroned Pope in Rome. In 1521 he excommunicated Luther from the Roman Catholic Church.

Thomas Cajetan
General of the Dominican Order and cardinal. In 1518 he tried in vain to persuade Luther to recant his theses.

Johann Eck
A Catholic theologian and opponent of Luther; he disputed with Luther in Leipzig in 1519.

Charles V
Spanish King from the House of Habsburg, Emperor of the Holy Roman Empire, he participated at the Diet of Worms, where Luther reaffirmed his position.

Frederick III
Frederick the Wise, Elector of Saxony, founded the University of Wittenberg; promoted and supported Martin Luther.

Lucas Cranach the Elder
Court painter of Frederick the Wise, Luther's friend and portrait painter of the Reformation.

Thomas Müntzer
Theologian, preacher, and rebel leader in the Peasants' War. He believed the Kingdom of God was imminent.

Florian Geyer
Imperial knight from Franconia. In the Peasants' War, he led the rebel Black Company (Tauberhaufen).

Götz von Berlichingen
Imperial knight from Franconia. Led a band of rebel peasants in Swabia and on the Tauber.

Georg von Waldburg-Zeil
Recruited mercenaries and led them into battle against the peasant insurrectionists.

Ferdinand I
Emperor of the Holy Roman Empire, he succeeded his brother Charles V and played an important role in the establishment of the Peace of Augsburg.

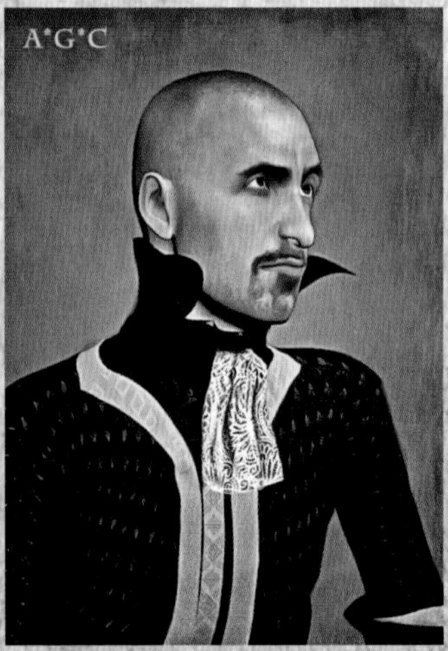
A·G·C

Andrea Grosso Ciponte is a Calabrian painter, graphic novelist, filmmaker, and illustrator. He is a professor of computer graphics and digital animation techniques at the Academy of Fine Arts in Catanzaro, Italy. Ciponte was born in Praia a Mare, Italy, in 1977. In 2011 his work was shown at the Venice Biennale. He lives in Rome.

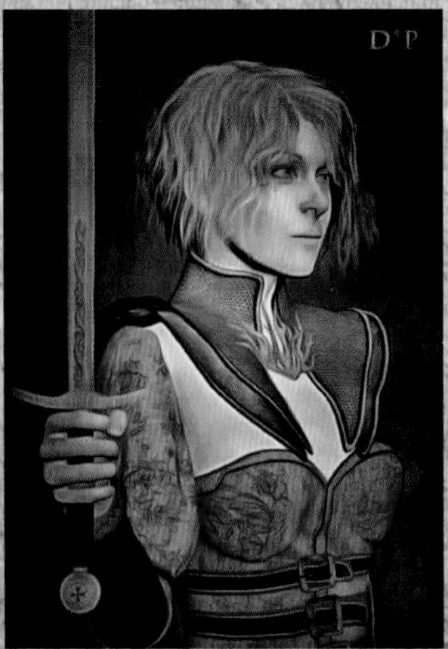
D·P

Dacia Palmerino has collaborated with Andrea Grosso Ciponte on six graphic novels since 2014. Formerly a professor at the Academy of Fine Arts in Foggia, Italy, she researches experimentation in audiovisual and multimedia art, curates film and video exhibits, and reviews emerging artists and musicians. Born in Milan in 1978, Palmerino lives and works in Catanzaro, Italy.